Rutherford Studies in Hi

Editors

DAVID F. WRIGHT
Professor of Patristic and Reformed Christianity,
New College, University of Edinburgh

DONALD MACLEOD
Professor of Systematic Theology,
Free Church College, Edinburgh

THOMAS CHALMERS:
ENTHUSIAST FOR MISSION

The Christian Good of Scotland and the Rise of the
Missionary Movement

Thomas Chalmers

THOMAS CHALMERS:
ENTHUSIAST FOR MISSION

*The Christian Good of Scotland and the Rise of
the Missionary Movement*

John Roxborogh

Published for Rutherford House

by

paternoster
press

British Library Cataloguing in Publication Data

A catalogue record for this book is available from
the British Library

ISBN 0-946068-49-6

Typeset by Rutherford House, Edinburgh
and Printed by
T.J. International, Padstow, Cornwall

In gratitude

CATHERINE ISABEL ROXBOROGH

CONTENTS

ACKNOWLEDGEMENTS

Thanks are due in many quarters. My mother made it possible for our family to extend our time in Scotland and has taken a constant interest in Chalmers and the land of our forbears. The Senatus of Knox Theological Hall, Dunedin, provided the scholarship which enabled the project to begin. Assistance from the Bruce and Fraser Scholarship Fund in Aberdeen and the Helmut Rex Trust in Dunedin is also acknowledged. Retyping into the computer was done by Mrs Beh Goh Peng and Miss Suzie Chan of Seminari Theoloji Malaysia. Those associated with Rutherford House have been long-suffering in the processes leading to publication. The support and attention to detail of Dr David F. Wright and Miss Lynn Quigley is particularly acknowledged.

It was a pleasure to experience the assistance of librarians around Scotland and further afield. Particular thanks are due to the staff of New College Library, Edinburgh, especially Mr John Howard, Mrs Margot Butt, Mr Iain Hope and Dr Murray Simpson. I am indebted to Miss Katharine F. Lambert, Sir Roderick Inglis of Glencorse, and Mr James C. Macnab of Macnab, who granted access to private papers in their hands. Miss Kathleen Cann of the Bible Society gave special assistance.

Andrew Walls as my supervisor was the source of extraordinary example, constant encouragement, searching questions, unusual information, unexpected contacts and thoughtful suggestions. Being a research student in the Religious Studies Department of the University of Aberdeen was enriching. Special mention must be made of Dr Harold Turner, Dr Jocelyn Murray and Dr Stuart Piggin. I was also helped in my understanding of the period by Dr Don Chambers, Professor Alec Cheyne, Dr Michael Laird, Mr Iain Maciver and Mr Donald Withrington.

Not least I remain thankful for the support of my wife Jenny, and our children Rachel, Joanna, Katie and Timothy. Since the original work was done I have been in parish ministry in Wellington and taught church history in Kuala Lumpur. I now teach mission studies at the Bible College of New Zealand. None has been spared hearing about Chalmers. Each has contributed to my understanding.

John Roxborogh
Bible College of New Zealand
June 1999

PREFACE

Many factors contributed to making Thomas Chalmers (1780-1847) the central figure in Scottish church life in the first half of the 19th century. He is inevitably linked with the Free Church of Scotland and remembered for church extension schemes, parish ministry in Glasgow, and support for overseas missions. His significance lies in a remarkable largeness of vision, Christian and social, which responded to the intellectual and social challenges of an age of rapid change in ways which were energetic, visionary and at times reactionary. He was held in great affection at the same time as his life was frequently marked by controversy. Not all his causes have been judged kindly by history, yet then as now his importance is more than Scottish or even British. His aphorisms appear unacknowledged in unexpected places and his name remains one to be conjured with. Churches around the world bear his name, as does Port Chalmers, in Otago, New Zealand.

The changes his lifetime embraced can easily be seen as they have often been portrayed, as being tied up with the demise of Moderate leadership and the rise of the Evangelicals. The Evangelical movement is then credited by some with the energy of a new mission commitment at home and overseas and blamed by others for lack of statesmanship when its enthusiasm and adherence to principle split the church.

There is truth in this, but only some. In the 19th century Evangelicals and Moderates both changed and both contributed. It was the church as a whole which needed to adapt and both parties felt the pain of adjustment. Both found their structures and their theologies inadequate. Both had to discern principles which could be more enduring. Neither succeeded fully, and if the Evangelicals succeeded the more, they did not do so on their own. Their achievements and failures alike owe much to the church as a whole and the opportunities and temper of the times.

As commonly perceived, both regard and distaste for Chalmers fail to do him justice. If some cannot come to terms with the fact that the central affirmations of his faith were combined with a relative liberalism in theology, others have difficulty seeing that behind the more obvious anachronisms of his parish schemes were principles and practices of abiding value. In Scotland it is easy to feel burdened by a surfeit of church buildings left over from an age of extension and duplication for which he is held responsible. It is all too easy to react against the adulation which he attracted in many quarters.

The revival of the early 19th century has too much to teach us to be trivialised in the service of other conflicts as has often been its fate. The period leading to and following the Disruption needs to be revisited not so much to prove the rightness or wrongness of particular groups and individuals, as to discover qualities of faith, commitment, and wisdom capable of rising above the challenges of the times and the weaknesses of those who wrestle with them in every generation.

Part of Chalmers' tension and genius was that he embodied so much of the process the whole church was going through in all its theological and political diversity. His story speaks to those who struggle with personal faith and its social outworking in every age. His solutions may have been partial and of their time, but he still has something to say to those concerned with science and faith, with cities and salvation, and with situations where the relationship of church and state needs sensitivity and understanding.

If he is set free from captivity to the mythologies of the Disruption, then the identity of Presbyterianism has to be drawn with firmer and broader strokes than has been customary. Chalmers' example addresses a tradition now less unique in its government and more diverse in its membership as it rediscovers commitments which rise above old polarities and adjusts to the realities of a multi-cultural and world-wide faith. If some Presbyterian homelands today feel their weaknesses, churches of the Reformed tradition in Asia and Africa know of growth and of missionary commitment. As partners in a world faith we recognize that the interplay of home and overseas mission must now be a universal Christian concern.

We live in an age which for all its differences appears to be revisiting all too many of the economic theories, social dislocations and theological uncertainties of Chalmers' own. All of us need a sense of identity which is authentic to the gospel we share and to the context in which we live. Chalmers may be seen as an example of the possibilities and risks of such a commitment.

The foundation of this book lies in my 1979 Aberdeen doctoral thesis which was originally researched in Aberdeen and Edinburgh from 1975 to 1978. Its underlying question was the way in which convictions about the mission of the church in a particular era were shaped by personal faith and social and religious change. It examines Chalmers' life and thought particularly in relation to the mission of the church first at home and then overseas.

Most attention is given to formative periods – his experience in the rural Fife parish of Kilmany, particularly his search for a theological identity after his conversion in 1811, and the interaction of the model and ideals these provided with the problems of unsettled industrial Glasgow after the Napoleonic wars. The continuity of his vision for the 'religious good of Scotland' is traced through the decade of the Voluntary Controversy, Church Extension Movement and Disruption to his hopes for the Evangelical Alliance and his final parish experiment in the West Port of Edinburgh.

Chalmers interacted at many points with the growth of the missionary movement in Scotland. Deciding positively to support missions was important for Chalmers' development after his conversion and the story of this movement and his involvement is traced in some detail. Bible and missionary societies caught his imagination while at Kilmany. At St John's they became part of his territorial plan and in St Andrews six of his students set their sights on missionary service.

Although he is less remembered as a theologian, the significance of his theology has been underestimated, particularly since his attitudes towards confessional standards anticipated views not widely accepted until later in the century. An attempt is made to justify this claim and explain the neglect of this aspect of his work.

Chalmers had a fine sense of what was of lasting importance. Impatient when it came to creeds and tolerant of Catholics, he was influenced by Methodists and Moravians, and was a friend of Anglicans, agnostics, Baptists, early charismatics, Quakers, a number of Moderates and not a few judged to be heretics. He was a warm conversationalist and loved children. He exasperated his friends, infuriated his opponents and colleagues and made fellow Evangelicals nervous. Students adored him.

Chalmers aimed to change both character and the environment by which character was formed. He believed in the Scottish parish and educational system and in the sending of missionaries, teachers and Bibles around the world. His judgement was at times imperfect, but his instincts were sound. It is a story worth telling.

ABBREVIATIONS

AGA	*Acts of the General Assembly of the Church of Scotland*
BFBS	British and Foreign Bible Society
BL	British Library, London.
BMS	Baptist Missionary Society
BOD	Bodleian Library Oxford
CBD	D. Patrick and F. H. Groome, *Chambers' biographical dictionary*, London, W. & R. Chambers, 1897.
CMS	Church Missionary Society
Correspondence	William Hanna, *A selection of the correspondence of the late Thomas Chalmers*, Edinburgh, Constable, 1853.
DNB	*Dictionary of National Biography*
EUL	University of Edinburgh Library
Fasti	Hew Scott, *Fasti Ecclesiae Scoticanae. The succession of ministers in the Church of Scotland from the Reformation*, Revised edition, Edinburgh, Oliver and Boyd, 7 vols, 1915-1928.
GUA	University of Glasgow Archives
Journal	Thomas Chalmers'manuscript diaries, NCL.
LMS	London Missionary Society
Memoirs	William Hanna, *Memoirs of the life and writings of Thomas Chalmers*, Edinburgh, Constable, 4 vols, 1849-1852.
NCL	New College Library, University of Edinburgh.
NLS	National Library of Scotland
NRA(S)	National Register of Archives (Scotland)
NSA	*New Statistical Account of Scotland*
OSA	*Statistical Account of Scotland*, 1791-1799 ('*Old Statistical Account*').
PLDU	William Perkins Library, Duke University, North Carolina.
SPCK	Society for the Propagation of Christian Knowledge
SRA	Strathclyde Regional Archives
SRO/GRH	Scottish Record Office, General Register House.
SRO/GRO	Scottish Record Office, General Register Office.
SRO/WRH	Scottish Record Office, West Register House.
SSPCK	Society in Scotland for the Propagation of Christian Knowledge
StAUL	University of St Andrews Library
T. C.	Thomas Chalmers
Works	Thomas Chalmers, *Works* [series title varies], 25 vols, Glasgow, William Collins, 1836-1842.

PART ONE

THE CHRISTIAN GOOD OF SCOTLAND

Who cares about the Free Church compared with the Christian good of the people of Scotland? Who cares about any church, but as an instrument of Christian good? For be assured that the moral and religious wellbeing of the population is of infinitely higher importance than the advancement of any sect.[1]

The high and holy mission...to which he devoted all the faculties of his vigorous intellect, and all the activities of his laborious life, was the christianizing of Scotland.... If his actings were many, his aim was one...to render Scotland over its length and breadth, a Christian nation.[2]

---

[1] Chalmers, 27 December, 1845. *Memoirs*, 4, 394.

[2] 'The late Rev Dr Chalmers', *Macphail's Edinburgh Ecclesiastical Journal*, 3(18), July 1847, 479f.

Chapter 1

'My travail is that both princes and subjects obey God'[3]
Church and society in Scotland

In the 1830s cries of 'spiritual independence' and 'non-intrusion' were a stand on principle against government and court interference in the heart matters of the Church. Behind them lay an 'unexamined question' concerning not the role of the State in the Church, but the role of the Church in the State – whether 'the historic Calvinist standpoint that the Christian Church...could so impress itself upon the surrounding community that the standards of the Gospel became the rule of life for society at large' was 'consistent with the New Testament and practicable or even realistic in a nineteenth century industrial situation'.[4]

In fact Scotland remains a place where it is not necessary to apologize for the social dimensions of the Christian gospel. However it is natural to question whether revival of the personal is likely to mean loss of commitment to the social. Chalmers' life is testimony to the complexity and interwovenness of these dimensions. It is true that some of the energy of mission in this period owed more than it should have to conflicts of party and class rather than convictions of faith, but overall the depth and scope of commitment was real enough. Although church and state drew the boundaries of their autonomy in different places, and the authority of the Church of Scotland was not to be what it once was, Christian concern for society remained wide and generally accepted. What is significant about Chalmers is not so much that this vision existed (though he certainly gave it fresh life and direction) but the energy and persistence with which it was worked out.

Convictions about the role of the church in society are deeply rooted. The Reformation was brought about against the wishes of the monarchy,

---

[3] John Knox, quoted by G. D. Henderson, *The claims of the Church of Scotland*, 1951, 157.

[4] A. L. Drummond and J. Bulloch, *The Church in Victorian Scotland 1843-1874*, 1975, 1.

rather than at its bidding, and reformers needed political influence to implement their ideals. The church as God's new People of Israel provided a rationale and a model.[5] John Knox gave many instances of being true to his remark quoted above. The *First Book of Discipline* spelt out that Christian rulers had a duty to support true religion and to bring the laws of the land into conformity with the standards of the Bible.[6] In the eyes of some ministers, even monarchs were subject to the discipline of the church.[7]

The Covenants of the 17th century were also a binding together of the nation and its faith. Rejection of episcopacy was coloured by feelings towards the English, but it was also related to a strong sense of the autonomy of the church in the full breadth of its concerns. The Westminster Confession noted the duties and obligations of the civil magistrate, and further reflected and reinforced the conviction that the whole of life in society ought to be ordered according to the will of God. At the end of the 17th century the failed Darien colonial scheme was a mission overseas of both church and state.

The union of 1707 left the General Assembly of the Church of Scotland as the nation's only forum for debate, and its meetings took on some of the functions and concerns of the parliament that moved to Westminster. Well into the 19th century members of parliament, leaders in the legal profession and numbers of the landed gentry were prominent in the lay membership of the Assembly.[8] Not surprisingly it represented these interests better than others, yet on occasion it was capable of condemning commercial injustice and 'the grinding of the faces of the poor by landlords'.[9]

In the 18th century there began a breakdown of the unity of the church. Social change made it difficult to keep up with population shifts, rises in new social groupings, the complexities of cities and of industrial and commercial life. Revolutions of mind, agriculture, and industry and the rapid growth of population in urban areas, could not leave the church unaffected.

For much of the century the General Assembly was dominated by the Moderate party who advised the government on church patronage and ceased to protest at infringements on the autonomy of the church. Intellectually Moderates reflected the spirit of the age more than their Evangelical opponents. Differences between these parties lay in the failings they were

---

[5] G. D. Henderson, *The nature of the church*, 1948, 38f.

[6] J. K. Cameron, *The First Book of Discipline*, 1972, 62-7.

[7] A. L. Drummond and J. Bulloch, *The Scottish Church 1688-1843*, 1973, 258.

[8] I. F. Maciver, 'The Evangelical Party and the eldership in General Assemblies, 1820-1843', *Records of the Scottish Church History Society*, 20(1), 1978, 1-13.

[9] S. Mechie, *The Church and Scottish social development 1780-1870*, 1960, 2.

prepared to tolerate, in emphases on the rights of people over against rights of patrons, and in orthodoxy as relating to an experience of faith and a particular understanding of the Bible, more than a symbol of loyalty to the government as much as to Christ. That the gospel itself and the role of the church were concerned for the whole of life and for all the people was not in doubt and neither was the value placed on education as a means of salvation both social and religious.

A cohesive role in society was well demonstrated under the threat of the ideas flowing from the French Revolution. When faced with invasion, the pulpits of Scotland were not slow in rallying the national spirit. However changes in government and society soon tested Moderate ability to relate to one and adjust to the other and while a comprehensive vision remained, its outworking could not be the same. Those whose intellectual heritage included a clear sense of the rights of the people in religious matters at least, were, once the threat of France had passed, more likely to understand and adapt to an Age of Reform.

Seceders had steadily increased in number for over half a century and in the first decade of the 19th century, Congregationalists,[10] Baptists and Roman Catholics also began to take on significant proportions. Population increase and urban migration taxed facilities for worship and blunted concerns about the growth of dissent at the same time as it made it difficult for the Church of Scotland to maintain its provision and control of education and poor relief.

The 1832 Reform Acts extended the franchise to sections of Scottish society which had the economic basis for supporting their own churches. It became impossible for governments politically dependent on dissenters to assist with the building or endowment of churches for what was now one group among several. The Church of Scotland might still be established, but government patronage now served its own ends best by offending as few as possible.

Even before the Disruption 'the time had gone when the Church of Scotland could be regarded more or less as the nation in its spiritual aspect'.[11] The loss of a third of its membership in 1843 for a time reduced it to one denomination alongside others. The lay membership of the Assembly had been declining in status, and it was no longer acceptable that an unrepresentative body should control major social functions. The fate of the Church of Scotland was not indicative of a decline in Christianity, but it contributed to the secularization of important parts of national life.

The post-Disruption Church of Scotland was shorn of functions it had carried out from before the Reformation, but all was not lost. In the late 1820s it launched a new mission in the Highlands, and in 1830 its first overseas missionary began work in India. By 1843 it had added a mission to

---

10 At first known as Independents.
11 Drummond and Bulloch, *The Scottish Church*, 1973, 220.

the Jews[12] and another in aid of colonial churches. Led by Chalmers, its programme of church building at home increased its charges by about 20% in less than a decade.

In developing this machinery the Church equipped itself out of its own resources to engage in new dimensions of mission at home and overseas. Only if the 18th century church had exercised its relationship with the government and society in a more critical way could this be described as a reduction in mission to functions which were narrowly religious. Fragmentation of commitment obviously made a difference, but the churches of Scotland still had a concern for the salvation of society. The threat of dis-establishment was also strongly felt. Chalmers was not alone in believing that this was a challenge to its religious mission, not just to its position in society. What was changing was less the fact of the involvement of Christians in the life of society than the way in which that involvement was structured.

The Church of Scotland had traditionally looked to the government and to wealthy patrons for its finance, but now money for new ventures had to be found by church members themselves. Financial involvement increased lay participation in congregations and the many-sided auxiliary associations which developed during this period. It was Chalmers' ability to mobilize these resources which financed church extension at home and overseas, and in due course the setting up of a new denomination.

In these processes, Chalmers played a prominent and frequently a leading part. He preached a personal experience of salvation and related it to the communal vision of his childhood and first parish which was never far away from his thinking. In Glasgow he fought to demonstrate the viability of rural Christian values in a growing industrial city. In his convenership of the Church Extension Committee and leadership of the Free Church of Scotland, he presented a comprehensive vision of a church taking shape around a mission to all the people.

---

[12]   D. Chambers, 'Prelude to the last things: the Church of Scotland's mission to the Jews', *Records of the Scottish Church History Society*, 19(1), 1975, 43-58.

Chapter 2

'A more beneficial member of society than a schoolmaster?'[1]
Chalmers at Anstruther and St Andrews, 1780-1799

Chalmers was born on March 17, 1780, in the small[2] fishing and ship-building town of Anstruther Easter on the south-east coast of Fife.[3] The family had been in the area since his great-grandfather[4] became minister at Elie, six miles to the west, at the beginning of the century. One son succeeded to the parish[5] whilst his grandfather[6] settled in Anstruther as a ship-owner, merchant, dyer and threadmaker. His father[7] remained in the business and was provost on a number of occasions.

Thomas was the sixth child and the only one to find a career in the church, although one sister married a minister.[8] Of the nine brothers, James[9] was in business in Liverpool and then London. One died in infancy,[10] three went to sea,[11] one became a distiller in

---

1   T. C. student paper, NCL CHA 6.

2   In 1801 the population of Anstruther Easter was 969 and that of the neighbouring burgh of Anstruther Wester 297. *Comparative account of the population of Great Britain in the years 1801, 1811, 1821 and 1831*, 1831, 382.

3   *OSA*, 16, 1795, 243f. *NSA*, 9, 1838, 294-303. See also entries for Anstruther Wester. *OSA*, 3, 1792, 77-88. *NSA*, 9, 1838, 610-30. A. Thirkell, *Auld Anster*, 1976.

4   James Chalmers (c.1679-1741). *Fasti*, 5, 198f.

5   John Chalmers (1712-1791). *Fasti*, 5, 199, 210.

6   James Chalmers (1713-1788). Boog-Watson, Chalmers family tree, NCL.

7   John Chalmers (1740-1818), ibid.

8   Helen Chalmers (1786-1854) married the Revd John Maclellan of Kelton in 1826. *Fasti*, 2, 414f. Boog-Watson, Chalmers family tree, NCL.

9   James Chalmers (1722-1839), ibid.

10   John Chalmers (1785-1785), ibid.

11   George Chalmers (1777-1806), William Chalmers (1778-1800), and David Chalmers (1783-1811), ibid.

Wishaw,[12] one a surgeon in Kirkcaldy,[13] and Charles redeemed an unsettled youth by founding Merchiston Castle School in Edinburgh.[14] Three of the five sisters never married.[15] The youngest, Jean, married the factor on an estate in Somerset.[16]

Anstruther Easter and its neighbouring burgh of Anstruther Wester were of declining economy but rich in story and tradition. A few hundred yards from Chalmers' home was the church where John Knox had preached and the crowd tore down the altar screen.[17] James Melville[18] was later minister and the solid manse he built still contains timbers from the Spanish Armada.[19] In 1679 Archbishop James Sharp[20] spent his last night there before he was murdered. Anstruther supported the Covenants and many lost their lives at the battle of Kilsyth in 1645.[21] Nearby St Andrews was the cradle of the Scottish Reformation where George Wishart had been martyred and Cardinal Beaton killed in revenge. In Beaton's castle Knox had joined the reformers and was captured by the French.

From his youth Chalmers imbibed these traditions and the manifold associations of story and place. At an early age he play-acted as a preacher,[22] and the story told of many[23] indicated his career. Both parents were devout, particularly his father, though this took a long time to be reflected in the son. With no special religious commitment beyond a vague desire to enter the ministry[24] he went to St Andrews university at the age of 11. It was a less precocious age than it appears now, but even so it was unusually young.

From 1791-2 until 1794-5 he attended arts and philosophy and in November 1795 began divinity,[25] though his main interest was mathematics and issues such as free-will and determinism. He joined the

---

12　Patrick Chalmers (1790-1854), ibid.

13　Alexander Chalmers (1796-1829), ibid.

14　Charles Chalmers (1792-1864), ibid.

15　Lucy Chalmers (1773-1810), Barbara Chalmers (1775-1808) and Isabel Chalmers (1781-1864), ibid.

16　Jean Chalmers (1788-1864) married John Morton in 1812, ibid. *Memoirs*, 1, 270.

17　Thirkell, *Auld Anster*, 1976, 7.

18　Ibid., 9-13. *Fasti*, 5, 212f.

19　It remains the oldest inhabited manse in Scotland.

20　*Fasti*, 7, 326f.

21　*OSA*, 3, 1792, 86. J. Kinross, *Discovering battlefields of Scotland*, 1976, 19f.

22　*Memoirs*, 1, 8.

23　H. Watt, *Thomas Chalmers and the Disruption*, 1943, 14.

24　The intention was known to the family by the start of his second session, James Chalmers to T. C., 18 October 1792, NCL CHA 4.1.1.

25　*Memoirs*, 1, 15.

Theological Society in December 1795,[26] and took part in its weekly meetings. On each occasion there was a debate and a paper for discussion. Topics ranged widely and included mission overseas, the eternity of hell-torments and the immortality of the soul.

Chalmers debated church establishments, and at the end of his first session as a divinity student supported the proposition that 'a minister is a more beneficial member of society than a schoolmaster'.[27] The manuscript survives, and reveals more of a dislike for authoritarian schoolteachers than ideas about the ministry. Nevertheless the minister dealt with matters of eternity, visited the sick and administered charity. In contrast to the schoolteacher,

> the exaction of unlimited obedience from his parishioners is entirely beyond the power of the minister and (he) is therefore not so liable to acquire exalted ideas of his own superiority.[28]

It was an age of intellectual excitement stirred by the Scottish Enlightenment and ideas from France. Many subjects arose out of the students' Calvinist heritage. At this point they could debate with relative freedom, but once they became licentiates of the Church of Scotland, formal adherence to the Westminster Confession inhibited open speculation. It was taken for granted that those who could get churches would carry on the long-standing traditions of preaching, catechizing, baptizing, marrying and burying common to every other parish minister.

Scotland had seen political disturbances, but the revolt of the '45' had been in the Highlands and it already seemed a long time ago. Whatever the threats from France or the state of the economy, the stability of Moderate rule appeared assured. It was in keeping with their values of urbane learning rather than fervid faith that a number would have had ambitions for a university position, probably in conjunction with a nearby parish.

Chalmers was not alone in coveting such a career, nor entirely unique in having the professor's chair of his dreams not one in some field more obviously related to the ministry, but in mathematics. In his theology course it is probable he attended George Hill's lectures on church government.[29] Hill's main concern was the credentials of presbyterianism relative to episcopacy, independency and quakerism. As later with Chalmers,

---

26   Theological Society minutes, 2, 1786-1823, StAUL UY 911.

27   T. C. student paper, NCL CHA 6.

28   Ibid.

29   Unless he missed them while absent during the first two months of his final session at St Andrews. The lectures can be found in book 6 of G. Hill, *Lectures in divinity*, 1854, 520-96, and are likely to be those delivered during the 1790s. These were published in 1817 and follow exactly the outline in Hill's *Theological Institutes* of 1803.

there was little treatment of the nature and purpose of the church, although he acknowledged Christianity made universal claims. However gradual, he looked to its eventual world-wide propagation. Church government was

> one branch of the provision which is made in the gospel for propagating and maintaining the truth, for restraining vice, for assisting Christians in the discharge of their duty and for promoting the universal practice of virtue.[30]

Hill's lectures became a standard theological text and are still notable for their clarity and measured analysis. At the time Hill seemed to Chalmers to be chiefly interested in moral theology. In the Moderate tradition it was not difficult to conceive the mission of the church as first of all that of trying to make people good. With such an understanding Chalmers began work in his first parish.

---

[30] Hill, *Lectures*, 1854, 571. In article 18 of the Scots Confession of 1560, the purpose of ecclesiastical discipline was stated to be the repression of vice and the nourishment of virtue.

Chapter 3

'The malignant touch of ordination'[1]
Minister at Kilmany, 1803-1809

Chalmers' first charge was the parish of Kilmany, about nine miles west of St Andrews, where he was ordained on 18 May 1803. A distant cousin[2] had held the position briefly in the 18th century. The chief attraction was proximity to the university and the prospects for advancement which might be there.

The parish was triangular, six miles long and four miles across at the widest point. During Chalmers' time the population remained at about 780 including about 150 families.[3] Ministers before[4] and after[5] Chalmers took a

---

[1] (T. Chalmers) *Observations on a passage in Mr Playfair's letter to the Lord Provost of Edinburgh relative to the mathematical pretensions of the Scottish clergy*, 1805, 48.

[2] John Adamson (1742-1793) was at Kilmany from 1764 to 1772. *Fasti*, 5, 161, 235 and 240.

[3] In 1801 the population was 787, in 1811, 781. By 1821 it had declined to 751 and this gradual reduction in population continued thereafter. *Comparative account of the population*, 1831, 383.

[4] John Cook (1771-1824) was at Kilmany from 1793 to 1802. He was subsequently Professor of Hebrew and then of Biblical Criticism at St Andrews. *Fasti*, 7, 429f.

[5] Henry David Cook (1791-1857) was at Kilmany from 1815 to 1857. *Fasti*, 5, 162. He was a younger brother of John Cook. Their father, John Cook (1739-1815), was Professor of Moral Philosophy at St Andrews from 1773 and had married the sister of Principal George Hill whose talents for nepotism were proverbial. At one stage six of the 13 members of the senatus were his relatives (R. G. Cant, *The University of St Andrews*, 1970, 99). Another of John Cook's sons, George, succeeded Chalmers to the chair of moral philosophy in 1828. He became leader of the Moderate party during the 1830s and was frequently in conflict with Chalmers. See also H. R. Sefton, 'St Mary's College, St Andrews in the eighteenth century', *Records of the Scottish Church History Society* 24(2), 1991, 161-180.

keen interest in farming which was the main source of employment.[6] His predecessor emphasized the need to plant trees and lamented the effects of improving agriculture. The substitution of unmarried men for families as farm labourers meant 'the healthiest and purest nursery of the most vigorous and innocent class of our countrymen has...been much depopulated'.[7]

> Religion will be found here to be much more than mere speculation; it has great influence on the conduct; it concurs, with unseducing situation, to preserve the manners simple, and to make the morals pure; and it yields support in the hour of distress, which the stoutest hearts might wish to have.[8]

The school and the church provided some community focus and the nearest market-town was five miles away at Cupar.[9] It is not clear whether there was a public house in Chalmers' time; by 1838 there was 'now only one'.[10] Those who looked to the Kirk Session for poor relief were few and were said to be reluctant to compromise their pride and independence.

> They very seldom and with much hesitation ask; their wants must be noticed and supplied. These two happy consequences...arise from hence. The rich are roused to that care of their brethren which anticipates the wishes of the needy, which is man's best acquisition and a source of pure enjoyment while the poor lose not that withdrawing declining modesty to which it is so pleasant to afford assistance.... The reluctance not merely to solicit, but often even to receive aid, shows that delicate sense of dignity which poverty may so keenly feel; of which nothing can divest a man but the meanness of his own soul; and which is much desiderated amongst the lazy, importunate beggars of large towns.[11]

This was not Chalmers' writing, but it could easily have been – and the romantic picture was one he never lost. It had a certain dignity, but it concealed both need and causation. Neither was the lack of seduction complete, although the 3.5% of baptisms entered in the parish register in Chalmers' time as 'natural'[12] was not bad by the standards of rural

---

6   *OSA*, 19, 1797, 420-33. *NSA*, 9, 1838, 532-57.
7   *OSA*, 19, 1797, 430.
8   Ibid., 432.
9   There was no fair or market in Kilmany.
10   *NSA*, 9, 1838, 557.
11   *OSA*, 19, 1797, 431f.
12   The only surviving parish records for this period are the register of baptisms and the parish accounts, Scottish Record Office, General Register Office, Edinburgh, POR 437/1. These give little indication of Kirk Session

Scotland.[13] If the figures given in the *New Statistical Account* are to be believed, in the 1830s about 17% of births were illegitimate.[14]

The only ecclesiastical competition was a congregation of Seceders which dated to 1762 and met a mile and a half away at Rathillet. In 1797 'several families'[15] worshipped there, but it must have taken more than that to support the minister, James Johnston (1759-1812).[16] After 1815 his successor benefited from Chalmers' move to Glasgow, owing to distaste for the Moderatism of Chalmers' replacement.[17] The three hundred reported as attending the Secession that year were over a third of the population.[18]

Most people were connected with the land. There was no nobility and of the ten proprietors five were resident farmers on their own estates. In 1838 there were 12 tenant farmers and about a hundred cottars, ten weavers, 23 wrights and smiths and six millers. There were three teachers and a beadle.[19]

Chalmers had been licensed by the Presbytery of St Andrews in July 1799[20] and preached his first sermons while visiting England a month later. His brother James reported he leaned to the practical rather than the doctrinal and did not take much care of his appearance for the pulpit despite the best efforts of his friends. He was more interested in mathematics than religion.[21]

The winters of 1799-1800 and 1800-1801 had been spent in Edinburgh attending lectures in chemistry, moral philosophy and natural philosophy. The summer of 1801 brought the prospect of an assistantship at Cavers near

---

13   discipline, although the accounts show on occasions the entry of a fine. A separate discipline book had been started in 1749 but it was not kept up until the 1830s. *NSA*, 9, 1838, 542.

A typical level was 5-6%, the highest 15-17%. T. C. Smout, 'Aspects of sexual behaviour in nineteenth century Scotland', A. A. MacLaren, ed., *Social class in Scotland: past and present*, 1977, 63.

14   *NSA*, 1838, 545. Over a three and a half year period.

15   *OSA*, 19, 1797, 431.

16   R. Small, *History of the congregations of the United Presbyterian Church from 1733 to 1900*, 1, 1904, 178f.

17   According to one of Chalmers' parishioners, John Tindall (1782-1836), the Secession minister who took over Rathillet in 1814, was impressive. By contrast Chalmers' successor might as well have preached in Greek. 'We could make nothing of it at all.' J. Balfour to T. C., 1815, NCL CHA 4.4.1.

18   Small, *United Presbyterian Church*, 1, 1904, 178.

19   *NSA*, 9, 1838, 546. The figures for the trades include 'masters, workmen and apprentices'.

20   *Memoirs*, 1, 33. Watt, *Chalmers*, 1943, 18f. Chalmers was two years younger than the normal minimum of 21. His case was argued on the grounds that he was 'a lad o' pregnant parts' and that the church allowed discretion for those of 'singular and rare qualities'.

21   James Chalmers to John Chalmers, 3 September 1799, *Memoirs*, 1, 38.

Hawick and a few months later news of the vacancy near St Andrews.[22] In November 1801 he went to Cavers and remained there until September 1802. He entered into his duties with energy, enjoying the hospitality of the local farmers and the annual parish visitation which involved dividing it into districts and staying overnight with farmers in each area.[23]

He preached regularly and assisted with the sacrament in neighbouring parishes. Nevertheless his main interests lay elsewhere. The chance arose of becoming assistant to the Professor of Mathematics at St Andrews,[24] and with the vacancy at Kilmany also looking hopeful, his future seemed assured. In April 1802 he was successful in both applications and the summer at Cavers was spent preparing lectures.

At Cavers Chalmers was left to his own devices, and little mention is made of the minister Thomas Elliot (c.1732-1808)[25] who 'possessed considerable attainments as a mathematician and astronomer'.[26] Of more significance was his relationship with Samuel Charters of Wilton (1742-1825).[27]

Returning to Fife in September Chalmers took up his mathematical appointment at the beginning of the winter session. However, having criticized his professor in public,[28] at the end of the session he found himself relieved of the post.

As this situation developed, parental disquiet over his attitude to the ministry expressed itself in the suggestion he spend some time in a spiritual retreat prior to his ordination. It drew a sharp reply.

> I hope that my principles...are already established, and that they do not require any extraordinary exercises of reflection at present.... It is my decided opinion that the charge of a congregation is of the first importance...it is vain to think that the extraordinary effort of a few

---

22 *Memoirs*, 1, 53. Charles Wilson, Professor of Church History, died on 5 September 1801. *Fasti*, 7, 432.

23 T. C. to John Chalmers, 13 January 1802, *Memoirs*, 1, 54f. T. C. to John Chalmers, 19 February 1802, *Memoirs*, 1, 55.

24 Professor Vilant employed a succession of assistants who undertook virtually his full duties. In February 1801 Chalmers had written to his friend James Brown (1763-1836), *Fasti*, 5, 197, that it would be 'an employment very suited to my wishes and may perhaps prepare for others of greater importance'. Brown had been an earlier holder of the position and Chalmers' own mathematics teacher. T. C. to James Brown, 28 February 1801, EUL Dc.2.57.50.

25 Chalmers' appointment was as 'assistant' and the position was entirely in the hands of the minister and himself. If it had been 'assistant and successor' it would have been permanent and involved the patron as well.

26 *Fasti*, 2, 106.

27 *Fasti*, 2, 143f.

28 *Memoirs*, 1, 66.

days will very essentially contribute to preparation or to improvement.[29]

Asking to be spared a 'painful and unmeaning solemnity' Chalmers replied that suspicions about 'indifference to parochial duties' might be better founded after he had been in the position for a while – as indeed they were.

Chalmers entered his first parish at the age of 23 with his self-assurance seemingly scarcely rippled by the fiasco over the mathematics lectureship and with views of Christian commitment radically different from those of his father.

In the summer of 1803 he visited the 150 families of the parish and settled into the routine of services, baptisms, marriages and burials. At the same time he decided to return to St Andrews and lecture during the winter whether he held the position or not. He wrote home that it would mean being non-resident for six months of the year.

> My chief anxiety is to reconcile you to the idea of not confining my whole attention to my ministerial employment. The fact is that no minister finds that necessary.[30]

His lectures began on the first of November and his teaching gifts and audacity attracted students. The university was unimpressed and fought back by switching lecture times. In December he began chemistry which did not compete with anything official and this gradually won acceptance.

For the winter of 1803-4 Chalmers lived at St Andrews, returning to Kilmany for little more than the Sunday service. Parishioners had to be content with this brief appearance to deliver sermons prepared that morning. These lacked content, but he was capable of being inspiring on occasion.[31] His heart lay in mathematics and chemistry where he showed something of the eloquence and social concern that was later to characterize his ministry.

> Philosophy is never more usefully and never more honourably directed than when multiplying the stores of human comfort and subsistence – than when enlightening the humblest departments of industry – than when she leaves the school of declamation and descends to the walks of business, to the dark and dismal receptacles of misery, to the hospitals of disease, to the putrid houses of our great cities, where poverty sits in

---

29   T. C. to John Chalmers, 28 April 1803, *Memoirs*, 1, 67.

30   T. C. to John Chalmers, 18 October 1803, *Memoirs*, 1, 73.

31   The principal heritor of Kilmany, David Gillespie of Mountquhannie, asked for a copy of his fast-day sermon on October 20, 1803. *Posthumous Works*, 6, 40. ('Fast-days' were observed as additional Sundays in times of national emergency, as in this case when Britain was again at war with France.)

lonely and ragged wretchedness, agonized with pain, faint with hunger, and shivering in a frail and unsheltered tenement.[32]

A minister holding a second job in some form of pluralism was hardly unprecedented. It was the manner as much as the fact of it which drew comment at Presbytery meetings in May and September 1804.[33] Chalmers replied that 'after the punctual discharge of his professional duties his time was his own'.[34]

Only in the narrowest sense could Chalmers remotely claim that he was covering what was required. In 1804 he conducted his first sacrament of communion[35] and continued every summer as was normal. In 1804 the church was 'without sermon' for three Sundays and that year he carried out 16 baptisms and attended to 3 marriages and 10 burials.[36] He challenged the Presbytery to send somebody to investigate.

> Let the gentleman traverse the boundaries of my parish; let him begin with the houses of my wealthy proprietors and descend to the lowest tenements of poverty and disease. I will defy him to find a single individual who can substantiate the charge of culpable negligence against me. I will defy him to find a single individual who will say that I have been outstripped by any of my predecessors in the regularity of my ministerial attentions.[37]

The following winter he reduced his lecturing to chemistry and his absence from Kilmany to two days a week. However in November 1804 the Professor of Natural Philosophy died and Chalmers was quick to declare himself a contestant for the position. What mattered was not academic knowledge. It was said that mathematics, for example, could readily be picked up by a 'man of decent abilities'.[38] What was important was loyalty to the government and the superiority of the Moderates. Chalmers'

---

[32] *Memoirs*, 1, 79. This was a lecture in chemistry.

[33] *Memoirs*, 1, 82-9. The minutes of the Presbytery of Cupar are not among those held in the Scottish Record Office.

[34] *Memoirs*, 1, 87.

[35] SRO/GRO, OPR 437/1, Kilmany Old Parochial Register 1706-1819. No sacrament was held in 1809, no doubt because of his illness which would also explain its being delayed until December in 1810. Services were held on Wednesday or Thursday (the fast-day), Saturday, Sunday itself, and on the Monday. The attendance was considerably greater than at ordinary services (about three to five times greater from 1804 to 1811, and about twice in Chalmers' last years reflecting the greater attendance at his ordinary services after his conversion. See Appendix 1).

[36] SRO/GRO, OPR 437/1, ibid.

[37] *Memoirs*, 1, 89.

[38] G. Hill to H. Dundas, Lord Melville, StAUL 4802.

theological sympathies were Moderate, but in behaviour he was far from being part of the establishment. His scientific ability was as irrelevant as his general attitudes were a liability, and he was dismissed as 'an eccentric mathematician who comes in from his parish...to read lectures in chemistry in our town hall'.[39]

It was only a month before a similar vacancy occurred in Edinburgh. He was no more successful, but in the 'Leslie controversy'[40] which developed over the appointment it was said that mathematics and the ministry were incompatible. To Chalmers this was a 'cruel and illiberal insinuation', an attempt to deny ministers 'the pride and consolation of...the hope of literary preferment'.[41] In his first publication he wrote:

> The author...can assert from what to him is the highest of all authority, the authority of his own experience, that after the satisfactory discharge of his parish duties, a minister may enjoy five days in the week of uninterrupted leisure for the prosecution of any science in which his taste may engage.[42]

A parish minister had more free time for mathematics than a professor. The two days that had to be spent on clerical duties were only such as to make the intellectual exercise of mathematics a refreshing change.

> There is almost no consumption of intellectual effort in the peculiar employment of a minister. The great doctrines of revelation, though sublime are simple.... A minister's duty is the duty of the heart. It is his to impress the simple and home-bred lessons of humanity and justice and the exercises of a sober and enlightened piety. It is his to enlighten the sick-bed of age and infirmity; to rejoice in the administrations of comfort; to maintain a friendly intercourse with his people, and to secure their affections by what no art and no hypocrisy can accomplish – the smile of a benevolent countenance, the frank and open air of an undissembled honesty.[43]

Chalmers regarded the ministry as little challenge for a man of his talents. Without the hope of a university chair he was

---

[39]   Ibid.

[40]   I. D. L. Clark, 'The Leslie controversy, 1805', *Records of the Scottish Church History Society* 14(3), 1962, 179-97. J. B. Morrell, 'The Leslie affair: careers, kirk and politics in Edinburgh in 1805', *Scottish Historical Review*, 54, 1975, 63-82. Henry, Lord Cockburn, *Memorials of his time*, 1946, 122-5.

[41]   *Observations on a passage in Mr Playfair's letter*, 1805, 10.

[42]   Ibid.

[43]   Ibid., 12.

one of those ill-fated beings whom the malignant touch of ordination has condemned to a life of ignorance and obscurity; a being who must bid adieu, it seems, to every flattering anticipation and drivel out the rest of his days in insignificance.[44]

Insignificance was to be avoided at all costs. No doubt speaking autobiographically, he wrote of ministers that

> the choice of their profession often depends on the most accidental circumstances, a whim of infancy, or the capricious destination of parents.[45]

If it did not realise his academic ambitions, nevertheless 1805 did provide other interests. Before the battle of Trafalgar in October, the threat of French invasion was real. Chalmers enrolled in a corps raised in St Andrews and held commissions as lieutenant and chaplain. When he resigned he gave his uniform and sword to a former student and according to the son-in-law of the recipient, 'the coat and breeches once fitted a very portly gentleman'.[46]

That year he was still lecturing in chemistry and gave demonstrations round the district in Cupar, Kirkcaldy and Kilmany. Sometimes people got apologetics as well as science. He 'revered' Christianity

> because it is built on the solid foundations of impregnable argument – because it has improved the world by the lessons of an ennobling morality, and because by the animating prospects which it holds out, it alleviates the sorrows of our final departure hence, and cheers the gloomy desolation of the grave.[47]

By 1806 his absenteeism from the parish was again increasing.[48] He had given up chemistry lectures at St Andrews, but now the state of the manse made him live elsewhere during the winter. In October he reported an interest in botany[49] and the garden displayed a wide range of plants, which testified to his mathematical interests by their geometrical layout.

---

[44] Ibid., 48.

[45] Ibid., 47.

[46] *Memoirs*, 1, 95f. Henry Grafton to John Chalmers Morton, 4 July 1859, Gloucestershire County Record Office, D1021/3/3.

[47] *Memoirs*, 1, 145.

[48] In 1803 Chalmers was absent for eight out of the 32 Sundays after his ordination in May. In 1804 there were three 'no sermon' Sundays. In 1806 this increased to nine, and to 15 the following year, after which the figure steadily dropped apart from the period of his illness in 1809-10. SRO/GRO, OPR 437/1. See Appendix 1.

[49] T. C. to James Chalmers, 29 October 1806, *Memoirs*, 1, 100.

In April 1807 he went on an extended visit to London and did not return until July. While he claimed he returned 'more of the country parson than I ever was in my life before, quite devoted to the sober work of visiting and examining',[50] his mind was well away from the religious state of either himself or his parishioners.

In November 1806 Napoleon had placed an embargo on trade with Britain. It was not clear what the effects would be, but people were worried. By September 1807 he half-completed a book on the subject.[51] *An inquiry into the extent and stability of national resources* appeared at the end of March, 1808.[52] It did not sell well despite the efforts of his friend David Wilkie (1785-1841), then in London establishing his reputation as a painter.[53]

The *Inquiry* was a venture into a subject he would later teach and was not without relevance to his later success as a preacher. Whatever might be said for the reasoning,[54] he was grappling with a current topic. A writer in the Dundee paper complained the press was 'teeming with productions on "national wealth", "internal resources", "foreign commerce"'.[55] Chalmers' *Inquiry* sought to reassure people like his own parishioners that they had nothing to fear.

By the winter of 1808 the condition of the manse could no longer be ignored and in December the heritors[56] agreed to build a new one.[57] Chalmers took lodgings, and when the manse was demolished in March,[58] moved to a farm outside the parish, but not very far from the church.

After five years Chalmers' burning ambition to find significance in life no longer drove him to behaviour which was quite so reckless. His decision to pursue the replacement of the manse showed he had come to accept that, for the present at least, his future lay within the parish and not somewhere else. It also meant that if he was to succeed in getting the heritors to pay for it, it would be necessary for him to be more diligent in carrying out his duties. Whatever energies had been diverted to the *Inquiry*, the number of

---

50   T. C. to James Chalmers, 9 September 1807, *Memoirs*, 1, 121.

51   Ibid. T. C. to T. S. Hardie, 9 September 1807, NCL CHA 3.12.7.

52   *Memoirs*, 1, 132.

53   *Memoirs*, 1, 132-6. Wilkie's father was minister of the neighbouring parish of Cults.

54   *The Eclectic Review* gave credit to his eloquence but the writer was 'probably young in years...certainly young in this kind of speculation'. 'His command of language is probably a fatal snare...for as he seems to be at no loss for words, he is led to mistake fluency of expression for fertility of thought.' July 1808, 576-89.

55   *Dundee, Perth and Cupar Advertiser*, 14 April 1808.

56   Landowners.

57   T. C. to John Chalmers, 1 December 1808, NCL CHA 3.4.19. T. C. to John Chalmers, 15 December 1808, NCL CHA 3.4.21.

58   T. C. to John Chalmers, 20 March 1809, NCL CHA 3.4.25.

Sundays the pulpit was vacant in 1808 suggests greater commitment, and the weekly collections for the poor were consistent with improving attendance.[59]

Chalmers also realized that within a few years he would be able to apply for an increase in his stipend.[60] He took a close interest in an act of parliament to regulate the augmentation of stipends.[61] He noted that the period between augmentations, set as 20 years, was in practice dated from the last decision. If the court took several years to reach a verdict, the period between augmentations was increased accordingly.

---

[59]   See Appendix 1.

[60]   He was also in debt: £355 on his twenty-ninth birthday, 17 March 1809. Account notebook NCL CHA 6.25.3.

[61]   Since the Union of England and Scotland in 1707, matters concerning the legal status of parishes including the determination of the stipend and alterations in boundaries were under the jurisdiction of the Court of Session sitting as the Commissioners for the plantation of kirks and valuation of teinds. The system of paying the ministry defies simple description. Broadly speaking in rural parishes the stipend was paid out of the teinds (tithes or tenths) of the parish, at one stage literally a tenth of the produce of the land collected in kind. Following the appointment of commissioners by Charles I this was commuted into a money payment expressed in terms of meal and paid at rates (the 'fiars prices') which were set annually. The amount of meal available for paying the stipend was calculated as one fifth of the rental value of the land as determined by Charles' commissioners. This rental was not altered in subsequent centuries, although stipends changed with the price of meal. Not all the teinds were applied to the stipend as the commissioners also determined what the stipend should be within the teinds available. There remained 'unexhausted teinds' which went into different hands depending on the history of the parish. Often it went to the patron as in Kilmany. In this case the patron was the United College of St Salvator and St Leonards at the University of St Andrews, but usually the patron was a local heritor. Hence heritors had an interest in resisting any augmentation to stipends. Since 1790 the Court of Session sitting as Commissioners for the plantation of kirks and valuation of teinds had been granting augmentations at an increasing rate. In Ayr resolutions were passed lamenting 'the hardships inflicted on the landed interest' by 'a perpetual tax...of at least £45,000 a year' being the amount of augmentations granted by the court since 1790 (G. Hill to H. Dundas, Lord Melville, 17 March 1808, StAUL 4830). In response to pressure the Government prepared a bill to regulate the situation. The General Assembly of the Church of Scotland kept a watch on the progress of the bill from 1807 onwards. J. Connell, *Treatise on the law of Scotland respecting tithes and the stipends of the parochial clergy*, 1815. N. Elliot, 'Teinds or tithes and church property in Scotland', in R. H. Story, ed., *The Church of Scotland: past and present*, 1890, 5, 557-96. J. N. Wolfe and M. Pickford, *The Church of Scotland. An economic survey*, 1980, 21, 219f.

The Presbytery did not think Chalmers had much chance of getting the General Assembly to ask parliament to amend the bill, but they were willing to let him try.[62] On 25 May 1809 he presented an overture[63] from the Presbytery of Cupar as his maiden speech to the Assembly. As predicted he was unsuccessful, but the effort served to introduce him to a young Evangelical, Andrew Thomson.[64] Chalmers agreed to the suggestion that the speech be published,[65] particularly as there was competition to pay for the privilege.[66]

Chalmers' arguments were shaped by the matter in hand, but showed he was still grappling with the significance of parish ministry. Whereas in 1805 the lack of the prospect of a university chair threatened any hope of a meaningful life, now it was the lack of an adequate stipend. Ministers were entitled

> to maintain their rank in the country, and be rescued from that insignificance in which they would otherwise be infallibly left by the progress of every other order in society.[67]

They had to fight to 'reach that genteel independence...which should be the inheritance of every public instructor'.[68] Politicians should recognize the church was

> a most essential part of the political fabric; a powerful instrument of security against the disaffection of the people, in so far as it propitiates the attachment of an enlightened order, whose business it is to nurse a numerous population in the solid principles of virtue and patriotism.[69]

This could not be maintained without status, and that meant stipend.

---

62   The Presbytery met at Cupar on May 9, 1809.
63   'Overture' is the technical term for a motion of recommendation from a lower court in the church to a higher one.
64   Andrew Mitchell Thomson (1778-1831) was a minister in Perth. He later became leader of the Evangelical party and editor of *The Edinburgh Christian Instructor*, founded in August 1810 as its semi-official mouthpiece. In May 1810 he transferred to New Greyfriars Edinburgh, and in 1814 to St George's in Edinburgh New Town. *Fasti*, 1, 105f.
65   T. Chalmers, *The substance of a speech delivered in the General Assembly, on Thursday the 25th inst. respecting the merits of the late bill for the augmentations of stipends to the clergy of Scotland*, 1809. This was republished in 1818 and inadvertently omitted from the *Works. Memoirs*, 1, 142.
66   T. C. to John Chalmers, 30 May 1809, NCL CHA 3.4.26.
67   *Substance of a speech*, 1809, 8.
68   Ibid., 15.
69   Ibid., 25.

It is quite ridiculous to say that the worth of the clergy will suffice to keep them up in the estimation of society. This worth must be combined with importance. Now, it is the part of the Court of Teinds to supply the element of importance. Give both worth and importance to the same individual and what are the terms employed in describing him? – a distinguished member of society – the ornament of a most respectable profession – the virtuous companion of the great – and a generous consolation to all the sickness and poverty around him.[70]

Chalmers was disappointed that his motion was not put to the vote – an indication whose interests the Assembly represented – but his concern was minuted.[71] The speech is further evidence that he now saw his future within the church. The role of the ministry was to help people accept society as it was and the sufferings they experienced. When he returned to Kilmany in June 1809 he was sick for over a year and left in a fragile state of health for long after. He feared for his life and began to ask whether the comfort he offered to others was all there was to Christian faith.

---

[70] Ibid., 29, *Memoirs*, 1, 141.

[71] *AGA*, 1809, session seven. Out of the agitation over stipends in these years the government eventually enacted in 1810 to grant £10,000 for the augmentation of stipends in parishes where the teinds were exhausted (50 Geo.III., c.189). In 1824 this was increased to £24,000 p.a.

Chapter 4

'A higher respect for the peculiar doctrines'[1]
The conversion years, 1809-1811

In September 1811 Chalmers asked his mother to tell his father that he had

> at length come into his opinion that the peculiar business of his profession demands all the time, all the talents and all the energy that any minister is possessed of.[2]

It was a change which had begun to be apparent to others and may not have been as much news as Chalmers thought. It involved his emergence from a period when his life seemed threatened, the fragility of his self-confidence was exposed, and his underlying ability and sincerity reached out for something more.

When he returned from the General Assembly in the summer of 1809 he had no more than a sore throat.[3] It was not long before he was sick again, apparently with a liver complaint, and his parish duties were suspended completely. For several months in the winter of 1809-10 he was confined to his room. At the end of January he was able to get down to the dining room and by April could 'creep out of doors'.[4] At the beginning of May 1810 he took his first service after taking ill.[5] A year later he still did not consider it wise to venture far.[6]

From mid-1809 to early 1811 a revolution took place in Chalmers' religious outlook. He was not one to identify a time and place of conversion, and it was clearly a process not just an event. Nevertheless his journals and letters provide an unselfconscious record of significant change.

---

[1] Journal, 30 January 1811.
[2] T. C. to Elizabeth Chalmers, 5 September 1811, *Memoirs*, 1, 217.
[3] T. C. to John Chalmers, 8 June 1809, NCL CHA 3.4.28.
[4] T. C. to J. Nairne, 3 April 1810, NCL CHA 3.4.37.
[5] T. C. to John Chalmers 1 May 1810, NCL CHA 3.4.42.
[6] T. C. to James Chalmers, 15 July 1811, NCL CHA 3.5.16.

In its effects it deserves to be compared with the experiences of Augustine and Wesley.

Following some experiences of doubt as a student,[7] Chalmers had long been settled in his basic conviction that Christianity was true.[8] During his sickness he was forced to think again as to what that might mean. Earlier he had dissociated himself from evangelical writers[9] and emphases.[10] By the second half of 1809 a number of factors combined to question his convictions.

In December 1806 his brother George died in Anstruther confessing his faith and having had the sermons of John Newton read to him as he weakened with tuberculosis.[11] In August 1808 the death of his sister Barbara from the same cause prevented him going to London to do something about sales of the *Inquiry*. During the summer of 1809 his favourite uncle,[12] after whom he had been named, died on his knees at prayer at the age of seventy-

---

[7]   In 1795 Chalmers had been swayed by William Godwin's *Enquiry concerning political justice*. He was then inspired by Jonathan Edwards and for about a year entered a period of almost mystical ecstasy in contemplation of the Godhead holding all things in balance and in being. At the end of his divinity course his reading of D'Holbach, *The system of nature*, resulted in a crisis of belief. D'Holbach argued that matter had always existed and contained its own principles of action within itself. There was no need to invent God as the creator and sustainer of the universe; he was a product of fear and ignorance. These doubts were dispelled by Joseph Butler, *Analogy of religion*, and the common-sense Philosophy he learnt in Edinburgh. The 'Scottish Philosophy' came particularly through contact with John Robison (1739-1805) and his lectures in natural philosophy. James Beattie, *Essay on truth*, also helped. *Memoirs*, 1, 14f and 43-6.

[8]   Chalmers may have taken the suggestion of a spiritual retreat as asking him to consider the truth of Christianity. Since this was not then an issue it seemed a waste of time.

[9]   One sermon admonished 'Many books are favourites with you, which I am sorry to say are no favourites of mine. When you are reading Newton's sermons, and Baxter's Saints rest, and Doddridge's Rise and progress, where do Matthew, Mark, Luke and John go?' *Memoirs*, 1, 102.

[10] 'The tenets of those whose gloomy and unenlarged minds are apt to imagine that the Author of Nature required the death of Jesus merely for the reparation of violated justice, are rejected by all free and rational enquirers', *Memoirs*, 1, 147.

[11] *Memoirs*, 1, 101f. George had been a sailor which may have contributed to his appreciation of John Newton (1725-1807), the slave captain who became an evangelical minister. Newton was a favourite author of Chalmers' father whose dying wish was that his children should read him. *Memoirs*, 2, 180, 183.

[12] Thomas Ballardie, RN. He left his house and furniture to Chalmers, but this made little impression on Chalmers' financial difficulties.

seven. When his own illness showed no signs of improvement it looked as if he might be next.[13]

He began to read on Christian evidences. He had been asked to write on trigonometry for the *Edinburgh Encyclopedia*, but after Barbara died he asked[14] instead to be able to do the entry on Christianity.[15] It was not until a year later that he began, and it was not completed until 1812. Its importance for what was to follow was real even if not the decisive element.[16] In assuring himself of the integrity of the Bible he was not breaking new ground, but he was rediscovering a basis for considering the obligations of an historically credible Christian faith.

During the winter of 1809-10 he read Pascal's *Thoughts on religion*. Here was a man of science like himself. Yet Pascal put mathematics aside for the sake of Christianity. Chalmers wrote to a friend:

> You know his history – a man of the richest endowments, and whose youth was signalized by his profound and original speculations in mathematical science, but...who could resign all the splendours of literary reputation...and resolve to devote every talent and every hour to the defence and illustration of the gospel.[17]

This challenged his residual assumptions about where significance might be found in life. Faced with the prospect of dying with the ambitions of his youth unfulfilled, his sense of perspective began to alter. He later explained:

> My confinement has fixed on my heart a very strong impression of the insignificance of time.... This should be the first step to another impression still more salutary – the magnitude of eternity. Strip human life of its connections with a higher scene of existence and it is

---

13 It was another sister, Lucy, who died next, in December 1810 at the age of thirty-eight. *Memoirs*, 1, 182.

14 Brewster (1781-1868) trained for the church but became editor of the *Edinburgh Magazine* before embarking on the encyclopedia. He invented the kaleidoscope and a system of lenses for lighthouses. Later he was principal of the United College at St Andrews and then of Edinburgh University. He was a life-long, though not especially close, friend of Chalmers.

15 *Memoirs*, 1, 142. D. Brewster to T. C., 3 September 1810, NCL CHA 4.1.15.

16 Watt, *Chalmers*, 1943, 27-40.

17 T. C. to G. Carstairs, 19 February 1810, *Memoirs*, 1, 152. Hanna dates this letter 1809, but the contents and address require it to be 1810. The original is not in New College Library.

the illusion of an instant, an unmeaning farce, a series of visions and projects and convulsive efforts which terminate in nothing.[18]

On his thirtieth birthday, 17 March 1810, he began a regular diary journal.[19] He felt two-thirds of his last 15 years had been 'uselessly or idly spent' and that for the most part there had been 'a total estrangement...from religious principle'. He visualized his journal as a record of 'errors and deviations', a means of bringing his behaviour 'under the habitual regulation of principle' and making his mental labours 'subservient to the interests of the gospel'. There was no sense in which he intended it to be seen by others and not all he noted in these diary entries survives.

While classic in many ways, it was also one of the more unusual repentances of Christian history in that he began this new phase of his life by planning to give up mathematics and completing a review of a book of sermons he had begun some years earlier.[20] More conventional decisions followed. He determined to get out of debt[21] and resolved to be more patient with the elderly and deaf,[22] particularly his parents.

He had not lacked company during his illness and convalescence. An aunt, some of his sisters, occasionally his two younger brothers, a pupil and a servant all shared his accommodation. Visitors dropped in constantly, but those he felt free to share deeply with about his pilgrimage were few. Preparation for the article on Christianity provided a sense of elation, and when his friend James Smith[23] called, Chalmers challenged him.

---

[18] T. C. to G. Carstairs, ibid.

[19] There are fragments from earlier periods, and from this time onwards he kept a diary (referred to as his journal) fairly regularly except apparently for 1817-21 and 1834-37. Extracts are in the *Memoirs* without indication where passages were omitted. In a few instances the *Memoirs* contain sections later excised from the manuscript copies. Unless otherwise stated all references and quotations are from the manuscript originals in New College Library.

[20] Journal, 17 March 1810. The sermons were by Samuel Charters.

[21] Journal, 19 March 1810.

[22] Journal, 20 March 1810.

[23] James Smith (1797-1856) was a teacher at Gauldry (two miles from Kilmany) from October 1807 until September 1810. He developed a friendship with Chalmers and acted as amanuensis for the *Enquiry* and for part of the article on Christianity. He became minister of the Secession church at Dunning in March 1812. They met often enough but Smith was not interested in serious conversation. Small, *United Presbyterian Church*, 2, 1904, 590, writes of the influence of Chalmers on Smith rather than the other way. I have not been able to locate any correspondence between Chalmers and Smith, but Smith did provide some reminiscences for the *Memoirs*. *Memoirs*, 1, 145f. Journal, 17 March to 5 September 1810.

> Tell me all that you ever heard against Christianity from its enemies: I
> am more than able to refute them all. The evidences of our religion are
> overwhelming.[24]

Although much of what was going on he kept to himself, others could not
escape hearing something. When his brother James was suffering from
depression, Thomas advised:

> I can assure you from experience that occasional reading upon grave and
> moral and religious subjects has a wonderful effect in giving a tone and
> elevation to the mind.... Light reading is only a relaxation for the
> moment – profound reading fatigues.... Morals and practical divinity
> are precisely that species of literature which without any painful effort
> to the understanding has the effect of engaging and tranquillizing the
> heart.[25]

Applied theology could be useful even if it was still not an intellectual
challenge. Among the books recommended were Blair's sermons[26] and 'the
good honest Bible'. He was especially keen to introduce James to Christian
evidences.

> It is not any mystical controversy that I recommend. This is hateful
> and repulsive. It is that liberal and enlightened enquiry which has led
> the greatest philosophers of the last century to acquiesce in the
> scriptures as a divine revelation. Read Paley's evidences[27] and you will
> be astonished at the strength of the argument.[28]

The seriousness was sustained, though not without struggle. This showed in
impatience with others and irritation was doubled by an inability to control
his reactions. He frequently confessed 'evil speaking' in regard to a legal
agent in Edinburgh and the mother of a girl in Anstruther who had caused

---

[24]   *Memoirs*, 1, 194.

[25]   T. C. to James Chalmers, 4 April 1810, NCL CHA 3.4.39.

[26]   Hugh Blair (1718-1800) was minister at St Giles and Lecturer in Rhetoric
and Belles Letters in the University of Edinburgh. His *Sermons* (5 volumes,
Edinburgh 1777, London 1790) epitomized the age of the Moderates,
attained wide popularity and earned a pension from George III. *Fasti*, 1, 68.

[27]   William Paley (1743-1805) was Archdeacon of Carlisle from 1780 and
famous for his *View of the evidences of Christianity* first published in 1790.
Chalmers made enthusiastic reference to Paley in a sermon in 1802
(*Memoirs*, 1, 143f.) and lectured on him when Professor of Divinity at
Edinburgh (*Posthumous Works*, 9, 82-128).

[28]   T. C. to James Chalmers, 4 April 1810, NCL CHA 3.4.39.

their relationship to be broken off early in 1810.[29] Spring and summer that year were marred by the residue of this love affair, and until June 1812, when Miss Grace Pratt of Kilmany eventually accepted his proposal,[30] he was easily distracted by a propensity for infatuation. One example of the entries in his journal[31] must suffice.

> After tea had a call of Miss June Balfour and Miss Margaret her niece – a lovely interesting girl – full of talent and full of serious principle. Her deafness is an objection to her – her manner is somewhat too decisive – and in her conversation disposed to censoriousness. She is quite young and highly improvable – a most interesting object of course – but I should not be so unguarded in my attentions to her. I feel my error is, that when I feel an attachment my manner carries too open and decided an expression of it. Now this ought to be kept under unless I mean to follow it up. Till I take my determination I should restrain my attentions – and though the restraint be painful I ought to submit to it as an exercise of principle.[32]

Another worry was his finances, not helped by losing at cards.[33] If ambition was no longer a burning issue,[34] there were now a host of other pressures to contend with. Chalmers began to discover spiritual resources of which he had been previously unaware. His journal records prayers written as he sought help for the re-ordering of his life. When a Miss Gardner gave him a piece of her mind at Sunday dinner Chalmers was pleased to find himself capable of restraint and noted:

> I pray God that I may keep all my irritable and malignant tendencies under the control of principle. I have to bless his holy name for the peace and piety and regulated feelings of this day.[35]

Many of the prayers published in the *Memoirs* make little sense apart from the problems which gave rise to them. They lose a good deal of their unearthly piety when the struggles he was going through are examined. Elderly and deaf parents and aimless younger brothers were a severe test of a slender patience and his sister Jane contributed bouts of 'religious melancholy' to manse life. If he was going to find a religious solution, he

---

[29] For example, Journal, 11 June 1810.
[30] Journal, 27 June 1812.
[31] None of which appear in the *Memoirs*.
[32] Journal, 3 May 1810.
[33] Journal, 17 December 1810.
[34] Journal, 18 May 1810.
[35] Journal, 17 July 1810.

needed something which would enable him to come to terms with these problems in a way his earlier faith and efforts at self-reformation had not. In September 1810 he again determined to drop 'severe mathematics' and devote more time to theology. He now believed, 'eminence in two departments is scarcely attainable, let me give my main efforts to religion'.[36] If it was still eminence he was after, now he was prepared to seek it where he had thought it impossible. While he wished to concentrate on the 'defence of Christianity, the exposition of its views and maintenance of its interests as affected by the politics or philosophy of the times', other subjects were still relevant.

> Political economy touches upon religious establishments and a successful or original speculation in this department may throw an *eclat* over my ecclesiastical labours.[37]

By October 1810 he was well enough to take a holiday in Edinburgh and at Cavers. For a week he based himself with Samuel Charters at Wilton while he visited old friends. He had great admiration for the elderly Charters and one night 'sat up till one in the morning in an intimate and confidential conversation'.[38] The following day Charters began to show impatience at the flow of questions.[39] He was an important influence but as far as Chalmers' more personal quest was concerned does not appear to have been much help.

On his way south Chalmers had been impressed with the 'manly and vigorous orthodoxy'[40] of Andrew Thomson, and met him again briefly when in Edinburgh on his return journey.[41] These meetings could be construed as steps in an evangelical direction, but although Chalmers' religious seriousness was deepening, he was essentially bent on self-reformation.

Some of his problems were alleviated by changed circumstances and when he returned to Kilmany to enter the new manse for the first time, he found mental and spiritual equilibrium easier to achieve when some of the relatives stopped living under his roof. Later, marriage was a help in more ways than one as Miss Pratt's dowry covered his debts. Meantime he was to learn that however much other things might improve, his essential religious problem remained. Like Augustine and Luther he was to discover the need to see changes in himself as the product of faith rather than the means of

---

[36]   Journal, 21 September 1810. This is incorrectly dated in the *Memoirs*, 1, 176.

[37]   Journal, 21 September 1810.

[38]   Journal, 1 November 1810.

[39]   Journal, 2 November 1810.

[40]   Journal, 28 October 1810.

[41]   Journal, 9 and 13 November 1810.

justification. An important influence was William Wilberforce's *Practical view of the prevailing religious system of professed Christians in the higher and middle classes of society contrasted with real Christianity*.[42]

He had begun reading Wilberforce on Christmas Eve 1810 after returning to Anstruther following the death of his sister Lucy.[43] He hoped to be 'much the better' for the *Practical view* and the following day recorded he was delighted with the book.[44] His journal contains few other references to Wilberforce,[45] but there is no doubt the *Practical view* was decisive. He frequently recommended it to others[46] and in 1829 wrote that 'next to the Bible it was the most instrumental in effecting a great change on my views of scriptural and divine truth'.[47] In 1820 he wrote to his younger brother Alexander explaining more fully what this had involved.

> The effect of a very long confinement...was to inspire me with a set of very strenuous resolutions, under which I wrote a journal and made many a laborious effort to elevate my practice to the standard of the divine requirements. During this course, however, I got little satisfaction, and felt no repose. I remember that somewhere about the year 1811 I had Wilberforce's *View* put into my hands, and as I got on in reading it, felt myself on the eve of a great revolution in all my opinions about Christianity. I am now most thoroughly of the opinion...that on the system of 'Do this and live', no peace and even no true and worthy obedience can ever be attained. It is 'Believe in the Lord Jesus Christ and thou shalt be saved'. When this belief enters the heart, joy and confidence enter along with it. The righteousness which we try to work out for ourselves eludes our impotent grasp.... The righteousness which, by faith, we put on, secures our acceptance with God...and gives us a part in those sanctifying influences by which we are enabled to do with aid from on high what we can never do without it.[48]

---

42 First published in 1797.
43 Journal, 23, 24 December 1810.
44 Journal, 25 December 1810.
45 Journal, 29, 30 December 1810, 17 March 1811.
46 James Anderson to T. C. 8 August 1811, *Memoirs*, 1, 286. T. C. to John Honey, 2 May 1812, *Correspondence*, 266.
47 T. C. to J. Sinclair, 9 February 1829, BOD MS Wilberforce C.3 fol.251.
48 T. C. to Alexander Chalmers, 14 February 1820, *Memoirs*, 1, 185f. As Watt noted, it is a question whether, or to what extent, this letter used evangelical stereotypes acquired after the event *(Chalmers, 1943, 35)*. Judging by the journal the terminology is consistent with language Chalmers was capable of using at the time.

From the new year of 1811 Chalmers' thinking and allegiance began to move rapidly in an evangelical direction. On 7 January he noted 'the futility of resting a man's hope of salvation upon mere obedience'. Two weeks later he reflected that in his preaching he needed to 'enter more earnestly and particularly into the peculiar doctrines'.[49]

Towards the end of the month, a childhood friend came to stay for a few days and had 'much conversation about religion'.[50] Mary Wood annoyed him with her talkativeness and her attempts to organize his household, but nevertheless he wrote in his journal:

> Through her I have enlarged my observations on religious sentiments. I have imbibed a higher respect for the peculiar doctrines. I feel more cordially than ever that my sufficiency is of Christ, and that faith in him is the most comprehensive principle of practice.[51]

The message of the *Practical view* was getting home. He was invited to take the Thursday fast-day sermon at the nearby parish of Dairsie for their mid-February communion. Chalmers was impressed by the elderly Robert M'Culloch (1740-1824),[52] only son of William M'Culloch, the minister of Cambuslang during the revival of the 1740s.[53] In turn M'Culloch and his widowed daughter, Janet Coutts (1776-1849), were appreciative of Chalmers – 'the kind of testimony that two years ago I would have despised'.[54] Mrs Coutts wrote to a friend:

> On the fast-day we had a new miracle of divine grace in a Mr Chalmers of Kilmany, a great philosopher, but once an enemy avowedly to the peculiar doctrines of the gospel. For a year back the Lord has been teaching him by the rod. Confinement and the death of a beloved sister in the triumphs of faith, together with his studying the evidences of Christianity and the Bible itself seem to have been eminently blessed to change his views.[55]

A week later Chalmers began the autobiography of the evangelical Anglican, Thomas Scott (1747-1821). Scott's *Force of truth* described his pilgrimage, while a curate, through unitarianism to evangelical Calvinism. If 15 months earlier Pascal had mirrored Chalmers' situation by being the

---

[49] Journal, 18 January 1811.
[50] Journal, 28 January 1811.
[51] Journal, 30 January 1811.
[52] *Fasti*, 5, 148.
[53] *Fasti*, 3, 237f. A. Fawcett, *The Cambuslang revival*, 1971.
[54] Journal, 14 February 1811.
[55] Janet Coutts to Jane Burns, 19 February 1811, W. M. Hetherington, *Memoir and correspondence of Mrs Coutts*, 1854, 123.

scientist who gave up science for the sake of the gospel, now Thomas Scott was the parish minister who discovered he lacked the faith he was appointed to proclaim.

Scott thus provided Chalmers with the example he needed to bring into focus the ideas expressed by Wilberforce and embodied in the M'Cullochs, Andrew Thomson and his own father. Chalmers was soon to share their religious experience.[56]

The day after beginning Scott, a letter from Andrew Thomson confirmed a fear that a review of Charters' *Sermons* for the *Edinburgh Christian Instructor* was not satisfactory.[57] He had not drawn attention to Charters' lack of evangelical sentiment.[58] Chalmers saw this as saying something about himself and felt he was on 'the eve of some decisive transformation in point of religious sentiment'.[59] Within a week he accepted Christianity as offering forgiveness before it asked for reformation rather than the other way around. On 26 February 1811 he read of the conversion of Paul.

> The verse, Acts 26.18, has struck me this night as a compendious expression of Christianity – the object of which is to give forgiveness of sins, and inheritance among them that are sanctified by faith that is in Jesus.[60]

It is natural to ask if there were individuals he knew personally who were of importance in his conversion. His manuscript journals suggest there was no one particular mentor.[61] Although Andrew Thomson's comments on the review of Charters' sermons certainly spoke to Chalmers, Thomson was in Edinburgh and they had met only once or twice. He had contact with the Secession minister of Rathillet, James Johnston, but there is no indication of their being very close.

The Evangelical who seems to have had the earliest real contact was M'Culloch of Dairsie, but not before Chalmers assisted at his sacrament.

---

56 The significance of Thomas Scott is also shown by Chalmers' introductory essay to an edition of Scott's *Tracts* published in 1826. Chalmers dealt extensively with the *Force of truth*, and referred at length to the futility of self-reformation. The language is similar to that in the letter to his brother Alexander concerning Wilberforce cited above.

57 A. M. Thomson to T. C. 18 February 1811, NCL CHA 4.1.57.

58 Thomson eventually accepted the review and added a footnote lamenting the neglect of the 'peculiar doctrines'. *Memoirs*, 1, 198f.

59 Journal, 23 February 1811.

60 Journal, 26 February 1811.

61 This is based on examination of the journals, correspondence and *Fasti* entries relating to Chalmers and his colleagues in the Presbytery of Cupar. It was also the view of Watt, *Chalmers*, 1943, 37.

Chalmers realised that they now had something vital in common, but nevertheless he remained uncomfortable with M'Culloch's piety. Some he knew during this period later joined the Free Church, such as John Fleming (1785-1857) of Flisk[62] and Andrew Melvill (1775-1848) of Logie[63] and might be thought of as Evangelicals at this time were it not for Chalmers' journals which indicate he did not see them in that light at Kilmany. Chalmers enjoyed talking science with Fleming but found him frivolous when it came to religion. He had been at university with Melvill who preached at his ordination, but although his wife had evangelical interests which Chalmers noted in 1811 he still shared the attitudes of their youth.

The one person Chalmers really looked to was Samuel Charters of Wilton and he learned much from his wise and cultivated Moderatism even if Charters could not help him in his quest for justification by faith. The religious conversation with Mary Wood noted above seems to have been an isolated instance. Given the thorough documentation available for these years, it seems reasonable to assume that if there was some individual guiding him towards an evangelical conversion they would have been identified. His closest friend was someone who ultimately never shared his faith. It is consistent with his life-long behaviour that so much of basic thinking developed in interaction with books and situations. It was his own judgement that he trusted more than others.[64]

One of those situations was the state of society, which may also have been a contributing factor. His conversion has been seen as

> related to the malaise of the time, to the strain of war and the general revulsion against the 18th-century intellectualism which was now associated with irreligion and social disorder. The search for a deeper basis of authority and a more spiritual guidance had thus a social as well as an individual urgency.[65]

Chalmers' world was under threat quite apart from what was happening to society, and a feature of Chalmers was how much 18th-century intellectualism he retained. He was confident in his ability to cope with the malaise of the age. It was personal crises which shook his confidence and fuelled the process leading to his conversion.

On the other hand his experience of personal salvation did say something about the salvation of society. His period of turmoil was important for the consolidation of his social attitudes. He had not read

---

[62]   *Fasti*, 4, 302f.

[63]   *Fasti*, 5, 164.

[64]   John McCaffrey, 'The life of Thomas Chalmers,' in A. C. Cheyne, ed., *The practical and the pious. Essays on Thomas Chalmers (1780-1847)*, 1985, 35f.

[65]   L. J. Saunders, *Scottish democracy 1815-1840*, 1950, 210.

Wilberforce in search of social philosophy, and the *Practical view* echoed his own attitudes as much as they were a reflection of the thinking of many others. The role of Christianity was to deal with the failings of individuals and to make the inequalities of society bearable in a transitory world. The adequacy of this might be questioned, but it was not out of touch – as Wilberforce's political career should indicate. What Wilberforce did has to be read alongside what he wrote. Both influenced Chalmers, who read in the *Practical view* that Christianity teaches

> Affluence...to be liberal and beneficent authority to bear its faculties with meekness.... Thus softening the glare of wealth and moderating the insolence of power she renders the inequalities of the social state less galling to the lower orders.[66]

It has been noted that the *Practical view* contained 'the blue-print for the social concern' which Chalmers later evinced.[67] One might add it was a blue-print he had found earlier in Charters. Of greater importance at this stage was Wilberforce's message that a different order of personal commitment was necessary if any of this was actually to happen. Christianity should address itself 'to the particular mode of selfishness' to which each class in society was prone. In order to realize 'the blessed effects of Christianity on the temporal well-being of political communities', it needed to be 'real, not nominal, deep, not superficial'.[68]

The *Practical view* was a remarkable book, and Chalmers may also have learnt from it the value of addressing the section of society which happened to hold power. Wilberforce appealed to ideals to which the upper and middle classes paid lip-service and concentrated on essential issues to the exclusion of less relevant points of contention. He did not hound heretics or get involved in theological disputes. It was, in one sense, an astutely political piece of theology. Chalmers' eventual success as a preacher and writer was also related to the audiences he addressed, the issues he chose to tackle and those he decided to ignore.

In July 1811 the review of Charters' sermons was eventually published.[69] It showed how he had been thinking through problems of the scope of Christian preaching and the difficulty of holding together

---

[66]   W. Wilberforce, *Practical view*, 1833, 315.

[67]   W. Ferguson, 'Social problems of the nineteenth century' (review of S. Mechie, *The church and Scottish social development*), *Scottish Historical Review*, 41, 1962, 58.

[68]   Wilberforce, *Practical view*, 1833, 316.

[69]   *Edinburgh Christian Instructor*, July 1811, 45-53. *Works*, 12, 299-322.

Evangelical and Moderate emphases. It is clear Charters' example was important.[70]

> His great aim is to bring forward Christianity to the walks of ordinary business, and to send home its moral principles to the understanding and experience of ordinary men.... He carries out religion from the house of prayer and into the shop, the market and the family.[71]

This was the ideal Chalmers adopted,[72] not least because in doing so he was keeping together the best of both traditions.

> There is a most unfortunate distinction kept up...betwixt moral and evangelical preaching. The mischief of this is incalculable. It has the effect of banishing Christianity altogether from the system of human life.... It is the happy combination of evangelical piety with the familiar, wholesome and experiential morality of human life which to our taste constitutes the peculiar charm and excellence of the sermons before us.[73]

A second review Chalmers wrote for the *Edinburgh Christian Instructor* appeared earlier, in May 1811.[74] This also showed concern for the place of Christianity in society.

> Believing as we do in the supreme...importance of religion, we would be untrue to our principles were we not to contend for its pre-eminence in all the possible varieties of business and of life. As the true disciples of Christianity we cannot in conscience surrender the universality of its empire.[75]

The book he was reviewing, *Hints on toleration*,[76] was concerned for the rights of dissenters in a world of established churches. Chalmers rejected the

---

70   Charters' influence on Chalmers was ignored by Hanna and most of Chalmers' other biographers. Those who noted his importance include M. F. Conolly, *Eminent men of Fife*, 1866, 114, and (James Hamilton), *North British Review*, 7 August 1847, 561f.

71   *Edinburgh Christian Instructor*, July 1811, 44. *Works*, 12, 302f.

72   *Posthumous Works*, 9, 382-7.

73   *Edinburgh Christian Instructor*, July 1811, 51f. *Works*, 12, 318-20.

74   It was not included in the *Works* although the points made are found throughout his writings, particularly those relating to establishments.

75   *Edinburgh Christian Instructor*, May 1811, 315. Charters wrote that it was 'the only good article of late'. S. Charters to T. C., 10 July 1811, NCL CHA 4.1.33.

76   Philagatharches, *Hints on toleration in five essays suggested for the consideration of the Right Hon. Lord Viscount Sidmouth and the*

idea that religion was no business of parliament and established churches were invalid forms of Christianity. Dissenters were entitled to toleration but that was best achieved by positive legislation. The key point, and a conviction for the rest of his life, was that parliament had a duty to underwrite the provision of the gospel for all the people. What was at stake was

> whether in...our perfect security that through every district of the land there is a church to which the people may repair and a minister to expound the word of truth and preside over the exercises of social piety...the spiritual interests of the people are not far better provided for than if so important a concern had been abandoned to the uncertain elements of individual character.[77]

His concern for mission was greater than his interest in particular denominations, even if the government should support one of them and not others. Having an established church was more important than the form of Christianity it embodied.

> It is not the Church of England, or the Church of Scotland, that we feel ourselves *at all events* interested in defending it is for a church in both these countries that we plead.[78]

Mindful of his own failings and how they had contributed to the growth of a Secession congregation in his parish, he analysed what it was that encouraged dissent. It is hard not to read this as autobiographical.

> It is not in the doctrine or the constitution of the church that the mischief originates. It is in the laxity of those ministers who have swerved from the pure and evangelical doctrine of their own standards; or, who by the negligent performance of their duties have disgusted and alienated men who would have gladly ranked themselves amongst the most loyal and devoted adherents of the church. The reformation wanted is not in the liturgy or constitution of the establishment; it is a personal reformation that is called for.[79]

Dissenters, 1810. Chalmers received this from Thomson on 23 February 1811 and completed his review by 4 April. Sidmouth's Protestant dissenting ministers bill was given a first reading in the Lords on 9 May 1811 and later defeated without a division. D. M. Thompson, *Nonconformity in the nineteenth century*, 1972, 20f, 29.

77   *Edinburgh Christian Instructor*, May 1811, 316.
78   Ibid., 319.
79   Ibid., 320.

Throughout 1811 Chalmers' return to health proceeded as did the increasing openness of his evangelical convictions. Once he trembled to be identified with people regarded by some of his parishioners as fanatics, but in March he held a collection for the Bible Society[80] and in May noted 'a growing partiality...on the part of the evangelical clergy'.[81] His friendship with Robert M'Culloch and Janet Coutts developed as he read the books they lent him.[82] His theological reading now took in Richard Baxter,[83] Matthew Henry,[84] the Scottish Evangelical Robert Walker[85] and Hannah More's *Practical piety*.[86]

During his illness the pulpit had been supplied by and later shared with Andrew Thomson of Balmerino, an adjacent parish which was having a new church built. Chalmers realized how much he had to catch up on the neglect of the past two years and the failings of his ministry before then. In September 1811 he wrote home to tell of his new commitment[87] and in October told his brother James of a desire to get back to the day-to-day round among his parishioners.

> There is a justice due to them – and the very first I ought to make of my health is to go round them ministerially. The good old custom of visiting and examination still lingers amongst us – and I should be sorry to see it falling into desuetude. The cause of Christ is more effectively served by daily and familiar conversation...than by weekly exhibitions from the pulpit.[88]

For a time he had taken in a pupil and acted as tutor but that too was a distraction he could no longer afford.

---

[80]   Journal, 21 March 1811.

[81]   Journal, 1 May 1811.

[82]   T. C. to J. Coutts, 24 October 1811, *Correspondence*, 66.

[83]   Chalmers began the '*Body of practical divinity*' (sic; perhaps he meant *Christian Directory*) in July 1811 and the *Call to the unconverted* in September. Journal, 18 July, 13 September, 1811.

[84]   Chalmers was 'much impressed' with the *Life of Matthew Henry* which he finished in October. Journal, 28 August, 4 October 1811.

[85]   Robert Walker (1716-1783) was colleague and Evangelical counterpoise to Hugh Blair in St Giles. Chalmers looked for and received 'a great confirmation of evangelical principles' in Walker's *Sermons on practical subjects*, 4 vols., 1775-96. He was taken with the comment 'we are commanded to believe'. This meant that it was not presumptuous to do so. Journal, 15, 17, May 1811.

[86]   Chalmers received a copy on 20 May 1811 and recommended it to Janet Coutts and Samuel Charters. *Correspondence*, 66, S. Charters to T. C., 19 September 1811, NCL CHA 4.1.34.

[87]   T. C. to Elizabeth Chalmers, 5 September 1811, *Memoirs*, 1, 217.

[88]   T. C. to James Chalmers, 30 October 1811, NCL CHA 3.5.29.

I have given too much of my time to extra-professional employments. I have got rid of my young cousin...and have closed the door against all similar applications by stating...the positive impossibility of a clergyman taking himself up with anything that lies beyond the limits of his professional duty and at the same time executing this duty aright.... My sentiments on this head were at one time different.[89]

The arrangement with Balmerino came to an end in November[90] and he returned to full duties. He was now able to demonstrate his new convictions in the pulpit and in pastoral work. Evangelicalism had given him a personal faith; the Moderate Samuel Charters was a model of the loyal pastor concerned for the whole of society – qualities he began to appreciate afresh. He buried himself in study and pastoral work as he forged his own synthesis of the mission of the church and what it meant to be a minister.

---

[89] Ibid.
[90] *Memoirs*, 1, 227.

Chapter 5

'A free, unshackled and scriptural divinity'[1]
Minister of Kilmany, 1812-1815

Chalmers' new energy was in sharp contrast to his earlier ministry. His preaching gained acceptance in Kilmany and further afield and he was pressed for sermons in Dundee, Dunfermline and Edinburgh. Out of his reading came the beginnings of a successful and life-long literary output. In four years he published five review articles,[2] three sermons,[3] three pamphlets,[4] and a book.[5] His growing reputation meant the possibility of a call to a city church.

---

1   *Journal*, 23 August 1813.

2   *Sermons*, by Samuel Charters, *Edinburgh Christian Instructor*, July 1811, 43-53, *Works*, 12, 299-322. Philagatharches, *Hints on toleration*, *Edinburgh Christian Instructor*, May 1811, 311-20. *Essays in a series of letters to a friend*, by John Foster, *Edinburgh Christian Instructor*, May 1813, 327-39, *Works*, 12, 221-50. *Essay on the theory of the earth translated from the French of M Cuvier*, *Edinburgh Christian Instructor*, April 1814, 261-74, *Works*, 12, 347-72. *Journal of a voyage*, by Benjamin Kohlmeister and George Kmoch, missionaries of the...United Brethren, *Eclectic Review*, 1815, 1-13, 156-73, *Works*, 12, 251-98.

3   *The two great instruments appointed for the propagation of the Gospel*, 1813, *Works*, 11, 315-44. *A Sermon preached before the Society for the Relief of the Destitute Sick*, 1815, *Works*, 11, 221-46. 'Speech to the Fife and Kinross Bible Society', *Edinburgh Christian Instructor*, January 1813, 64-9.

4   *The influence of Bible societies on the temporal necessities of the poor*, 1814, *Works*, 12, 123-60. *Scripture reference: designed for the use of parents, teachers and private Christians*, 1814. *The duty of giving an immediate diligence to the business of the Christian life: being an address to the inhabitants of Kilmany*, 1815, *Works*, 12, 69-120.

5   *The evidence and authority of the Christian revelation*, 1814 (substantially his entry 'Christianity' in the *Edinburgh Encyclopedia*). A revised version was incorporated in *Works* 3 and 4.

It was part of the testing of his new commitment that he became a convert to Bible societies and convinced of the world-wide missionary obligations of all Christians. The courts of the Church also presented responsibilities he could not neglect. He served his turn as moderator of presbytery, and took part in debates over pluralities, the amalgamation of parishes, slavery and Roman Catholic emancipation.

His preaching now laid the foundation of an increasing reputation. He had always been capable of oratory, but his new effectiveness was not unrelated to the fresh language in which he clothed his theological heritage and applied it to contemporary issues.

Involvement with Bible societies not only reflected his heightened appreciation of the Bible, but by their organization in parish associations helped establish convictions about the ability of all members of a parish to participate in the mission of the church. The missionary movement widened his horizons and provided evidence which confirmed his own conversion. This encouraged the application of the same principles in his parish. The way to achieve the morality Christianity demanded was to begin with salvation offered to all through the atonement of Christ.

In the face of objections to the relaxation of civil disabilities against Catholics,[6] Chalmers maintained the Bible alone was the only legitimate means for combating Roman Catholicism.[7] Proposals to amalgamate parishes and combine a university and parish appointment were resisted because of the dilution in pastoral care which would result.

Although development took place after he left Kilmany, it is important to note these formative years, his theological study, parish work, preaching and involvement in poor relief, Bible and missionary societies and the courts of the Church.

The search for a theological identity

Chalmers' conversion brought a profound sense of the inability of people to save themselves and of the free offer of salvation in Christ as the basis of moral reform. Pascal, Wilberforce and Scott had each been helpful, but Chalmers believed it was the Bible which brought these views to him with greatest impact. This led him to expect it to have the same effect on others. Yet he was far from rejecting everything about his past. His friendships across a wide theological spectrum were of great significance and as had been the case with his conversion, much of his inspiration came from reading.

---

6   In May 1813 the General Assembly petitioned parliament 'that none of the bulwarks of the constitution, ecclesiastical or civil be on any account exposed to hazard'. *AGA*, 1813, 14.

7   What was intended as a speech became three anonymous letters to the *Dundee Perth and Cupar Advertiser*, 7, 14 and 21 May 1813.

He looked back on his student days as a time when he shared the rejection of Evangelicalism which pervaded Moderate St Andrews.[8] While there he had encountered one person of evangelical faith who commanded respect although nobody could understand how such beliefs were possible,[9] and his borrowings from the library included works by Philip Doddridge[10] and Robert Walker.[11] This was when he first read Jonathan Edwards on the freedom of the will and for a time he was impressed. The reasonable Calvinism of his theological professors was something he came back to. Like his preaching during his first seven years at Kilmany which shared the tendency to concentrate on behaviour more than faith, these were things not so much to be repudiated as to be built upon.

It was fortunate that in Charters and M'Culloch, Chalmers was able to form friendships with those who represented the better features of Scottish Moderatism and Evangelicalism. M'Culloch was the only minister within the Presbytery of Cupar of unequivocal Evangelical commitment. Chalmers also developed relationships with Walter Tait (1775-1848) of Tealing,[12] Malcolm Colquhoun (1758-1819) of Dundee,[13] George Muirhead (1764-

---

[8]   'St Andrews was overrun with Moratism, under the chilling influences of which we all inhaled, not a distaste only, but a positive contempt for all that is properly and peculiarly gospel.' *Sermons by the late Rev Robert Coutts, Brechin, with a preface by Thomas Chalmers*, 1847, vii.

[9]   'Mr Coutts may be said to have stood almost alone; and I can well remember that, with all our respect for his general abilities, we juniors were in the habit of viewing him as a rare and inexplicable phenomenon.' Ibid.

[10]   Chalmers borrowed Doddridge's *Lectures* during the 1795-96 session. StAUL borrowing record. Philip Doddridge (1702-1751) was an English non-conformist who trained students at Northampton. Following Richard Baxter (1615-1691), he was a moderate Calvinist.

[11]   Chalmers borrowed a volume of Walker's *Sermons* during the 1796-97 session. StAUL borrowing record. Robert Walker (1716-1783) was a leading Church of Scotland Evangelical and minister of the Canongate from 1754. *Fasti*, 1, 60.

[12]   Chalmers began corresponding about Bible societies with Tait in March 1812 and visited him when across the Tay. Chalmers was impressed by his pastoral work and wrote that he was 'experimentally conversant in the work of close dealing with souls' (T. C. to T. S. Jones, 12 February 1813, *Correspondence*, 61). Tait moved to Trinity Church, Edinburgh in November 1813. *Fasti*, 1, 128; 5, 164.

[13]   Colquhoun was minister of the Church of Scotland Gaelic chapel in Dundee and having been the first president of the Dundee Missionary Society then served as its secretary for many years. After one visit Chalmers noted that 'Mr Colquhoun and Mr Tait have been of great use to me.' Journal, 5 November 1813, *Fasti*, 5, 333.

1847) of Dysart[14] and Thomas Snell Jones (1754-1837) of Lady Glenorchy's Chapel in Edinburgh.[15]

Charles Stuart[16] (1745-1826), a leading Baptist layman in Edinburgh, was also an influence. He arranged for missionaries to visit Kilmany, sent reports of Baptists in India, encouraged a petition over the 1813 East India Company charter renewal, and kept a critical eye on Chalmers' theology. Among the many Moderates in the Presbytery of Cupar, Chalmers had relations that were usually cordial with Michael Greenlaw (1722-1815) of Cults[17] and George Campbell (1747-1824) of Cupar.[18]

Many of those with whom he was in almost daily contact were less pronounced in their ecclesiastical allegiance, for example Andrew Thomson[19] (1746-1836) of Balmerino and Andrew

---

[14] Chalmers corresponded with Muirhead about Bible societies, and enjoyed visiting Dysart (Journal, 27 June 1811). Muirhead was later minister at Cramond and was the oldest to join the Free Church at the Disruption. *Fasti*, 1, 12; 5, 87.

[15] Jones was an influential Edinburgh Evangelical. Born in Gloucester, brought up a Methodist and educated at Trevecca, he was ordained by the Presbytery of London and appointed by Lady Glenorchy to her chapel in 1779. As a minister of a chapel-of-ease he was not a member of the courts of the Church until 1834, yet his influence on the Evangelical revival in Scotland was considerable. Chalmers preached for Jones in the summer of 1812 and they maintained contact thereafter. Chalmers liked Jones' preference for exegesis over systematic theology and experimented with his testimony to the value of cold baths. Journal, 23, 24 August 1813, *Memoirs*, 1, 505-14. D. P. Thomson, *Lady Glenorchy and her churches*, 1967, 41-3.

[16] Stuart was a son-in-law of John Erskine and for a few years minister at Cramond, but he resigned from the Church of Scotland in 1776. In 1796 he was co-founder with Greville Ewing of the *Missionary Magazine*. Chalmers first met Stuart in July 1812. H. Escott, *A History of Scottish Congregationalism*, 1960, 54, 58. *Fasti*, 1, 12. *Memoirs*, 1, 370.

[17] After some effort Chalmers managed to get Greenlaw to be vice-president of the local Bible Association. Chalmers put his reluctance down to his age 'and perhaps a slight tinge of that coldness which is the characteristic of a Moderate clergyman', Journal, 9 March 1812. Greenlaw officiated at Chalmers' marriage in August 1812. *Fasti*, 5, 137.

[18] *Fasti*, 5, 144.

[19] Not to be confused with Andrew Mitchell Thomson the editor of the *Edinburgh Christian Instructor* and later minister of St George's Edinburgh. Thomson and Chalmers were in and out of each other's manses. When presbytery met, Thomson would breakfast with Chalmers at Kilmany before they walked over the hill to Cupar. Thomson looked after Chalmers' parish during his illness and his congregation shared the Kilmany church while theirs was being rebuilt. Chalmers sat under a good many of Thomson's sermons. Despite occasional appreciative comments after hearing

Melvill[20] (1775-1848) of Logie. The ministers of the Anstruther parishes, Robert Wilson[21] (1764-1839) and Andrew George Carstairs[22] (1780-1838) were also middle-of-the-road. Wilson and Carstairs were family friends and Chalmers saw them on visits home to Anstruther. Whatever sort of Evangelical Chalmers was to become, the fact that he maintained relationships with people who did not share his religious experience helped ensure he took seriously a wide range of theological and ecclesiastical allegiance.

Despite his resolutions to give up mathematics, Chalmers' reading was not purely theological. He continued to receive the *Edinburgh Review*,[23] read Boswell[24] and Walter Scott[25] and was familiar with Burns[26] and Wordsworth.[27] Bible and missionary societies produced their own lines of enquiry. He received Bible Society reports, read Claudius Buchanan's *Christian Researches* twice and Thomas Clarkson on the *History of the abolition of the slave trade*. As well as Baptist and Moravian *Periodical accounts*, he read William Brown, *History of the propagation of Christianity*, and Jonathan Edwards' *Life of Brainerd*.

He found inspiration in English Evangelical and Puritan traditions. Thomas Scott and Wilberforce had helped his conversion, but equally formative were Hannah More,[28] Richard Cecil[29] and John Newton.[30] Philip

---

Thomson preach, there is no mention of any serious conversations and Chalmers once prayed 'that Mr Thomson could be awakened out of sleep' (Journal 11 July 1810). Thomson was upset with Chalmers over the India petition and Bible societies but this may have been due to Chalmers' advocacy more than the causes themselves. Journal, 1 May 1813. *Fasti*, 5, 129.

20   Like Thomson, Melvill held a parish contiguous to Kilmany and there was visiting between manses. *Fasti*, 5, 164.

21   Wilson was minister of Anstruther Easter from 1795. *Fasti*, 5, 181.

22   It was to Carstairs at Anstruther Wester that Chalmers wrote in 1810 of his interest in Pascal (*Memoirs*, 1, 152), but there is little evidence of more than social interaction during this period. They became closer at St Andrews from 1823. *Fasti*, 5, 184.

23   In 1843 Chalmers' library contained '38 volumes and many numbers' of the *Edinburgh Review*. Catalogue of books, p.50, NCL CHA 6.3.12. There are several references to the *Edinburgh Review* in his journals for 1810-1815.

24   *Life of Johnson*, Journal, 18 November 1813. *Journal of a tour to the Hebrides*, Journal, 12 January 1814.

25   *Lady of the lake*, Journal, 16 March 1811. *Marmion*, Journal, 16 March 1812.

26   *Memoirs*, 1, 297.

27   *Edinburgh Christian Instructor*, July 1811, 44 (review of Charters' *Sermons*).

28   Chalmers began More's *Practical piety* in May 1811 and finished it by October. He recommended it to others and had to stop his aunt lending his

Doddridge[31] and Richard Baxter[32] were life-long influences as were Joseph Alleine,[33] Matthew Henry[34] and John Owen,[35] all of whom he read during his last years at Kilmany.

Another who may have had more impact than has been realized was Bishop Beilby Porteous (1731-1808). In 1812 Chalmers read two of Porteous' works and the biography[36] of this 'almost Evangelical' bishop of broad sympathies who strove to improve the effectiveness of his London

copy before he had got through it. Journal 20, 23 May, 14, 21 June 1811. S. Charters to T. C., 10 July 1811, NCL CHA 4.1.33, *Memoirs*, 1, 236.

29 Chalmers completed the *Remains* by 16 March 1813 and wrote out several extracts in his commonplace book. NCL CHA 6.2.5.

30 Chalmers used Cecil's life of John Newton for reading to his household. Journal 8, 21 December 1813.

31 In 1806 *The rise and progress of religion in the soul* was disowned by Chalmers from his pulpit. In 1812 he read John Osten's *Life of Doddridge* and recommended the *Rise and progress* to others. Journal 26 February, 12 March, and 3 June 1812. T. C. to J. Honey, 2 May 1812, *Correspondence*, 266.

32 Baxter was probably the single most important writer for Chalmers during this period and it was said he exchanged a horse for one of his works (*Memoirs*, 1, 282). He read Baxter's *Body of practical divinity* [sic], *Call to the unconverted*, and *Life* at this time though it appears he did not read the *Reformed pastor* before the late 1820s. The journals contain many references to being impressed by Baxter. Chalmers used the *Call* as a tract, and gave copies to a painter working on the manse (Journal, 9 May 1812) and to several parishioners. The outline 'heads of doctrines' in the *Call* provided the structure of Chalmers' sermon on Isaiah 27.3-5, 'Fury not in God' (*Posthumous Works*, 6, 422-40). Preached on seven occasions in and around Kilmany during 1814-15, in the last years of his life Chalmers rediscovered this sermon and delivered it all over the country. He was thus indebted to Baxter for his most characteristic evangelical statement.

33 Alleine's *Alarm to the unconverted* was read in January 1815 and used for his first communicants. He described it as 'a very close and vigorous performance', but had to overlook 'its occasional coarseness of imagery and expression' (T. C. to Mrs Glasgow, 13 August 1819, *Correspondence*, 113).

34 He began Matthew Henry's *Life* in August 1811, and a year later his work on prayer. In May 1813 he began Henry's *Commentary* and by August 1814 finished volume 1 on the Pentateuch. In 1825 he was impressed by Matthew Henry's life of his father, Philip Henry.

35 Between September and December 1814 Chalmers read Owen on indwelling sin, temptation and mortification, Journal, 13 September, 3 October, 24 December 1814.

36 Chalmers bought Porteous' *Lecture on the transfiguration* in January 1811 and in November noted he was 'much delighted with it'. In April 1812 he finished *Lectures on Matthew* and between September and October completed Hodgson, *Life of Porteous*.

parishes. Moravians were important for their piety, their missionary commitment and their missionary methods. In 1813 he read 'almost all' of A. G. Spangenberg, *An exposition of Christian doctrine as taught in the Protestant Church of the United Brethren*, and completed it the following year.[37]

Scottish evangelical writers were also important. He read Thomas M'Crie's *Life of John Knox* late in 1812 and like Wesley and Whitefield was influenced by the memoirs of Thomas Halyburton.[38] The sermons of Robert Walker, which he first looked into while a divinity student, were now seen in a different light. The *Marrow of modern divinity* recalled the early 18th-century controversy in which pietist 'Marrow men' were censured by the General Assembly. Chalmers described the *Marrow* as masterly, found it helpful on faith,[39] and believed he would have been among its supporters in 1722.

What he did not read is also striking. Thomas Boston's *Memoirs* and *Fourfold state* appear not to have been looked at until 1826 and 1828 respectively. The *Pilgrim's progress* is not in the catalogue of Chalmers' library nor in the exhaustive references to his reading in the journals.[40] Samuel Rutherford's *Letters* are another omission.

That all this included little systematic theology was partly due to the general absence of such writing in the Scottish theological tradition. Many factors had combined to produce this situation, not least that the interests of the 18th century lay elsewhere and theological differences were associated with religious wars. Chairs of divinity in Scotland were often held by parish ministers, which affected the time available for writing and ensured they tended to avoid speculative issues in favour of matters more practical. The links of church, university and government could be an advantage; they also had their costs.

The Westminster Confession was also inhibiting. Familiarity with the Shorter Catechism helped produce theological acuteness more than creativity. The *Theological institutes* of George Hill had been published in 1803, but contained only the headings of his lectures and the text was not brought out till years later. George Campbell of Aberdeen's *Lectures on systematic theology and pulpit eloquence* had been published 20 years earlier and Chalmers borrowed a copy,[41] but they contained little more than advice

---

37 Journal, 16 May 1813, 3 September 1814. On 30 August 1814 he was 'soothed and edified with the Moravian doctrine' and the day after that he could 'feel the impulse of Spangenberg'.

38 Halyburton (1674-1712) was Professor of Divinity at St Andrews from 1710. *Fasti*, 7, 429.

39 Journal, 23 August 1812.

40 Although he had read it at some stage. T. C. to J. Anderson, 18 December 1811, *Memoirs*, 1, 249.

41 StAUL borrowing record, 28 June 1815.

on constructing a theological system from a reading of the Bible with suggestions on sermons ranging from the 'controversial' to the 'pathetic'.[42]

As a divinity student at St Andrews Chalmers learnt the distinction between theology as a means of organizing Christian belief and what was helpful from the pulpit. Predestination was not, although Hill recommended students read Calvin for themselves.[43] Chalmers questioned Hill's commitment to Calvin and complained about the requirement to sign the Confession.

> Here order and method is as proper as in any other branch of science...it is both our duty and interest to pay to divinity our most unremitting attention. How inconsistent...with reason and conscience, after we have finished our course at the Divinity College, to subscribe our assent to the Confession of Faith after a superficial examination of its tenets and doctrines.[44]

It was about this time he was inspired by Edwards, and Theological Society discussions inevitably included the doctrine of election. In March 1796 he opened the debate 'Can man be held accountable for wrong belief?' In February 1798 he presented a discourse on predestination and a year later 'Is man a free agent?'[45]

The assumption is common that the Evangelical revival in Scotland had at its centre a revival of confessional orthodoxy.[46] The claim that Chalmers was central to this, says more about the conflicts of the Disruption than the reality of the decades before the 1840s. The only reference to the Westminster Confession in Chalmers' journals is on 4 July 1811 when he noted he 'looked into the Confession of Faith' and resolved to 'give it an attentive perusal'. Not long after he wrote to James Anderson of Dundee.

> My Christianity approaches nearer, I think, to Calvinism than to any of the *isms* of Church History: but broadly as it announces the necessity of sanctification, it does not bring it forward in that free and spontaneous manner which I find in the New Testament.... It is laid before me as part of a system.... I feel the influence of these systems

---

[42] Campbell, *Lectures*, 1824, xii.

[43] 'I do not know a more useful book for a clergyman in the country. It may be purchased for a trifle, and it is the best body of divinity.' Hill, *Lectures*, 1854, 172.

[44] T. C. to John Chalmers, 24 November 1796, NCL CHA 3.1.17.

[45] St Andrews University Theological Society Minutes, 2, 1786-1823, StAUL UY911.

[46] For example, Iain Murray, 'Biographical introduction', William Cunningham, *Historical theology*, 1, 1960, v-xxvi.

to be most unfortunate in the pulpit.... Is not this scrupulous orthodoxy of Calvin a principle altogether foreign and subsequent to the native influence of divine truth on the heart?[47]

In other words, not only had Chalmers been unable to discover justification by faith in the moral preaching of Moderatism, he also could not find it in scholastic orthodoxy. It was a different form of Evangelicalism which had led to his conversion and now shaped his faith. In March 1812 he began to read Calvin's *Institutes*, at first in Latin, and from November in English.[48] A year later he reached the end of Book Three, but found Book Four on the church 'heavy and uninteresting' and decided to give it up.[49] Where once the idea of all things being in God's grand design filled him with ecstasy, now he found systematic theology oppressive. When Thomas Snell Jones visited and preached, Chalmers noted:

> I hope that his free, and unshackled, and scriptural divinity, will help to overthrow the spiritual tyranny of systems over me.[50]

It was Charters who told him he was going too far in his distrust of systematic theologies, and wrote that whatever their deficiencies 'a professional man should know one or two of them'.[51] Instead of the Evangelical Chalmers enthusiastically advocating the Westminster Confession and orthodox Calvinism, we have a Moderate clergyman telling him to pay them more attention.

In 1814 with the encouragement of Charles Stuart,[52] Chalmers took up Jonathan Edwards for the first time since the 1796-97 session at St Andrews. He began in March with Edwards' life[53] and worked through his major writings. By July he had completed the posthumous sermons,[54]

---

[47] T. C. to J. Anderson, 2 November 1811, *Memoirs*, 1, 241f.

[48] Journal, 24 March, 10 November 1812.

[49] Journal, 22 March 1813. In the *Memoirs* Hanna gives part of this entry, but not the telling phrase 'I have resolved to give him up.' *Memoirs*, 1, 327.

[50] Journal, 23 August 1813.

[51] S. Charters to T. C., 16 February 1814, NCL CHA 4.3.24.

[52] C. Stuart to T. C., 29 April 1813, NCL CHA 4.2.41. T. C. to C. Stuart, 24 May 1813, NCL CHA 3.5.79. T. C. to C. Stuart, 18 May 1815, NCL CHA 3.7.23. Copies of Edwards on religious affections and his posthumous sermons were lent by Stuart. William M'Culloch of Cambuslang had been one of Edwards' correspondents.

[53] Journal, 15 March 1814. Chalmers later owned the 1834 two-volume edition of *The works of Jonathan Edwards*. It is not always certain which of Edwards' writings Chalmers is referring to as he used abbreviated titles.

[54] Journal, 27, 28, 29 June 1814. There are five collections of sermons included in the 1834 *Works of Jonathan Edwards*, and it is not clear to which or how many of these Chalmers refers.

account of the conversions in New England,[55] and life of Brainerd.[56] Chalmers enjoyed Edwards but felt the close reasoning got in the way of what Christianity was really all about.

> I suspect both Edwards and Brainerd impair the freeness of the gospel offer and may embarrass and restrain a young convert in the outset of the work of seeking after God.[57]

A few days later he began Edwards on religious affections[58] but again came to the conclusion 'there is a tendency in it to unsettle gospel faith'.[59] He went on to the life of the Methodist John Fletcher (1729-1785), by whom he was 'edified and impressed'.[60] In March 1813 when he began Richard Cecil's *Remains,* he found a kindred spirit and copied out a lengthy extract.

> The right way of interpreting Scripture is to take it as we find it without any attempt to force it into any particular system.... Many passages speak the language of what is called Calvinism and that in almost the strongest terms. I would not have a man clip and curtail these passages to bring them down to some system...but let him look out as many more...which speak the language of Arminianism, and let him go all the way with these also. [61]

In February 1812 Chalmers spent a week with Samuel Charters at Wilton. A previous visit had been a few months before his conversion; but this was a year after and Chalmers soon found they did not get on so well as they used to.[62] He hoped Charters' use of 'a language and a mode of conception different from my own' did not mean the absence of 'vital Christianity'.[63] When Chalmers preached on the Sunday the gap widened further still.

> My principles on the incompetency of reason to decide upon the subject of revelation from previous and independent materials of its

---

[55] Journal, 2 July 1814. It is not clear whether this is the 'Narrative of surprising conversions' (*Works of Jonathan Edwards*, 1, 1834, 344-64) or 'Thoughts on the revival of religion in New England' (*Works of Jonathan Edwards*, 1, 365-430).

[56] Journal, 9, 29 July 1814. *Works of Jonathan Edwards*, 2, 1834, 213-458.

[57] Journal, 29 July 1814.

[58] Journal, 1 August 1814, *Works of Jonathan Edwards*, 1, 1834, 234-343.

[59] Journal, 14 August 1814.

[60] Journal, 7 October, 15 December 1814, 17 March 1815.

[61] Commonplace book, 1813, NCL CHA 6.2.5. *Memoirs*, 1, 322.

[62] Journal, 13 February 1812.

[63] Journal, 14 February 1812.

own are evidently most troublesome and offensive to Dr Charters. I was commented on with passion and severity in the evening.[64]

Shortly afterwards Charters wrote of their differences:

> Your sermon reminded me of a book that once made some noise, *Christianity not founded on argument,* to which Dr Doddridge made a good reply. It is right to avow your own sentiments, but is it right to announce hostility against Clarke, Butler and Locke's reasonableness of Christianity – men who assuredly believed, and whose writings have aided the belief of many?[65]

Despite Charters' irenical letters it took a while before some of the old trust was restored. He reminded Chalmers that the pulpit was an inappropriate place for airing differences[66] and suggested they 'agree to differ about the use of reason in religion and write in the same faith and hope'.[67] In the long run Chalmers took more notice than he appeared to at the time.

It is not easy to get to the bottom of their argument.[68] One would expect that following his conversion Chalmers might have been sceptical about the place of reason in religion. After all a 'reasonable' faith had not helped him when faced with a series of personal problems. Against this, he was finishing his article on Christianity for the *Edinburgh Encyclopedia* which was criticized for neglecting internal evidences. In arguing with Charters, Chalmers was also arguing with himself, but it is possible that what he objected to at Wilton was not the use of reason in assessing claims to authenticity, but the use of reason in formulating natural theology out of one's own self-consciousness. Chalmers chose to announce his rejection of natural religion from the pulpit of an elderly minister who had lived through more than a half of the century which held such an approach to be not merely normal but essential.

Later Chalmers gave considerable attention to natural theology. His acceptance of the Chair of Moral Philosophy at St Andrews in 1823 involved formulating the relationship between natural and revealed ethics. His commission in 1830 to write the first of the Bridgewater treatises produced a successful volume in its own right which in turn formed the basis of the two volumes on natural theology with which his *Works* commenced.

---

[64]   Journal, 16 February 1812.
[65]   S. Charters to T. C., 29 February 1812, NCL CHA 4.2.3.
[66]   S. Charters to T. C., 13 March 1812, NCL CHA 4.2.4.
[67]   S. Charters to T. C., 20 June 1812, NCL CHA 4.2.5.
[68]   Chalmers did not record the text of this sermon at Wilton and it is not known just what he said.

While in Kilmany these developments were in the future. At that point he was torn between dissociating himself from natural theology as a means of bringing people to God and the value of Christian evidences as confirming faith. The fact that in working this through he wounded the feelings of one of his most respected mentors may have sown the seeds of the more balanced assessment of the relationship between the 'natural' and the 'revealed' which he later adopted.

With the publication in 1815 of *An address to the people of Kilmany. The duty of giving an immediate diligence to the business of the Christian life,*[69] Chalmers was again involved in controversy. He re-asserted the moral imperatives, almost priorities, of his pre-conversion period and stated that those serious about their religion should get on with obeying God. Those nurtured on a stricter Calvinism were sensitive to nuances of which he was careless[70] and he had difficulty convincing his evangelical friends. Although after intense discussion Janet Coutts eventually agreed,[71] Charles Stuart had the advantage of not dealing with Chalmers in person and did not. Others said prayer was sinful in the unregenerate.[72] When he argued people ought to put themselves in the way of receiving God's grace by doing what they knew to be right he appeared close to justification by works. To Chalmers such responses were further examples of theological systems getting in the way of Scripture.

> Man may attempt to *do* for his acceptance with God – and in this attempt there is presumption and delusion. Or he may attempt to *do* in submission to the gospel and for the purpose of accommodating himself to its economy. The second set of doings have a character altogether distinct from the first. But they have been so confounded that a kind of sacrilegious dread of doing has got hold of the mind of many

---

[69] First published in 1815, the 'Kilmany address' was reprinted in 1816 and twice printed in America in 1817. It was included in the *Works*, 12, 69-120. Reviews in the *Christian Observer*, the *Edinburgh Christian Instructor* and the *Glasgow Herald* were friendly (*Correspondence*, 64f.), but the Glasgow Evangelical Robert Balfour was unhappy with it, as was Charles Stuart who had been corresponding with Chalmers on the issue for some time. Two pamphlets were published in refutation. W. Braidwood of the Scots Baptist Church in Edinburgh wrote *Faith and works contrasted and reconciled in six letters to a Christian friend*, Glasgow, 1816, and a Dublin minister, John Walker produced *The faith and hope of the gospel vindicated*, Glasgow, 1816. See also *Memoirs*, 1, 425f., 2, 17, 491-4.

[70] He took as his proof texts, John 7.17 'If any man will to do God's will, he shall know of the doctrine whether it be of God', and Psalm 50.23 'To him that ordereth his conversation aright will I show the salvation of God'. *Memoirs*, 1, 425.

[71] J. Coutts to T. C., 3 March 1815, StAUL 30385.189.

[72] J. Anderson to T. C., 16 July 1812, *Correspondence*, 7.

an enquirer and the work of Christian ministration has been reduced to a
bare inefficient exposition of articles on the one hand, and a fruitless
speculative orthodoxy on the other.[73]

Chalmers believed that he was true to biblical precedent, and that he avoided
the antinomianism some thought inherent in the free proclamation of
justification by faith. He insisted on justification and sanctification being
closely related and this became a recurrent theme.[74] For him it was a major
event

> when made to understand both the indispensable need of morality and
> the securities that we had for its being realized...notwithstanding the
> doctrine that by faith, and by faith alone, we were justified.[75]

It is perhaps difficult to share the sense of this being the 'greatest
enlightenment and enlargement'[76] he ever experienced, but it can be seen to
have been important in the way it functioned for him. If the Calvinism of
Scotland seldom precluded preaching of the gospel, nevertheless there were
barriers of habit and attitude to be broken down, much as in England
Particular Baptists had to escape from the inhibitions of hyper-Calvinism
before the Baptist Missionary Society could come into being. The Kilmany
address represented a breakthrough parallel to that of Andrew Fuller's
Gospel worthy of all acceptation. Chalmers needed and found a way to
preach freely the gospel that worked in his own experience. Thomas Snell
Jones was one who believed the Kilmany address made a significant break
with the past.

> The affectation of orthodoxy of some ministers on the point...has made
> them conceited, proud, arrogant,...censorious,...cold, dry, lukewarm
> and useless. And among the people this species of orthodoxy has made
> some of them dark...lifeless, inactive.... Others of them it has made
> careless, presumptuous and both theoretical and practical antinomians.
> This subject was much controverted from thirty to sixty years ago by
> your hair-splitting divines under the question 'Was faith a duty?'
> 'Should the unconverted be addressed and required to believe?' ... Verily
> you are not a bold man merely, but a very daring one...to thrust your
> hand into the viper's nest.[77]

---

[73]   T. C. to C. Stuart, 12 November 1818, NLS 2618 f.188.
[74]   *Memoirs*, 1, 425.
[75]   *Posthumous Works*, 9, 376. *Memoirs*, 1, 425.
[76]   Ibid.
[77]   T. S. Jones to T. C., 29 September 1815, StAUL 30385.428.

The evangelical preacher

From 1811 attendance at public worship in Kilmany rose steadily. Except for some annual communions when Chalmers recorded the numbers of tokens issued,[78] exact figures are not available. A reasonable estimate would be that on ordinary Sundays numbers increased from less than 70 in the early years of his ministry to about 200 in 1814.[79] The average number of communion tokens issued from 1812 to 1815 was 363 and the typical number of new communicants was 10. At his last communicants' class there were 23 attending including a Roman Catholic.[80]

As his reputation increased, so did the number of visitors from around Fife and beyond. In September 1813 Lord Leven asked him to preach at Monimail and in 1814 there was talk of him taking one of the services before the High Commissioner at the General Assembly.[81] His abilities as a fund-raiser were demonstrated by the Dundee Missionary Society in October 1812 and he refused several other requests.[82]

He had never lacked the ability to make an impression, but now he was burning with a much more explicitly religious message. He preached with energy, to the extent that he sometimes rebuked himself for doing so. He tried to adapt his sermons to his congregation and in one instance carried this as far as preparing more than one address and taking them both into the pulpit before deciding which to use.

Although not in his 'element where work and work people are concerned',[83] he struggled to make himself intelligible to the farm workers who formed a good proportion of the congregation. One of his first converts was a ploughman who became a city missioner in Edinburgh,[84] though this was not typical. Chalmers realized that there was a problem which was not just with the lower classes and not just due to his personal deficiencies. It was partly his background, but it was also a matter of the language in which the gospel was expressed. Evangelical formulations could be as inappropriate as those of the Moderates.

---

[78] Communicants 1810-15, NCL CHA 6.2.3.

[79] Based on a comparison of the collections at sacraments compared with ordinary services, and the quantity of communion tokens. See Appendix 1. Two hundred would have more than filled the small church, even with its galleries, and Chalmers noted it was crowded. Journal, 23 May 1813.

[80] T. C. to J. Coutts, 1815, *Correspondence*, 70.

[81] Journal, 13 May 1813.

[82] Journal, 6 October 1812.

[83] Journal, 9 October 1811.

[84] J. Baillie, *The missionary of Kilmany, being a memoir of Alexander Paterson*, 1854.

I feel that I do not come close enough to the heart and experience of my hearers and begin to think that the phraseology of the old writers must be given up for one more accommodated to the present age.[85]

In his contact with Janet Coutts and her elderly father Robert M'Culloch, Chalmers was exposed to traditional evangelical language and piety. It provided a sufficiently accurate description of his own religious experience for him not to reject it out of hand, but he soon wondered whether it was as much an integral part of the gospel as they assumed.[86] He was aware that such language was offensive to many and often stood in the way of communication.

One writer in particular helped in this area. In November 1811 'with great relish and excitement'[87] he finished John Foster, *Essays in a series of letters to a friend*, having been particularly struck by one 'on the aversion of men of taste to evangelical religion'. Chalmers warmly recommended Foster[88] and in January 1813 began reading him again in preparation for a review in the May *Edinburgh Christian Instructor*.[89]

He now felt confident enough to complain of Evangelicals for whom 'even orthodoxy is not welcome unless she presents herself in that dress in which she is familiar'. Insistence on traditional language indicated a lack of the very faith and spirituality they were anxious to proclaim. The principle of 'being all things to all men' would have to be abandoned if they were to continue a 'style tainted with all the obsolete peculiarities of a former age and disfigured by all the uncouthness of a professional dialect'.

Following Foster he was especially concerned with the effect of this on the middle and upper classes and asked whether it was not right that 'every man should be addressed in his own language' and 'proselytes attempted from every quarter of society'. This would not be possible if the language of Evangelicals continued to be 'below the elegant and cultivated phraseology of critics upon other subjects'.

Improving the language of the preacher would not of itself change a person's alienation from God, but it would be the removal of a barrier. Just as going to church was not 'an infallible specific for conversion' it did make it more likely. From his own experience Chalmers knew conversion could

---

[85] Journal, 7 March 1813.

[86] 'Though in substantial sentiment I trust we are the same, there is a certain want of congeniality in the modes of expression.' T. C. to J. Anderson, 18 December 1811, *Memoirs*, 1, 248.

[87] Journal, 11 November 1811.

[88] T. C. to J. Coutts, 24 October 1811, *Correspondence*, 66. T. C. to J. Honey, 2 May 1812, *Correspondence*, 266.

[89] *Edinburgh Christian Instructor*, May 1813, 327-39. *Works*, 12, 221-50, retitled 'On the technical nomenclature of theology'.

make matters of taste irrelevant, but that was no reason for avoiding clearing away whatever prevented people from understanding the gospel.

His argument was with a Calvinism which took refuge in predestination when challenged to modify traditional language. Yet more was at stake. In interaction with Foster and in the thinking that lay behind his *Kilmany address* he was wrestling with the role of man in a salvation which was all of God. However high its doctrine of election the Westminster Confession declared 'God in his ordinary providence maketh use of means',[90] and Chalmers strove to identify his responsibility in providing the 'means' that 'God in his ordinary providence' could use.

Over a long period his addresses on missions dealt with this question. In October 1812 he spoke to the Dundee Missionary Society on 'The two great instruments appointed for the propagation of the gospel' – namely Bibles and missionaries. In May 1824 he preached for the Scottish Missionary Society 'On the necessity of uniting prayer with performance for the success of missions'. Chalmers' distinction between the sovereign work of God and man's responsibility for the provision of Bibles and preachers (and in consequence schools and churches) meant he was free to take an activist role not only in providing these means, but also in giving attention to a matter of detail such as religious language. In this way Evangelicalism could work out of a Calvinistic tradition and meet missionary opportunities at home and abroad.

The evangelical pastor

From the spring of 1810 Chalmers had begun taking a more active interest in the pastoral needs of his parishioners. Visiting the sick became a priority and he sought to include prayer as part of his calls. However, with his extended convalescence it was not until December 1811 that he reinstituted systematic visitation of the whole parish. Earlier it took only a matter of weeks, now it became a more or less continuous process, calling together groups of people on farms, catechizing children and speaking to adults.

If this was different in degree rather than in kind from what was normally expected in a rural parish, in other respects his pastoral work was more distinctive. He started a Bible Association as is discussed below, and in 1812 he also began to make use of tracts. Late in 1813 he began a successful Saturday school on alternate weeks. An attempt to hold an adult class did not get off the ground.[91] A prayer or lay-fellowship meeting was also contemplated. He sought advice on running them[92] after attending a

---

[90]   Chapter 5.3.
[91]   Journal, 5, 7 June, 8 July 1812.
[92]   T. C. to J. Coutts, 19 December 1814, *Correspondence*, 67f. T. C. to (crossed out) 23 November 1814, NLS 10997 f.63.

Methodist prayer-meeting and class-meeting in Dundee[93] and a prayer-meeting in George Muirhead's parish at Dysart.[94] Despite Janet Coutts' lament that 'social meetings for prayer have become so infrequent in our day' and her reminder that 'in every revival of religion...a spirit of prayer appears...to have preceded or accompanied it',[95] nothing more was heard of the idea.

The Kilmany Bible Association

Chalmers was not long in showing that he saw the support of Bible societies as a part of his renewed commitment. His activity on their behalf reflected a conviction that the Bible contained a message applicable to people everywhere and that making Bibles available was a responsibility which every person could share. The methods of fund-raising this entailed gave him experience and ideas of crucial importance when it came to raising funds for church extension in the 1830s and for the Free Church of Scotland after the Disruption.

At a fast-day service in March 1811 Chalmers dedicated the collection to the Bible Society.[96] Probably due to failure to warn people beforehand this drew criticism, but he resolved 'to carry through what is right and religious in opposition to every discouragement'.[97] In May and September he was impressed by *Bible Society Reports* and began to think of organizing something himself.[98] He was encouraged by James Johnston, the Secession minister at Rathillet,[99] and in November got involved in founding a society in Anstruther.[100] The following month he began sounding out heritors and other parishioners in Kilmany but was frustrated when Johnston went ahead among the members of his chapel.[101]

Chalmers was insistent that if they were to 'secure the credit of liberality'[102] there should be one society for the whole parish. In March 1812 the Kilmany Bible Association came into being with support of both

[93] Journal, 26 April 1814.
[94] Journal, 4 January 1814.
[95] J. Coutts to T. C., 26 December 1814, StAUL 30385.188.
[96] Journal, 2 March 1811.
[97] Ibid.
[98] Journal, 31 May, 10, 11 September 1811. It is not clear whether Chalmers is referring to the British and Foreign Bible Society or the Edinburgh Bible Society. At least one was the Edinburgh Bible Society.
[99] Journal, 7 November 1811.
[100] Journal, 20 to 26 November 1811.
[101] Journal, 9 to 11 January 1812.
[102] T. C. to J. Johnston, 11 January 1812, NCL CHA 3.6.50.

church and chapel,[103] as well as the patronage of Kilmany's Episcopalian chief heritor, David Gillespie.

To the annoyance of fellow ministers, Chalmers was active in neighbouring parishes[104] and he encouraged his Dundee friend James Anderson who had the idea of publicizing the cause through letters to the *Dundee, Perth and Cupar Advertiser.*[105] The Dundee Auxiliary Bible Society was formed on 24 February 1812, though there was controversy whether it should affiliate with the Scottish Bible Society or the British and Foreign.[106]

In 1809 the Scottish Bible Society had been founded by the Presbytery of Edinburgh in opposition to the Edinburgh Bible Society which was affiliated to the British and Foreign Bible Society in London. Nationalism was a factor which would later reassert itself in the Apocrypha Controversy, and Moderate churchmen did not want to be swamped by laymen and members of other churches.[107]

For Chalmers, mission was more important than party spirit. He believed association direct with London[108] would be more effective.[109] In common with most societies in Scotland at the time, Dundee aligned with London.

The British and Foreign Bible Society had come into being in March 1804 and although it received remarkable support, it had already faced criticism. In England some objected that it was a rival to the SPCK and was not established by law or by the Church of England. It was said that Bibles should not be circulated apart from the interpretation provided by the Book of Common Prayer, and that it was an unbiblical method of evangelism unheard of in the early church and in the Reformation. As with Scottish Moderates some objected to an organization which included laymen and dissenters. Others speculated on its seditious potential.

---

103 Journal, 2 to 10 March 1812.

104 In late March Chalmers attributed the 'cold and resentful' attitude of some of his fellow ministers to his keenness in promoting Bible societies. It cannot have been helped by getting Logie and Dairsie included in a list of parishes with societies published before the ministers had made up their minds. Journal, 16 and 26 March 1812.

105 The initial series of letters were published over the signature '*Amicus*', on 31 January and 7, 14 and 21 February 1812.

106 J. Anderson to T. C., StAUL 30385.13 and 5 February 1812, StAUL 30385.18. T. C. to J. Anderson, 22 February 1812, *Correspondence*, 1-3.

107 Similar attitudes were seen in the Synod of Dumfries on 16 October 1810. *Edinburgh Christian Instructor*, 1810, 276ff.

108 J. Anderson to J. Owen (secretary of the British and Foreign Bible Society), 21 March 1812, Bible Society Archives. T. C. 'On the Bible Society', NCL CHA 6.

109 W. Tait to T. C., 30 March 1812, NCL CHA 4.2.20.

Generally speaking, the reception in Scotland was very different.[110] The SSPCK welcomed it as an ally rather than a rival and within a few years collections were being taken on its behalf by a majority of presbyteries. Auxiliary societies began to form from 1809 onwards, as they did in England, though most reserved the right to the independent allocation of some of their funds. In 1811 societies were formed in Montrose, Brechin, and Forfar as well as in Aberdeen, Arbroath, Dumfries and Glasgow, where members of the nobility agreed to head up the lists of patrons. By 1815 there were 45 auxiliary Bible societies in Scotland, many with smaller societies affiliated.[111] It would have been surprising if Fife did not come to be included at some stage and Chalmers' enthusiasm has to be seen alongside that of others.

In March 1812 he was writing round his friends to express fears that a Fife and Kinross Society might detract from those at parish level,[112] but eventually supported the regional body. Muirhead of Dysart believed parish associations would bring in the contributions of ordinary people, but larger societies were a way of tapping the resources of the rich.[113] Chalmers attended a preliminary meeting of ministers[114] and spoke at the inauguration of the Fife society in July 1812.[115] He brought the Kilmany Bible Association under its umbrella and though impatient of their lack of zeal became a member of the Cupar district committee.[116]

In his enthusiasm Bible societies were 'the most magnificent scheme that ever was instituted for bettering the moral condition of the species'.[117] He encouraged other associations in the district and joined Anstruther committee meetings when he visited home.

The simplicity of the aim of the British and Foreign Bible Society to 'encourage a wider circulation of the Holy Scriptures without note or comment' was a key to its success. There was no question of wanting to accompany Bibles with the Westminster Confession or the Shorter Catechism. The Scots had an attachment to the Bible and a high degree of

---

110   W. Canton, *A History of the British and Foreign Bible Society*, 1, 1904, 84-99. G. A. F. Knight, *The History of the National Bible Society of Scotland*, typescript, n.d., 7-24, National Bible Society of Scotland.

111   Canton, *Bible Society*, 1, 1904, 482f.

112   Journal, 13, 18, 19 March 1812. G. Muirhead to T. C., 27 March 1812, NCL CHA 4.2.10. W. Tait to T. C., 30 March 1812, NCL CHA 4.2.20.

113   G. Muirhead to T. C., 27 March 1812, NCL CHA 4.2.10.

114   Journal, 15 April 182.

115   *Edinburgh Christian Instructor*, September 1812, 212f., January 1813, 64-9.

116   Journal, 8 February 1813 to 7 January 1815. *Report of the Bible Society of Fife and Kinross Shires for the year ending 24 August 1813*, Cupar, 1814, 46.

117   *Memoirs*, 1, 263. *Edinburgh Christian Instructor*, January 1813, 67.

literacy. There was a common expectation that people should own their own Bibles and take them to church.

Outside Gaelic-speaking areas there was little scope for supplying Bibles in Scotland,[118] and societies found their main function to be the supply of cheap Scriptures in England, Ireland, the Highlands and overseas, with some going to French prisoners in Scotland. When he read the second annual report of the Edinburgh Bible Society in May 1811,[119] what impressed Chalmers was the potential for involving even the poorest people. The Aberdeen Female Servants Society for Promoting the Diffusion of the Scriptures[120] organized a penny-a-week scheme, and he was not slow calculating that if extended to every householder in Britain it could bring in half a million pounds a year.[121]

Penny-a-week societies were designated by London as 'Bible associations'[122] and it is more accurate to describe Chalmers as an enthusiast for these rather than societies,[123] which were less concerned about the contributions of the poor. He maintained that many and regular small donations would outweigh occasional large gifts from the wealthy, and the Kilmany Bible Association raised £52 in just over a year mostly from donations of less than 10s 6d.[124]

Accused of taxing the poor and placing a burden on the charity which maintained them, he replied that the penny-a-week system helped prevent poverty as it raised people to the status of givers and encouraged moral improvement by the regular management of their money. His defence was published in January 1814 as *The influence of Bible societies on the temporal necessities of the poor*[125] and became his best known statement on

---

[118]   In 1822 the parish of Fenwick could only find six poor people without a Bible in a population of over 1800. Fenwick Auxiliary Missionary Society Minutes, 11 March 1822, NRA(S) 797.6.

[119]   Journal, 31 May 1811.

[120]   *Edinburgh Bible Society second annual report*, May 1811, 8, 43f. Chalmers did not specify which Bible society report he was reading, but it was the Aberdeen Female Servants Society which caught his attention, and it was in the Edinburgh Society's report that the letter from the Aberdeen Female Servants Society detailing their activities first appeared, although it was reprinted in other publications (e.g. *Christian Observer*, October 1811, 601-3).

[121]   *Memoirs*, 1, 267.

[122]   Canton, *Bible Society*, 1, 1904, 54-7.

[123]   The term 'society' was commonly used by Chalmers and others when referring to what was technically an 'association'.

[124]   *Report of the Bible Society of Fife and Kinross*, 1814, 19, 45.

[125]   It reached four editions by 1818 and was published in America in 1826. Slightly amended it was included in the *Works* as 'The influence of parochial associations for the moral and spiritual good of mankind', *Works*, 12, 123-60. *The influence of Bible societies* was favourably

Bible societies, although it is hard to find any publication from his last years at Kilmany which does not contain some reference to them.

As in later writings, his argument that regular giving reduced poverty overshadowed other points of at least equal merit. He was not alone in being attracted by the simplicity and comprehensiveness of the aims of the British and Foreign Bible Society. Although insistent that there should not be a separate Secession society in his own parish, he gave little emphasis to its ecumenical potential.[126] It was not sectarianism which the Bible societies wished to circulate, but 'the pure Christianity of the original record'.[127] The free provision of Bibles was the mighty engine which would bring down the remnants of popery.[128] Bibles and schools had been the means of civilization in Britain, especially Scotland, and this was an experiment repeatable anywhere in the world.[129]

Missionary experience provided evidence that 'the Christianity of the Bible gains a readier access into the hearts of the ignorant than the Christianity of sermons and systems and human compositions'.[130] People paying for Bibles for others were more likely to take its message seriously for themselves.

Bible societies helped introduce Chalmers to the missionary movement, and it was not long before he saw them as one aspect of the

---

reviewed in the *Edinburgh Christian Instructor*, February 1814, 126-33; the *Evangelical Magazine*, 22, 1814, 187f.; and the *Baptist Magazine*, 1814, 253-5. In his *History of the origin and first ten years of the British and Foreign Bible Society*, 2, 1816, 548f., the secretary John Owen paid tribute to Chalmers' pamphlet and included extracts. Excerpts were reprinted in the reports of the Edinburgh Bible Society in 1814 and the Liverpool Auxiliary Bible Society in 1818. Andrew Thomson wrote to a friend that it was 'good, though not quite so good as expected' (A. M. Thomson to R. Lundie, 20 January 1814, NLS 1676 F.95.). The *Evangelical Magazine* thought Chalmers was fighting an imaginary enemy, though that was not the view of John Owen. In 1818 the issue was alive in two Bible Associations in the London area (personal letter, Miss K. J. Cann, Archivist, Bible Society, 10 February 1977). Chalmers was confronted with the issue again when president of the St Andrews Missionary Society in 1825.

126 George Muirhead pointed out that 'meeting on this common ground, other grounds of difference may be softened down'. G. Muirhead to T. C., 27 March 1812, NCL CHA 4.2.10.

127 'Speech of the Rev Mr Chalmers of Kilmany at the institution of the Fife and Kinross Bible Society', *Edinburgh Christian Instructor*, January 1813, 67.

128 *Edinburgh Christian Instructor*, January 1813, 66f.

129 Ibid.

130 T. C. to the secretaries of the Fife and Kinross Bible Society, 20 October 1813, *Correspondence*, 267.

larger movement. In 1813 the Kilmany Bible Association gave £25 to the Baptist Missionary Society[131] and £15 to the Moravians the following year.[132] In *The influence of Bible societies* he made it clear he was concerned for more than Bible societies[133] and in the *Works* changed the title to 'parochial associations'.

The parish association and penny-a-week scheme meant the participation of every member of the parish in the mission of the church had great potential not only for particular causes, but for the social, moral and spiritual life of the parishioners. The work of the church was no longer something to be left to the state or to the rich; it involved everybody, including the poor.

The relief of the poor

Until 1845 poor relief in Scotland was the joint responsibility of heritors and kirk sessions and was generally exercised through the ministers. It was a part of the mission of the church which had long interested Chalmers. When he arrived in Kilmany he had been struck by the contrast in the standard of living of the poor there compared with Hawick where they received higher allowances. Was there an explanation?

Hawick raised its money by a poor rate not by donations, and Chalmers believed the impersonal nature of this funding and its seemingly limitless supply encouraged people to stop looking to their own resources and increase their expenditure.[134] Once formulated, it was an explanation he thereafter collected evidence to support. He found confirmation of his ideas in Malthus,[135] and in July 1808 had told his congregation that it was 'in the power of charity to corrupt its objects'.[136] He believed he saw this in those

---

[131] *Report of the Fife and Kinross Bible Society*, 1814, 45.

[132] C. I. Latrobe to T. C., 13 March 1814, NCL CHA 4.3.33.

[133] 'I should be sorry if the Bible Society...were to occupy the whole ground and leave no room for other institutions.' *Works*, 12, 157. This annoyed 'An old member of the committee of the British and Foreign Bible Society' who wrote *Remarks on a late publication of Rev Dr Chalmers entitled 'The influence of bible societies...,' showing the dangerous tendency of some clauses in that work*, 1819 (Miss K. J. Cann, personal letter, 10 February 1977).

[134] *Memoirs*, 1, 379.

[135] Chapter 5 of T. R. Malthus, *An essay on the principle of population*, 1798. All checks to population could be resolved into misery and vice, and by their very nature poor laws had a powerful tendency to defeat their own purpose. Chalmers probably read Malthus in preparation for his *Enquiry*. He made reference to him in a letter in 1811 (T. C. to J. Morton, 7 February 1811, *Memoirs*, 1, 382). Chalmers later defended Malthus and corresponded for a period.

[136] *Posthumous Works*, 6, 60. *Memoirs*, 1, 381.

who moved from Kilmany to Dundee where a poor-rate also operated. When they returned, any hesitancy about asking for help had gone and relief was demanded from the church as of right.[137]

When his brother-in-law moved from Fife to Somerset there was further opportunity for comparison between the English and Scottish systems. In February 1811 Kilmany was supporting the poor with £24 a year. Although the collection might increase, that was 'scarcely desirable'.

> Not that I could not get poverty enough in the parish to absorb it, but that, let you extend this fund as much as you please, the poverty will extend along with it, so as to press as hard upon the supplies as ever. And if ever they come to be augmented to such a degree as to be counted upon by the lower orders, there is an end to that industry and virtuous independence which have so long formed the honourable distinction of our Scottish peasantry.[138]

To some this sounds harsh, not to say condescending, to others no more than realistic. It was not very remarkable in its time and might suggest that laws attributed to Northcote Parkinson[139] go back some way. When Chalmers heard from Somerset that a rural parish with the same population as Kilmany had a poor rate of £1260[140] he might be forgiven for believing that his diagnosis was all too accurate.

He believed in private charity and sought to practise it,[141] but was against giving people a sense of security outside their own efforts. Wandering beggars did not get much out of him.[142] When he preached for the Destitute Sick Society in Edinburgh,[143] it was to advocate charity as something deliberate rather than casual or sentimental. The Society operated through a committee whose members visited each applicant and enquired into their situation. These visits were followed up weekly. This meant that 'every precaution which prudence can suggest is adopted to prevent impositions'.[144] The Destitute Sick Society is the probable source of the

---

137   *Memoirs*, 1, 380f.

138   T. C. to J. Morton, 7 February 1811, *Memoirs*, 1, 382.

139   C. N. Parkinson, *The law and the profits*, 1963, 9-23.

140   *Memoirs*, 1, 383. The parish was Kingbrampton.

141   Journal, 25 December 1811.

142   Journal, 26 March 1810, 19 March 1811.

143   *A sermon preached before the Society for the Relief of the Destitute Sick, in St Andrew's Church, Edinburgh on the Lord's Day, April 8, 1813*, Edinburgh 1813. *Works*, 11, 283-314. It was published through the efforts of Charles Stuart despite Chalmers' objections, and an American and second British edition were brought out in 1817. It was reviewed in the *Edinburgh Christian Instructor*, December 1813, 394-404 and the *Evangelical Magazine*, 21, 1813, 306f.

144   *Edinburgh Christian Instructor*, December 1813, 401.

investigative methods Chalmers later implemented in Glasgow. In April 1813 Chalmers also emphasized the need for the 'trouble of examination'.

> It is not enough that you give money, and add your name to the contributions of charity. You must give it with judgement. You must give your time and attention…. You must rise from the repose of contemplation and make yourself acquainted with the object of your benevolent exercises. Will he husband your charity with care, or will he squander it away in idleness and dissipation?[145]

Such investigation meant thinking of more than just the effects of being too generous.

> You must go to the poor man's sick-bed. You must lend your hand to the work of assistance. You must examine his accounts. You must try to recover those wages which are detained by the injustice or rapacity of his master. You must employ your mediation with his superiors.[146]

Religious needs should not be forgotten and he saw the Society providing evangelistic opportunities. It was short-sighted to make a man content on earth and forget the longer future ahead. 'The man who considers the poor will give his chief anxiety to the wants of their eternity.'[147]

Chalmers regarded his pamphlet on Bible societies as a manifesto on poor relief, not just Bible societies.[148] It set forth the idea that a compulsory poor rate was demoralizing because it undermined self-reliance. Regular donations to an organization such as a Bible society placed people in the position of being givers rather than receivers.

He never conceded that more might be involved in this. Charters considered poor rates 'the least of two evils because without them the poor must perish',[149] but Chalmers stuck to his belief that if a parish was functioning properly they would not perish and the dangers of a publicly advertised fund were too great. He warned against the system in 'such full and mischievous operation in England', and of the day

> when the yearly assessment comes to be established and the provision of a mistaken benevolence is made known and the poor have found their way to it – they will set upon you in thousands; and the money which is withheld from the endowment of more schools and more churches and more ministers to meet the moral and religious wants of

---

[145] *Works*, 11, 320f.
[146] Ibid., 303.
[147] Ibid., 306.
[148] *Poor law enquiry (Scotland)*, Appendix, part 1, 1844, 271.
[149] S. Charters to T. C., 16 February 1814, NCL CHA 4.3.24.

an increasing population will be as nothing to hungry and
unquenchable demands of a people you have seduced from the principle
of independence which Christianity teaches.[150]

The threat of a disordered society was a theme which was easy to return to.
The preacher speaking to the needs of the day became fused with the social
conservative fearing the old order was on the eve of destruction. He was
arguing for an existing system, the main alternative was English, and he
was not inclined to examine deeply whether or not there was more than one
Christian principle at issue. His use of texts was selective as he asked
people to 'remember the words of the Lord Jesus how he said, "it is more
blessed to give than to receive"',[151] and warned that 'if any provide not for
his own, and especially for those of his own house, he hath denied the faith
and is worse than an infidel'.[152]

Once these convictions were established, he resorted to eloquence and
illustration without regard for how strong the arguments really were. Yet the
problem was not so much that his point of view was totally wrong, or that
it was especially novel, but that it was limited by considerations he failed to
take seriously.

At the same time one cannot say that Chalmers considered only
personal factors and not social ones. Both those he allowed for and those he
did not, can be found in each category. A great deal of the strength of his
convictions and the response which they drew, can be attributed to perfectly
worthy qualities which the rural society of Kilmany did exemplify.
Something was being lost when community spirit disappeared and people
did not know or care for one another. Personal pride and self-reliance were
desirable values. How they ought best be preserved, and how needs could be
met which they could not address were another matter.

As noted, his predecessor had written of the poor who 'very seldom and
with much hesitation' asked and who kept a 'withdrawing declining modesty
to which it is so pleasant to afford assistance'.[153] Kilmany was not
economically vulnerable; it neither attracted nor retained large numbers of
poor and the one regular and seven occasional poor on the roll of the kirk
session were only one percent of the population. They subsisted on their

---

[150]   *Works*, 11, 427f. Similar points were made in another sermon reported in
the *Dundee, Perth and Cupar Advertiser*, 14 July 1815. Although
unidentified as such it was published in the *Works*, 18, 375-99 and is an
important statement from immediately prior to Chalmers' transfer to
Glasgow.

[151]   Acts 20.35, *Works*, 11, 401.

[152]   1 Timothy 5.8, *Works*, 18, 375.

[153]   *OSA*, 191, 1797, 431.

own resources, informal charity from friends and neighbours, and £12 a year which the church divided among them.[154]

Their relief was neither a preoccupation for the minister nor a burden for heritors[155] obliged to make up any short-fall in church offerings, rent of the mort-cloth for burials, fines for immorality and interest on a legacy of £200. Shortly before Chalmers' arrival the heritors assessed themselves for £35 to build up the funds,[156] but they repeated this only once during his time and that was for a period of special need and against his wishes.[157]

When Chalmers later spoke of the insignificance of the task of administering poor relief in Kilmany,[158] he failed to note the warning this held for generalizations from this experience. Kilmany's small size, the trivial amount involved, and the fact that few heritors were absentees meant extrapolation to larger situations was difficult.[159] There was little danger of insufficient funds since they had the interest of a legacy and as attendances improved collections increased dramatically. Also the stigma attached to 'going on the parish' could operate in a small community in a way it never could in a city.

To help protect a traditional sense of independence, Chalmers went to considerable lengths to maintain even an illusion of its reality. Even when it was kirk session money he was distributing he sometimes made it anonymous and entered the recipient as 'industrious and deserving poor'.[160] One gift was administered separately because 'many who felt a reluctance to drawing anything out of the session's funds...did not feel the same reluctance to a present from an individual'.[161] By this means he was able to

---

[154]   *Third report from the select committee on the poor laws (1818), with an appendix containing returns from the General Assembly of the Church of Scotland*, 26 May 1818, Appendix, 66. This is said to be inaccurate, but in the case of Kilmany the figures correspond with Chalmers' recollections. *Works*, 16, 302. The discrepancy between the figure of £12 here and the £24 above is due to one family which at the earlier period required as much aid as the rest put together.

[155]   In the 1970s the cost of social welfare in Fife was said to be lower than other areas of Scotland.

[156]   SRO/GRO OPR 437/1, Kilmany old parochial register, 196, 23 August 1801.

[157]   *Works*, 16, 304.

[158]   *Journal*, 306.

[159]   Chalmers never accepted that when a large number had left the established church, it was inequitable for those who remained to be responsible for all the poor, a situation made worse by absentee landowners not contributing to local funds. A legal poor rate or assessment was one solution.

[160]   SRO/GRO 437/1, 231.

[161]   Ibid., 231.

claim that some who were on the 'very verge of sessional relief' were kept from being a permanent charge on the session.[162]

The good of religion

A number of incidents show that Chalmers had become sensitive to any reduction in the ratio of ministers to people. Late in 1811 a proposal to amalgamate the parishes of Moonzie and Creich found general support in Presbytery and among heritors. To Chalmers it was making 'religion give way to a mere secular accommodation'[163] and he was disappointed by the attitude of his fellow ministers. However the heritors changed their minds and the danger passed.[164]

The second matter was a case in which a minister would be given a university position while still in his parish – a situation in which he was not without experience. In 1813 it was proposed that the Professor of Civil History at St Andrews, William Ferrie[165] (1789-1850), should be appointed to Kilconquhar without resigning his chair. The Presbytery did not favour the proposal, but the General Assembly ordered the appointment to go ahead.

The matter came before Synod in October 1813 where Chalmers failed to block the move. He then supported moves to get the General Assembly to prevent any further such appointments. In a speech to the Assembly of 1814[166] he argued that the 'single object' of the Assembly in enacting legislation should be the 'good of religion'.[167]

This phrase is less trite than it appears, and is the ancestor of his more famous slogan 'the Christian good of Scotland' which still finds its place in Scottish vocabulary. In entering what was to prove a long-running conflict, Chalmers was insisting that his own repentance, from thinking that ministers had five days of the week to do what they liked, should be shared by the church as a whole. Doing so under the cry 'the good of religion', he also made it clear that whatever other functions the church might fulfil in society, its religious purpose was paramount. It also indicated that it was the religious good of society, not just of individuals, that was his concern.

It is perhaps significant that when reading Calvin he had given up when he reached the section on the church. He believed Christianity was concerned for the whole of society and its mission was worldwide, and this and much else of what he advocated was not in question theologically. It might be debated in terms of practice and tradition, but biblical or

---

[162] Ibid.
[163] Journal, 2 December 1811.
[164] Journal, 4-13 December 1811.
[165] *Fasti*, 5, 210.
[166] *Memoirs*, 1, 398-402.
[167] *Memoirs*, 1, 497, 499-500.

theological argument was only necessary if an issue needed that authority, and where what the Bible taught was defined by Confession and Catechism, that would not be easy. As it happened, neither was it altogether necessary. Chalmers felt supported by precedent and the Scottish way of life, and reflection on the nature of the church need not be particularly deep.

Where tradition did get in the way, if it could not be remoulded, perhaps it could be ignored. He believed the gospel needed to be freed from systematic theology and outdated language to function freely as a 'scheme of reconciliation for sinners'.[168] It was 'a simple offer on the one side and a simple acceptance on the other'.[169] His task as a minister was the 'great work of preparing a people for eternity'[170] but how they should live in the meantime was also a question he could not avoid.

---

[168] Journal, 23 April 1811.
[169] T. C. to J. Morton, 21 April 1812. *Memoirs*, 1, 348.
[170] Journal, 17 November 1811.

Chapter 6

'Seizing stubborn, knotty problems with his teeth'[1]
The Tron Church Glasgow, 1815-1819

Call to the city

For some time Chalmers had been marked out for something more influential than a tiny parish in rural Fife. He had no hesitation declining a call from London in 1813,[2] but the following year the central city charge of St Mary's Tron Glasgow was not so easy to refuse. Among the visitors to Kilmany had been a young Glasgow elder, William Collins (1789-1853), who returned to organize a Town Council deputation[3] to hear Chalmers for themselves.

An evangelical tradition had been established at the Tron under Stevenson Macgill (1765-1840).[4] With his appointment to a divinity chair at the end of 1814, there was anxiety it be maintained. Chalmers was interested, but hesitated. Glasgow itself was a drawback, and the secular duties expected of city ministers were a worry. In the end, urged by friends in Glasgow and Edinburgh, he saw it as a matter of 'duty and usefulness'[5] and allowed his name to go forward.

There were three candidates and canvassing was intense. Chalmers had the unanimous support of the kirk session and a petition of 245 signatures from the congregation,[6] although he refused to say if he would accept the call. On 25 November his supporters got a majority[7] and he was deluged

[1]   William Hazlitt, *The spirit of the age*, quoted in the *Glasgow Herald*, 14 April 1915.

[2]   *Fasti*, 7, 491. Journal, 30 June, 13 July 1813.

[3]   The patronage of the burgh churches in Glasgow was exercised by the town council which paid the stipends of the ministers.

[4]   *Fasti*, 7, 401f. R. Burns, *Memoirs of The Rev Stevenson Macgill*, 1842.

[5]   T. C. to R. Tennent, 21 November 1814, NCL CHA 3.6.61; *Memoirs*, 1, 444, 447.

[6]   R. Renwick, *Extracts from the records of the Burgh of Glasgow*, 10, 1809–1822, 1905, 271. (4 November 1814).

[7]   Ibid., 273f. (25 November 1814). *Memoirs*, 1, 448.

with letters. One pled he 'come over to Macedonia and help'.[8] Independents and Seceders were enthusiastic and Thomas Snell Jones reported it was a joy shared in Edinburgh.[9] To Robert Balfour, who had earned for Glasgow Evangelicals the nickname of 'Balfourites',[10] the election was 'a great day of Christian triumph'.[11] Chalmers still hesitated and when he finally agreed, delayed leaving until the summer of 1815.

Parish and congregation

St Mary's was known as the Tron Church because it was behind the Tron Steeple where the public weights ('tron') were kept. It dated from 1484[12] and had been converted to Presbyterian use in 1592.[13] Rebuilt in 1794 it could seat about 1300. It was one of eight parish churches within the Royal Burgh, though the larger community which centred on Glasgow included the parishes of Barony and the Gorbals.

The church was just outside the boundaries of the parish – indicative of the extent to which the concept of the church at the centre of the community had broken down.[14] Until mid-1819 the parish was the south-eastern segment of the Royalty of Glasgow running east from the Saltmarket and south from the Gallowgate. The boundary to east and south was that between the city and the Barony, a line which meandered across street and tenement in seemingly arbitrary fashion.[15] The parish ran about a mile from west to east and its width varied from almost nothing to a quarter of a mile. It was shaped like an elongated figure eight and the Calton area, otherwise part of the same natural community, was excluded by the city boundary. When Chalmers began to complain that it was impossible to create the sort of parish he wished, it was not just secular distractions he had in mind, but the effects of the disjoining of church, congregation, parish and community.

The population was about 11,000 in some 2,200 households. About 45% of households were Dissenters, 29% had seats in a congregation of the

---

[8]   J. Love to T. C., 28 November 1814, NCL CHA 4.3.24.

[9]   T. S. Jones to T. C., 26 November 1814, StAUL 30385.424. *Memoirs*, 1, 448-50.

[10]   *Memoirs*, 1, 449.

[11]   R. Balfour to T. C., 28 November 1814, NCL CHA 4.3.5.

[12]   J. Cleland, *Statistical tables relative to the city of Glasgow*, 1823, 166.

[13]   Ibid., 171. *Fasti*, 3, 473.

[14]   This was common. St Andrew's Church was inside the Tron parish; St George's had parts which were disjoined from one another as well as from the church itself. The Barony church was located near the cathedral, but its parish was an enormous area encircling the northern half of the city. The pre-1819 boundaries are described in the Glasgow Town Council Records, SRA A2/1/3, 186.

[15]   See map, Appendix 4.

Church of Scotland and 28%, including some of the Dissenters, had no seats anywhere. Roman Catholics were about 6%.[16]

The parish, though not the congregation, was working class. About 3% of the families in the parish, or 1% of its population, held sittings in the church.[17] It was on a growing edge of the city and the housing density varied considerably. Much had been built in the previous decade though open spaces still remained. Towards the east end there were rope works, weaving factories, potteries, brick works and a foundry. On the western side towards the city centre, the tenements with their crowded closes and wynds were tightly packed. The population was largely artisan, the most common trade being weaving, and there were a good many widows.[18] That this was not an affluent area was clear enough, that it was therefore also a very poor one – despite Chalmers' later claims – did not necessarily follow, although when he began a parish survey he was asked for money on just over 9% of his visits.[19]

The congregation could hardly have been in greater contrast. He conducted services in a building outside the parish, with a congregation more than 90% of whom were not of the parish either. Only 63 individuals came from the parish.[20] The great majority who were attracted in by his ministry and that of his predecessor were from the relatively affluent middle-classes among whom business and professional men predominated. This meant that Chalmers was minister of a working-class parish and a preacher to a middle-class congregation. He sought to make himself as available and intelligible to his working-class parishioners as to his better-off

---

[16]   These figures are partly based on Chalmers' surveys between November 1815 and November 1817 (*Memoirs*, 2, 109. *Works*, 11, 48. Notebook of marriages and sacraments 1815-1821, NCL CHA 6.20.38). These are consistent with the growth in the city between 1811 and 1821, but the rationalization of parish boundaries in 1819 makes exact comparison impossible. Chalmers' early categories were neither fully comprehensive nor mutually exclusive but his figures are comparable to Cleland, *Statistical tables*, 1823, 6f.

[17]   Description of the proportions of St John's parish, 3, NCL CHA 5.1.12. In this printed circular Chalmers included a summary of a survey of the new parish carried out immediately prior to his taking up appointment as its minister. Of a total population of 10,304, 6,148 were from the old Tron parish. Of these 63 individuals from 29 families had held seats in the Tron church.

[18]   R. A. Cage, *The Scottish poor law, 1745-1845*, University of Glasgow PhD thesis, 1974, table 24. This table of occupations relates to St John's parish in mid-1819 which included a fair amount of the old Tron parish and may be taken as a guide to the Tron generally.

[19]   T. C., Notebook of marriages, NCL CHA 6.20.38.

[20]   Out of 29 seat-holding families. Descriptions of the proportions of St John's parish, 3. NCL CHA 5.1.12.

congregation, but it was inevitable that he viewed the needs of the parishoners through the eyes of those who filled the church Sunday by Sunday. It was their values and fears to which he gave voice and leadership.

His last years in Fife had provided a model of a parish church as a caring community where the minister had leisure to pursue his interests, now theological rather than scientific. His first years at Glasgow gave broader scope for relating an evangelical gospel to increasing social needs and scientific awareness. It also gave him the middle-class support to try an experiment where he might bring together church and community, parish and congregation as he had known it in Kilmany. At the Tron he gained experience in the use of laymen in parish visitation and Sunday schools. Alarming as the problems of industrial Glasgow might appear to his middle-class supporters, his first few years in Glasgow only made him more convinced that the solution was to be found in his rural parish ideal and the energies of those laymen themselves.

City minister

It was said Chalmers 'disclaimed all responsibility for any pastoral oversight'[21] of the congregation of 1500 and concentrated on the 11,000 who made up the parish. In a sense this was true and he never went on a systematic visitation of his middle-class seat-holders who lived outside the parish. However it was to their country houses he went when he wanted to get away from the city and they provided the elders and Sunday-school teachers with whom he developed close working relationships. It was from among them rather than his parishoners that he gained friends and correspondents whom he retained for the rest of his life.

At the Tron he developed methods of carrying out pastoral care among a large working-class population. The essential elements were a parish survey, the use of Sunday schools and gathering people together from a locality for informal services. There were also duties associated with marriages, baptisms and burials. Less congenial were responsibilities for poor-relief administration, membership of committees of city charities, and endless requests for signatures to attest the identity of parishioners in receipt of money from the government.

Among his duties as a minister was the examination of first communicants. The sacrament was celebrated twice a year in April and November and those receiving communion for the first time averaged about 35.[22] The usual pattern of Scottish communions in this period was followed, with services on Thursday, Saturday, Sunday evening and Monday in addition to the communion itself on the Sunday morning. About 12 tables were served, although a few years later Chalmers instigated serving

---

[21]　Watt, *Chalmers*, 1943, 51.

[22]　T. C., Notebook of marriages, loc. cit.

people in pews rather than at tables in the aisle.[23] He was assisted in the preaching by as many as eight other ministers over the four days.

Baptisms were performed privately and in his first six months in Glasgow he carried out just over a hundred. He recorded only 18 marriages in the year from June 1816,[24] and kept no note of burials. There would have been about 240 a year in the parish, but how many he would have been associated with and what they entailed is not clear. Fear of praying for the dead meant the Church of Scotland did not permit prayers at the graveyard and while the well-known might achieve mention in a sermon the following Sunday, in general the role of the minister was confined to comforting the relatives and arranging the provision of a coffin if they happened to be poor.

The visitation of everybody in the parish was a normal duty for ministers, but in large towns the size of the population, the numbers of Dissenters and the scattered membership of gathered congregations generally made it impracticable. After his conversion, Chalmers regarded visiting as vital. Faced with a population nearly 14 times the size of Kilmany he was still determined to find some way of doing it.

His initial visitation was a survey begun in November 1815 and completed two years later. In all 32 days were spent on the task, mostly during the first and the last six months. Elders were already allocated to districts or 'proportions' for administration of poor-relief (he neither invented elders' districts nor their designation in Glasgow by the word 'proportion'[25]). Typically in company with the elder for the proportion he visited about 70 families a day for three days. He recorded the statistics of each household and special needs which required further visits. To begin with he was faced with frequent requests for money and for a while noted how often people brought up the subject of their 'temporalities'.[26] He generally declined to offer prayer and confessed to 'putting butter very thinly on the bread',[27] but believed that if he spent time with any but the most urgent cases he would never get finished.

Mid-week services were arranged in conjunction with the visitation of each proportion. For many people these were the only services they were ever likely to attend, and at them he also conducted examinations on set passages from the Bible.[28] Again this was not so novel except in the

23   *Memoirs*, 2, 389-95. Anderson, *Reminiscences*, 1851, 120-22. W. D. Maxwell, *A History of worship in the Church of Scotland*, 1955, 171f.
24   T. C., Notebook of marriages, NCL CHA 6.20.38.
25   J. Cleland to T. C., 26 June 1819, NCL CHA 4.10.53. In this circular asking city ministers to conduct a census, Cleland asked them to divide their parishes 'into such proportions as you may think proper'.
26   T. C., Notebook of marriages, NCL CHA 6.20.38.
27   *Memoirs*, 2, 110.
28   Tron Church examinations, NCL CHA 6.17.12.

context where he was determined to make it part of the normal activity of the church.

If the knowledge of the working classes gained from these exercises can be criticized as in some ways superficial, what is remarkable is that he achieved as much as he did. From early on it was clear that even with an active eldership it was impossible to give anything like adequate pastoral care. Mindful of the religious ignorance his visits uncovered, he saw in a network of Sunday schools a potent means of meeting these deficiencies.

Sunday schools

Sunday schools had been started in Scotland about 1760,[29] 20 years before Robert Raikes began putting them on an organized footing in Gloucester. They suffered a set-back in 1799 with the adoption by the General Assembly of a report concerning 'vagrant teachers and Sunday schools',[30] designed to check the evangelistic activities of the Haldane brothers and their Society for the Propagation of the Gospel at Home.

At Kilmany Chalmers instituted classes for religious instruction which met on Saturday evenings. He had hesitated on the grounds that this was the responsibility of parents[31] and Sunday schools might encourage religious neglect of children. In some communities to send your children to Sunday school was open confession of such dereliction.

In Glasgow Sunday schools had begun in 1786 and in 1790 the Magistrates and Council granted a seal to the Glasgow Sunday School Society.[32] Their work was financed by the General Session[33] and by June 1819 they had 11 schools and 650 children. Methodist and Congregationalist societies also came into existence in 1806 and 1809. By 1819 the Methodists supported one school and the Congregationalists 23. Between 1814 and 1818 five schools were started by the Glasgow Sabbath School Association under the presidency of John Lockhart[34] (1761-1842), the parish minister of Blackfriars. In 1815, John Pollock (1762-1820) of Govan wrote *An enquiry into the expediency of Sabbath schools in Scotland.*[35]

This suggests that there is nothing very remarkable about Chalmers encouraging Sunday schools. What was noteworthy was the philosophy he had for going about it. Previously they had been established either to cater for very specific groups of children (such as those who went to week-day

[29] By David Blair (1701-1769) of Brechin. *Fasti*, 5, 376.

[30] *AGA*, 1799, 42-5.

[31] T. C. to J. Morton, 6 November 1812, *Memoirs*, 1, 351.

[32] J. Cleland, *The rise and progress of the city of Glasgow*, 1820, 228f.

[33] A meeting of the ministers of the city churches.

[34] Father of the biographer of Sir Walter Scott. *Fasti*, 3, 399.

[35] *Fasti*, 3, 413.

charity schools) or else for any who were prepared to come some distance.[36] In order to cope with a parish of 11,000 people[37] Chalmers insisted each teacher have a restricted catchment area which they visited repeatedly. He succeeded in attracting outstanding teachers and in establishing a large number of schools. The 'locality principle' meant each teacher had a defined manageable task, and the benefits of the teaching were made available to more than just those who were prepared to go out of their way to attend.

Among the teachers was William Collins, who had been instrumental in bringing him to Glasgow, and who was at this time the successful proprietor of a private school. Another was David Stow (1793-1864), later one of the leading educationalists of his generation.[38] Stow had been running his own local Sunday school when Collins introduced him to Chalmers. Although Stow gave Chalmers credit for insisting on the value of local rather than 'general' Sunday schools there is little doubt that Chalmers picked the idea up from Stow.[39]

In December 1816 a Sunday school society was founded in the Tron Church[40] and was soon one of Chalmers' favourite projects. Its success dwarfed all his other efforts and by the time Chalmers left in 1819 there were 47 schools in the society, almost half the total number in Glasgow.[41] Chalmers gave a large amount of his energy and enthusiasm to the Sunday school society and its corps of young teachers. What these 'young men of religious character and education, chiefly in the middle and upper ranks of life'[42] learnt was not the least of his achievements. A number later became ministers. All received first-hand experience visiting working-class homes, getting to know people and the conditions in which they lived, and trying to make Christian faith intelligible among what cannot have been the most orderly and compliant groups of children. The locality principle and Chalmers' close personal interest helped retain teachers and the success led to their imitation.[43]

---

36   Cleland, *Rise and Progress*, 1820, 228f.
37   *Memoirs*, 2, 129.
38   W. Fraser, *Memoirs of the life of David Stow*, 1868.
39   Ibid., 27. *Memoirs*, 2, 127.
40   *Memoirs*, 2, 122f.
41   Cleland, *Rise and Progress*, 1820, 228f. With Chalmers' move the 35 Sunday schools in the part of the Tron parish which went into St John's became the St John's Parish Sabbath School Society, and the remaining 12 became the Saltmarket-Street Sabbath Society.
42   Cleland, *Statistical tables*, 1823, 123.
43   *Scottish Missionary Register*, 1821, 7-10, 131-6.

The secularization of the ministry

Chalmers had doubts about non-ministerial duties in Glasgow right from the beginning. Answers to his enquiries did not satisfy him and he wrote to one of the town councillors:

> The secular employment laid upon your clergy to the degree mentioned by you will not restrain me from accepting it. But I will not oblige myself to any portion of such employment, however small.... The purity and independence of the clerical office are not sufficiently respected in great towns. He comes among them as a clergyman, and they make a mere churchwarden of him. I have much to say upon this subject...it shall be my unceasing endeavour to get all this work shifted upon the laymen.[44]

Assurances were forthcoming from Robert Balfour, but again not to Chalmers' satisfaction. It was

> a matter of greater magnitude than I can make it appear to the bulk of my clerical acquaintances.... Now it is not enough to be told that the business of my parish will not take up beyond two hours a day. I perceive that in addition to this the clergy are the trustees of charities and charity-schools.[45]

The reply was no more reassuring.[46] Balfour was a fellow Evangelical, but had a different outlook. It would be a great loss if Chalmers did not go to Glasgow, but Balfour could not see what he was fussing about. Dispensing poor-relief was part of being a minister of the established church. Other ministers, many of them pious, did not complain; why should Chalmers? If Chalmers had expected that Balfour at least might understand, he was disappointed. Robert Burns of Paisley was more sympathetic and recalled the sign Cotton Mather fixed to his door: 'Be short'.[47]

Just before he left Kilmany, Chalmers preached[48] that the business of the ministry 'is not to perform good works, but to multiply the workers'.[49]

---

[44]   T. C. to Robert Tennent, 21 November 1814, NCL CHA 3.6.60. In reply to R. Tennent to T. C., 17 November 1814, *Memoirs*, 1, 440.

[45]   T. C. to Robert Balfour, 4 December 1814, NCL CHA 3.6.63. This was in reply to R. Balfour to T. C., 28 November 1814, NCL CHA 4.3.5.

[46]   R. Balfour to T. C., 7 December 1814, NCL CHA 4.3.7.

[47]   R. Burns to T. C., 15 March 1815, StAUL 30385.107.

[48]   'The example of the apostles a guide and an authority for the conduct of clergymen in the administration of public charities', *Works*, 18, 377-399. *Dundee, Perth and Cupar Advertiser*, 14 July 1815.

[49]   *Works*, 18, 380.

'The time of a Christian teacher is too precious to be taken up with the business of any public ministration.'[50]

In the event Glasgow was everything he feared. People pressed him for money and his signature was necessary on innumerable documents. In October 1815 he wrote back to Fife after an hour spent deciding the future of a drain.

> I am gradually separating myself from all this trash, and long to establish it as a doctrine that the life of a town minister should be what the life of a country minister might be, that is, a life of intellectual leisure…and his entire time disposable to the purposes to which the apostles gave themselves wholly, that is the ministry of the word and prayer.[51]

Through 1816 his dissatisfaction mounted and his feelings showed frequently in correspondence,[52] a speech at the General Assembly,[53] and an address to the annual meeting of the Glasgow Auxiliary Bible Society.[54] He appealed to laymen to take a greater role running religious societies and get away from the idea that every meeting required a clerical presence to do its business.[55] He vented his frustration from his pulpit[56] and complained that the minister 'instead of sitting like his fathers in office, surrounded by the theology of present or other days…must now turn his study into a counting room'.[57]

He was giving his signature 70 times a day and if he went to all the meetings he was sent notice of he would never do anything else. If ministers were looking more and more like 'surveyors and your city clerks, and your justices and your distributors of stamps', it was small wonder people had 'lost sight of us altogether as their spiritual directors'.[58] He harked back to when the minister was the man

> whose business it was…to prepare for your Sabbath instruction, and to watch over your souls, and to hold individual conference with every earnest enquirer, and to ply his daily attendance upon your deathbeds, and by his yearly presence to shed a holy influence over your streets

---

50   Ibid., 394.
51   T. C. to D. Watson of Leuchars, 27 October 1815, *Memoirs*, 2, 21.
52   T. C. to J. Morton, 5 January 1816, *Memoirs*, 2, 22-5.
53   *Memoirs*, 2, 68.
54   *Glasgow Courier*, 13 June 1816. *Memoirs*, 2, 120f., 501-6. (Hanna gives the impression that this took place in 1817.)
55   *Memoirs*, 2, 505.
56   *Posthumous Works*, 6, 330-47. *Memoirs*, 2, 113-20.
57   *Posthumous Works*, 6, 334.
58   *Posthumous Works*, 6, 346.

and your families, and to brandish all that spiritual armour which the great Master of the Church has put into his hand for reclaiming the profligate and overawing the audaciously wicked, and arresting the mad career of licentiousness, and so manifesting the truth to the conscience of men as to force their willing consent to the faith and obedience of the gospel.[59]

The Tron congregation was alarmed, doubly so when the Stirling Town Council offered to deal with his complaints if he went there. The Tron offered an assistant and a supplement to his stipend as well as freedom to escape to the country. In January 1817 he ended the suspense by declining the approach from Stirling. He accepted the offer of pulpit assistance[60] and in December wrote to Samuel Charters of an improvement in health:

> Partly I believe from having betaken myself to horsemanship, partly from having shaken from me that load of secular duties which in the shape of attendance on the various institutions of the place, and of ministering in things temporal to the needs of a crowded population frittered away all the time and vulgarized all the habits and put to flight all the literature and all the spirituality of our clergymen.... All my fears before I entered Glasgow...were fully realized.[61]

Of greater significance than opting out of committee meetings and trying to minimize verifying the identity of his parishioners (made worse by the end of the Napoleonic wars) was the formation of the Sunday school society and the ordination of additional elders to share the pastoral load.[62] He looked to the day when an order of deacons might be revived[63] but in the meantime the eldership had both spiritual and temporal duties to perform. He encouraged them to undertake 'the practice of our ancestors'

> of ministering from house to house in prayer and in exhortation and in the dispensation of spiritual comfort and advice among the sick or the disconsolate or the dying.[64]

Chalmers called new elders to civility and firmness in administering poor relief so that real need would be met but 'unseasonable applications' refused.

---

[59] *Posthumous Works*, 6, 332.
[60] T. C. to William Roger, 25 January 1817, NCL CHA 3.7.46. Wrongly dated by Chalmers as 1816.
[61] T. C. to S. Charters, 26 December 1816, NCL CHA 3.7.57. *Correspondence*, 275.
[62] *Memoirs*, 2, 121, 507-11.
[63] *Memoirs*, 2, 509.
[64] Ibid., 508.

If it were possible to find work for those in need, or provide private help to tide them over, that would be better than public charity.

By the beginning of 1817 his ministry at the Tron had passed its first crisis. There were still fundamental problems in the relationship of parish to church and the management of poor relief which required a more radical solution. When the Town Council began taking steps for going ahead with the formation of a new parish in the city, one appeared to be within reach.

The popular preacher

It was said of Chalmers at the Tron that 'from his very first sermon his name was made as a preacher.'[65] It is true his preaching had led to his appointment, but accounts of enthusiastic crowds fail to indicate how Chalmers' popularity developed further afield. He may well have charmed the Tron congregation from the first, but a wider reputation was not instantaneous.

At Kilmany he attracted little attention in the religious and secular press before his appointment to Glasgow. The *Dundee, Perth and Cupar Advertiser* reported his election to the Tron,[66] his farewell sermons at Kilmany[67] and a charity sermon in Dundee about the same time.[68] Before this the only references had been reviews in the *Evangelical Magazine* and the *Edinburgh Christian Instructor*.[69]

Once in Glasgow reporting of his preaching says as much about the newspapers as it does about the interest he generated. Neither the *Glasgow Herald* nor the *Glasgow Courier* carried much local news and a great deal depended on being provided with copy. Even when well-established he was often reported in Glasgow newspapers only when he published a sermon, or preached out of town and they were able to reprint accounts from other papers. However meagre the home coverage, no other minister received a fraction of it.

Chalmers' first sermon in Glasgow was for the Society of the Sons of the Clergy,[70] and was given a few months before leaving Kilmany. It got a brief mention in the *Glasgow Herald*[71] and the *Glasgow Courier* called it

[65]   Watt, *Chalmers*, 1943, 41f.
[66]   *Dundee, Perth and Cupar Advertiser*, 2 December 1814.
[67]   *Dundee, Perth and Cupar Advertiser*, 14 July 1815.
[68]   Ibid.
[69]   *The two great instruments appointed for the propagation of the gospel* and *A sermon preached before the Society for the Relief of the Destitute Sick* were noticed in the *Evangelical Magazine*, 1813, 136ff., 178f., 306 and reviewed in the Edinburgh Christian Instructor, 1813, 391-404.
[70]   *Memoirs*, 2, 1.
[71]   31 March 1815.

'excellent'.[72] In July the *Courier* reported that his appointment had given 'peculiar satisfaction'[73] to the congregation and described his farewell sermon in Kilmany, where he preached from the window of the church because of the crowd of 'all ranks and many religious sects'.[74]

Some time elapsed before his name appeared again. In February 1816 the *Courier* gave a column extract from a sermon on universal peace delivered in January and just published.[75] An indication his reputation had not been standing still came during the 1816 General Assembly when he preached for the Society of the Sons of the Clergy in Edinburgh the same sermon delivered in Glasgow the year before.[76] The *Glasgow Courier*[77] reprinted an account from the *Edinburgh Correspondent*. The audience was 'very crowded and elegant'. Many were standing, and Chalmers excelled himself.

> Probably no congregation since the days of Massilon[78] ever had their attention more completely fixed, their understanding more enlightened, their passions more agitated and their hearts more improved.[79]

The same account was given by the *Glasgow Herald* the day after.[80] A day later again the *Courier* made reference to him in connection with the debate on pluralities[81] and on 28 May reported his sermon before the High Commissioner. The service was at eleven. By nine o'clock a crowd had gathered.

> When the doors opened at half past ten the rush…[was] so great that several persons, particularly females, were hurt, and many had their clothes torn. There never was such an immense audience in this church, and it was even with difficulty the commissioner, judges, magistrates, etc. could reach their seats.[82]

---

72 1 April 1815.
73 22 July 1815.
74 25 July 1815.
75 *Thoughts on universal peace: a sermon delivered on Thursday, January 18, 1916, the day of national thanksgiving for the restoration of peace*, 1816. *Works*, 11, 55-86. *Glasgow Courier*, 15 February 1816.
76 *Memoirs*, 2, 64. *Works*, 11, 387-435.
77 23 May 1816.
78 Jean Baptiste Massilon (1663-1742) was a preacher at the French court and Bishop of Clermont.
79 *Glasgow Courier*, 23 May 1816.
80 24 May 1816.
81 25 May 1816.
82 *Glasgow Courier*, 28 May 1816.

The reporter compared Chalmers to Cicero and Demosthenes and counted himself 'fortunate to hear once more this surprising man.... His oratory is so totally different from anything we have ever heard.'[83] Waking up to the impact of their man from Glasgow the *Courier* gave a fuller account of his speech on pluralities. Mainly verbatim, at one point the reporter lost track as Chalmers broke into

> a torrent of eloquence which seemed to astonish the house, and which has, in the opinion of the best critics and judges, perhaps never been exceeded.[84]

From this point the Glasgow press took greater interest. Within two weeks of the 1816 Assembly the *Courier* covered the annual meeting of the Glasgow Auxiliary Bible Society including Chalmers' speech on the need for the laity to take a larger role.[85] The Chalmers phenomenon went to London in May 1817 where he preached at the annual meetings of the London Missionary Society and on three other occasions,[86] all widely reported in the London and Glasgow papers.[87]

Enthusiasm in London for the 'justly celebrated preacher'[88] was warm[89] but not unanimous. The *Public Ledger* thought not all the praise was deserved:

> We may allow that he is a man of no ordinary powers, and he has done more to overcome the obstacles of a provincial education, an ungraceful person, and an unharmonious voice, than could have been expected....
> Among the honourables who listened to his late discourses we observed Lord Elgin,...Lord Castlereagh, Mr Canning, Mr Wilberforce and a

---

83 1 June 1816.

84 *Glasgow Courier*, 6 June 1816.

85 13 June 1816.

86 Chalmers preached for the LMS at Surrey Chapel on May 14, for the Scottish Hospital, again at the Surrey Chapel on May 22, and on Sunday May 25 in the morning at London Wall for the Hibernian Society and in the afternoon at Swallow Street. He spoke at the annual dinner of the SSPCK on May 21. *Memoirs*, 2, 98-103.

87 Reports include: *Evening Star*, 15, 23, 26 and 27 May, 1817; *Glasgow Courier*, 20, 27, 29 May and 3 June 1817; *Glasgow Herald*, 26 and 30 May 1817; *Morning Chronicle*, 26 May 1817 (*Memoirs*, 2, 103f.); *Public Ledger*, 29 May 1817 (*Glasgow Courier*, 3 June 1817); and the *Sun*, 26 May 1817 (*Glasgow Courier*, 29 May 1817).

88 *Glasgow Courier*, 20 May 1817.

89 J. W. Cunningham to T. C., 12 August 1817, NCL CHA 4.6.8.

long list of M.P.'s which we have not been much accustomed to elbow at a place of divine worship.[90]

Chalmers discovered openings to members of parliament and the nobility. The *Glasgow Courier* wrote of 'our own Chalmers'[91] and the *Edinburgh Star* referred to 'perpetual triumph', the effects of which 'scarcely seem to be accounted for on human principles'.[92] Within a year of coming to Glasgow he had become the most renowned preacher in Scotland and within two London experienced thousands being turned away wherever he preached.[93]

Among the curious who attended his first sermon in Glasgow in March 1815 was the young J. G. Lockhart, who a few years later gave a classic description of his unpromising style. Chalmers ignored that most cardinal of Scottish rules by reading from a manuscript, but that was not all.

> His voice is neither strong nor melodious, his gestures are neither easy nor graceful; but, on the contrary, extremely rude and awkward; his pronunciation is not only broadly national, but broadly provincial, distorting almost every word he utters into some barbarous novelty....
> He commences in a low drawling key, which has not even the merit of being solemn, and advances from sentence to sentence, and from paragraph to paragraph, while you seek in vain to catch a single echo that gives promise of what is to come.... But then, with what tenfold richness does this dim preliminary curtain make the glories of his eloquence to shine forth....
> I have never heard either in England or Scotland, or in any other country, any preacher whose eloquence is capable of producing an effect so strong and irresistible.[94]

In November 1817 *Blackwood's Edinburgh Magazine* began a series of articles on the pulpit eloquence of Scotland with an assessment of Chalmers.[95] Again the beginnings were notable for their 'tame and unhurried monotony'. Yet as he got on

> Our souls are quickened with a more vigorous sense of life; our heartstrings vibrate with unknown intensity of emotion. He carries our

---

90   *Glasgow Courier*, 3 June 1817.
91   28 October 1817.
92   *Glasgow Courier*, 30 December 1817.
93   *Sun*, 26 May 1817. *Evening Star*, 26 May 1817.
94   W. Ruddick, ed., *John Gibson Lockhart, Peter's letters to his kinsfolk*, 1977, xii, xvi-xxi, 171f. *Memoirs*, 2, 4f. Lockhart had studied in Glasgow and Oxford and visited Germany. *Peter's letters* was anonymous, scandalizing and satirical, but his assessment of Chalmers was sincere.
95   *Blackwood's*, 8(2), November 1817, 132-140.

enthusiasm along with him in flights…. We are willing to confess that
we have never lived before, and would sacrifice ages of earthliness for
one moment of rapture so divine.[96]

Six months later *Blackwood's*[97] considered Chalmers had 'a more vigorous
style and a more energetic imagination' than any other preacher, though his
reasoning was 'lame and weakly' compared with Butler and Paley; his
erudition 'nothing to that of a Lardner,[98] a Warburton[99] or a Horsley'[100]
and his eloquence 'jejune when set by the side of Barrow'.[101] Still he was
'assuredly a great man'.[102]

Why was it that Chalmers should have gained acclaim long denied
other Evangelicals who did not read their sermons or suffer the handicap of a
provincial accent full of 'barbarous novelties'? Why was it that it was he
rather than someone else who received the dubious accolade of the
mimicking of his vocabulary and rhetoric by preachers[103] and others?[104]

Despite its drawbacks, his style had a certain novelty.[105] It was
energetic and dramatic – a dusty pulpit cushion could produce ludicrous side-

---

[96]   Ibid., 136.

[97]   'Letters to the supporters of the *Edinburgh Review*. No. 1 – To the Reverend
Thomas Chalmers,' *Blackwood's*, 3, May 1818, 155-62. According to
Anderson, *Reminiscences*, 1851, 41, this (like *Peter's letters* quoted above)
was written by J. G. Lockhart. Lockhart was attacking the *Edinburgh
Review* and its Whig supporters. Chalmers was lending his name to a
periodical known for scepticism. Ruddick, *John Gibson Lockhart,* 1977.

[98]   Nathaniel Lardner (1684-1768).

[99]   Bishop William Warburton (1698-1779).

[100]   Bishop Samuel Horsley (1733-1806).

[101]   Isaac Barrow (1630-1677).

[102]   *Blackwood's*, 8(2), November 1817, 155.

[103]   A correspondent in the *Edinburgh Christian Instructor* wrote of 'the
pigmy race of rising divines' who thought it 'indispensably necessary that
they should ape the manner of Dr Chalmers'. *Edinburgh Christian
Instructor*, November 1819, 755-8.

[104]   'Chalmerianism' infected not only clerics, but also newspaper editors and
legal and medical writers. 'Dr Cross on the foot and leg', *Blackwood's*,
August 1819, 532-4: 'we heard conversations carried on…whereof both the
matter, the style, and the enunciation, testified the prevalence of this
alarming disease'. It was worst amongst Chalmers' own profession and the
imitators were 'successful only in copying those things about that great
man which ought not to be copied'.

[105]   G. D. Henderson, 'Thomas Chalmers as a preacher', *Theology Today*, 4(3),
1947, 346-56. As noted by Watt, *Chalmers*, 1943, 51, the description by
John Brown, *Horae Subsecivae*, second series, 1861, 57-96, recaptures
Chalmers' impact.

effects.[106] His pictorial imagery; his positive, hopeful, authoritative tone, and the way he engaged mind and emotion on central issues – all suited an age in which old landmarks were under threat. Chalmers aimed to convince and believed the standards of the preacher could not be less than in other fields.[107] In terms of accepted conventions his were, but it did not matter.

His basic method was to take one idea at a time, explore its possibilities and hammer home his response with illustration after illustration. The message could not be called anything other than evangelical, yet its language and application was far from traditional. His interests had long been broad, including science and economics and the state of society. He added the insights of his own pilgrimage in faith and the piety and missionary vision of the Moravians whom he much admired. He showed some of the strategic sense of tact learned from Wilberforce.[108] He preached on the depravity of man, but affirmed natural virtues. He addressed issues of the day, astronomy, commerce, poor-relief, but could relate them to personal faith in Jesus Christ. He called people not to be afraid of 'doing' as well as 'believing'. Christianity was about living in this world as well as preparing for the next.

Lockhart addressed him in *Blackwood's*:

> If there is one thing more than any other characteristic of you as a preacher, it is the zeal with which you are never weary of telling your audience, that Christianity should exert an intense and pervading influence, not only over their solemn acts of devotion, but over their minds, even when most engaged with the business and the recreations wherein the greater part of every life must of necessity be spent.[109]

---

[106] In 1880 Sir James Moncrieff recalled Chalmers in the High Church, Edinburgh. 'In those days his action was violent in the extreme. The whole energy of the man seemed to be thrown into his limbs: the pulpit cushion got such a dusting as it had not known since the days of John Knox. He was enveloped in a cloud of dust – his gown flew around his shoulders; but he held his audience rapt until one was unconscious of time and space.' *The Chalmers centenary. Speeches delivered in the Free Assembly Hall Edinburgh on Wednesday, March 3, 1880*, 1880, 59.

[107] In one Kilmany sermon Chalmers tried 'to maintain...the forms and the phraseology of a philosophical argument'. *Posthumous Works*, 6, 180.

[108] He admired the preaching of the Edinburgh Evangelical, Thomas Snell Jones, who 'had escaped from the monotony of observation into which the training of a scholastic orthodoxy has drawn so many of our theologians'. 'Sermons, by Thomas Snell Jones', *Eclectic Review*, September 1816, 238-51.

[109] *Blackwood's*, May 1818, 156.

Chalmers was dealing with issues that were relevant, and drew people into the battle. As was remarked during the centenary of his arrival in Glasgow, what he did was master

> the art of making thinking a strenuous, vital and terribly earnest thing, so that the audience appreciates the magnitude of every successive difficulty that arises, and is made to face it and to overcome it along with the preacher.[110]

The Astronomical Discourses

The first mention of Chalmers' mid-week sermons on Christianity and astronomy was in the *Courier* for 12 September 1816. The Tron was 'crowded to the door and it was with much difficulty we could get standing within reach of the preacher's voice'. The discourse[111] was an 'intellectual treat' to which words could not do justice.

Chalmers' first love had been mathematics and he had lectured in mathematics and chemistry, so it is not surprising he felt able to explore questions about religion and science. Scientific method and inductive philosophy were basic to his epistemology, and he believed the methods of science were applicable in theology. These were lifelong traits and though the relationship between religion and science was not static, the emerging problems of this approach were not issues he felt particularly strongly. Nevertheless as the century progressed, he perceived that while science could still be a useful aid to Christian apologetics, more and more it also held the potential to be a challenge.

At the beginning of his career he had been confident the onus was on science to demonstrate its conformity with accepted interpretations of the Bible. Forty years later when organizing the training of ministers for the Free Church of Scotland, he was anxious that New College have a special chair to deal with the threat of modern science as well as ways in which it was still of help to the Christian apologist.[112]

By the turn of the century it was clear the earth was much older than the dates of Archbishop Ussher had led people to think. In his chemistry lectures Chalmers gave his solution to the problems raised:

> There is a prejudice against the speculations of the geologist which I am anxious to remove. It has been said that they nurture infidel

---

[110] 'A great career, the life and work of Thomas Chalmers.' *Glasgow Herald*, 14 April 1915.

[111] 'On the knowledge of man's moral history in the distant places of creation,' *Works*, 7, 90-112.

[112] J. Fleming to T. C., 18 August 1843, NCL CHA 4. H. Watt, *New College Edinburgh. A centenary history*, 1946, 53-8.

propensities. By referring the origin of the globe to a higher antiquity than is assigned to it by the writings of Moses, it has been said that geology undermines our faith in the inspiration of the Bible, and in all the animating prospects of immortality which it unfolds. This is a false alarm. The writings of Moses do not fix the antiquity of the globe. If they fix anything at all, it is only the antiquity of the species.[113]

Chalmers suggested that there could be a large period of time after 'God created the heavens and the earth' and before the rest of creation described in Genesis. This was set out in his article on Christianity for the *Edinburgh Encyclopedia,* which was published separately in 1814,[114] and in April that year it also appeared in his review of Cuvier's *Essay on the theory of the earth.*[115] He was confident Moses was more reliable than the conflicting theories of science and found Cuvier supported his ideas. He was pleased to note 'the transition of the genera into one another is most ably and conclusively contended against'[116] since their separate existence required the positive activity of God to bring them into being.[117]

Another source of doubt was provided by astronomy. A week after arriving in Glasgow he took his turn preaching a mid-week sermon in the Tron Church.[118] This came round again in September[119] and on the third[120] occasion, in November, he began the first of seven sermons which ran through 1816 and became known as the *Astronomical Discourses.* The basic idea came from the Baptist Andrew Fuller[121] who had visited him in Kilmany in 1813, but the eloquence and illustration were his own.[122] Fuller

---

113 *Memoirs,* 1, 80f.

114 *The evidence and authority of the Christian revelation,* 1814, 184f., *Memoirs,* 1, 386.

115 *Edinburgh Christian Instructor,* April 1814, 261-74. *Works,* 12, 347-72. See also A. M. Thomson to T. C., 19 November 1813, NCL CHA 4.2.47. Journal, 24 November 1813, 17 March 1818.

116 *Works,* 5, 365. See also *Works,* 1, 161-87, 228-58. *Posthumous Works,* 7, 81-9. Chalmers' *Daily Bible readings* and *Sabbath Bible readings* are also of interest for his understanding of the first chapters of Genesis. *Posthumous Works,* 1, 1-15, 5, 1-15.

117 C. C. Gillispie, *Genesis and geology,* 1959.

118 Journal, 27 July 1815. *Works,* 8, 141-64. Midweek sermons by city ministers were all preached on Thursday forenoons in the Tron Church.

119 Journal, 21 September 1815. This sermon, on 1 Corinthians 3.1, was never published.

120 Not the first as stated by Hanna, *Memoirs,* 2, 87.

121 'Fuller in the "Gospel its own witness" gives a chapter to this discussion. I enter more at large into it.' T. C. to S. Charters, 26 December 1816, NCL CHA 3.7.57. *Correspondence,* 275.

122 *Memoirs,* 1, 335-9.

had attacked Thomas Paine's[123] observation that a vast universe and the probable existence of life on other planets made the idea of redemption through the death on earth of the Son of God absurd.

In elaborating his answer, Chalmers attracted enormous attention. His sermon before the Lord High Commissioner at the General Assembly in 1816 had been a summary of the early part of the series. When the series was printed in January 1817[124] it made publishing history. Until then the most popular sermons on sale in Scotland had been those of the Moderates, Blair and Charters.[125] Within ten weeks the *Astronomical Discourses* sold 6,000 copies. By the end of the year there were nearly 20,000 in circulation[126] and it had been reprinted in America.[127] They were widely and generally favourably reviewed[128] although some pamphlets were critical.[129]

---

123   *Age of Reason*, 1796.

124   *A series of discourses on the Christian revelation viewed in connection with the modern astronomy*, 1817. *Works*, 7, 1-200.

125   T. C. to S. Charters, 26 December 1816, NCL CHA 3.7.57. *Correspondence*, 275.

126   *Memoirs*, 2, 89. D. Keir, *The house of Collins*, 1952, 31f. It reached 12 editions by 1834 and was translated into Welsh in 1846. It was last reprinted separately in 1871. Extracts can be found in unexpected places, for example, *The Saturday Magazine*, 369, March 1838, 128.

127   It reached 13 editions by 1860.

128   Including: *Eclectic Review*, September, October, November, 1817. 205-19, 354-66, 464-76 (by John Foster); *Blackwood's*, April 1817, 73-5; *Glasgow Herald*, 21 February 1817; *Scots Magazine*, 79, 1817, 122-7, and *Evangelical Magazine*, 25, 1817, 267-70. Hanna mentions notices in the *British Review, Christian Observer, Edinburgh Christian Instructor* and *Monthly Review*; but observes their lack in the *Edinburgh Review* and *Quarterly Review*. *Memoirs*, 2, 499-501.

129   Hanna lists: *Plurality of worlds; or, some remarks, philosophical and critical in a series of letters to a friend occasioned by the late 'Discourses on the Christian revelation viewed in connection with the modern astronomy'*, London, 1817; John Overton, *Strictures on Dr Chalmers's discourses on astronomy*, 1817; and A Scotch Presbyter (possibly Bishop George Gleig of Brechin), *An examination of the astronomical and theological opinions of Dr Chalmers*, Edinburgh 1818. *Memoirs*, 2, 501. It is probable that the first of these was by Alexander Maxwell, a London bookseller, who published further pamphlets with similar titles in 1817 and 1820, a revised edition of which appeared in 1872. Other pamphlet critiques of the Astronomical discourses include: Menippus (Duncan Mearns of Aberdeen), *A review of Dr Chalmers' Astronomical Discourses*, 1818; Samuel Noble, *The astronomical doctrine of the plurality of worlds irreconcilable with the popular systems of theology...a lecture delivered April 13, 1828, at the New Jerusalem Church, Cross Street, Hatton Garden*, 1828; and a scathing commentary on Chalmers' English as well as his astronomy: *A free critique on Dr Chalmers' Discourses on astronomy; or,*

A number were not convinced about the seriousness of the question,[130] though they paid tribute to Chalmers' eloquence. Coming from an Evangelical the impact was unprecedented, not only in the number of copies sold, but in the people who read them.

> These sermons ran like wild-fire through the country, were the darlings of watering-places, were laid in the windows of inns, and were to be met with in all places of public resort.... We remember finding the volume in the orchard of the inn at Burford Bridge, near Boxhill, and passing a whole and very delightful morning in reading it without quitting the shade of an apple tree.[131]

So wrote Hazlitt, and he was a long way from being the only one to find them compelling reading. The pioneer missionary to China, Robert Morrison, devoured them at a sitting and made a special trip north when he was home on furlough.[132] In 1830 Chalmers' eldest daughter talked with a coach traveller who had sat up a whole night to read them while a student at Cambridge.[133] A student at Glasgow was thrown 'into a state of chronic ecstasy which lasted all summer',[134] and late in life Chalmers heard from an American who traced his conversion to a copy borrowed from an employee.[135] They were among the best sermons Chalmers ever wrote, though he came to accept the comment of John Foster in the *Eclectic Review* that they were in need of editing.

It says as much of the age as of Chalmers that they achieved the popularity they did. Here was evangelical faith addressed to feelings of awe and wonder – it was no accident this was also the age of Romanticism. It

---

an English attempt to 'grapple it' with Scotch sublimity, 1817. A more recent analysis is David Cairns, 'Thomas Chalmers' Astronomical discourses: A study in natural theology', *Scottish Journal of Theology*, 9, 1956, 410-21. Republished in C. A. Russell ed., *Science and religious belief*, 1973, 195-204.

130 Whatever his popularity, the issue cannot have been completely irrelevant for the *Astronomical Discourses* to produce the effect they did, both in preaching and in publication. The question is a recurring one. See also the review of W. Whewell, *Plurality of Worlds*, 1853, and Sir David Brewster's reply, 'More worlds than one', *The British and Foreign Evangelical Review*, 4, 1855, 75-108. See also Drummond and Bulloch, *Scottish Church*, 1973, 169-71.

131 *Memoirs*, 2, 89.

132 R. Morrison to T. C., 11 November 1827, NCL CHA 4.81.19.

133 *Letters and Journals of Anne Chalmers*, 1922, 181.

134 G. Gilfillan, *Life of William Anderson*, 1873, 34.

135 F. A. Rope to T. C., 28 March 1847, NCL CHA 4. Another conversion was the author of CXS of Brighton to T. C., December 1826, NCL CHA 4.51.15.

was a period of changing sentiment reflected in what were seen as appropriate Christian convictions and concerns. Chalmers was able to use his lifelong interests to address yet another level of application of the gospel. The *Astronomical Discourses* marked a point in the revival of evangelical fortunes in the Church of Scotland. They created for Chalmers and for the evangelical cause an audience prepared to take more seriously an outlook hitherto out of fashion.

The Tron sermons

The success of the *Astronomical Discourses* created a situation to be exploited for both commercial and evangelistic[136] reasons, and Chalmers and his publisher were keen to produce another volume. During 1818 he was preoccupied with a possible transfer to a new parish[137] and only when this was postponed was he able to gather together a number of other Glasgow sermons for publication. *The Sermons preached in the Tron Church, Glasgow,*[138] appeared in February 1819,[139] but the popular following he had acquired was not sufficient to compensate for the lesser appeal of more general topics.

One outcome was that he blamed the publisher, John Smith, for the slow sales, and then used the profits from the *Astronomical Discourses* to set up William Collins as a publisher who would take special interest promoting his writings.[140] The story of the break with Smith does him little credit, but the alliance with Collins was mutually fruitful.

Despite the slow sales a second edition was required in two years,[141] and they were not without impact. They got lengthy and on the whole favourable comment from reviewers,[142] though some such as the *Edinburgh Magazine* were unhappy about his emphasis on depravity:

> we do not like Scripture to be made a vehicle for a libel upon human nature. Let the doctrine of the original corruption of our nature be what it may, we are persuaded that it does not by any means amount to that utter depravity and monstrous alienation from the Divine Being –

---

[136] J. W. Cunningham to T. C., 2 May 1819, NCL CHA 4.10.54.

[137] St John's.

[138] *Works*, 8, 1-164, 183-309, 331-53. *Works*, 9, 66-133.

[139] *Memoirs*, 2, 206.

[140] Keir, *House of Collins*, 1952, 32-52.

[141] In America it ran to only two editions by 1822.

[142] Including: *Blackwood's*, July 1819, 462-8, *Christian Observer*, 1819, 386-99, 443-57; *Eclectic Review*, December 1819, 501-17; *Edinburgh Christian Instructor*, 19, 1820, 251-8, 315-36, and the *Edinburgh Magazine and Literary Miscellany*, 4, 1819, 243-5.

which Dr Chalmers is so fond of insisting upon, – in terms, too, which, in our humble opinion, are neither scriptural nor decent.[143]

In this regard the *Christian Observer* preferred the language of the Book of Common Prayer, that man was 'very far gone from original righteousness',[144] as did Chalmers' friend John Strachan, then on his way to becoming a Bishop in Toronto.[145] For others this doctrine in Chalmers' hands led to 'serious thought'[146] and for one minister of the Church of Scotland it resulted in a conversion similar to Chalmers' own.[147] J. W. Cunningham of Harrow reported hearing 'all sorts of opinions'.

> The religious people of the higher and more thinking class are, as far as I can see, much pleased with them – our highly doctrinal are not likely to be satisfied with anything of so neutral a cast as to some disputed points. The worldly think them eloquent in expression, but a little 'wild' in sentiments.[148]

It was Chalmers' belief that

> if there be one truth which, more than another, should be habitually presented to the notice, and proposed to the conviction of fallen creatures, it is the humbling truth of their own depravity.[149]

While this doctrine was 'most urgently and most frequently insisted on'[150] from the Tron pulpit Chalmers had other things to say as well. He was not interested in condemning people without explaining the remedy the gospel offered. There were also those who thought he was in fact soft on depravity. As far as he was concerned faith was not an end in itself but a means to practical holiness.[151]

The muted interest in these sermons also indicated that such revelations were not what everybody wanted to read; yet Chalmers earned some right to be critical by his insistence on the recognition of good qualities people had quite apart from being religious. The sermons show his ability to take a traditional and unpalatable stance and make it one which many felt

---

143 *Edinburgh Magazine and Literary Miscellany*, 1819, 243.

144 *Christian Observer*, 1819, 389.

145 J. Strachan to T. C., 27 September 1819, NCL CHA 4.13.51.

146 W. Innes to T. C., 30 June 1823, NCL CHA 4.26.58.

147 T. Gillespie of Cults to T. C., 18 March 1819, StAUL 30385.368.

148 J. W. Cunningham to T. C., 2 May 1819, NCL CHA 4.10.54.

149 *Sermons preached in the Tron Church*, 1819, xi.

150 Ibid., v.

151 Ibid., viii.

compelled to listen to even if they were not necessarily converted to his point of view.

The Commercial Discourses

Human depravity also loomed large in his third volume of sermons. Although they did not appear until 1820, the *Commercial Discourses*[152] date from the same period as many of the Tron sermons and to a large extent reflect the same concerns. Chalmers had preached the last of the *Astronomical Discourses* at the end of 1816, and from then on his rostered midweek services turned to the moral problems of a middle-class business community. The eight discourses are more loosely related than the earlier series and like the Tron sermons did not attain the same level of popularity. Yet he regarded them as the more important series, and reviewers[153] acclaimed his efforts to apply an evangelical gospel in neglected areas. If not a best-seller, the volume sold well enough and ran to four editions in the year of publication. The sermons were translated into French in 1824 and reached seven editions in America by 1855. Among those influenced was William Ewart Gladstone.[154]

Chalmers dealt with the relationship between Christianity and natural goodness, particularly the 'mercantile virtues' encouraged by enlightened self-interest, and attempted to deal with the criticism that Christian values were incompatible with the motivation essential to success in a competitive business world.

> An affection for riches, beyond what Christianity prescribes, is not essential to any extension of commerce that is at all valuable or legitimate; and, in opposition to the maxim, that the spirit of enterprise is the soul of commercial prosperity, do we hold, that it is the excess of this spirit beyond the moderation of the New Testament which…is sure, at length, to visit every country where it operates with the recoil of all those calamities, which, in the shape of beggared capitalists and unemployed operatives, and dreary intervals of

---

[152] *The application of Christianity to the commercial and ordinary affairs of life*, Glasgow, 1820. *Works*, 6, 1-208 ('Commercial Discourses').

[153] Including: *Baptist Magazine*, 8, 1821, 297f.; *Blackwood's*, November 1820, 178-85; *British Critic*, 23, 1838, 104ff.; *Christian Recorder*, 1, 1821, 94-109, *Methodist Magazine*, NS 18, 1821, 452-5, 517-31.

[154] M. R. D. Foot and H. C. G. Matthew noted frequent references in Gladstone's diaries, *The Gladstone diaries, 3, 1840-47*, Oxford 1974, xxxviii. Gladstone's notes on the *Commercial Discourses* are in the British Library, BL Add MS 44737 f.203.

bankruptcy and alarm, are observed to follow a season of overdone speculation.[155]

Although his knowledge of commercial affairs and of the larger temptations faced by his audience was limited, he was not without experience either. That his family had been shop-keepers and ship-owners for several generations was not irrelevant; neither were the difficulties he had had as executor of an estate in 1810. The significant thing was not that he was able to identify all or even the major issues, but that he sought to do so and that his knowledge and ability were greater than many of his fellow-ministers. He sensitized consciences[156] who were thus more likely to apply the gospel in areas where they, rather than he, had competence to determine what was required of serious followers of Christian standards.

Christianity and society

Blackwood's observed that 'one most remarkable peculiarity of the works of Dr Chalmers' was

> the close adaptation of all that he says and writes to the actual condition of the people he is addressing and the circumstances of the times in which he lives.[157]

Certainly the relationship between his ideas and their social context is as apparent in Glasgow as it had been in Kilmany. His beliefs about society and the way Christianity applied to it were well developed by the end of his ministry in the Tron Church, but it is useful to consider not only the period 1815 to 1819, but also some statements from earlier and later years.

In May 1843, at the opening of the Free Church General Assembly, Chalmers spoke out

> against all participation in the lawless and revolutionary politics of those who speak evil of dignities and are given to change.[158]

He then informed ministers fresh from their exodus from the 'Auld Kirk' that the lessons they were to inculcate were to be 'all on the side of peace

---

[155] *The application of Christianity to the commercial and ordinary affairs of life*, 1820, v-vi. *Works*, 6, vi-vii.

[156] Drummond and Bulloch, *Church in Victorian Scotland*, 1978, 197.

[157] 'Review of the *Commercial Discourses*', *Blackwood's*, November 1820, 179.

[158] *The addresses delivered at the commencement and conclusion of the first General Assembly of the Free Church of Scotland*, 1843, 8.

and loyalty and order'.[159] Later at the laying of the foundation stone for the
New College in 1846 he cautioned:

> Nothing will ever be taught, I trust, in any of our halls, which shall
> have the remotest tendency to disturb the existing order of things, or to
> confound the ranks and distinctions which now obtain in society.[160]

At the Disruption Chalmers wished to calm those who could 'spy
democracy'[161] in the movement to assert the rights of the church over
against the state, but three years later he had no such excuse and statements
like these are often seen as evidence of his reactionary conservatism. The
quotations cannot be denied. On other occasions he would say that
revolution against a tyrant was not something he would rule out as never
permissible in any circumstances, but he *was* a social conservative,
whatever his schemes for change.

Nevertheless the description[162] can be misleading. Chalmers spoke
often and with passion of 'the essential equality of human souls'.[163] He
believed less that the social order was immutable because God had ordained
it to be the way it was, than that attempts to change it were often
impractical and impious and did not deal with matters of character and
community with which he was primarily concerned. Those Chalmers had in
view as 'given to change' appeared ignorant of human nature and idealistic
about inequalities in society he believed to be inevitable.

Although he was sceptical about the Reform Bills[164] and only a
reluctant supporter of factory reform,[165] whatever he said about others he
himself was frequently 'given to change'. In his willingness to tackle social
problems he was a prominent figure; he was a vocal supporter of Catholic
emancipation and took the revolutionary step of separating more than a third
of the Church of Scotland from its centuries-long connection with the state,
an irony not lost on Chalmers or his critics. Yet he had some justification
claiming his schemes were meant to restore things to a natural state and, the
Disruption and Catholic emancipation apart, he frequently insisted that even
restorative changes should be done gradually.[166]

---

[159] Ibid.
[160] Watt, *New College Edinburgh*, 1946, 3f.
[161] T. C. to J. Strachan, 1 May 1843, *Correspondence*, 361.
[162] J. H. S. Burleigh, *A church history of Scotland*, 1960, 316.
[163] Watt, *New College Edinburgh*, 1946, 4.
[164] Watt, *Chalmers*, 1943, 91f. *Memoirs*, 3, 299, 312f., 405.
[165] J. T. Ward, 'The factory reform movement in Scotland,' *Scottish Historical Review*, 41, 1962, 119.
[166] For example his proposal for gradually emancipating West Indian slaves. This pleased nobody. *Works*, 12, 399-408. *Eclectic Review*, June 1826, 549-59.

It is probable that his ambivalence about social change derived from experiences going back to his years as a student at St Andrews. During his third session, 1793-94, he joined the Political Society,[167] and frequently met in the evenings with a group of 'marked men, ultra Whigs, keen Reformers...what would now be called Radicals'.[168] These included John Leslie (1766–1832),[169] James Mylne[170] and the mathematics assistant, James Brown (1763–1836),[171] who like others were attracted by the ideals if not the realities of the French Revolution.[172] At the time this marked a significant break with the politics and the religion of his parents.[173]

During the university session following, he read and admired William Godwin's *Enquiry concerning political justice*,[174] before getting caught up in the defence of Britain against threatened invasion by the French. By 1805 when he joined the St Andrews' volunteer corps, he held rather different views. From the Kilmany pulpit he informed people of the lengths to which his patriotism was prepared to go:

> May that day when Bonaparte ascends the throne of Britain be the last of my existence; may I be the first to ascend the scaffold he erects to extinguish the worth and spirit of the country; may my blood mingle with the blood of patriots; and may I die at the foot of that altar on which British independence is to be the victim.[175]

The events on the Continent stimulated both desire for change and excuse enough for repressing such inclinations. Chalmers' 1808 *Enquiry into the extent and stability of national resources* was also concerned with danger from France, and following his conversion he lost nothing of his dedication to his country, its monarchy and the way of life it represented. Yet uncertainty remained about how much British society could be improved in its social structure and political institutions.

---

[167] *Memoirs*, 1, 20f.

[168] *Memoirs*, 1, 11.

[169] Of 'Leslie controversy' fame; from 1805 to 1819 Professor of Mathematics at Edinburgh, then Professor of Natural Philosophy until his death.

[170] Later Professor of Moral Philosophy at Glasgow.

[171] Brown was an important influence on Chalmers over a considerable period and a close friend until his death. *Memoirs*, 1, 461-9. *Fasti*, 5, 197. Edinburgh University Library has 27 of Chalmers' letters to Brown, EUL Dc.2.57.

[172] W. L. Kirkland, *The impact of the French Revolution on Scottish religious life and thought, with special reference to Thomas Chalmers, Robert Haldane and Neil Douglas*, University of Edinburgh PhD thesis, 1951, 36-52.

[173] *Memoirs*, 1, 14f.

[174] *Memoirs*, 1, 14, 45.

[175] *Memoirs*, 1, 95f. *Posthumous Works*, 6, 49.

While there was nothing remarkable in this, politically Chalmers stood in contrast to many of his colleagues. His underlying Toryism was common in the Moderate party; his new-found Evangelical friends were mostly Whigs.[176] In some ways he was closer in his social and political attitudes to English Evangelicals like Simeon, Wilberforce and the Methodist Jabez Bunting, than to many of his colleagues in Scotland. The contrast with Andrew Thomson is striking. The old appellation of the Evangelicals as Populars applied accurately to Thomson – something which could never be said of Chalmers. Thomson had a sense of justice and of rights, Chalmers one of fairness and order. Thomson was more radically anti-slavery than Chalmers ever was, and an implacable foe of patronage – a position to which Chalmers was a late and reluctant convert. Thomson was ready to scent, even in government requests for services, threats to the independence of the Church. Chalmers was more trusting until that trust was betrayed. He could be defensive, touchy and sensitive, but people perceived him as fundamentally benign. Thomson was belligerent and a controversialist, though arguably a cooler politician. It is not surprising they worked uneasily together.[177]

Chalmers came to Glasgow with a combination of politically conservative and religiously liberal ideals. His respect for the institutions of the land found obligatory expression in the oath of allegiance,[178] and his understanding of the way society functioned was shaped by his interest in political economy. From Adam Smith and Malthus he acquired a pessimistic view of what could be done about society, and from Wilberforce took the view that the role of Christianity was to soften rather than remove the inequalities they analysed. In Kilmany both the analysis and the prescribed role for an active Christianity seemed credible enough. In Glasgow he found a situation that was vastly different, but the viewpoint was not lightly to be surrendered.

It was not just the population, the industry and the squalor, but the political turmoil which disturbed him when he reached Scotland's

---

[176] The correlation of Moderates with Toryism and Evangelicals with Whiggism broke down during the next 20 years. *Journal of Henry Cockburn*, 1, 1874, 183 (4 June 1838). D. Chambers, *Mission and party in the Church of Scotland*, 1810-1843, University of Cambridge PhD thesis, 1971, 162.

[177] 'Chalmers had little sympathy with the rights of the people, but he earnestly desired their well-being.... Thomson, on the other hand, was the friend and consistent advocate of popular right. It is unquestionable that benevolence was more an actuating principle with Chalmers than a sense of justice.' R. S. Candlish, quoted in Adam Philip, *Thomas Chalmers Apostle of Union*, 1929, 133.

[178] T. C. to Moderator of the Presbytery of Glasgow, 28 March 1815, NCL CHA.

metropolis of the West. He arrived within a month of Waterloo. Before long fears were expressed for the effects on business of the transition from a wartime to a peace-time economy. In a sermon on the day of national thanksgiving[179] he showed some understanding of these apprehensions, but countered that the 'interest of trade' had long been used as an excuse for ignoring the 'interests of humanity'.[180] It was 'not fair to make others bleed that you may roll in affluence'.[181] There were other fears as well. As had been observed, 'after the peace it became feasible to relight the torch of political radicalism',[182] and Chalmers spoke of

> the utter repugnance that there is between the spirit of Christianity and the factious, turbulent, unquenchable, and ever-meddling spirit of political disaffection.[183]

The economic effects of peace hit all levels of society.[184] In February 1816 Chalmers wrote of the 'depressed state of the agricultural interest' and the effects in the city where 'this day there have eight principal houses stopped payment'.[185] Depression spread steadily. In April the *Glasgow Courier* noted 'the embarrassment in the commercial world still continues',[186] and in June Chalmers reported that the 'distressed state of the operative classes' was 'occupying the serious attention of the community'.[187] In the early autumn there were riots[188] and in late October a rally of 40,000 within the boundary of the city.[189] Speakers called for the reform of parliament and the burghs,

---

[179]   *Thoughts on universal peace. A sermon delivered on Thursday, January 18, 1816*, 1816, *Works*, 11, 55-86. This ran to a second edition and created interest in Canada and America where it was published in 1817 and 1869. Secretary of the Massachusetts Peace Society to T. C., 31 March 1818, NCL CHA 4.9.51. J. Strachan to T. C., 27 September 1819, NCL CHA 4.13.51. *Memoirs*, 2, 74. Chalmers was awarded a DD by the University of Glasgow two weeks after the sermon was published. *Memoirs*, 2, 63.

[180]   *Works*, 11, 81.

[181]   *Works*, 11, 83.

[182]   T. C. Smout, *A history of the Scottish people 1560-1830*, 1972, 417.

[183]   *Works*, 11, 69.

[184]   For what follows, besides sources quoted, the following have also been consulted. W. Ferguson, *Scotland 1689 to the present*, 1968, 273-84. W. L. Mathieson, *Church and reform in Scotland, 1797 to 1843*, 1916, 141-62.

[185]   T. C. to R. Edie, 13 February 1816, J. Baillie, *The Missionary of Kilmany*, 1854, 33.

[186]   *Glasgow Courier*, 20 April 1816. This conveys what Chalmers would have known about many of these events.

[187]   Ibid., 29 June 1816.

[188]   Ibid., 3 August 1816.

[189]   Ibid., 2 November 1816.

and declared that the distress was caused by the 'unnecessary, ruinous and sanguinary war' which had only resulted in 'the re-establishment everywhere of that bigotry and despotism which disgraced the darkest period of European history'.[190] These relatively peaceable calls for reform met with a reactionary response and government spies were not slow uncovering deeper plots which led to a series of political trials during 1817.

The citizens of Glasgow raised a subscription of £10,000 and distributed it among 23,000 unemployed.[191] In March 1818 the lower classes in Glasgow were the main victims of a typhus epidemic.[192]

This state of affairs brought home events which were taking place elsewhere. In Scotland political disturbance and economic depression were concentrated in the western-central area where there had been the heaviest industrialization and the most rapid growth in population.[193] Worse was to come in 1819 and 1820, but several different lines of response were emerging.

Chalmers' ideas were developed in competition with a range of remedies from various quarters. Radicals called for the reform of parliament and the burghs and complained of extravagance in high places. Robert Owen[194] of New Lanark publicized model industrial communities by pamphlets[195] and meetings in London.[196] In parliament, besides the employment of spies and agents provocateurs, the arranging of trials and the passing of repressive legislation,[197] attention was given to the poor laws[198] which were manifestly inadequate, and in January 1818, another approach was called for: the building of additional churches.[199]

Repressive activity aside, Chalmers' ideas had elements which can be found in each of these responses except the first, though he had his own critique to make of what those in high places failed to do. Like Owen, Chalmers was interested in the closely integrated community, but its basis was to be Christian and not secular and its model rural, not industrial. Chalmers was also deeply interested in the poor laws though his ideas tended more to their abolition than their reform; and he too saw the building of more churches as essential.

---

190   Ibid.
191   Cleland, *Statistical tables*, 1823, 197.
192   Ibid.
193   Smout, *History of the Scottish People*, 1972, 419.
194   S. Pollard and J. Salt, eds, *Robert Owen, prophet of the poor*, 1971.
195   *Glasgow Courier*, 17 August 1816.
196   Ibid., 29 July 1817. 19, 26, 28 August 1817.
197   Ibid., 8, 18, March 1817.
198   Ibid., 16, 19 August, 13 September 1817. Cleland, *Statistical tables*, 1823, 150-58.
199   *Glasgow Courier*, 31 January 1818.

His ideas had a peculiarly Scottish reference, but they were intended for the whole of Britain. The details of his scheme for a solution to irreligion, poverty and social disaffection must wait for the next chapter, but the leading principles found frequent expression during his time at the Tron and can be considered here. Compared with rural Fife what struck him about Glasgow was the isolation of one class of society from another. He criticized the upper-classes and royalty for being remote from the people; but the key person for the restoration of relationships was the parish minister. There was

> no other way of preventing the danger arising to the good order of society from the hostile attacks of an illiterate rabble, than by the kindly and unwearied attentions of their pastor among them. This would reclaim them when the gibbet with all its terrors would have no effect.[200]

Chalmers believed it was only necessary for as little as 'one tenth of the labouring population' to be acting on Christian principles to have a widespread effect.[201]

The most comprehensive statements of social philosophy from his period at the Tron can be found in his sermons on the death of Princess Charlotte, and that of her grandmother, Queen Charlotte, twelve months later. In November 1817 ministers were called to play their part in national mourning for the loss of the most popular member of an otherwise unpopular royal family. His sermon on the day of the funeral of Princess Charlotte[202] is significant, not only for its immediate impact and the subsequent controversy[203] and its appeal for the building of 20 more churches in Glasgow, but for the exposition of the prophetic role of ministers. True to form he advised hearers 'to meddle not with those who are given to change'[204] and maintained it was in the interests of the nation to 'Christianize her subjects', since 'a permanent security against the wild outbreakings of turbulence and disaster' was only to be obtained

> by diffusing the lessons of the gospel throughout the great mass of our population – even those lessons which are utterly and diametrically at

---

[200] *Memoirs*, 2, 68, Speech at General Assembly, May 1816.

[201] *Edinburgh Review*, March 1817, *Works*, 20, 285.

[202] *A sermon delivered in the Tron Church, Glasgow, on Wednesday November 19, 1817, the day of the funeral of Her Royal Highness the Princess Charlotte of Wales*, 1817. *Works*, 11, 11-54.

[203] Chalmers was accused of exploiting the situation to preach politics. *Memoirs*, 2, 137-40. *Dundee, Perth and Cupar Advertiser*, 28 November 1817.

[204] *Works*, 11, 22.

antipodes with all that is criminal and wrong in the spirit of political disaffection.[205]

This was not to say Christianity ought to be uncritical of society. While 'the only radical counteraction' to political disloyalty was 'the spirit of Christianity', at the same time

> though animated by such a spirit, a man may put on the intrepidity of one of the old prophets, and denounce even in the ear of royalty the profligacies which may disgrace or deform it – though animated by such a spirit, he may lift up his protesting voice in the face of an unchristian magistracy and tell them of their errors.[206]

One can detect an echo of John Knox,[207] but one wonders how much Chalmers saw himself in this role beyond calls for closer intimacy with the people he addressed and his criticism of upper-class irreligion.[208]

When Queen Charlotte died Chalmers again presented a summary of his beliefs about the relationship between Christianity and the existing order of things.

> There appears to be nothing in the progress of religion which is at all calculated to level the graduations of human ranks, or to do away with the distinctions of human society. Not to annihilate poverty, for it is said of the poor, that they shall be with us always; not to bring down from their eminence the authorities of the land, for there is positively nothing in the Bible that can lead us to infer that even under the peace and righteousness of a millennial age there will not be kings and queens upon the earth; and certain it is that they will be the instruments of helping forward this great moral consummation – the former being the nursing fathers and the later the nursing mothers of the church. The utopianism which would regenerate the world by political and external revolutions, is, I trust, at this time of day pretty generally exploded. The kingdoms of earth may become the kingdoms of God and of his Christ with the external framework of these present governments, and at least with all those varieties of outward condition which are offered at this moment to the view of the observer. There must therefore be a way in which Christianity can accommodate itself to this framework – a mode by which it can animate all the parts and all the members of it – a mode by which, without the overthrow of existing distinctions, it can establish a right reciprocity of feeling and

---

[205] *Works*, 11, 22f.
[206] *Works*, 11, 23.
[207] Thomas M'Crie, *Life of John Knox*, 1812. Journal, 25 November 1812.
[208] For example, *Works*, 6, 364f.

conduct between them – a charm by which it can divest grandeur of all its disdainfulness, and poverty of all its violence, and chasing away all the asperities of party from the land, can, from the monarch's throne to the peasant's hovel, bind together the whole of a Christianized nation under the influence of one common charity.[209]

Kings and queens did not have as much to fear from Chalmers as from John Knox, and this was true for the upper classes generally, although he had less respect for them than he reserved for royalty. Christianity permitted them 'to maintain...rank and distinction', and they could be reassured that the New Testament recognized the 'gradations of society and...the rich and the noble among the disciples of the Saviour'.[210]

Perhaps he found it convenient not to mention how many such people Paul found among one of his congregations at least,[211] but despite these affirmations, Chalmers' relationship with the upper classes was less than straightforward. He was scornful of those who courted their influence, but from 1817 onwards gathered a widening circle of friends whom he did not hesitate to call upon. While in London in May that year he met Wilberforce and Lord Sidmouth, and on the way home through Liverpool made a good impression on the Gladstones.[212] About this time he began a long association with Lord and Lady Elgin, Sir Robert Maxwell of Pollock, and the Glasgow cotton magnate Kirkman Finlay MP.

This was a modest beginning to a list which lengthened considerably during the next 20 years.[213] Nevertheless, as with the working classes, Chalmers saw the upper classes through middle class eyes and never really understood them, nor they him. Only one of the Scottish nobility supported the Free Church at the Disruption, and more than once Chalmers berated the upper classes for their lack of interest in the cause.

More frequently Chalmers has been criticized for the limitations of his attitudes towards the working classes. Drummond and Bulloch are not among the most unkind.[214]

---

[209] *Memoirs*, 2, 202f.

[210] *Works*, 11, 415.

[211] 1 Corinthians 1.26.

[212] Mrs Gladstone to Thomas Gladstone, 12 June 1817, S. G. Checkland, *The Gladstones*, 1971, 87.

[213] T. C. to W. E. Gladstone, 10 February 1835, BL 44,345 f.172. The Gladstone papers detail Chalmers' lobbying for state endowment of new churches.

[214] See, for instance, D. C. Smith, *The failure and recovery of social criticism in the Scottish Church 1830-1950*, University of Edinburgh PhD thesis, 1964. Since published as *Passive obedience and prophetic protest. Social criticism in the Scottish Church 1830-1945*, 1987.

He had boundless pity for the poor, but little understanding. The craftsman's standards and interests, his pride of work, traditions of group action, his intellectual independence, and exposure to the harsh pressure of unemployment, vile housing, and sudden illness were things of which he was little aware. In his eyes irreligion was the source of all their ills.[215]

This is less than accurate. He was not saying[216] irreligion was the source of *all* ills of the working class, but that it was the root cause of radical disaffection – 'the great moral distemper' of 'impetuous defiance to all that wears the stamp of authority in the land'.[217] It is not true that he was little aware of the standards of craftsmen and the squalor of the unemployed. The former were the very sort of artisans with which he could identify because they had all the associations of independence and self-reliance he prized. He had systematically visited thousands of Glasgow working-class homes and was familiar enough with the effects of unemployment. He may have recoiled from aspects of what he found, but he showed a remarkable commitment to observing it for himself. His ideas as to what should be done about it had imperfections, but they were not the schemes of an armchair theorist.

---

[215] *The Scottish Church*, 1973, 165. The phraseology resembles Saunders, *Scottish democracy*, 1950, 211.

[216] *The importance of civil government to society and the duty of Christians in regard to it. A sermon preached in St John's Church, Glasgow, on Sabbath the 30 April, 1820*, 1820. *Works*, 6, 335-77. *Memoirs*, 2, 268. See also *The Scotsman*, 27 May 1820, *Glasgow Courier*, 16 May 1820, *The Glasgow Herald*, 19 May 1820, and *The Literary and Statistical Magazine for Scotland*, August 1820, 275-81.

[217] *Works*, 6, 367. The occasion was the execution of the 'Cato Street conspirators', who with one exception refused to make peace with God beforehand. *Glasgow Herald*, 5 May 1820.

Chapter 7

'Effectual contact with the minds of the population of an assigned district'[1]

St John's Church Glasgow, 1819-1823

In the autumn of 1819 Chalmers moved to the newly created parish of St John's. He remained there until 1823 when he escaped from the turmoil of Glasgow to the Chair of Moral Philosophy at St Andrews. Generations of students later learned of the 'St John's Experiment' from its chief architect and defender, discussed principles of parish management and with probably more admiration than conviction listened to his passionate rebuttal of criticism.

If not as a model, then certainly as an inspiration, St John's has continued to have influence. The general features of elders' and deacons' districts, schools and poor relief, are well known. No attempt will be made to describe every aspect in detail but it is necessary to consider the debated issues without losing sight of Chalmers' religious interest.

In many respects Chalmers had been unhappy at the Tron from the start. In April 1816 there had been talk of building a church more to his liking, but the building itself was really the least of his problems.[2] Although he was devoted to pastoral work and Sunday schools, and preaching brought him fame, his frustrations over secular duties and the effects of the disjointed congregation and parish continued to mount. One could say the main trouble with Glasgow was that it was not Kilmany. If he could not return to the community life of rural Fife, perhaps he could recreate it where he was. In October Chalmers vented his feelings in sermons and a move to Stirling seemed possible. The Tron congregation

---

[1] T. C. to J. Ewing, 9 March 1818, *Memoirs*, 2, 521.

[2] Some of his friends wanted to lend the Town Council £6,000 for this purpose as his health was 'much impaired' by preaching in the Tron. The offer was declined. Renwick, *Extracts*, 10, 1905, 326 (5 April 1816).

were alarmed, petitioned him to stay, and did what they could to improve conditions, though many of the problems were outside their control.[3]

For some time the Glasgow Town Council had been planning a new church in the east of the city, and Chalmers saw it might provide what he was looking for. Subject to negotiation with the Council it could free him from a number of annoyances, and it held possibilities for his ideal of a town parish on a rural model. It was an advantage that, because of the redrawing of parish boundaries, he would be able to retain half his existing parish instead of having to cope with an entirely new one.[4] In June 1818 he got the appointment and, following a year's delay due to construction problems, was inducted into St John's in September 1819.

From the time of its inception, St John's received critical attention which has continued to the present day.[5] Poor-relief involved secular authorities and affected public finances, so it is not surprising it drew public comment. It also attracted attention because Chalmers embarked on a campaign not just for one parish in Glasgow, but to rescue Scotland in general from English pauperism and if possible save England as well.[6] His claim to have demonstrated that any parish was capable of looking after its own poor without a poor-rate invited debate and can be discussed in quantitative terms. This did not prove as conclusive as it might, and the mathematics of poor-relief has less relevance for the significance of the whole than he or others recognized. Other aspects of St John's were distinctive and influential. Like many of his schemes, a lot depends on what is looked for and whether one is impressed only by quantifiable results. If poor-relief has distorted the significance of the St John's experiment, the history of the discussion makes it difficult to avoid joining in the debate.

Other things also stand in the way of a fair assessment of St John's. Chalmers should not be held responsible for everything we may happen to dislike in his lifetime. Chalmers has been blamed for views for which he is

---

3   The ventilation was improved and he accepted offers of pulpit supply and an escape to the countryside when Glasgow got too much. He declined a free manse (not part of the job) and a supplement to the stipend. The offer of a full-time assistant was held over.

4   Appendix 4. Map of the Tron and St John's parish boundaries.

5   R. A. Cage and E. O. A. Checkland, 'Thomas Chalmers and urban poverty: the St John's parish experiment in Glasgow, 1819-1837', *Philosophical Journal*, 13(1), 1976, 37-56. A. C. Cheyne, '1815: Chalmers in Glasgow's time of turmoil,' *Life and Work*, July 1978, 23-4, 28. S. Mechie, *Scottish social development 1780-1870*, 1960. L. J. Saunders, *Scottish democracy 1815-1840*, 1950. D. C. Smith, *Passive obedience and prophetic protest. Social criticism in the Scottish Church 1830–1845*, 1987. Watt, *Thomas Chalmers*, 1943.

6   Especially from 1822 to 1824.

no more than a representative figure,[7] and it is sometimes forgotten in how many respects he was simply a person of his time.

At St John's his basic principles were little more than the determined application in an urban situation of a commonly accepted rural parish ideal – his singularity was trying to put them into practice in an unpromising and complex situation. Later in life, when he was the figurehead of the church extension movement of the 1830s and of the Free Church of Scotland after 1843, while his actions were often congruent with others', his principles were often different from those he represented.

The St John's experiment stands as a distinct phase in Chalmers' career and not surprisingly one in which elements of continuity from the past and into the future are evident. Kilmany provided a model which it was impossible to replicate in his first years in Glasgow. In the context of economic crisis and political instability, the Tron contributed the authority of further fame as a preacher and the incentive of increasing frustration. When he moved to St John's, he took with him much of the Tron, including half of the kirk session, a majority of the congregation and about half the population and territory of the old parish. St John's not only enabled him to do something new, it permitted him to do so without parting with much of what he had already been doing.

In particular it provided freedom to administer church collections for poor-relief independently of other Glasgow parishes. With the redrawing of parish boundaries the church was located in the parish rather than outside it and he was thus in a position to try and bring back together church, congregation, parish, and community in an effort to meet their religious and social needs in one comprehensive plan. It remained to be seen how successful he could have been, given Glasgow's mobile population, the diversity of its religious commitment, and the lack of it altogether in many areas. He was not easily deterred and went to work with a remarkable 'agency' of elders, deacons, and Sunday-school teachers. Among much else they founded four schools, a parish-wide network of local Bible and missionary societies, and a savings bank.

By the time he left in 1823 Chalmers had made a name for himself as a parish minister quite apart from his fame as a preacher. He hoped his leaving would prove the system could carry on without him at the centre – many said his ideas were fine, they just needed Chalmers to make them work – and that others would imitate the pattern of organization he had demonstrated. Some did, but the influence of the scheme was wider in its inspiration and component parts, than as a comprehensive model to be copied – least of all with regard to attempts at self-sufficiency in poor-relief. Chalmers gave the laity an active role in the mission of a parish church, and at his hands

---

[7]   Smith, *Passive obedience*, 1987.

generations of students were to imbibe his convictions that parish ministry in cities demanded everything they could offer.

The origins of the St John's experiment

Contrary to what is often said, the actual building of St John's had nothing to do with Chalmers; it is not true to say that it was 'a concession to his demands' by a Town Council which was 'anything but enthusiastic'.[8] The pressure of population and the challenge of dissenting congregations had long been felt. In 1812, the Town Council responded to a memorial from the Presbytery[9] by purchasing a site for a new church.[10] It had been 30 years since a new parish church had been erected and although three chapels-of-ease had been built[11] during that period, the population had increased two and a half times to reach 110,000.[12] There were more than one and a half times as many sittings available outside the 18 Church of Scotland places of worship in greater Glasgow than there were inside.[13] In 1813 the Town Council prepared a parliamentary bill to raise a local tax for new churches.[14] There was an outcry from property-owners, business-men and Dissenters. Most objections were at root financial, but the need was also disputed.

> There is not a city or town in the British empire having a population so numerous and so much employed in manufactures where there is so general a diffusion of religious knowledge, and where, under the hardships and privations of the late distressing times, the labouring classes conducted themselves in a more loyal, peaceable, and exemplary manner.[15]

In other words, if the working classes were not causing trouble, there was no point in building churches – a social commentary in itself. One writer argued that the parish churches were not full in any case. 'If I go into any of

---

8   This common error is repeated by Drummond and Bulloch, *The Scottish Church,* 1973, 172.

9   J. Lapslie, *Letters addressed to the Magistrates and Council of Glasgow and the heritors and landward parishes within the bounds of the Presbytery of Glasgow, anent accommodation in parish churches,* 1811.

10   Renwick, *Extracts,* 10, 1905, 120 (20 March 1812); 145 (25 September 1812).

11   See Appendix 3.

12   See Appendix 2. This includes the parishes of the Barony and the Gorbals.

13   Based on Cleland, *Statistical tables,* 1823, 33. In 1819 the nominal membership of the Church of Scotland was 55%. Appendix 5, table 2.

14   Renwick, *Extracts,* 10, 1905, 190 (10 September 1813); 197 (22 October 1813); 198 (2 November 1813).

15   Memorial to the Town Council, Renwick, *Extracts,* 10, 1905, 204 (12 November 1813).

them, I shall find a pew for myself, another for my hat, a third for my stick and another for my dog.'[16] Petitions and meetings were organized and the Council had to let the bill drop.[17]

Within three years the end of the Napoleonic wars meant the situation had changed and the religiosity and political stability of Glasgow lost credibility as reasons for delaying church extension. The increase in population was apparent and Chalmers at least had a parish church crammed to its doors. By 1816 it was felt the funds of the city were sufficient to start building on the site acquired,[18] and the foundation stone was laid in April the following year.[19]

Planning for a new parish was thus well in hand when in March 1817 Chalmers first made mention, in an unsigned article in the *Edinburgh Review*, that there ought to be 30 parish churches in the city, not 10.[20] By November when he repeated this appeal in a sermon on the death of Princess Charlotte,[21] the building was well advanced. It was intended to open the new church in the summer of 1818 and only from the beginning of that year is there any suggestion that Chalmers might be the minister.

Negotiations over this possibility occupied two distinct stages. Those during the first half of 1818, until the last-minute discovery that much of the church was going to have to be rebuilt, are important for their indication that at the time of his appointment he had not achieved any agreement about poor-relief. Between July 1819 and the delayed opening in September, there was a second phase which also requires examination for details of just what it was he eventually obtained by way of special conditions.

During 1817 Chalmers had been developing ideas about more churches in Glasgow and had corresponded with Sir John Gladstone about patronage arrangements for chapels he had built in Liverpool and Seaforth.[22] Chalmers had also been exchanging ideas with friends in Glasgow when the death of Princess Charlotte provided an opportunity to state openly what was on his mind. People feared for a revolution, yet on a day of national mourning there was no room for the working-classes in the city churches any more

---

[16] *Examination of the eight resolutions adopted by a meeting of gentlemen in the Tontine Room, Glasgow, 3 November 1813, after discussing the merits of a bill brought into parliament, anent building and endowing additional churches in the city of Glasgow. Addressed to Robert Muirhead. Preses of that meeting*, Glasgow, 1813, 43.

[17] Renwick, *Extracts*, 10, 1905, 202–5 (26 November 1813); 205 (7 December 1813); 208 (28 December 1813).

[18] Ibid., 318 (23 January 1816); 324f. (26 March 1816).

[19] Ibid., 382f. (21 April 1817).

[20] *Works*, 20, 293.

[21] *Works*, 17, 37.

[22] J. Gladstone to T. C., 12 August 1817, NCL CHA 4.6.16.

than on a Sunday.[23] The sermon was published, and in an appendix he expanded on church reform and church extension as a means of stabilizing society. He wanted more churches, ministers freed from civic duties, a priority for parishioners in allocating seats, and 'wealthy individuals who would willingly undertake the expense and hazard of the erection of as many churches as would be called for'.[24]

During 1817 there had been talk in parliament of additional churches in England, but nothing came of it until the speech from the throne in January 1818.[25] Chalmers took a close interest because he did not trust the arrangements for patronage which might be made, and believed that rather than just make grants, it would be better for the government to encourage local initiatives like Gladstone's.[26]

In Scotland the response was different from what might have been expected. The Commission of the General Assembly was summoned in April to ensure Scotland did not miss out,[27] but although information was gathered showing the need for more churches in many of the cities, particularly in the West of Scotland,[28] the only real enthusiasm came from the Highlands, where vast parishes were unworkable not because of population, but distance.[29]

As a result efforts were concentrated on getting grants for the Highlands, but despite the Government promising £100,000 in May 1818, it was six years before an act of parliament was obtained. By this time England was on the point of getting its original grant of a million pounds increased by half as much again. As far as Scottish cities were concerned there was a strange complacency, and in Edinburgh Evangelicals were

---

[23]   *Works*, 11, 39.

[24]   Ibid., 52f.

[25]   *Glasgow Courier*, 31 January 1818, M. H. Port, *Six hundred new churches*, 1961. I. F. Maciver, *The General Assembly of the Church, the State and Society in Scotland 1815-1843*, University of Edinburgh M Litt thesis, 1976.

[26]   T. C. to W. Wilberforce, 9 February 1818, *Correspondence*, 93-6. J. Gladstone to T. C., 17 February 1818, NCL CHA 4.8.1; 26 February 1818, NCL CHA 4.8.2; 23 March 1818, NCL CHA 4.8.3. *Works*, 14, 227.

[27]   *Glasgow Courier*, 4 and 7 April 1818.

[28]   NCL CHA 5.

[29]   Memorial presented to the Chancellor of His Majesty's Exchequer by the Commission of the General Assembly of the Church of Scotland in April 1818, SRO/GRH CH1/2/143. D. Dewar, *Letter to Sir James M. Riddell, being a brief memorial on the state of the Highlands, and the objects to which the parliamentary grant of one hundred thousand pounds for building churches in Scotland should be applied*, 1819. A. Irvine, *Substance of a speech delivered before the Commission of the General Assembly of the Church of Scotland which met in April last*, 1819.

instrumental in blocking a proposal for a chapel-of-ease on the grounds that it was 'unnecessary and inexpedient'.[30]

In Glasgow Chalmers turned his attention to the one new church that was being built, and began to sound out people to see whether he might be permitted to implement his ideas if it were offered to him. To gain control of his own poor-relief he needed agreement from the Town Council as patrons, from the Town Hospital or poorhouse, and also from the General Session of city ministers.

The system of poor-relief was complex. Funds for church expenses came from pew rents. Church collections were entirely for the relief of the poor and were pooled in a central fund administered by the General Session. This was reallocated back to kirk sessions depending on the number of poor supported. Cases which were too expensive for a kirk session were sent to the Town Hospital for indoor or outdoor relief financed by the annual 'assessment' or poor-rate.

The first outcome of Chalmers' enquiries was a proposal in a Town Hospital report on 7 January 1818. Chalmers had written to the chairman, James Ewing, who was also a senior member of the Town Council, and asked

> That on condition of his being allowed to retain the collections at his own church; of seats being provided for his own deacons; of the residing parishioners having the preference as vacancies occur, and of his having the protection of the laws of residence, he is willing, not only to meet the wants of all the existing sessional poor in his own parish, but to engage, that not a single new pauper shall be sent from it to the hospital during his incumbency; it being understood, that as the old hospital cases die out, a proportional sum shall be remitted from the assessment.[31]

The fate of this overture is uncertain, but Chalmers was now in view as the future minister of St John's, and in February the Town Council had a clause permitting special arrangements for poor-relief included in the decreet of the Court of Session authorizing the new parish.[32]

The main interest of the Town Hospital was financial, and the Council no doubt shared the view that whatever the details of Chalmers' ideas, 'the ulterior abolition of the rates…is a consummation devoutly to be wished'.[33]

---

[30]   *Glasgow Courier*, 14 March 1818. Andrew Thomson objected because of unlet sittings in existing churches. *First report of the Commissioners of Religious Instruction, Scotland*, 1837, 328-30.

[31]   *Statement from the Session of St John's parish, Glasgow, to the directors of the town's hospital, in regard to the management of their poor*, 1836, 3.

[32]   Renwick, *Extracts*, 10, 1905, 435 (5 June 1818); 506 (18 August 1819).

[33]   *Statement from the Session of St John's*, 1836, 3.

In March he again wrote to Ewing and sought the understanding that if his experiment did not work the poor should be able to fall back on the Town Hospital. He believed success depended on a law of residence and a reduction of the parish poor-rate as the number of paupers supported by the Town Hospital began to decrease.[34]

Although Chalmers wished Glasgow would restore to its ministers 'the same unfettered and independent parishes that they have in the country',[35] he would be content with whatever he could get.

> I have resolved not to contest any one matter relative to my parish – though if all the elements of my own arrangement were easily granted to me I would set about it with great pleasure.[36]

Within two months he decided there was, after all, one matter to insist on, and he made his acceptance conditional on seat-holders at the Tron being given first preference for seats in St John's.[37] Since few lived in the parish, this was contrary to his oft-repeated principle that hearers and parishioners ought to be the same set of people.

He was in some difficulty but argued he needed to begin with a 'wealthy day congregation' if he was to restore the parish to its natural state. If he took up the Tron congregation's earlier offer to pay for an assistant, then he could hold evening services for the parishioners until they supplanted the morning congregation. It would be possible to use any surplus from the morning collections to build schools and the poor would be supported entirely out of the evening collections. That at least was the theory.

Part of this letter was read to the Town Council[38] on 5 June 1818 and had the desired effect. They agreed to give Tron seat-holders the preference Chalmers sought, and elected Chalmers to be the minister.[39] At their next meeting they recorded his letter of acceptance:

---

[34] T. C. to J. Ewing, 9 March 1818, *Statement from the Session of St John's*, 1836, 7. *Memoirs*, 2, 519-22. This letter was published in a Town Hospital report.

[35] T. C. to J. Peddie, 14 March 1818, NLS 3704 f.72.

[36] Ibid.

[37] T. C. to J. Ewing, 23 May 1818, NCL CHA 3.8.43.

[38] There is no mention of any letter in the Council minutes, but a letter of Chalmers to the Provost a year later refers to one having been read on this occasion. Hanna believed this to have been Chalmers' letter of 9 March 1818, but it was probably that of 23 May 1818. This puts the understanding Chalmers reached with the Council in a different light from that in the *Memoirs*, 2, 214.

[39] Renwick, *Extracts*, 10, 1905, 434f. (5 June 1818). *Memoirs*, 2, 208, gives the impression that St John's parishioners had first preference. That was

It is true that I could not have taken St John's without such a preference being allowed my present hearers.... I felt it impossible to abandon the congregation with which I am connected.[40]

Although Chalmers' proposals for special poor-relief arrangements had been widely canvassed, no doubt including while he was on a Town Hospital committee reviewing its general administration,[41] at the time of his election he did not attempt to achieve formal agreement with his ideas. The only special condition he obtained was one which flatly contradicted something he had previously advocated.

His bargaining position was weakened, but he returned to the fray in July and managed to enlist the support of the Glasgow MP Kirkman Finlay,[42] if not that of the General Session.[43] However it was not long before his transfer to St John's was postponed by the discovery that the new building was unsafe.

Almost a year later, on 3 June 1819, he was formally admitted to St John's, although the re-building prevented the church from being opened until late September. These months were used in a further attempt to gain special arrangements. This time he was more successful, probably helped by Edinburgh Evangelicals trying to get him for Playfair's chair of natural philosophy.[44]

Chalmers spent 10 days from 27 July in active negotiation with the Town Council, and on 3 August wrote to the Provost with his proposals.[45] Rather hopefully he believed that because a letter of his had been read to the

---

what the Council had earlier decided, but Chalmers' ultimatum resulted in a change of decision.

40 Ibid., 440f. (16 June 1818).

41 R. A. Cage, *The Scottish poor-law, 1745-1845*, University of Glasgow PhD thesis, 1974, 85.

42 *Memoirs*, 2, 174.

43 T. C. to J. Peddie, 14 March 1818, NLS 3704 f.72. *Memoirs*, 2, 176f.

44 Chalmers did not make his intentions clear and got the criticism he left himself open to. To the successful candidate, John Leslie, the idea of Chalmers in the chair was 'absurd and preposterous' and 'the conduct of Dr Andrew Thomson and one or two more pretended saints has been more atrocious than anything ever acted in the darkest days'. J. Leslie to A. Leslie, 13 August 1819, EUL Phot. 1144/1 f.60. Chalmers published an explanation, but his conduct was less justifiable than understandable. *Memoirs*, 2, 223-6. *Glasgow Courier*, 25 September 1819. Edinburgh Evangelicals were keen to get Chalmers in their midst, but as well as a weak sense of strategy, some had a poor appreciation of his principles. David Brewster wrote that Chalmers could easily cope with both a chair and a parish. For many years pluralism had been anathema to Chalmers. D. Brewster to T. C., 1819, NCL CHA 4.10.15.

45 *Memoirs*, 2, 214-17.

Council before his election, they must have agreed with what was in it. What he now sought was a 'deed of consent' for the 'separate and independent management...of the fund raised by the collections at the church door', and permission to use them not just for poor-relief, but for the building of schools. He would not press immediately for a law of residence to operate between the Glasgow parishes.[46] There is no mention of his hopes for a rebate on the assessment for the Town Hospital collected from within the parish.

This letter was minuted at the Town Council meeting of 18 August 1819 and the Council 'approved highly of the general tenor of the plan now and formerly suggested by Dr Chalmers'[47] – a resolution which allowed ample scope for misinterpretation. They agreed to his control of the collections, but reserved 'for further consideration the other matters noticed in Dr Chalmers' letter.'[48] Some months later they allowed him to use surplus collections for schools, but in the meantime the General Session had reacted bitterly and described the decision by the 'magistrates who are so willing to gratify the doctor' as 'premature and illegal'.[49] The Council defended itself, but there was no question of further concessions. The response of the General Session was commentary on Chalmers' inability to carry his fellow-ministers.

The aims of the experiment

For Chalmers, the function of the ministry was to 'bring the lessons of Christianity into effectual contact with the minds of the population of an assigned district'.[50] Its teachings were 'preparatives for death'[51] and the church a 'school for immortality'.[52] Post-Napoleonic Glasgow saw a succession of riots and demonstrations, a long period of economic depression and high unemployment, and it seemed as if revolution was not far away. In this atmosphere Chalmers was mindful of other functions of the church's presence in the community. Christianity inculcated loyalty and required from upper classes the morality and participation in worship they were keen to see in lower ranks of society.

Conscious of irreligion and social instability, Chalmers saw that the ministry needed to be reorganized if it was to be capable of meeting

---

[46]   Quite apart from the doubtful practicalities it would not have been legal because the City of Glasgow was one parish *quoad civilia*, and the division into parishes was only *quoad sacra*.

[47]   Renwick, *Extracts*, 10, 1905, 504–6 (18 August 1819).

[48]   Ibid., 507.

[49]   Ibid., 508–11 (7 September 1819).

[50]   T. C. to J. Ewing, 9 March 1818, *Memoirs*, 2, 521.

[51]   *Memoirs*, 2, 550.

[52]   Ibid.

religious needs quite apart from social ones. While this might go some way towards alleviating the malaise of society, other changes in the social and economic environment were also required. His key principles were to insist on dealing with the population in defined and manageable units of territory (the 'locality principle') and to provide a setting where different classes of society could accept one another as human beings. He also believed it was necessary to change environmental factors which discouraged poorer classes from being economically self-reliant, kept their wages low and their cost of living high.

He divided the parish into districts each with its own elder, and in each appointed one or more Sunday-school teachers, a deacon to administer new cases of poor-relief, and a Bible and missionary society to be run by the parishioners themselves. The parish was thus divided into 25 Christian cells. Chalmers also sought to provide schooling of a quality which would attract the better-off at a price the poor could afford to pay.

A central feature was the administration of poor-relief in the context of personal relationships with the office-bearers of the church. By lobbying members of parliament, and by writing and speaking, Chalmers sought to influence decisions beyond the parish. He called for the abolition of the corn-laws, the removal of competition faced by Scottish workers due to lower wages in England, and the reform of taxation. He wanted the gradual abolition of public poor-relief funds raised by compulsory assessment, but failing this he tried to insulate St John's from the effect of this arrangement as it existed in Glasgow.

In terms of more specifically religious functions, Chalmers had already implemented most of his ideas at the Tron, but he did hope (despite the contrary nature of his initial arrangements) eventually to draw his congregation from the parish itself rather than outside, and he looked to a more spiritually effective eldership relieved of its poor-relief duties to help achieve this. In the formation of local Bible and missionary societies he sought to harness missions overseas to assist mission at home. His poor-relief scheme apart, once the new boundaries were created in 1819, Chalmers could have done all this while at the Tron, and in almost every respect his shift to St John's can be described as a way of *not* moving to a new situation.

Some have claimed the origins of his schemes can be found in Simeon's Cambridge in the case of his pastoral care,[53] and a German model in respect of his poor-relief arrangements.[54] Despite parallels with Simeon's visiting schemes and Van Voght's descriptions of poor-relief in Hamburg[55]

---

[53] H. E. Hopkins, *Charles Simeon of Cambridge*, 1977, 48.

[54] H. D. Rack, 'Domestic visitation: a chapter in early nineteenth century evangelism', *Journal of Ecclesiastical History*, 24, 1973, 359.

[55] Baron Caspar van Voght, *Account of the management of the poor in Hamburg since the year 1788. In a letter to some friends of the poor in*

there is no evidence to support these suggestions. The principles employed were commonly known if not commonly practised and Chalmers' interest in the Edinburgh Destitute Sick Society[56] and his expressed intention of assimilating a town to a country parish make doubtful the necessity of going further afield in search of sources. What was distinctive at St John's was less his ideas than the determination with which he enacted them. He took 'the traditional features of parish life more seriously, and dealt with them more efficiently than had perhaps ever been done before'.[57]

The parish agency

Chalmers was a superb organizer with ability to lead and inspire. He provided a plan in which each man or woman had a definite task with a clear relationship to the whole. They were motivated by an atmosphere of idealism, energy and encouragement. He took intense interest in details; yet was willing to let others get on with the job once they understood his basic methods.

Those who worked with him felt they were part of a magnificent mission to change the face of their parish in the name of Christ and to provide a model for the city and nation. If their years at St John's had the glories and excitement of an army on the march, that was in part because it was indeed an army. Each of the 25 proportions[58] had an elder, a deacon and at least one Sunday-school teacher, sometimes several and at full strength an 'agency' of lay men and women which numbered close on a hundred. They met as a body every quarter, but there were also meetings of their own groups, frequently round Chalmers' meal-table.

> Every Monday morning in his own house there was an agency breakfast, to which a general invitation was issued, and at which from six to eight of his elders, deacons, or Sabbath-school teachers were generally present. More special invitations to tea were also given, and

---

Great Britain, 1795. Hamburg was divided into 50 districts, in each of which poor-relief was administered through an investigative team of three citizens. They attempted to meet real needs without giving anything a person could earn himself. The impression is of improvement in care but no great reduction in cost.

56   *Works*, 11, 283-314.

57   A. C. Cheyne, '1815; Chalmers in Glasgow's time of turmoil', *Life and Work*, July 1978, 24.

58   Five of the proportions were transferred to St James in 1820. The remainder were subsequently reduced in size, and by 1825 there were 27.

that with such frequency, that there was scarcely an agent who was not asked to the house once in six weeks.[59]

One later recalled:

Our meetings were very delightful. I never saw any set of men who were so animated by one spirit, and whose zeal was so uniformly sustained. The Doctor was the very life of the whole, and everyone felt himself as led on by him, committed to use his whole strength in the cause.[60]

Chalmers began with 17 elders, 12 of whom transferred with him from the Tron, and five who were appointed in October 1819.[61] The full quota of 25 was not made up until 1821.[62] Although they still had the care of the poor who had been obtaining sessional relief before the parish was formed, Chalmers was principally interested in their spiritual duties.[63] Addressing the five new elders in 1819 he reminded them that not until

God put it into the hearts of men to go forth among our heathen at home with the same zeal and enthusiasm which are expected of missionaries who go abroad, will there be anything like a revival of religion throughout the mass of our city families.[64]

As visitors they could expect a welcome in people's homes, but they should not think this necessarily reflected religious interest. People would be obstinate in spite of all 'proofs and earnestness'.[65] This was added reason for Sunday schools, but they ought not give up on anyone. Their confidence should not be in efficient organization, but in the 'essential influence' which only God could supply.

We may just as well think that a system of aqueducts will irrigate and fertilize the country without rain, as think that any human economy

---

[59]   *Memoirs*, 2, 289.

[60]   *Memoirs*, 2, 288.

[61]   St John's Kirk Session minute book, SRO/GRH CH2/176/1, 9 October 1819.

[62]   Ibid., 7 May 1821, 6 August 1821. The 13 new elders comprised three manufacturers, three merchants, two clerks, an accountant, a grocer, a clothcapper, a saddler and a clerk.

[63]   For a parallel interest in reviving the spiritual functions of the eldership see R. Burns of Paisley, *An essay on the office and duties of the eldership in the Church of Scotland*, 1818.

[64]   *Memoirs*, 2, 293.

[65]   *Memoirs*, 2, 295.

will Christianize a parish without the living water of the Spirit....
Still it is right to have a parochial constitution, just as it is right to
have aqueducts.[66]

Chalmers often visited in company with his elders, assisted in surveys of
their proportions and involved them in arranging of local mid-week services.
Besides spiritual oversight, their duties included functions such as the
organization of tract distributors.[67] As was common enough, a large amount
of the business at kirk session meetings arose from cases of discipline. That
of Janet Reid was typical of the two or three which came up every month.
She appeared at the meeting of 3 January 1820 and

> Acknowledged that she had brought forth a child in fornication and
> accused David Paterson Wright, who...had left the place and gone to
> England, as father of the child. She was taken upon discipline and the
> Session accordingly appointed Mr John Brown and Mr Robert Neilson
> to converse with her and report at the next session.[68]

At the meeting in March she again appeared and was 'rebuked, admonished
and absolved' by the Moderator.[69]

Kirk-session discipline had mellowed from its most inquisitorial days,
and matters were treated with some compassion and discretion. It is probable
that cases only came to the session when a girl required financial help
because the father had disappeared, or a couple desiring regular marriage were
obliged to confess 'antenuptial fornication'. The concern of Chalmers to
involve elders in positive outreach was a move away from their standing
role as moral policemen and heralded a change in the nature of parish lay
leadership and understanding of mission.

His quarterly addresses to the agency gave Chalmers the opportunity to
equip lay workers with a coherent philosophy of what they were about. On
3 January 1822 he dealt with 'the likeliest methods of Christianizing a
given district of population'. At their next meeting in March that year he
referred to nine fellowship meetings being held and how they demonstrated
the best features of both the 'aggressive principle' of going out and bringing
people into the life of the church, and the 'attractive principle' which made
the church somewhere they would feel at home.[70]

He used mid-week meetings to reach those who were unlikely ever to
go to church on a Sunday. The people 'assembled in a cotton-mill, or the
workshop of a mechanic, or the kitchen of some kindly accommodating

---

66   *Memoirs*, 2, 295f.
67   *Method of circulating tracts in St John parish*, NCL CHA 5.1.17.
68   Kirk Session minute book, SRO/GRH CH2/176/1, 3 January 1820.
69   Ibid., 6 March 1820.
70   St John's quarterly addresses. NCL CHA.

neighbour' and heard Chalmers give impromptu evangelistic addresses which many believed had more impact than his pulpit sermons.[71]

In December 1821 these attacks on the religious life of the parish were further extended by the founding of the St John's Parish Association for Religious Purposes.[72] This was a development of the Bible Association founded in Kilmany in 1812 and the auxiliary missionary societies encouraged throughout Britain by the London Missionary Society and the Church Missionary Society. Chalmers organized the St John's Association so that in each proportion people would arrange collections of a penny-a-week and distribute missionary literature. He was anxious to make the overseas missionary movement work for the church at home so that those living in working-class Glasgow would not only 'wonder at the ignorance and barbarity of heathen lands' but be impressed

> with the blessings which Christians hold of the gospel, and when they see the knowledge and improvement which follow...[understand] the order and beauty which will overspread their own lives if they will walk in the ways of God.[73]

Each proportion met quarterly to allocate its funds and an annual parish meeting was also held. In the first year an association functioned in every proportion except two and raised £150,[74] but the year after he moved to St Andrews it fell to £70[75] and this part of the St John's experiment did not long survive his absence.

In August of 1820 he rented a room in the middle of the parish and wrote to his wife:

> I spend four days a week visiting the people in company with the agents of the various districts.... This I have generally done with in the forenoon, and then dine either at the vestry or in a friend's house. In addition to this I have had an agency tea every night except yesternight; and in a few evenings more I expect to overtake the whole agency of my parish. At nine I go out to family worship in some house belonging to the district of my present residence, where I assemble the people of the land or close vicinity.... I have generally Mr Newbigging...to accompany me...in the capacity of a precentor, and to drink a tumbler of rum toddy with me ere I go to bed.[76]

---

71   *Memoirs*, 2, 285f.
72   *Scottish Missionary Register*, 3(2), February 1822, 41-3.
73   *Scottish Missionary Register*, 3(2), February 1822, 41f.
74   *Scottish Missionary Register*, 4 March 1823, 105f.
75   *Scottish Missionary Register*, 5 April 1824, 155f.
76   *Memoirs*, 2, 279.

There were four services every Sunday, though the burden of them, and much of the visiting, was shared with Edward Irving[77] (1792-1834), who joined him as assistant shortly after he began at St John's. Still the pace could not continue, and Chalmers felt torn between pastoral work and a desire to publish his ideas further afield.[78] In October 1821, after two years, he announced he was cutting back on his parish visiting and that he considered the parish was still three times too large for one minister.

The Town Council could not be expected to build more churches in the area[79] so he began to contemplate[80] a privately constructed chapel-of-ease to take over about 3000 of the St John's population. In March 1822 the kirk session appointed a committee to investigate[81] and in May the permission of the General Assembly was obtained.[82] Chalmers persuaded 11 of his friends to take £100 shares in the chapel in addition to £500 he himself subscribed[83] and £1000 he obtained from the Douglas family of Cavers.[84] Tenders were called in August 1822 and the building was opened for worship in May the following year.

This was his first venture into church extension and financially it was a failure. So far from getting interest on their investment as intended, subscribers found themselves assessed for contributions to clear debts.[85] People could be drawn to worship, but they were not interested in paying seat rents.[86]

After he left Glasgow Chalmers often returned to preach in aid of the chapel, but it was a losing battle and the disappointment was bitter. He attached a good deal of the blame to the minister,[87] but there were a number of circumstances which made its financial viability doubtful from the start.

Until 1834 it was not possible for a chapel-of-ease minister to have his own kirk session and thus he could not develop his own leadership of an 'agency' independent of that of St John's. As a Church of Scotland chapel

---

[77]   *Fasti*, 7, 279. Irving still awaits his modern biographer, but see G. Strachan, *The Pentecostal theology of Edward Irving*, 1973. Chalmers and his family continued to think affectionately of Irving. He was sympathetic with Irving's views on the gifts of the Spirit and miracles, and was influenced by his teaching on prophecy. He avoided involvement in Irving's deposition, but was consulted by Irving's congregation at the time of the presbytery trial. He was not perturbed by Irving's Christology.

[78]   *Memoirs*, 2, 320-24.

[79]   Kirk Session minute book, SRO/GRH CH2/176/1, 4 March 1822.

[80]   Journal, 12 January 1822.

[81]   Kirk Session minute book, SRO/GRH CH2/176/1, 4 March 1822.

[82]   *Works*, 16, 141-214.

[83]   *Memoirs*, 2, 380f.

[84]   Lady Grace Douglas to T. C., 16 April 1822, NCL CHA 4.19.55.

[85]   Minute book of St John's chapel. SRO/GRH CH2/176/5.

[86]   Ibid., 22 March 1829. Anon to T. C., (1823), NCL CHA 4.102.20.

[87]   *Memoirs*, 2, 381-7.

the collections had to go to the parish poor, and it was not the sort of area where much income could be expected from seat-rents, as events proved. Evening services ceased at St John's when the chapel was built, so that what the chapel did was to take over the evening congregation with few advantages to set against the expense of an additional building. Chalmers was to claim the St John's experiment showed a working-class area could support its own poor. What it showed was that even if they could they were unlikely to be able to support a minister as well.

One wonders if Chalmers realized just how difficult a task he had set himself. He and his elders and deacons visited every household and claimed they were made welcome in virtually all of them. Yet when they began their work only 24% of households held seats in any congregation of the Church of Scotland,[88] and even by 1825 only 6% of the population held seats in St John's church or chapel.[89]

The diversity of church-going was amazing in an age of little public transport. In 1819, in one proportion of 69 households, seats were held in 22 different churches, including nine belonging to the Church of Scotland.[90] This may not have been unrelated to the high mobility. In this same proportion in 1823, only 43% of householders had been resident there four years previously.[91]

The extent of non-churchgoing can be variously estimated. An 1819 survey managed to find some nominal religious affiliation for every inhabitant in Glasgow,[92] and 61% of St John's householders had one seat somewhere,[93] even if only 28% of the total population of the parish were seatholders.[94]

During Chalmers' incumbency, some increase in church-going was achieved. In the proportion referred to above, in 1823 9% of those who held seats anywhere did so in St John's,[95] and 12% of those who had some sort of church affiliation said it was with the parish church.[96] St John's obtained its local church-goers mainly at the expense of other churches[97] and non-seatholders remained a steady 72% of the population.[98] Like a good many

---

88 Appendix 5, tables 3, 6.
89 Ibid., table 7.
90 Ibid., table 10.
91 M. Montgomery, W. Mathieson and J. Cunningham, St John's survey notebook (proportion 7, 1823); Statistical, moral and educational survey of St John's parish Glasgow for the year 1819. NCL CHA 5.1.14.
92 Cleland, *Statistical tables*, 1823, 7.
93 Appendix 5, table 12.
94 Ibid., table 3.
95 Ibid., table 8.
96 Ibid., table 9.
97 Ibid., table 8.
98 Ibid., table 3.

exercises in Christian outreach, the St John's experiment was more effective at redirecting the interests of those already partially committed than it was at drawing in those who were completely outside.

The most dramatic change in the pattern of religious behaviour was the improved position of the Church of Scotland relative to Dissent, yet the long-term effect was no more than to bring the situation almost level with that of Glasgow as a whole, where in 1836 12% of the population held seats in the Church of Scotland, 14% in Dissenting churches, and 74% had no seats at all.[99] This did show Dissent was vulnerable to revival in the Church of Scotland. Additional establishment places of worship altered the balance of allegiance, even if the challenge was not so great after Chalmers left.[100]

Education

A school in every parish had been the vision of John Knox, and one shared by his countrymen ever since. In St John's Chalmers lost no time setting about providing for the education of his parishioners and the day after the church opened a committee was formed to raise funds.[101] He wrote a pamphlet to help the cause[102] and began seeking subscriptions.[103] A site was purchased opposite the church and two schools and a school-house erected. Great care was taken with the selection of teachers and the schools opened in July 1820. It was immediately necessary to begin planning for two more and by 1823 the parish was catering for around 800 pupils.[104]

Chalmers visited the schools almost daily and regarded them as showpieces where the only inequality was 'such as arises from the diversity of talent and diligence and personal character'.[105] He was anxious to ensure that they attracted all classes of society, even if the mix available was not very wide.[106] Children of rich and poor needed a shared educational experience to learn 'the lesson of respect for our common nature…that neither talent nor character are the prerogatives of rank alone'.[107]

To achieve this it was necessary to set the fees low enough for the poor to afford (he was not alone in believing fees were necessary if people were to

[99] Appendix 5, table 3.
[100] Ibid., tables 3, 4, 5.
[101] *Memoirs*, 2, 233.
[102] *Works*, 12, 191-219.
[103] Record of transactions connected with the establishment of parish schools in St John's, 1819, Chalmers' commonplace book, NCL CHA 5.1.13.
[104] *Memoirs*, 2, 236.
[105] *Memoirs*, 2, 239.
[106] Appendix 5, table 13.
[107] *Memoirs*, 2, 241.

value education),[108] and also ensure that the quality of education was high enough for the better-off not to send their children elsewhere. Nevertheless there was criticism that he was educating the poor above themselves.

> We have never hesitated on the question of popular education; and when it is asked, how far should the illumination of the lower orders in society be permitted to go – we do not scruple to reply that it should be to the very uttermost of what their taste and their time and their convenience will permit. There have been a dread and a jealousy upon this topic wherewith we cannot at all sympathize.[109]

If some still believed education to be the seed-bed of sedition, for Chalmers the 'true way of disarming' radical influences was 'to educate the people up to them'.[110] He noted that poorly educated cotton spinners, although reasonably paid, 'were greatly more disaffected and mischievous than our weavers with bad wages'.[111] It was to a 'growing virtue and intelligence and worth'[112] among the working-classes that he looked when he predicted they were 'destined to attain a far more secure place of comfort and independence'[113] in society.

Next to the church itself, the schools were the major institutional component of the St John's experiment, and their success was the least ambiguous. Their functions were widely accepted, well supported and integrated into the overall aims of the parish. Here children learned to read their Bibles and some better-off as well as the poor mixed to break down social distance. Children were taught not only character and self-reliance, but skills to help maintain their independence in a competitive society.

The right management of the poor

Chalmers had long believed any form of compulsory public poor-fund was detrimental to the best interests of the poor themselves and of society. It

---

[108] Chalmers has been criticized for excluding the very poor by his insistence on fees. Saunders, *Scottish democracy*, 1950, 217. If he had not set fees Chalmers would have lost the more well-off and destroyed a major social function of the schools. The fees were below those charged elsewhere in Glasgow (Cage and Checkland, 'Thomas Chalmers and urban poverty', 1976, 50). Saunders is wrong to suggest the pupils came from outside the parish. The schools were strictly parochial – unlike the congregation. *Memoirs*, 2, 235.

[109] *Works*, 6, 289.

[110] T. C. to W. Wilberforce, 25 April 1820, *Memoirs*, 2, 265.

[111] Ibid.

[112] *Memoirs*, 2, 245.

[113] Ibid.

was his intention to demonstrate that, even in a working-class area, church collections could provide for poor-relief. He obtained the authority of the Town Council for independent control of these funds, but to complete his scheme he needed to ensure they would be properly managed. He turned to the provision for deacons which had long existed in the Church of Scotland, but which had seldom been implemented. Also for the improvement of the economic situation of parishioners was the founding of a parish saving bank.[114]

In January 1820 he ordained 15 of the 25 deacons needed,[115] and gave them responsibility for using the collections from the evening congregation to provide for new cases of pauperism. The deacons were expected to make themselves known among the people of their proportion so that when applications arose they would know whom they were dealing with. They were equipped with verbal advice and written instructions. They were to check if work might be found for any applicant, whether there were relatives or friends who could assist and, if the applicant was a Dissenter, whether or not their own church would contribute.

It was necessary to make certain that the legal requirement of three years residence in Glasgow had been met, and that people were not already obtaining relief from another parish or from the Town Hospital. Enquiries were to be checked by another deacon, after which a recommendation would be made to the deacons' meeting which would decide on the aid to be granted.[116]

It is ironical that in wanting a system inspired by the personal knowledge and relationships found in a small rural community, Chalmers was forced to design something formal and bureaucratic which by its very existence would seem to make the source of the funds allocated irrelevant. The distance between donor and recipient was already there because of the scale of the situation, never mind the fact that most of those who provided the money were non-resident in the parish.

Chalmers' methods were not as harsh in their application as has been portrayed, as those with experience of social welfare would recognize. Deacons were authorized to give 'discretionary aid' while cases were being investigated,[117] and private charity could be administered more freely again.[118] There were enough instances of deception to justify

[114]   *Works*, 15, 304-33. *The Times*, 8 October 1823. The idea was pioneered by Henry Duncan (1774-1846) of Ruthwell in 1810. *Fasti*, 2, 255f.

[115]   Kirk Session minute book, SRO/GRH CH2/176/1, 3 January 1820.

[116]   *Memoirs*, 2, 299.

[117]   Ibid.

[118]   T. C. to W. Matthews, 10 December 1822, NCL CHA 3.9.82.

caution[119] and Chalmers' correspondence with deacons is a fair guide to how the system worked.

In August 1823 he received a report of a visit to a recent applicant:

> She is a widow left with 4 children and will soon have a fifth. The oldest child, a girl [who] is 12 years of age, and a boy of ten, have been weaving since May last. Their earnings seem to be about 3/- to 3/6 per week. The mother winds for them which brings about 1/3 more, making in all about 4/9.
>
> The girl she intends to send to service as soon as the time of her confinement is past, and she intends to send the boy to another trade as she has no person to instruct them in weaving since their father's death about 3 weeks ago.
>
> The expenses of the husband's funeral she paid by selling his watch and some pieces of furniture. The looms in the weaving shop are her own, she has not yet got her husband's loom let, for which she expects 8d a week....
>
> She ought to be put on the highest list which is about 2/6 per week.... Mrs McInlay's character seems respectable among her neighbours. Her landlord, William Nelson, says her husband's character was equally good; although in a bad state of health for twelve months he died without debt which shows a correct disposition. He was I think 6 weeks confined to bed before his death which took all the trifle he had saved to support himself and family.[120]

The system continued after Chalmers left St John's, but the financial situation deteriorated and in 1837 the session was forced to ask the Town Hospital to take over its more expensive cases. The question which had long been asked about the practicality of Chalmers' ideas again came to the fore. A key feature of the St John's experiment had ended after 18 years; did that mean it had also failed?[121]

Chalmers had been writing in defence of St John's from its inception,[122] and took advantage of the superficiality of much of the

---

[119] *Memoirs*, 2, 302. Nor did the deacons always detect them. A. Ranken, *A letter addressed to Dr Chalmers on the subject of pauperism in the city of Glasgow*, 1830, 27.

[120] W. Ramsey to T. C., 19 August 1823, NCL CHA 4.29.4.

[121] In 1836 Chalmers was preparing for the inevitable, but wanted to make sure it would be for the 'right' reasons. T. C. to W. Buchanan, 19 April 1836, GUL MS Gen 1036.

[122] The main works are: *Christian and civic economy of large towns*, 1819-1826, *Works*, 14-16. *A speech delivered on the 24th of May 1822, before the General Assembly of the Church of Scotland explanatory of the measures which have been successfully pursued in St John's Parish Glasgow*

criticism to avoid that which was more searching.[123] The debate, including his advocacy of traditional methods of Scottish poor-relief, is an aspect of the history of the poor-laws during his life-time.[124]

The ability of a parish to meet the cost of its own poor-relief depended on the amount of poverty it had to cater for and its capacity for raising funds. Chalmers argued that St John's was the poorest parish in Glasgow and that therefore his principles had been vindicated in the most unfavourable of circumstances. Hence it is necessary to note where the funds for St John's poor-relief came from, what the level of poverty actually was, and whether the collections for the poor did in fact exceed expenditure on their behalf.

In September 1837, despite a refund from the Town Hospital of £462, which St John's had earlier paid towards the upkeep of paupers from before the parish was founded, the parish was over £200 in deficit.[125] Chalmers pointed out that the accounts included other things besides poor-relief, in particular a large amount spent on education, and claimed that over the 18

---

for the extinction of its compulsory pauperism, 1822, Works, 16, 141-214. Statement in regard to the pauperism of Glasgow, from the experience of the last eight years, 1823, Works, 16, 215-84. 'Evidence before the Committee of the House of Commons on the subject of a poor-law for Ireland', (May 1830), *Works, 16, 285-421.* 'Reflections of 1839 on the now protracted experience of pauperism in Glasgow', (1839. MSS copy in Mitchell Library Glasgow, MS98), *Works, 16, 422-4. The sufficiency of a parochial system, without a poor-rate, for the right management of the poor, Works, 21.* See also Chalmers' evidence before the 1843 Poor-law Commissioners, *Report from Her Majesty's Commissioners for enquiring into the administration and practical operation of the poor laws in Scotland, 1844,* Appendix, part 1, 266-80.

[123] For example: A. Ranken, *A letter addressed to Dr Chalmers on the subject of pauperism in the city of Glasgow,* 1830. W. P. Alison, *Observations on the management of the poor in Scotland,* 1840. W. P. Alison, *Reply to Dr Chalmers' objections to the improvement of the legal provision for the poor in Scotland,* 1841. R. A. Cage and E. O. A. Checkland, 'Thomas Chalmers and urban poverty: The St John's parish experiment in Glasgow, 1819-1837'. *Philosophical Journal,* Glasgow, 13(1), 1976, 37-56, would have found it helpful to consult the minutes of the Glasgow Town Council. See also John F. McCaffrey, 'Thomas Chalmers and social change', *Scottish Historical Review,* 60, 1981, 32-60.

[124] R. A. Cage, *The Scottish poor law 1745-1845,* University of Glasgow PhD, 1974, for a critique of which see R. Mitchison, 'The making of the old Scottish poor law,' *Past and Present,* 63, May 1974, 58-93. See also Cage's reply and a rejoinder from Mitchison, *Past and Present,* 69, November 1975, 113-21. An analysis of issues between 1815 and 1841 is contained in *Report...into the poor laws in Scotland,* 1844.

[125] *Works, 21, 134.*

years of the experiment the collections amounted to £1100 more than what had been paid out to the poor.

This much said, Chalmers needed to have done better than scrape home financially if the case he wished to make was to be a strong one. If his scheme had worked as well as it was meant to, the cost of schools and the expenses of 'foundlings, illegitimates, and the families of runaway parents',[126] imports from other Glasgow parishes,[127] and those who were already on the Town Hospital in 1819, would have been easily catered for.

If St John's needed a Chalmers to run it successfully, after 18 years that carried less weight than the underlying fact that it was not the working-class parishioners who were supplying the funds, but a relatively well-off congregation drawn from further afield. Chalmers had insisted on starting St John's with a 'wealthy day congregation'[128] and for the first few years managed to keep the cost of new cases within the collections from the evening congregation which was entirely from the parish itself. However this arrangement came to an end with the building of the chapel, and the proportion of parochial seat-holders in both church and chapel remained low – it was only 18% in 1836, although it had been higher in some intervening years.[129]

This failure to obtain a parochial congregation answers the complaint of Chalmers that he never obtained a concession for parish rate-payers to compensate them for not sending new cases to the Town Hospital.[130] Perhaps a rate concession would have attracted people to St John's, but it is unlikely it would have made any difference. It is difficult to see how he could go on saying this was 'obviously equitable'[131] when on his own admission the 14% of the city population living in the parish contributed only 1.5% of the assessment,[132] and on top of that at best only 6% of them held seats in either the church or the chapel.[133]

Chalmers' repeated claim that St John's was the poorest parish in Glasgow[134] carried the implication not only that there was less money available from collections, but also that the amount of poverty to be dealt with was greater than in other parishes. The largely non-parochial nature of the congregation made the economic state of the parish irrelevant as far as

---

[126] *Works*, 21, 136.
[127] *Works*, 16, 424.
[128] T. C. to J. Ewing, 23 May 1818, NCL CHA 3.8.43. In 1822 the St John's collections were the largest in Glasgow and 50% greater than the second in the list. Cleland, *Statistical tables*, 1823, 110.
[129] Appendix 5, table 7.
[130] *Works*, 16, 425.
[131] *Works*, 21, 130.
[132] *Works*, 16, 220. This was in 1819.
[133] Appendix 5, table 7.
[134] *Works*, 16, 318. Other instances can be multiplied.

income was concerned, but was his claim correct at least with respect to the amount of poverty?

He noted there were very few families who were not working class, about 1%, and that the number of servants was low compared with most other Glasgow parishes.[135] The small amount of the assessment collected from St John's was an indication that there were few people with property.

As information this is not open to dispute, but his deductions are questionable. While a working-class population may include a large number of paupers, it is not a necessary consequence. St John's was not an inner-city parish, but on the eastern outskirts. It was not rich, or middle class, but it was not destitute either. When St John's was established it had the third *lowest* ratio of sessional poor to population among city parishes,[136] and its 49 paupers on the Town Hospital were less than a third of the number which would have been expected if it had only an average amount of pauperism.[137] In terms of the poverty its collections would actually be called upon to meet, St John's had one of the lightest burdens in Glasgow.

Both the true nature of the congregation and the actual amount of poverty there was to relieve make St John's far removed from the situation Chalmers portrayed, and this destroys his case. Whatever else it did, the St John's experiment did not demonstrate 'the sufficiency of a parochial system without a poor rate for the right management of the poor'.

If Chalmers had really wanted a poor parish to experiment on, he should have stayed minister of the Tron. After the Glasgow parish boundaries were redrawn in 1819 it was that parish which had the greatest amount of poverty in the city.[138] It is open to question whether, if he had remained at the Tron, it would have proved impossible to obtain the independent management of the poor he sought. His earliest proposals made no mention of a new church at all.[139]

The assertion that St John's was the poorest parish in Glasgow was Chalmers' reply to criticism of his having broken up the system of the pooling of funds which the General Session had previously operated. He had no answer to the fact that his action resulted in an increase of costs for Glasgow rate-payers, not a decrease as predicted. Once kirk sessions functioned independently, those with surplus poor funds could retain them while those in deficit were obliged to seek grants from the Town Hospital, thus increasing the assessment.[140]

---

135   *Works*, 16, 218-20. Cleland, *Statistical tables*, 1823, 6.
136   Appendix 5, table 15.
137   Ibid., table 17. *Works*, 16, 233.
138   Appendix 5, tables 14, 15.
139   T. C. to J. Ewing, Town Hospital report 7 January 1818, *Statement from the Session of St John's parish, Glasgow, to the Directors of the Town's Hospital in regard to the management of their poor*, 1836, 3.
140   Ranken, *Letter addressed to Dr Chalmers*, 1830, 7f.

Those completely convinced about 'the sufficiency of a parochial system' in this respect have never been numerous, but the claim to have reduced the cost of poor-relief has been widely accepted by those more and less critical alike. Although at times he gave his figures some of the qualifications their origins demanded, no one reading Chalmers' many accounts of St John's would doubt he believed he had reduced the expense of pauperism in the parish from around £1400 to the region of £300 a year.[141]

The later figure cannot be seriously questioned, but the same cannot be said for the estimate of the cost of poor-relief before he took over. He calculated this as a proportion of the total expense of the Glasgow sessional and Town Hospital poor, but on this basis it can be readily computed to be about £1760.[142] In fact the actual cost was nothing like either figure. St John's began with 125 sessional poor who required £225 per year for their maintenance.[143] There were 49 poor supported by the Town Hospital, and these would at the average rate for 1819[144] have required a further £330 to make a total of only £555.

At the very most, Chalmers could claim to have almost halved the cost of poor-relief in four years. This is more credible than his own estimate and also takes some of the sting out of the accusation that he used draconian methods. This is even more apparent when the reduction is set against the background of the falling level of poverty in Glasgow after 1820. By 1823 the assessment for the Town Hospital poor was 83% of its 1819 level and 63% of its peak in 1820.[145] Several other Glasgow parishes also achieved substantial reductions in the cost and number of their poor during this period,[146] although Chalmers might claim in some instances this was due to his example.[147]

There have been other criticisms. It was said the poor were starved out of St John's, but as one critic conceded, the fact that the 'imports' of poor from other parishes were double those 'exports' who felt constrained to leave,[148] helped vindicate him from this particular charge. Another accusation was that he achieved success through wealthy deacons relieving the poor out of their own pockets, thus doctoring the experiment to please its author. If it had been realized what the reduction in poor-relief actually was, people might have been less concerned, but in 1841 Chalmers was

---

[141] *Works*, 16, 233 gives the figure as £308; *Memoirs*, 2, 307 mentions £280 which is the more widely quoted figure.

[142] Appendix 5, tables 1, 14, 17.

[143] *Works*, 16, 221. Cleland, *Statistical tables*, 1823, 110.

[144] *Works*, 16, 233. Appendix 5, table 17.

[145] Appendix 5, table 17.

[146] Ibid., tables 14, 15, 16.

[147] Chalmers' principles were tried in a number of parishes. See footnote 161, below.

[148] Ranken, *Letter addressed to Dr Chalmers*, 1830, 17, *Works*, 21, 117.

sufficiently worried by the question to inquire from Glasgow.[149] W. Buchanan, who had been an office-bearer at St John's from the beginning, replied:

> I have just to repeat what I am sure I have stated a hundred times, that the private relief afforded to the poor in the parish has been immensely overrated.... Had the deacons of St John's opened their purses and been so liberal as the enemies of our system say they were, then I consider that they would have been doing the system a very great injury and the people no permanent good, as our great aim was to encourage the people to industrious habits and to get their children taught to read the word of God.[150]

A more modern complaint is that Chalmers 'ignored the social or non-individual factors in the poverty around him'.[151] It would be more accurate to say he was not realistic about sources of poverty. The St John's experiment was in many respects an attempt to change 'social or non-individual factors', not just personal ones, and one reason it did not succeed was because to do so is extraordinarily difficult. He tried to re-create an environment which would eliminate the need for people to be dependent on other than mutual charity and the church plate. He never saw poverty simply in terms of individual failure, though the individual should look to their own resources and relations to try to cope. At the same time he did what he could to influence decisions which could only be made at a national level. His correspondence with Wilberforce,[152] his 1820 *Edinburgh Review* article on 'The state and prospects of manufacturers',[153] and his books[154] and articles[155] on political economy, should be evidence enough that he sought to grapple with the social salvation of the nation as well as with the religious salvation of its citizens.

Chalmers has also been criticized for not doing what he never intended. It has often been observed that St John's could not handle destitution arising

149   T. C. to W. Buchanan, 2 January 1841, GUL MS Gen 1036.
150   W. Buchanan to T. C.. 7 January 1841, GUL MS Gen 1036.
151   Mechie, *Scottish social development*, 1960, 60.
152   *Memoirs*, 2, 249-60.
153   *Edinburgh Review*, May 1820, 382-95. *Works*, 20, 365-94.
154   *An enquiry into the extent and stability of national resources*, 1808. *Political economy in connection with the moral state and prospects of society*, 1832. *Works*, 19-20.
155   'Tracts on the corn trade', *North British Review*, 1, May 1844, 67-98. 'The political economy of the Bible', *North British Review*, 2, November 1844, 1-52. 'Stirling's *Philosophy of trade*', *North British Review*, 6, November 1846, 87-116. 'Political economy of a famine', *North British Review*, 7, May 1847, 247-90.

from industrial recession, also that it 'could deal with honest poverty but did not know "what to do with immorality and drunkenness"'.[156] William Collins, who made this later remark, was concerned with the intractability of alcoholism, not the deficiencies of St John's,[157] and it ought to be remembered that there were certain things which the experiment was never designed to cope with. Chalmers had explained in August 1819:

> I here beg it to be distinctly understood, that I do not consider the revenue of the kirk-session to be at all applicable to those extraordinary cases which are produced by any sudden and unlooked for depression in the state of our manufactures.[158]

Nevertheless in the long run the poor-relief scheme achieved neither what its author had hoped nor what he subsequently claimed, and one is left wondering not only why it failed in this respect, but why Chalmers could never admit that it had. The first is the easier question, and the answer can be seen in the impracticality of trying to treat a mobile and religiously diverse city population as if it were a country parish which was not even a town, and in the futility of trying to isolate one part of the city from the rest, especially when there was no natural sense of community to reinforce the role of the parish church – even with the redrawn parish boundaries. In more ideal circumstances the scheme was still fragile. It was tried in Dunfermline for 20 years with 'great success', but

> it ultimately failed, not in principle, but because some of the heritors withdrew their voluntary subscriptions and wholly deranged the plan. The deficiency of Dr C's conception was that it did not, perhaps could not, keep alive this application of charity where personal intercourse and sympathy could not be established – and that impulse failing, there was little appeal otherwise for the exercise of the virtue of charity.[159]

The failure of Chalmers to accept a negative verdict is a sorry story of muddle and self-deception, yet there were other reasons as well. Behind arguments about sums were values he believed in deeply, and it was those he was really fighting for. Their rightness however could not carry what he built upon them. Despite his mathematical abilities, he was easily carried away by his own rhetoric. He could not see why principles which had worked in Fife would not do so in Glasgow, especially when the state of society was a strong incentive for wanting to demonstrate they had. He did pioneering work in parish surveys and dug out copious figures from parishes

---

[156] Ferguson, *Scotland, 1689 to the present*, 1968, 313.
[157] *Report from the select committee on inquiry into drunkenness*, 1834, 145.
[158] *Memoirs*, 2, 215.
[159] *Letter to Sir John J. Maxwell of Pollock*, 19 March 1840, SRA T-PM-117.

all over Britain, yet he used this information to illustrate conclusions already reached more than to test them.[160]

His ever-hopeful personality, his lofty principles which appeared to accord with Christian faith and relate to or rise above conventional economic philosophy, and his powers of profuse illustration, combined with the apparent authority of scientific data to discourage most from daring to suggest he might after all be wrong. Few could dig their way through all the data even if they had access to it. Doubts expressed were sometimes due to a better perception of the realities of the situation; often as not they arose out of a suspicion that a cause which required so much passion in its defence was the less likely to be proved correct in the end.

The St John's poor-relief scheme had few imitators in Scotland besides Dunfermline,[161] but of more lasting and positive impact was the influence of the philosophy Chalmers spun around descriptions of the experiment. Norman Macleod of the Barony believed he found evidence of Chalmers' ideas in Germany[162] and in this he was followed by Stewart Mechie.[163]

A more certain influence was on the Charity Organization Society, founded in London in 1869. Of this Chalmers became virtually the patron saint,[164] and through it his writings and principles took on a new life divorced from the need to prove the financial success of the experiment which gave them birth. The Charity Organization Society arose out of a concern that indiscriminate charity caused as much poverty as it relieved. Chalmers' principles of locality, personal knowledge of applicants, close examination of people's situation, the encouragement of independence, the importance of character, the training of lay workers, and the regarding of public funds as an avenue of last resort,[165] all found fresh relevance and gave

---

[160] Similar problems are apparent in the work of the Poor Law Commissioners of 1832-34, and there are many parallels with Chalmers' values and ideals. See the introduction to S. G. and E. O. A. Checkland, *The poor law report of 1834*, 1974, 9-59.

[161] In Glasgow it was tried in the Outer High, St David's-Ramshorn, St Enoch's, St George's and St James. It was also contemplated for the Canongate Edinburgh, and St John's Edinburgh was founded on Chalmers' principles in 1840. *Poor law report*, 1844, Appendix 1, 87-94, 270, 277. D. K. and C. K. Guthrie, *Autobiography of Thomas Guthrie and memoir*, 1874. In Langholm, W. B. Shaw was 'vexed and disappointed' at the failure of a scheme modeled on St John's. W. B. Shaw to T. C., 9 April 1830, NCL CHA 4.148.8.

[162] *Good Words*, 1 January 1860, 5-8. The parallels are undoubted, but the connection is uncertain and German sources are more likely.

[163] *The Church and Scottish social development, 1780-1870*, 1960, 61.

[164] C. L. Mowat, *The Charity Organization Society*, 1961, 10f.

[165] Mechie, *Scottish social development*, 1960, 63.

his work significance in the history of the theory and practice of social welfare in Britain.[166]

Around the turn of this century his writings on poor-relief enjoyed another revival in the context of a re-examination of the British poor laws,[167] and despite their very particular origins in a tiny village in rural Fife and two parishes in post-Napoleonic Glasgow, his ideas continue to speak to those sensitive to the tendency of public funds to stimulate as well as alleviate social needs. He failed to demonstrate that the poor generated by industrial society could be supported by traditional charity, but in the attempt showed how poor relief could be administered with a more human face. Despite his intentions his methods pointed to the future he resisted more than to the past he wished to preserve.

The Christian and civic economy

Coincident with the opening of St John's in September 1819,[168] Chalmers brought out the first of a series of quarterly papers later published as the *Christian and civic economy of large towns*.[169] His standing as a preacher and the state of society ensured a ready audience. The first issues dealt with the essential features of the St John's experiment – the model of a rural parish, the locality principle, ideas on the eldership and deacons, Sunday schools and, of course, pauperism.[170]

---

[166]   Karl de Schweinitz, *England's road to social security*, 1943, 112-13, 148-53. For a critique of the Charity Organization Society, much of which applies also to Chalmers, see D. Leat, 'Social theory and the historical construction of social work activity; the role of Samuel Barnett,' in P. Leonard ed., *The sociology of community action,* Sociological Review Monograph, 21, University of Keele, November 1975, 21-37.

[167]   N. Masterman, *Chalmers on charity*, 1900. *How best to reduce the rates or, Dr Chalmers and the Elberfield system of poor-relief*, 1909. W. Harper, *The social ideal and Dr Chalmers' contribution to Christian economics*, 1910. G. C. Wood, *Dr Chalmers concerning political economy and social reform*, 1912. H. Hunter, *Problems of poverty, Selections from the economic and social writings of Thomas Chalmers*, 1912.

[168]   *Memoirs*, 2, 223, 319.

[169]   They were published together in 1826 and included as volumes 14-16 of Chalmers' *Works*. They were published separately in 1856 in Britain and in 1900 in America.

[170]   Although he claimed pauperism occupied 'but a part and the smaller part of these volumes' (*Works*, 14, xvi), 19 of 28 chapters were overtly concerned with pauperism and related aspects of political economy which he was teaching at the time he finished the series.

Response to his articles in the *Edinburgh Review* in 1817 and 1818 had been mixed,[171] and that was also the case with the *Christian and civic economy*, though its positive influence was more apparent. Within Scotland,[172] *Blackwood's*[173] was not hopeful that a town parish could be operated as if it was a country one and considered the system 'simple and obvious...owing little to the ingenuity of invention and claiming everything from the energy of performance'.[174] The principles were sound, but how successful the experiment would be was another question.[175] The *Edinburgh Magazine*[176] saw Chalmers 'at the post in which even his eccentricities work for good' since they 'only give an air of romantic irregularity to the grandeur of his undertakings'.[177] Glasgow's 'radical war' had not reached its height, but faced with the challenge of radicalism,

> It is not to a Wellington we are to look for redress...so much as a Chalmers. It is not the magistrates of Manchester, with their yeomanry corps who are to do the business – it is the magistrates of Glasgow, with their corps of parochial agency and a Christian hero at their head.[178]

In England the 'locality principle' drew favourable comment and specific action. The *Christian Observer*[179] and the *Methodist Magazine*[180] drew

---

[171]   'Helvidius Priscus,' *Glasgow Chronicle*, 21 November 1817, referred to the first as a 'hobbling rumbling essay' of 'dreamy, drunken stuff'. A minister in Aberdeen took a while to discover Chalmers was the author, but was forced to print a reply as people were using the article as an excuse for not subscribing for poor-relief. (S. Ogilvey, *To the heritors and gentlemen of the parish of Old Machar*, 1817. S. Ogilvey to T. C., 16 October 1817, NCL CHA 4.6.41.) The Editor of the *Edinburgh Review* wrote of more favourable reactions and asked Chalmers to speed the second part. F. Jeffrey to T. C., 25 July 1817, NCL CHA 4.6.21.

[172]   See also *Glasgow Sentinel*, 29 May, 5 June, 14 August, 1822.

[173]   *Blackwood's*, 7, 1819-1820, 18-24, 176-83, 419-27.

[174]   Ibid., 182.

[175]   Ibid., 183.

[176]   *Edinburgh Magazine*, November 1819, 432-6; February 1820, 106-11; August 1821, 113-16.

[177]   Ibid., 5 November 1819, 435.

[178]   Ibid.

[179]   Its reviews included: 1821, 160ff., 490ff., 555-70; 627ff., 707ff.; 1822, 39-48, 105-17; 1823, 627-45. *The Christian Observer* made a special point of promoting Chalmers' 'benevolent plans'. C. Simeon to T. C., 23 November 1821, NCL CHA 4.18.39.

[180]   Its reviews included, 1822, 3rd series, 1, 40-46, 105-11, 174-7, 237-42. These were by Richard Watson and reprinted in his *Works*, 7, 1835, 264-90.

attention to this old idea to which Chalmers had given fresh life.[181] In Edinburgh a Sunday school society[182] and a juvenile missionary society[183] were founded on his principles. In Islington, the future missionary bishop, Daniel Wilson, started local Sunday schools in the poorest areas 'all on the system recommended by Dr Chalmers'[184] and the Methodist leader Jabez Bunting wrote:

> Your plan of *locality* has made a powerful impression on many persons here; and there is a strong disposition to apply it to some of the most wretched districts of our metropolis. A beginning, on a small scale, has been made in the parish contiguous to St Giles, and I believe in Spitalfields also; and already enough has been seen to induce the belief that your principle is the only one that will effectively reach the mass of our ignorant and vicious congregation.[185]

Chalmers' views on compulsory assessments were not shared by his fellow Evangelicals, Robert Burns of Paisley,[186] Stevenson MacGill[187] and Andrew Thomson;[188] but they restored his relationship with the Moderate friend of his youth, W. B. Shaw of Langholm.[189] Henry Cockburn favourably commented on the St John's experiment in the *Edinburgh Review* in 1824.[190] Bishop J. B. Sumner (1780-1862) of Chester was 'especially keen on District Visiting societies rather on the model of Chalmers'.[191] Malthus called Chalmers his 'ablest and best

---

[181] *Christian Observer*, September 1821, 556-8. R. Watson, *Works*, 7, 1835, 281-3.

[182] *Scottish Missionary Register*, January 1821, 7-10; April 1821, 131-6.

[183] Ibid., April 1821, 123.

[184] J. Bateman, *Life of Daniel Wilson*, London, 1861, 1, 184, quoted by H. D. Rack, 'Domestic visitation: a chapter in early nineteenth century evangelism,' *Journal of Ecclesiastical* History, 24, 1973, 357-76.

[185] J. Bunting to T. C., 27 February 1822, StAUL 30385.87.

[186] R. Burns, *Historical dissertation on the law and practice of Great Britain and particularly of Scotland with regard to the poor*, 1819.

[187]   S. Macgill, *Discourses and essays on subjects of public interest*, 1819, 361-475.

[188] A. M. Thomson to Lundie, 14 June 1819, NLS 1676, f.172.

[189] W. B. Shaw to T. C., 27 October 1823, NCL CHA 4.29.27. Shaw had helped Chalmers obtain his assistantship at Cavers in 1801, but Chalmers' conversion cooled their friendship.

[190]   'Review of T. Chalmers, *Statement in regard to the pauperism of Glasgow from the experience of the last eight years*, 1823,' *Edinburgh Review*, 81, October 1824, 228-58.

[191] G. F. A. Best, *Temporal pillars*, 1964, 163. J. B. Sumner shared similar views on science and religion as well as interests in political economy and the updating of the parochial system to meet the needs of the age (R. S.

ally'.[192] Although some raised questions, he got enough reinforcement not to waver in his resolve.

Conclusion

It is unfortunate that so much has to be said in rebuttal of much that Chalmers and others have written about St John's, as it overshadows what he did achieve. It is the way he mobilized laity and put new life into the parish system in an industrial city, rather than how strained was his reasoning in defense of its poor-relief regime, which gives St John's its place in history.

The citizens of Glasgow were not blind to Chalmers' faults, but they mourned his departure and the Provost and Town Council held a public dinner in his honour. As remarked on a similar occasion marking the centenary of his arrival, Chalmers had 'warmed Glasgow'.[193]

Among the fruits of his evangelistic efforts were the conversion of people from many walks of life; the army, business, and university, from the working classes as well as the upper.[194] Glasgow was going through a change in its social habits which it shared with wider British society. In a few decades manners had altered. It was no longer the case that 'he who did not send his guest from his house in a state of intoxication was considered unworthy of genteel society', and 'swearing in good society' became 'seldom or ever heard'.[195] The upper and middle classes discovered a social conscience and renewed religious interest. These things Chalmers spoke to, encouraged and built upon, and it is in this context that Hanna's assessment of the more general effect of Chalmers' ministry in Glasgow is probably correct:

> When Dr Chalmers came to Glasgow, by the great body of the upper classes of society, evangelical doctrines were nauseated and despised; when he left it, even by those who did not bow to their influence, these doctrines were acknowledged to be indeed the very doctrines of the Bible.

Dell, 'Social and economic theories and pastoral concerns of a Victorian archbishop', *Journal of Ecclesiastical History*, 16, 1965, 196-208). Dell analyses Sumner's *Treatise on the records of creation*, which Chalmers read and noted (Journal, 6, 14, November, 1, 18, December, 1827). See also Rack, *Domestic visitation*, 1973, 364.

[192] T. R. Malthus to T. C., 23 August 1821, NCL CHA 4.18.21. See also T. C. to T. R. Malthus, 12 December 1821, NLS 3112 f.228 and T. R. Malthus to T. C., 21 July 1822, NCL CHA 4.21.51.

[193] Watt, *Chalmers*, 1943, 68.

[194] *Memoirs*, 2, 482f.

[195] Cleland, *Statistical tables*, 1823, 202.

Chalmers rescued Evangelicalism from 'drivelling sanctimoniousness' and 'sour-minded asceticism',[196] while filling his church and benefiting the Town Council by its seat rents. That much was not lost on them, whatever the other problems he had given them. It was now clearly in their interest to use their patronage to appoint younger Evangelicals who seemed to have the ear of their generation more than the Moderates, or indeed the Evangelicals, of an earlier era.

There were a good many who felt that leaving Glasgow for a chair of moral philosophy at St Andrews was a mistake if not an escape and Chalmers had to explain how it could be a sphere of Christian usefulness. He had hesitated about Glasgow in the first place and it is difficult not to think that having tried and failed to make it like Kilmany the solution was to go back to Fife. His achievement at St John's was impressive but controversial. His desire for a university chair may have been sanctified, but it was still there. For a few days in July 1817 he actively sought a chair of divinity in Edinburgh on the strength of a rumour that the professor, if not actually dead, was at least dangerously ill.[197] It had to be given up rather rapidly when the report proved false, but the incident revived old ambitions.[198] Now they were to be fulfilled.

In his old university he was not long in founding a Sunday school and getting involved in missionary societies, showing he had not lost his evangelistic zeal. He embarked on his courses with contagious enthusiasm. Yet still he was not where he really belonged. He was popular with his students but quickly alienated and isolated from his colleagues, most of whom were Moderates of the old school. After five years many were relieved to have him installed as Professor of Divinity at Edinburgh University in 1828. His time at St Andrews was important for many things, but its primary significance for our purposes lies in his involvement in an almost forgotten part of the rise of the missionary movement in Scotland.

---

196   *Memoirs*, 2, 482f.
197   T. C. to W. Wilberforce, 9 July 1817, PLDU.
198   T. C. to W. Wilberforce, 14 July 1817, PLDU.

Chapter 8

'Upholding the Christianity of our land'[1]
Chalmers in Edinburgh, 1828-1847

The debates which polarized Scotland during the years leading to May 1843 and the Disruption of the Church of Scotland are well known[2] and have been the subject of recent research.[3] This section will trace the key issues in relation to Chalmers' vision for the mission of the Church, something which stayed remarkably consistent through the diverse and often seemingly contradictory activities of the last decades of his life.

His aim was the Christianization of Scotland and he took as means to this end whatever instrument happened to be at hand – whether the material benefits of establishment, freedom from state connection, or the hope that evangelical churches could be persuaded to co-ordinate their efforts for pastoral work and evangelism. As well as the continuities of Chalmers' ideas, including his justification of established churches, particular attention will be given to the aims he held for the church extension movement, his reasons for supporting the Disruption, and his interest in Christian union and the Evangelical Alliance.

---

[1] *Memoirs*, 3, 109.

[2] Most works from the period are partisan. J. Bryce, *Ten years of the Church of Scotland*, 1850. R. Buchanan, *The ten years' conflict*, 1849. A. Turner, *The Scottish secession of 1843*, 1859. By contrast the *Journal of Henry Cockburn*, 1874, is more balanced. See also H. Watt, *Thomas Chalmers and the Disruption*, 1943, 96-314, and A. L. Drummond and J. Bulloch, *The Scottish Church, 1688-1843*, 1973, 220-65.

[3] Notably I.F. Maciver, *The General Assembly of the Church, the State and Society in Scotland: some aspects of their relationships, 1815-1843*, University of Edinburgh M Litt. thesis, 1976, but see also D. Chambers, *Mission and party in the Church of Scotland*, 1810-1843, University of Cambridge PhD thesis, 1971, and G.I.T. Machin, *Politics and the churches in Great Britain, 1832-1868*, 1977, 112-47.

An instrument for Christian good

In Chalmers' eyes, the primary justification of a religious establishment was its potential for the evangelistic mission of the church. In 1811 he could not see how else it was possible to ensure that 'through every district of the land there is a church to which the people may repair',[4] and this remained central to his thinking. It was widely shared, even by many Seceders who at that time still believed the support of the national church was a public responsibility.[5]

In contrast to England, Dissenters in Scotland suffered no 'grievances respecting baptism, marriage, burial and university degrees',[6] but there were signs that the question of dis-establishment might not remain dormant. The 'New Light' controversy among Seceders around the turn of the century indicated the possibility of change, and sensitivity to tangible complaint was indicated by opposition to the proposed Glasgow church-building tax in 1813.

In 1818 James Haldane[7] (1768-1851) criticized Chalmers' call for 20 more churches in Glasgow because they would be connected with the Church of Scotland and Jesus never intended national churches.[8] Haldane, one of the founders of Independency in Scotland, was by this time a Baptist and believed that, whatever people's dreams of 'creating a supply for religious instruction',[9] the necessity of supporting a particular government inevitably corrupted an established church's life and doctrine.

At that time the *Edinburgh Christian Instructor* declined to be drawn into the debate and hoped Chalmers would show restraint.[10] He was preoccupied with St John's and the nearest thing to a reply to Haldane was a few pages in the *Christian and civic economy* for June 1820.[11] Given the growth of other churches and the political reforms being talked about, restraint on both sides could not last and the issue began to find an audience.

Controversy would have been stimulated sooner if Scotland's cities had earlier received government money for church-building as in England, and it was perhaps sensing this that in 1821 the Moderate leader, John Inglis, published *The importance of religious establishments*.[12] Government grants

---

4   *Edinburgh Christian Instructor*, May 1811, 316.

5   Drummond and Bulloch, *The Scottish Church*, 1973, 232.

6   Machin, *Politics and the churches*, 1977, 26.

7   A. Haldane, *The lives of Robert Haldane of Airthrey and of his brother James Alexander Haldane*, 1855.

8   *Two letters to the Rev Dr Chalmers on his proposal for increasing the number of churches in Glasgow, by an observer*, 1818. An enlarged 1820 edition was not anonymous.

9   Ibid., 1818, 22.

10   *Edinburgh Christian Instructor*, February 1819, 119-22.

11   *Works*, 14, 105-8.

12   *Fasti*, 1, 42.

for Scotland were delayed and restricted to 40 churches in the Highlands, where there were no Protestant Dissenters to offend and opposition from heritors for reasons financial or religious was precluded by endowment of the stipends.

Late in 1827 Chalmers brought out a small work *On the use and abuse of literary and ecclesiastical establishments*.[13] Again his apologetic was pragmatic. Established churches were necessary

> to secure over the whole length and breadth of the land, such a juxtaposition between the gospel and every human creature, as will never be accomplished in any other way.[14]

As his evidence before the Scottish Universities Commission in August of that same year indicated, this support was conditional.

> I have no veneration for the Church of Scotland merely *quasi* an establishment, but I have the utmost veneration for it *quasi* an instrument of Christian good: and I do think that with the means and resources of an establishment, she can do more, and does more, for the religious interests of Scotland, than is done by the activity of all the Dissenters put together. I think it a high object to uphold the Church of Scotland, but only because of its subserviency to the still higher object of upholding the Christianity of our land.[15]

In 1820 the United Secession Church was formed out of the two largest groups of Seceders and evidence was soon forthcoming that their attitude to established churches was shifting. One of their ministers, J. Ballantyne of Stonehaven, in 1824 published a *Comparison of established and dissenting churches*,[16] and in 1829 Andrew Marshall of Kirkintilloch created a stir with *Ecclesiastical establishments considered*.[17] Marshall argued that the logical consequence of Roman Catholic emancipation was to establish Catholicism as the religion of Ireland. The only answer was to see all

---

13   *Works*, 17, 21-186. It did not go beyond a first edition, but was reviewed in the *British Critic*, 10, 1831, 301-29; *Christian Observer*, 1828, 642-9; *Quarterly Review*, 49, 1833, 198-211, and the *Edinburgh Christian Instructor*, November 1832, 775-95. Much of it had been tried out on Chalmers' political economy class at St Andrews. Journal 3 January, 19 March, 1827.

14   *Works*, 17, 117.

15   Ibid.

16   A. B. Montgomery, *The Voluntary controversy in the Church of Scotland 1829-1843*, University of Edinburgh PhD thesis, 1953, 32.

17   M'Kerrow, *Secession Church*, 1841, 725-9.

established churches for what they were: 'unscriptural, unjust, impolitic, secularizing in their tendency, inefficient and unnecessary'.[18]

The challenge was very real and strongly felt. Chalmers had also been thinking about emancipation and establishment, but believed, contrary to Marshall and also to some opponents of emancipation, that it was not inconsistent to support both.[19] At a charity sermon in May 1829 he gave a temperate reply,[20] repeated in 1830 in the improbable setting of the opening service for a Dissenting chapel near Bristol,[21] and again in London in 1833 when Bishop Blomfield persuaded him to publish it.[22] This was elaborated rather than developed in 1838 when he delivered a series of lectures[23] to enthralled if not always convinced[24] crowds of nobility and bishops in London.[25] The 1829 sermon can be taken as a reliable guide to his thinking for the decade following at least.

Chalmers rejected any idea of the relationship between church and state being modelled on the Old Testament. Church policy had to be determined by what was appropriate in a given set of circumstances. What was not positively forbidden by Scripture could be permissible. Establishments were not prescribed by the Bible, but neither were they prohibited, and expediency was not necessarily a bad principle of Christian behaviour. Corruption was no more intrinsic to church establishments than was its absence guaranteed by voluntary principles. Religion had to be 'aggressively' taken to people; it was not a commodity such as food or housing which could be left to supply and demand. Under Constantine establishment enabled missionary work begun on a voluntary basis to permeate the countryside. Although the church's aim[26] was 'preparation of citizens for heaven',[27] its effect on society gave reason for state support:

---

[18]   Ibid., 725.

[19]   Presbytery of Edinburgh, 1 April 1829, the Catholic claims. Newspaper cuttings 1816-1831, Charles Watson papers, NCL.

[20]   On religious establishments: a sermon preached in St George's Church, Edinburgh, before the Society for the Daughters of the Clergy, in May 1829, *Works*, 11, 437-62. It was not published before 1833.

[21]   *Memoirs*, 3, 266-8.

[22]   *Memoirs*, 3, 393. *Church establishments defended*, 1833. It reached four editions that year and eight by 1837. Not surprisingly it was never published in America.

[23]   *Lectures on the establishment and extension of national churches; delivered in London from April twenty-fifth to May twelfth, 1838*, 1838. *Works*, 17, 187-356.

[24]   Notably W. E. Gladstone, who was driven to reply with *The State in its relations with the Church*. J. Brooke and M. Sorenson, eds, *The Prime Minister's papers: W. E. Gladstone, I:Autobiographica*, 1971, 42f., 56-8.

[25]   *Memoirs*, 4, 36-46.

[26]   G. Kitson Clark considers that Chalmers 'fell short of Arnold's conception that a Christian establishment should serve a social purpose, for Chalmers

> In virtue of the blessings which Christianity scatters on its way do the princes of this world find that these are the best citizens of earth – and that the cheap defence of nations, the best safeguard of their prosperity and power, is a universal Christian education.[28]
>
> For the sake of an abundant gospel dispensation we are upheld in things temporal by the State. For the sake of a pure gospel dispensation we are left in things spiritual to ourselves.[29]
>
> There is not one thing which the state can do to our independent and indestructible Church, but strip her of her temporalities.[30]

Other reaction to Marshall was sharper. The Apocrypha controversy[31] had brought fresh stridency to religious debate, and it was no accident that Andrew Thomson lost little time escalating the conflict. A pamphlet war between himself and Marshall spread,[32] and by the early 1830s most Dissenters in Scotland were united in the view that the only valid form of church organization was voluntary association – hence their designation as 'Voluntaries'. In 1832 Voluntary church associations were formed in Edinburgh and Glasgow and the *Voluntary Church Magazine* launched, soon followed by other associations around Scotland.[33]

Given the passing of the Reform Bills, the democratic expectations aroused if not altogether satisfied, and the need for something to be done about the scandal of a Protestant establishment in Roman Catholic Ireland, the challenge to the very idea of establishment was serious. Evangelical and Moderate in the Church of Scotland joined in organizations of self-defence and literary warfare. In 1831 the *Presbyterian Review* began publication, and in 1833 the *Church of Scotland Magazine*. The Glasgow Society for Promoting the Interests of the Church of Scotland was formed in the same year. John Inglis brought out *A vindication of ecclesiastical*

---

clearly believed that the only purpose of a Christian establishment should be to teach the Christian religion'. *Churchmen and the condition of England,* 1973, p. 79. While this was the church's primary purpose for Chalmers, it was a long way from being its only function.

[27] *Works,* 11, 447.

[28] Ibid.

[29] *Works,* 11, 451.

[30] *Works,* 11, 460.

[31] This was one debate Chalmers took no part in. For details see H. F. Henderson, *The religious controversies of Scotland,* 1905, 95-110. G. A. F. Knight, *The history of the National Bible Society of Scotland,* typescript, 54-8, NBSS archives. W. Canton, *A history of the British and Foreign Bible Society,* 1, 1904, 346-8. W. J. Roxborogh, 'Apocrypha Controversy', in N. M. de S. Cameron, ed., *Dictionary of Scottish Church History and Theology,* 1993.

[32] J. M'Kerrow, *Secession Church,* 1841, 726-8.

[33] Ibid., 729-39.

establishments[34] and in 1836 Edinburgh Moderates began the *Church Review*. In 1834 the Edinburgh Young Men's Church Association held public lectures in competition with an impressive list of speakers organized by the Edinburgh Young Men's Voluntary Association. The *Scotsman*, *Scottish Guardian*, and *Edinburgh Advertiser* all played active and partisan roles.

Moderates and Evangelicals had different reasons for resisting the Voluntary challenge, but both felt threatened. Much of the creative energy as well as financial support flowing into the schemes of the Church of Scotland during the 1830s had roots in a desire to disprove the allegations of the Voluntaries. The speed with which Evangelicals acted to reform the church owed a lot to the taunts of those who queried its independence and said Chalmers was all that kept it from collapse.[35]

The Voluntary debate did not lack intensity, but it needed a substantive issue. That was soon supplied by a revolt in paying the Edinburgh Annuity tax.[36] To the extent that it could be collected it helped pay the stipends of the Church of Scotland city ministers. In 1833 there were 846 prosecutions for non-payment and some imprisonments, and the reformed town council which came into office at the end of the year was committed to finding a better arrangement. Ministers were anxious to be spared suing people of other denominations to pay themselves. Less wisely they allowed their case to be handled by Chalmers acting on behalf of Presbytery.

While he had some understanding of the injustice of the system he was intransigent when it came to accepting a reduction either in the number of ministers or the stipends paid them.[37] Both were things he had fought to increase and his fierce commitment to mission through the established church as the only institution capable of doing the job made him blind to the viewpoints of those who had a different political and religious vision. His judgement was not helped by unhappy experiences with the Edinburgh Town Council over his appointment as Professor of Divinity and his antipathy towards Whigs was heightened by government attitudes towards the Church of Ireland.

Chalmers would have done well to have heeded advice that the Church's case was weak and given that many churches had more than one minister little would be lost by a reduction in clergy in return for a politically less sensitive means of funding stipends.[38] Instead he construed the issue as a

---

34   *Fasti*, 1, 42.

35   S.H. Cox, *Interviews: memorable and useful: from diary and memory reproduced*, 1853, 49.

36   Maciver, *General Assembly of the Church*, 178-85. Machin, *Politics and the churches*, 114f. *Memoirs*, 3, 424-33. *Works*, 18, 157-273.

37   (T. Chalmers), *Replies to queries regarding the city churches, proposed by the committee of the Town Council to the Presbytery of Edinburgh*, 1834.

38   Maciver, *General Assembly of the Church*, 180ff.

matter of principle – which of course it was, but it was questionable whose principles were better – and was convinced the Town Council's proposals would prepare the way

> for the entire subversion of our Church, in a manner similar to that in which the appropriation of an alleged ecclesiastical surplus in Ireland prepares the way for the destruction of the Protestant establishment there.[39]

A battle of statistics developed, and Chalmers' remarks about 'bungling and hostile administrators'[40] on the Town Council were hardly helpful.[41] Walking home after reporting to the Edinburgh Presbytery in January 1834 he suffered a mild stroke.[42] When he began to recover it was to devote his energies towards more positive schemes.

'A sufficiently thick-set establishment'

Since 1828 the efforts of the Church of Scotland to obtain government grants for church building in cities and large towns had proved fruitless. The limited possibilities for enlarging churches by assessments of heritors of landward parishes had been blocked by a Court decision,[43] and the need to obtain the consent of three quarters of the owners of landed property of a parish before a new church could be built rendered that method of funding impotent.

The Moderate leadership of the Church Accommodation Committee[44] realized that a different approach was required, and noting examples of lay

---

[39]   T. C. to R. Peel, 22 April 1835, BL 40420 f. 49.

[40]   *Memoirs*, 3, 469.

[41]   During 1834 Chalmers published two lengthy pamphlets, *On the evils which the Established Church in Edinburgh has already suffered, and suffers still, in virtue of the seat-letting being in the hands of the magistrates; with remarks on the unjust and injurious tendency of a late document, published by their authority, on the subject of the unlet sittings* (*Works*, 18, 157-234), and *Re-assertion of the evils of the Edinburgh system of seat-letting; with new proofs adapted to recent objections. Works* 18, 235-74.

[42]   *Memoirs*, 3, 433-5.

[43]   Against the background of cases where the Court of Session had to decide whether a church should be rebuilt because it could not hold two-thirds of the examinable persons (those over twelve). By 1831 the Neilston case had determined that heritors were not obliged to enlarge a church unless it was first ruinous.

[44]   In 1835 Chalmers changed the name to Church Extension Committee to make it clear that it was not just about buildings and seats, but the whole apparatus of the Church.

initiative for church building in Glasgow and Aberdeen,[45] recommended to the 1834 General Assembly that Chalmers be appointed Convener of the committee to lead a fresh campaign, not just to the government, but to the people.[46]

Nothing could have been more congenial, and he immediately set to work with energy and skill if not always tact. At their first meeting he told the committee they had a task in which they were to persevere, even if it took a whole generation, till they had made the Church of Scotland 'a sufficiently thick-set establishment' and there was not a poor family in the country

> who might not, if they will, have entry and accommodation in a place of worship and religious instruction, with such a share in the personal attentions of the clergyman as to claim him for an acquaintance and a friend.[47]

The highest ground, as explained in the first of many circulars to ministers, was the needs of the multitude who 'with an eternity wholly unprovided for, live in irreligion and die in apathy or despair'.[48] However this was not the only ground, nor the one most likely to stimulate support. The challenge of Voluntaries required a demonstration that there was life in the Church of Scotland and that the Voluntary system was incapable of taking the gospel to all the people.

The methods of fundraising he had used in Kilmany and St John's were now applied to church extension. At the same time the Voluntary threat was a goldmine which could not be resisted. 'Every man who you succeed in gaining as a penny a week contributor, you will succeed in confirming as a friend to the Church of Scotland.'[49] The number of divinity students passing through his hands meant that there were more looking for positions than there were charges available. The state of society, as always, was something to be considered.

> Even to the mere politician and worldly philanthropist we can address the argument that a depraved commonalty is the teeming source of all moral and political disorder.[50]

---

[45] D. Chambers, 'The Church of Scotland's parochial extension scheme and the Scottish Disruption', *Journal of Church and State*, 16, 1974, 271-5.

[46] T. Chalmers, *Report of the committee of the General Assembly of the Church of Scotland on church extension, 28th May, 1835*, 1835, 17-20.

[47] *Memoirs,* 3, 452.

[48] Ibid., 453.

[49] Ibid., 458.

[50] Ibid., 453.

These were arguments which had swayed people after the Napoleonic wars; how much they still spoke to the fears of the middle-classes was yet to be demonstrated. Many who might be impressed did not necessarily believe an established church was the best solution, at least not with their money. Other echoes of Glasgow and St John's appeared, including the financial difficulties of its chapel, although poor-relief was put to one side. His aim was to create Christian communities small enough for the traditional parochial system to function and where the seat-rents would be low enough for all to afford them.[51] St John's also made a contribution through the Glasgow Church Building Society founded by William Collins with a call for 20 more churches in Glasgow. This owed not a little to Chalmers' similar appeal 15 years earlier and Collins' experience during those halcyon days.

In many respects Chalmers was ideally suited to lead what was not just a committee, but a movement. His popularity as a preacher was undiminished, and he had standing in the community as in the church. Following the death of Andrew Thomson in 1831, the unofficial mantle of Evangelical party leadership had fallen to him, confirmed by his election as Moderator of the 1832 Assembly. He had contacts with members of parliament and administrative abilities. He knew what he wanted and how he was going to go about it. He had conducted a remarkable if debated experiment in parish organization and written extensively on the subject. His mathematical abilities served him well, as did a variety of fund-raising experiences through the Kilmany Bible Association, the St John's Association for Religious Purposes, the St Andrews Missionary Society and the building of the chapel and schools at St John's.

There were other elements Chalmers brought to the task which could prove a liability. Despite popularity and admiration he was a controversial figure in an age of controversy. The Annuity-tax debate in Edinburgh showed a side of his personality which came to the fore if he felt crossed. In the position of power and influence he now held it was important that his judgement rise above the politics and personalities of the day. Given his rural and Tory inclinations and the urban and Whig leanings of most other Evangelicals, not to mention the government, this was not easy. It was asking him to be different from who he was in a way of which he was not consistently capable. That he was in tune with a good deal of the spirit of the age explains some of his success; that in other respects he was out of kilter with the tide of history indicates the tensions he experienced. A less passionate personality would not have motivated and achieved as he did, but there were hazards and some of them were in due course realized.

Consistent with the 'locality principle' was his belief that it was more important to stimulate local effort and initiative than to amass centrally

---

[51]   Ibid., 466.

controlled funds,[52] and this was of immense importance in generating widespread involvement. Working with large committees in Edinburgh and Glasgow and through a network of personal correspondents, he showed all his old ability to enthuse others by providing a clearly articulated purpose, achievable goals, a place in an overall team effort, and copious praise and encouragement.

Pressure for practical means of extending the Church of Scotland had been building up for some time, and Chalmers was able to bring together this frustrated demand for action with a sense of competition with the Voluntaries. Local interest in funding a new church could also arise out of dislike for an existing or new minister in the parish.[53] In the past a source of new churches for the Secession, this now operated to extend the Church of Scotland.

From 1838 Chalmers took his campaign round Scotland and spoke at public meetings, presbyteries, and fund-raising dinners all over the country. By that year nearly £200,000 had been raised and 187 churches were built, planned or under construction. When he retired from the convenership in 1841, the totals came to over £300,000 and 222 churches.[54] Nothing should detract from the magnitude of this result and the credit it devolved on Chalmers. The circumstances of the times may have been favourable, but no one else had the unusual set of abilities he employed in exploiting them.

However, while his efforts were successful in Scotland, it was different with regard to Westminster. The old Church Accommodation Committee had given up trying to get the government to pay for churches, but Chalmers' experience with the St John's chapel convinced him that unless seat rents were subsidized the poor would still not go to church and he looked to the government for £100 towards the stipend of each minister. It was a small amount relative to other sums, but for opponents and for Chalmers it was a matter of principle. He stuck to his demand and devoted considerable effort to campaigns of lobbying and petitions.

The first deputation went to London in July 1834 while Chalmers was convalescing from his stroke.[55] He advised them to make their case in terms of providing 'a cheap Christian education for the common people'.[56] A memorial[57] was presented to the government and the reception was not unfavourable.[58] However the proposal suffered one of the hazards to which

---

[52] T. C. to J. Thomson, 24 September 1834, NLS 10997. f.73. *Memoirs, 3*, 457.

[53] As in Inverness. J. Fraser to T. C., 8 July 1836, NCL CHA 4.

[54] *Memoirs*, 4, 87.

[55] *Memoirs*, 3, 458.

[56] T. C. to C. Ferguson, 2 July 1834, *Memoirs*, 3, 459.

[57] T. Chalmers, *Report of the Committee of the General Assembly of the Church of Scotland on Church Extension, 28 May 1835*, 1835, 22-5.

[58] *Memoirs*, 3, 461f.

Scottish measures are prone. Before anything could be done, parliament was prorogued at the end of August. In December the Whig administration was replaced by the Conservative government of Sir Robert Peel.

Chalmers found consolation in the prospect of dealing with Tories rather than Whigs and sought advice about seeing Peel and the value of petitions.[59] He received assurances that the Church of Scotland had 'few more attached friends' than Peel, and that the committee's proposals had been addressed to one 'favourably disposed to the entertainment of them and who will take them into very early consideration'.[60] This suggested more than it promised, but Chalmers wrote to Gladstone that 'nothing could be more satisfactory than Sir Robert Peel's communication'.[61] Hopes were further raised when the speech from the throne also suggested something would be done.[62]

Chalmers lobbied both houses of parliament,[63] and corresponded about the proposed bill[64] with the Lord Advocate, Sir William Rae. He expected some outcry from Dissenters, but hoped it would be short-lived and that the government would brave the storm in the cause of principle. Since the theology of many Voluntaries was indistinguishable from that of the Church of Scotland, and 'the evil of...present dissensions' was great, they 'should at length get quit of it by absorption'.[65]

This was not realistic. The Tories were not in a strong position and Chalmers underestimated Voluntary feeling which soon showed a capacity for petitioning and lobbying at least equal to his own. He read his own hopefulness into every cautious word from the government, but before its resolve could be tested, in April 1835 Melbourne and the Whigs returned to power.[66]

Publicity about church extension and the plan for government endowment served to bring the Voluntary controversy to a new height.[67] The amount involved financially was a fraction of what Voluntaries feared, but there was a point of principle, and supporters of church extension, including Chalmers, were not innocent of calculating the effects on Dissenting churches. Rae wrote that the Voluntaries believed that 'affording

---

[59]   T. C. to Sir George Clark of Penicuik, 17 December 1834, SRO/GRH GD 18.411.

[60]   R. Peel to T. C., 24 January 1835, BL 40411 f.200.

[61]   T. C. to W. E. Gladstone, 28 February 1835, BL 44354 f. 153.

[62]   *Memoirs*, 3, 462f.

[63]   T. C. to W. E. Gladstone, 10, 14, 16, 21 February 1835, BL 44354 ff. 172-7.

[64]   W. Rae to T. C., 29 January 1835, *Memoirs*, 3, 531-3. Reply, 31 January 1835, *Memoirs*, 3, 533-7.

[65]   *Memoirs*, 3, 534.

[66]   T. C. to R. Peel, 22 April 1835, BL 40420 f. 49.

[67]   *Memoirs*, 3, 463-9.

church accommodation at a cheap rate will cut up their congregations most materially', making clear that this was 'one of the very objects' held in view.[68]

With the return of the Whigs, Voluntary agitation carried even more political weight. Faced with a legacy of intentions from his previous administration and the opinions of Scottish supporters which could not be ignored, Melbourne took refuge in a commission of enquiry. When it was said that the commission was packed with Voluntaries,[69] Chalmers and others felt tricked, but he advocated co-operation believing it could not fail to lend authority to his demands.[70] The commissioners turned out to be impeccable in their impartiality, but more than impartiality was needed to solve the underlying issues.

Despite being reconciled to the royal commission, Chalmers had 'ceased to look for truth or justice or consistency' at the hands of Whigs,[71] and unwisely gave vent to these feelings. He had some ground for complaint but so did they, and he did not appreciate the difficulties of a government supported by a fragile coalition of Liberals, Radicals and Dissenters.

Whig churchmen in Scotland were also in an uneasy position, and Chalmers' use of all his influence in an uncalled-for but successful effort to prevent John Lee[72] (1779-1859) from being Moderator in 1836 had political overtones, quite apart from his complaint that Lee did not believe in territorial parishes and doubted the value of parish visitation.[73] His relationship with Whigs was further worsened when, in the Argyllshire election of 1836, he allowed the Conservative candidate to make use of a statement that if the government carried out 'their proposed act of violence against the Episcopal Protestant Establishment of Ireland', then 'the Presbyterian Establishment of Scotland' was 'not safe in their hands'.[74] He denied he was heading up a 'Tory church building scheme' but it cannot be wondered the accusation was made. A letter of a lay supporter to one of Chalmers' old heritors in Kilmany indicates careless speech as well as mixed motives:

---

[68] W. Rae to R. Peel, July 1836, BL 40339 f. 366. Quoted by Machin, *Politics and the churches,* 1977, 116.

[69] Maciver, *General Assembly of the Church,* 1976, 205.

[70] *Memoirs,* 3, 470–87.

[71] T. C. to J. Hope, BL 43202 f. 128.

[72] *Fasti,* 1, 73.

[73] Maciver, *General Assembly of the Church,* 1976, 205, 212-16. D. Shaw, 'The moderatorship controversy in 1836 and 1837', *Records of the Scottish Church History Society,* 1970, 115-29. *Established Church of Scotland Moderatorship controversy* (bound volume of cuttings and pamphlets), NCL Kc/6. T. C. to W. E. Gladstone, 25 July 1836, BL 44355 f. 97. Lee papers, NLS. 3441-2.

[74] T. C. to A. Campbell of Monzie, 22 July 1836, *Memoirs,* 4, 25.

Apart from the solemn religious obligation to send the gospel to our poor countrymen, its political importance claims attention. This vast and increasing mass of deserted and irreligious people, give almost all the inhabitants of our jails, and will give, if allowed to increase, a fearful power to the destructives and revolutionists. Dr Chalmers says that the poor people of the new Dean Church are actually turned Conservatives.[75]

Although evidence of the need for churches was collected by the commissioners, the Whig government was not to be moved and its proposals were feeble enough to ensure their rejection by the Church.[76] By 1840 church endowment was politically dead and the solidarity of Voluntaries as Whig voters ensured that nothing more was achieved than damage to the standing of the Church of Scotland. Chalmers was sorely tried by the Whigs, but his open criticism of them coupled with support for the Tories whom he courted, hardly helped. Given the political realities, the endowment campaign was certain to fail. Its main achievement had been to embitter Church relationships with Dissenters and with the government in Westminster. When still more fundamental issues arose, any good will which might have helped the Church had evaporated.

Of at least equal significance was a result of Chalmers' insistence on local organization. The machinery he created was adaptable for fighting new issues such as the 'non-intrusion' of ministers and spiritual independence, to say nothing of the creation of another church.[77]

Disruption

The events which led to 451 ministers of the Church of Scotland (just over 37%)[78] resigning their connection with the State and forming the Free Church of Scotland are well documented and the story does not need much re-telling. Given Chalmers' role it is important to consider how it was that the arch-defender of establishments found himself the most prominent figure in the largest voluntary[79] church in Scotland.

The forces which contributed to the Disruption were many-sided, but accounts which detail the history of the exercise of patronage in the Church of Scotland do not mistake one of the central issues. Abolished by the

---

[75]   D. Maitland Makgill of Rankeillor to H. Wedderburn, 31 October 1836, NRA(S) 783.

[76]   *Memoirs*, 4, 21-3.

[77]   Maciver, *General Assembly of the Church*, 1976, 230-34.

[78]   A. Turner, *The Scottish secession of 1843*, 1859, 359.

[79]   That is voluntary in its financing. The Free Church rejected the 'voluntary principle' that there ought not to be established churches, but necessity forced it to live by voluntary practice.

Revolution Settlement and restored in 1712, patronage gained the acceptance of the Moderate party in the church by the middle of the 18th century, and within another 50 years Evangelicals were almost as acquiescent.[80]

In the first decades of the 19th century a generation grew up in an era when democratic ideas had been canvassed and the end of Moderate domination could be foreseen. Many Evangelicals were no longer prepared to accept patronage, and during the years leading to the Reform Bill of 1832 they were taunted by Voluntaries about lack of independence from patrons with no necessary connection with the churches whose appointments they controlled.

Those like Chalmers who were more conservative politically, were less concerned and noted that in the cities the existing system favoured Evangelical appointments. However, given his leadership among the Evangelicals, Chalmers could not ignore demands for reform. His Whig predecessor Andrew Thomson had insisted that patronage be abolished.

In the 1833 General Assembly Chalmers proposed a compromise motion for the Evangelical factions.[81] It was defeated by the Moderates, but the following year the Evangelicals had a majority, and what became known as the 'Veto Act' was passed. By giving congregations the right to oppose a particular nominee, it enabled those such as Chalmers to support it because patronage was preserved. To others it was but a first step in its abolition.[82]

After a century of Moderate domination, the Evangelicals used their new power to give seats in courts of the Church to ministers of chapels-of-ease. It was an injustice to be remedied but these ministers were mostly of their own party and it served to increase their majority. As with the Veto Act they ignored cautions that as an established church the Church of Scotland was unwise to make unilateral changes where secular interests were involved.

There was, however, considered legal opinion to support the view that the Church was not exceeding its jurisdiction, and the government gave tacit approval by exercising its patronage in terms of the Veto Act. In general the Act worked satisfactorily with other patrons as well, but the exceptions, although few, had far-reaching consequences as cases started to come through the legal courts.

In 1838 the Court of Session decided that the Presbytery of Auchterarder had acted illegally by applying the Veto Act,[83] and the General

---

[80] By 1800 disputed settlements were a trickle. J. Wilson, *Index to the Acts and Proceedings of the General Assembly of the Church of Scotland*, 1871, 238-43.

[81] R. Burns to T. C., 29 September 1842, NCL CHA 4.

[82] Ibid., D. J. Withrington, 'Non-church-going, c. 1750–c. 1850: a preliminary study', *Records of the Scottish Church History Society*, 17(2), 1970, 108.

[83] *Memoirs*, 4, 91-5.

Assembly appealed to the House of Lords. Just before the following Assembly, the Lords upheld the Court of Session in terms which regarded the Church entirely as a creature of statute with no independent authority.[84]

Chalmers had expected the decision but not the terms in which it was delivered. He had intended to repeal the Veto Act, but now felt the integrity of the Church was challenged in such a way that to do so would be to concede the Church's loss of spiritual independence. In a three-hour speech to the 1839 Assembly he reaffirmed the principle of 'non-intrusion', that 'no minister shall be intruded into any parish contrary to the will of the congregation', and called for a committee to negotiate with the government to resolve the conflict of jurisdictions.[85] Despite his low standing in the eyes of the Whigs, inevitably Chalmers was appointed convener.

The difficulties of the Church were soon compounded by other decisions of the Court of Session. Almost immediately after the 1839 Assembly the Presbytery of Dunkeld was censured for disobeying an interdict prohibiting their carrying out an ordination and induction of the minister of Lethendy, despite a contrary instruction from the General Assembly Commission. In December the General Assembly Commission suspended seven members of the Presbytery of Strathbogie who in a similar predicament declared their intention of ignoring the instructions of the General Assembly in favour of those of the Court of Session. Further interdicts followed and Chalmers saw all his efforts for the revival and extension of the Church under a cloud. He wrote to Peel of his frustration:

> We were going on most prosperously recalling the Dissenters and reclaiming section after section [of] that outfield territory of irreligion and ignorance...till these proceedings of the Court of Session, which have ruined church extension and will if not redressed end in the severance of the Church of Scotland from the State.[86]

For a time it appeared as if the Whigs might be prepared to legislate to resolve the conflict. In July 1839 Chalmers and a deputation from the Non-intrusion Committee visited London. Although he did his best to keep a low profile, he did not escape being cut by Melbourne[87] who wrote, 'I think him a madman and all madmen are rogues.'[88] Still the deputation was

---

84   *Memoirs,* 4, 95f.
85   *Memoirs*, 4, 106. T. Chalmers, *Substance of a speech delivered in the General Assembly on Wednesday the twenty-second of May 1839, respecting the decision of the House of Lords on the case of Auchterarder*, 1839.
86   T. C. to R. Peel, 26 December 1839, BL 40427 f. 353.
87   *Memoirs*, 4, 121.
88   Melbourne to F. Maule, 28 October 1840, SRO/GRH G. D. 45/14/640. Quoted by Machin, *Politics and the churches*, 1977, 125.

listened to by both parties, and Chalmers reported to the August Commission of Assembly that he believed a bill was in the offing.

However uncertainty grew as time passed without the government making any moves besides occasional reassurance that something was being considered. Whigs had little reason to go out of their way to help the Church, and behind their procrastination lay the fact that they would suffer politically if they did so. One Whig churchman lamented that 'Dr Chalmers and his party' were 'hurting the interest of the Church' but warned the Lord Advocate that if the government interfered they would lose the support of Dissenters.[89] At the end of March 1840 Lord Aberdeen called the government's bluff and after extracting the confession that they no longer planned to act, announced his intention of bringing in a bill of his own.

Aberdeen had been corresponding with the Non-intrusion committee, but although Chalmers believed he had an agreement with Aberdeen over a form of legalization of the Veto, when he saw the actual bill he was disappointed and made sure the General Assembly gave it no support. The feeling was mutual and both Aberdeen,[90] and years later Chalmers' daughter,[91] published the correspondence between them in order to clear one or the other from responsibility for the misunderstanding.

Factors on both sides had contributed. Chalmers was more willing to compromise than his committee and frequently communicated privately with Aberdeen.[92] Things were not helped by the lack of precision in his language which was better suited to rhetoric than negotiation. On Aberdeen's part he was ill-served by the Dean of the Faculty of Advocates, John Hope, who had been responsible for encouraging many of the actions brought against the Church in the Court of Session. Of at least equal importance was Aberdeen's experience as a patron when his own nominee was objected to by a congregation.

Chalmers and the Non-intrusion committee wanted the simple existence of objections to be sufficient reason for a presbytery to reject a nominee, irrespective of the nature of the objections. To them this was the only way to prevent Moderate presbyteries regarding Evangelical objections as 'causeless prejudice'.[93]

---

[89] J. Veitch to Lord Rutherford, 28 March 1840, EUL Gen 1995/81.

[90] *The Earl of Aberdeen's correspondence with the Rev Dr Chalmers and the secretaries of the Non-intrusion committee: from 14 January to 27 May 1840*, 1840.

[91] *The correspondence between Dr Chalmers and the Earl of Aberdeen in the years 1839 and 1840*, 1893.

[92] J. Hope to Aberdeen, 12 February 1840, *Selections from the correspondence of the 4th Earl of Aberdeen relating to the Church of Scotland, 1838-1845*, privately published (copy in Aberdeen University Library), 37a.

[93] T. C. to R. Buchanan, 19 February 1840, NCL CHA 4.

When Aberdeen got to the root of the problem with his own nominee, he found their objections groundless.[94] The episode disturbed him and he related it to Chalmers, who must have been hopeful in thinking that Aberdeen would draft a bill which, had it been in operation, would have caused a person of his own choice[95] to be needlessly rejected.

With the failure of the Aberdeen bill the stage for the Disruption was set, although many thought the government would yet do something. Members of parliament found the threat of secession difficult to take seriously and seemed to think that if they ignored the problem it would go away. Chalmers retired from the Non-intrusion committee and took little part in further negotiations, letting it be known he had given up on both parties in parliament. Whigs had 'no great value for a church establishment at all' and Tories seemed to value it 'more as an engine of State than as an instrument of Christian usefulness'.[96] Although he rejected the suggestion that Evangelicals would be better out of the Church,[97] he also said that if Hope was correct in his doctrine of the Church, and such was the necessary consequence 'of an ecclesiastical establishment', then 'let our establishments perish'.[98]

Chalmers' earlier defence of establishments in the 1838 London lectures was now noted by others, but it disguised an allegiance which had always been conditional on established churches fulfilling their evangelistic function. In Scotland that was now in doubt. In May 1841 he wrote to Bishop Strachan of Toronto.

> National establishments of Christianity will and ought to be put down, not for a perpetuity, but till that period when the kingdoms of the earth shall become the kingdoms of our Lord and Saviour Jesus Christ.[99]

And in September he told George Sinclair:

> The truth is that I reserve myself for one emergency. Should there be a disruption of the Church I should feel it my duty to help forward the operations of a great home mission, which I have no doubt could take full possession of the country in a very few months.[100]

---

94   Aberdeen to J. Hope, 5, 12, 17 September, 14 October, 1839, *Selections from the correspondence of the 4th Earl of Aberdeen*, 18-23.

95   James Whyte (1809-1881) of Methlick, *Fasti*, 6, 200.

96   *Memoirs*, 4, 174.

97   *Memoirs*, 4, 137.

98   *Memoirs*, 4, 129.

99   T. C. to J. Strachan, 1 May 1841, *Correspondence*, 361.

100 T. C. to Sir George Sinclair, 27 September 1841, *Memoirs*, 4, 240.

Although further attempts at legislation were made, none stood as much chance as the Aberdeen bill might have had had it received the support of the Church. The legacy of the endowment campaign and pressure from Voluntaries, made it impossible for Whigs to aid the Church, and although Tories in opposition might have appeared more willing, in government any move approaching legalization of the Veto Act was too democratic. Church defiance of the Court of Session provided an excuse for inaction which was all too convenient.

Chalmers was now involved in events which cast the Church in the role of law-breaker. He had supported the suspension of the Strathbogie Seven for obeying the state rather than the Church and moved their deposition. Despite a personal interdict served on himself and others of the Evangelical party, he preached within the parishes of the deposed ministers. It was a choice between obedience to the Great Commission and the incompetent restriction of a secular court.

Despite his social conservatism, Chalmers allowed the possibility of civil disobedience.[101] If the apostles' defiance of the Jewish Sanhedrin was not precedent enough, there was ample in the history of the Scottish church. In his reading he made notes of ministers ejected after the Restoration,[102] and declared that like 'their fathers before them' the Evangelicals were prepared 'to renounce all for the integrity of the church'.[103]

It might have been wished that Chalmers and his colleagues could have found a way of demonstrating the Church's spiritual independence which gave less of a handle to their opponents. Perhaps with more imagination and a cooler determination it would have been possible to resist accepting the terms of the conflict dictated by the judges of the Court of Session and others, but it would have been difficult. The Church's actions, particularly in not repealing the Veto Act after it had been declared illegal, and in deposing the Strathbogie Seven, set the seal on the possibility of assistance from parliament. They also had important repercussions for relationships within the Church.

It was quickly forgotten that for much of the 1830s there had been reasonable harmony between Moderates and Evangelicals, helped by the need for a common front to further church extension and meet the challenge of the Voluntaries. It was also forgotten that within the Evangelical party there were divisions between Tories and Whigs.[104]

---

[101] In 1832 (advocating tolerance of lesser grievances) he told his students, 'I am far from saying that there is not a certain degree of tyranny in a State which would justify rebellion and that there is not a certain degree of corruption in a church which would justify schism.' *Posthumous Works*, 9, 430.

[102] Theological commonplace book III, 10-17, NCL CHA 6.

[103] *Memoirs*, 4, 195.

[104] Maciver, *General Assembly of the Church*, 1976, 38.

The issue of spiritual independence redrew these lines of co-operation and division. Evangelicals[105] were united among themselves and Moderates changed from co-operation to confrontation. More extreme Moderates such as John Hope and George Cook, who had influence in their party after the death of John Inglis, sought to re-establish links with the Conservative government. They were not of Inglis' character or vision, worked to undermine the remnants of Chalmers' endowment scheme,[106] and advised against legislation to resolve the conflict over non-intrusion, since it was bound to 'induce evils far more formidable than any justly chargeable upon the long-tried system now existing'.[107] They also wrote to advise Conservatives on 'the most likely means of creating disunion...in the ranks' of Evangelicals.[108]

In August 1840 Moderates overcame their deep-seated reluctance to popularize their views and formed a Constitutional Party, with the aim of raising funds for the Strathbogie Seven and encouraging others of similar principles.[109] After the Disruption the government passed Aberdeen's bill against their advice and selected its ecclesiastical advisers from less reactionary churchmen.[110]

Some of the division that some Moderates hoped to achieve came in the spring of 1842 with the formation of the Middle Party[111] or 'Forty' centred around Matthew Leishman[112] (1794-1874) of Govan, and William Muir[113] (1787-1869) of St Stephen's Edinburgh. Of Evangelical piety and Moderate churchmanship, in later years they would have been called high-church. They favoured Aberdeen's bill, and were ill at ease with the hardening pronouncements of Evangelical and Moderate as well as the Court of Session judges.

---

[105]   The motives were complex. R. Burns wrote to Chalmers, 'Anti-patronage men may *now* with perfect propriety withdraw their support from the Veto act inasmuch as its ineptitude to the end in view has been legally and beyond question established. While we thus resume our old ground, you, non-intrusionists, *must*, in your turn go along with us.' 29 September 1842. NCL CHA 4.

[106]   G. Cook to Lord Melville, 12 January 1839, NLS MS Acc 5106.

[107]   Declaration by eighty members of the Synods of Aberdeen and Moray, 26 February 1840, SRO/GRH GD 45.9.145.

[108]   J. Grant to Lord Melville, 25 June 1842, NLS MS Acc 5106.

[109]   George Cook, D. Macfarlan, *et al*, to Lord Melville, March 1841, NLS MS Acc 5106.

[110]   Maciver, *General Assembly of the Church*, 1976, 27f.

[111]   Ibid., 23-9, J. F. Leishman, *Matthew Leishman of Govan and the Middle party of 1843*, 1924.

[112]   *Fasti*, 3, 413.

[113]   *Fasti*, 1, 115f.

The existence of the Forty was seized on by the government as evidence that the Church would at last be compliant,[114] and Leishman went to some lengths to win Chalmers. Chalmers replied that he did not trust the promises of that government, 'I was once as sanguine as you are. But they have deceived me, and they will also deceive you.'[115]

It was no longer a matter of if there would be a disruption, but when and on what terms. The 1842 Assembly adopted a 'Claim of Rights' drafted in consultation with Chalmers,[116] and drew up a manifesto of the legal basis of the Church's complaints. He was determined that they would leave not just on the basis of harassment by the courts, but because parliament would not give redress.

In November 1842 Chalmers was the central figure in a Convocation of some 400 ministers who were prepared to leave the establishment if necessary, but issued another appeal to the government. In January 1843 the Court of Session declared the Chapels Act illegal. This final blow confirmed rather than provoked the action Chalmers and others were then taking for the creation of an independent church.

It is often said that Chalmers was the one person who could have stopped the schism in the Church which took place on the 18th of May 1843. If one individual could have altered the course of events, it was Chalmers, but the Disruption was the culmination of many events, and the product of the forces of ideas and principles operating on a large number of people. Behind them all lay the problem of maintaining an established church in what had become a pluralistic society – even if the pluralism in Scotland mostly meant Presbyterian churches of the same theological family. The adjustments for all, as the role of the national church in the life of the state was redefined, were necessarily complex. Chalmers felt he had to leave in order to make a point about spiritual independence and freedom for mission, but he still clung to the vision of what a no longer viable ideal of establishment could accomplish. The tension was not sufficient to halt the process for him any more than for others.

If Chalmers had had better relations with the Whigs, they may have been more helpful, but the political realities of their situation would have been unchanged. If he had supported the repeal of the Veto Act, that would have been one less reason for Tory inaction, but they had other reasons as well, and the same could be said for the suspension of the Strathbogie Seven. That Chalmers defied a court injunction by preaching in Strathbogie may have been a tactical error shared with others, but it was not the Evangelicals who dictated the terms in which obedience to the Court of Session would be interpreted.

---

[114] Sir James Graham to Lord Melville, 21 April 1842, NLS MS Acc 5106.

[115] Leishman, *Matthew Leishman,* 1924, 149.

[116] A. M. Dunlop to T. C., 12 May 1842, NCL CHA 4.

Chalmers did not join the Forty. However much one might sympathize with moderation in the face of competing extremes, they had not the experience of dealing with successive governments which had been Chalmers' lot. It should not be wondered at if he felt he had had his fingers burnt once too often.

Chalmers has been accused of being under the influence of more extreme men such as Candlish and Cunningham, and the point is given weight by the evidence of William Muir that he was 'open to mere impulses' and would 'change according to pressure'.[117] Under stress Chalmers could be emotional in his responses and was capable of being piquish as well as impetuous, but his major decisions were not ill-considered. One might wish Chalmers' statesmanship had been greater at a number of points but none of the principals in these events is conspicuous for having shown more.

Despite his position in the Evangelical party, he was not a party man. He was careful to set out his own reasons for courses of action and indicated how these differed from others in the party. An example is a speech in the 1841 Assembly supporting the abolition of patronage. He had never been against patronage in principle, but now saw it as laying the Church open to invasion by the courts, and the 'great originator of dissent'.[118]

If not responsible for causing, or at least not preventing, the Disruption, Chalmers' standing gave the Free Church cause a respectability it might otherwise have lacked, and he laboured for a more positive vision than mere protest. Spiritual independence expressed as vindicating the 'crown rights of the Redeemer' was far from unimportant, but to him the central issue was the mission of the church. He insisted that the Free Church aim at being a national church, undertake a 'great home mission' and 'take possession of the land'.[119]

Without his status, financial acumen and organizing ability, aided by the local societies built up through agitation over church extension and spiritual independence, the Free Church would never have had the base to undertake such a programme. That within a short time of its coming into existence it had around 800 congregations, supported probably the finest theological college in Britain, and took over the entire missionary staff of the pre-Disruption Church, is a tribute to Chalmers' abilities.

Christian union

If Chalmers led the Disruption out of frustration at the unwillingness of parliament to preserve the integrity and mission of the Church, equally he

---

[117] Leishman, *Matthew Leishman,* 1924, 117f.

[118] *Witness,* 27 May 1841.

[119] T. C. to J. Lennox, 31 December 1842, *Memoirs,* 4, 319.

saw freedom from the interdicts of the Court of Session as a chance to revive his vision for the evangelization of Scotland.

As a defender of establishments, the only way he could justify leaving the established church was by trying to ensure that despite fewer resources, the new church's sense of mission to all people and the means for carrying it out were not diminished. His fund-raising and organizational genius amazed supporters as much as it confounded critics, but the vision for a comprehensive home mission to Scotland was more difficult to communicate.

The problem took shape around details of the Sustentation Fund which Chalmers designed to guarantee a minimum stipend for every minister. Once the euphoria of the Disruption began to fade, it became easy for Free Church congregations to accept aid from others and relax their fund-raising efforts, or if they kept them up, effectively drive the working classes out of the church. Chalmers expressed his apprehensions in a pamphlet published in 1845 *On the economics of the Free Church of Scotland*, expanded the following year as an *Earnest appeal to the Free Church of Scotland on the subject of its economics.*[120]

Local studies made of Free Churches in Aberdeen[121] and Kirkcaldy[122] illustrate some of the effects of the need to raise large quantities of money. Critics taunted that in the Free Church it was no longer possible for the poor to hear the gospel 'without money and without price'. The point was polemical, but it was not wide of the mark. There is evidence that Free Church success in gaining the business community squeezed out the working class[123] despite Chalmers' vision and intentions.

He sought to avoid neglect of the poorer classes, but was disturbed to find a distortion of his financial policy attenuating mission to the section of society he was most anxious to regain. He lamented he had 'never been able to command an adequate sympathy on the subject of church extension',[124] and believed Free Church leadership was pre-occupied with internal affairs,[125] and ignoring 'the vast extent that remains to be possessed...the appalling city wastes...the many outfields of heathenism over the whole of

---

[120] Neither of these is in any of Chalmers' collected works. *The Earnest appeal* was republished in America in 1847 and 1852.

[121] A. A. MacLaren, *Religion and social class. The Disruption years in Aberdeen*, 1974.

[122] C. M. Bain, *The social impact of Kirkcaldy's industrial revolution, 1810-1876*, University of Guelph, PhD thesis, 1973, 54-71. (Kirkcaldy Public Library).

[123] 'The communion roll of Kirkcaldy Free Church contained the names of nearly everyone engaged in business in the town.' ibid., 62. See also A. A. MacLaren, *Religion and social class*, 108-13.

[124] T. Chalmers, *Earnest appeal to the Free Church*, 35.

[125] Ibid.

Scotland'.[126] They might keep their 'ground as a limited and sectarian institute' but as a 'national' one, they were in danger of breaking up.[127]

Although always enthusiastically received in the Free Church Assembly, it was clear the attention paid to Chalmers' concerns was limited. He was intent on the evangelization of Scotland while others were building a new denomination. He turned his hopes towards the proposed Evangelical Alliance and what was to be his final parish experiment, the West Port Church in Edinburgh.

> My expectation of what has long been the object of my existence – a universal Christian education – is transferred from the Free Church of Scotland to such a union of the really good and wise of all evangelical denominations as is now contemplated by many.[128]

Interest in Christian union had deeper roots in Chalmers' theology and experience than disappointment with the Free Church. From the time of his conversion he had friendships across a wide spectrum theologically and denominationally – Baptist, Church of England, Scottish Episcopal, Independent, Moravian and Quaker. Some like Irving had been forced out for heresy. Others like Erskine of Linlathen were on the fringe of orthodoxy, some friends of great mutual respect were doubters rather than believers. Chalmers saw the church as 'a family composed…of the professing of many different creeds',[129] and took seriously Andrew Fuller's comment that Christians agreed more than they differed, and too much attention was paid to the differences.[130] He believed toleration would aid resolution of differences,[131] and told his students denominations ought to be drawing more closely together.[132] Church government was something which seemed

> historically to have been changed and adapted according to the purposes of what may be termed Christian expediency and instead of being decisively settled in Scripture, left very much to the discretion of Christian men.[133]

If church government was relative to circumstances it was the more possible that Christians could co-operate, and the more necessary that they should. Chalmers was delighted with the return of the Original Burghers to the

---

[126]   Ibid., 22.

[127]   Ibid., 16.

[128]   T. C. to W. K. Tweedie, 29 November 1845, *Memoirs*, 4, 372f.

[129]   T. C. to Mrs Coutts, 4 January 1819, NCL CHA 3.9.1.

[130]   *Posthumous Works*, 9, 425.

[131]   *Works*, 22, 236–8 (Sermon preached on 16 July 1820).

[132]   *Posthumous Works*, 9, 425.

[133]   *Posthumous Works*, 9, 423.

Church of Scotland in 1839, but as disruption loomed the vision of a larger union began to appeal.[134] At a public dinner in September 1840, with the failure of the Aberdeen bill not long behind him, Chalmers was asked to propose a toast to the 'union of Evangelical Dissenters with the Church of Scotland' and declared that the greatest issues facing them were 'church union and church extension'.[135]

Meetings on Christian union were being arranged in different parts of Britain from this time onwards, and Chalmers was invited to Exeter Hall at the beginning of June 1843.[136] It was hardly feasible to attend, but the subject was not far from his mind. Two days after the Disruption he spoke to the Free Church Assembly of the need for 'the most entire co-operation' with other evangelical churches and asked that they consider Jesus' prayer in John 17 'where the success of Christianity in the world' was 'made to hinge not merely upon ostensible, but upon real and vital union among Christians'.[137] In July 1843, at the bicentenary of the Westminster Assembly, he took this point a stage further. What he looked for was 'co-operation now, and as soon as may be...incorporation afterwards'.[138]

One outcome of the Westminster Bicentenary was the compilation of *Essays on Christian Union* which appeared late the following year and included Chalmers as first among its contributors.[139] In August 1845, he lent his signature to a letter calling for a preparatory British conference to lay a foundation for the inaugural meetings of the Evangelical Alliance in 1846.[140] He published on what the Alliance should achieve and how,[141] regarding its potential for improving the effectiveness of evangelism as enormous if only unanimity could grow out of shared experience applying the gospel, instead of spending effort on doctrinal issues.

Chalmers believed the Alliance would be better called 'Protestant' than 'Evangelical', since the term was more precise and renascent Catholicism was a threat. His major concern was positive. If each affiliated church took responsibility for a defined area, they could cover the cities with territorial

---

[134] R. Rouse and S. C. Neill, eds, *A history of the ecumenical movement, 1517-1948*, 1954, 318-23.

[135] *Witness*, 30 September 1840.

[136] J. Leifchild, F. A. Cox, *et al.*, to T. C., 5 April 1843, NCL CHA 4. (This is clearly dated 1840, but internal evidence is more consistent with 1843.) Rouse and Neill, *Ecumenical Movement*, 1954, 319.

[137] *Witness*, 23 May 1843.

[138] Ibid., 15 July 1843, *Memoirs*, 4, 379.

[139] 'How such a union may begin and to what it may eventually lead', *Essays on Christian union*, 1845 (it was distributed in December 1844), 3-18.

[140] J. W. Massie, *The Evangelical Alliance: its origin and development*, 1847, 109-11.

[141] T. Chalmers, *On the Evangelical Alliance: its design, its difficulties, its proceedings, and its prospects: with practical suggestions*, 1846.

churches in a great home mission. The proportions of St John's could have national application.

Some leading Free Church members were prominent in the Liverpool preparatory conference and the Evangelical Alliance itself, but the Free Church Assembly of 1846 almost unanimously defeated the proposal that they be involved as a church.[142] Once churches were not to be involved as corporate bodies there was no way Chalmers' vision of a co-ordinated home mission by Evangelicals was possible.

After the Alliance met in August and September that year Chalmers wrote that because they refused to see 'action, not...as the end, but as the means to the end – that of perfecting the union of Christians', it had 'stepped back from a do-little to a do-nothing association' and was to be judged a failure.[143]

The final experiment[144]

In the summer of 1844 Chalmers launched a fresh effort to show what might be done with a territorial church in a working-class area. He began with lectures setting out his belief in the territorial system and lay involvement. Visitation of the West Port area of Edinburgh commenced in July. He marked off an area with a population of about 2000, and this time there was no question about its being destitute. The only place to start a school and conduct worship was a tannery loft in a close, well remembered for the Burke and Hare murders. The school was opened in November, and in December Chalmers again presented the scheme to a public meeting.[145]

Although he had difficulty recruiting lay visitors and the scheme was dependent on outside financial help, particularly from a congregation in New York,[146] the West Port experiment was a considerable achievement. Services began in the tannery loft in December 1844, and in April 1845 Chalmers obtained one of his top students, W. Tasker, to be the minister. Tasker persevered in frightful conditions and gradually built up a

---

[142]   *Witness*, 29 May 1846.

[143]   *Lowes Magazine*, NS 1(2), December 1846, 81-7.

[144]   S. J. Brown, 'The Disruption and urban poverty: Thomas Chalmers and the West Port operation in Edinburgh, 1844-47,' *Records of the Scottish Church History Society*, 20(1), 1978, 65-89. W. Tasker, *Dr Chalmers' territorial church, West Port Edinburgh*, 1851. J. Anderson, *Reminiscences of Thomas Chalmers*, 1851, 342-6. *Memoirs*, 4, 391-415.

[145]   T. Chalmers, *Churches and schools for the working classes. An address on the practicability of providing moral and religious education for the working population of large towns, as illustrated by the success which has attended the operations carried on in the West Port of Edinburgh, delivered 27 December 1845*, 1846.

[146]   See correspondence with J. Lennox, 1844-1847, NCL and *Correspondence*, 433-443.

congregation. The school was important, and there was added a library, savings-bank and washing-house. One tenement was fitted out as model-housing. In February 1847 a new church building was opened. For Chalmers it was the most joyful event of his life. For 30 years he had 'been intent...on the completion of a territorial experiment'.[147]

> I have got now the desire of my heart, – the church is finished, the schools are flourishing, our ecclesiastical machinery is about complete, and all in good working order. God has indeed heard my prayer, and I could now lay down my head in peace and die.[148]

[147] T. C. to J. Lennox, 27 February 1847, *Memoirs*, 4, 411.

[148] *Memoirs*, 4, 411.

PART TWO

SCOTLAND AND THE MISSIONARY MOVEMENT

There never was an age of the world in which a more effective machinery for conversion was, in the shape of schools and Bibles and missionaries, put into operation.

Chalmers[1]

---

[1] *Memoirs*, 2, 503.

Chapter 9

'Promoting Christian knowledge and increase of piety and virtue within Scotland'[2]
Scotland and missions before 1813

During Chalmers' life-time Scotland responded, in common with Britain, Europe and America, to the stimuli and opportunities which produced the modern missionary movement. Its special contribution lay not only in what was felt to be a high number of talented[3] and well-educated[4] missionaries, but in a distinctive philosophy in which a bias towards education was integrated with more direct forms of evangelism. This can also be found in some of the aspirations of the ill-fated Darien expedition to Central America at the end of the 17th century, traced through the involvement of the SSPCK in the Highlands of Scotland and among the Indians of North America in the 18th, and seen in the policies drawn up in the 1820s and implemented in the subsequent decade by the Church's India mission.

The absence of overseas mission before Darien and for long after has some obvious reasons. Scotland did not have anywhere it could send people. A look at involvement overseas during these centuries provides a large part of the answer, though it is conceivable enthusiasm might well have contrived an opening had it existed. Scots had been in contact with Europe and trading in the Baltic for a long period, and although there were Scots churches in parts of Europe this did not lead immediately to wider religious ambitions.

The role of Scots in defending and running the British empire makes it easy to forget that this was not always so. The first to go to America were

---

[2] Letters patent, 1709, bound in with SSPCK Records, Minutes of General Meetings, 1, 1709-1718. SRO/GRH GD 95.1.1.

[3] J. Calder, *Scotland's march past. The share of Scottish churches in the London Missionary Society*, 1945, 5, 10, 29.

[4] F. S. Piggin, *Making Evangelical Missionaries 1789-1858. The social background, motives and training of British Protestant missionaries to India*, 1984, 219-37.

those under banishment. In the aftermath of Darien there was resentment, and for a time legislation, about Scots holding positions of authority in English colonies. The Union of 1707 marked the beginning of change, but migration to North America and elsewhere was later as far as significant numbers were concerned. It was here that direct involvement in mission first became a possibility, and after the American revolution and a shift of British attention to India, interest in Asia also developed.

The SSPCK's work in America was respectable enough, and important because of that, but the suggestion of more widespread commitment was not at first welcome. Nevertheless in the three decades between the founding of the London Missionary Society in 1795 and the decision of the 1824 General Assembly that the Church of Scotland investigate a mission of its own, a considerable change in attitude took place. Chalmers himself changed from treating such things not very seriously to believing that the conversion of the world was an obligatory task requiring the involvement of all Christians. The role of the SSPCK meant that, for the leadership of the Scottish Church, at least thinking about mission had long been on their horizons. The question from the 1790s onwards was less about validity, than about seriousness of commitment and the priorities involved. The Scots did not come to the missionary movement in a theological vacuum or with theological barriers as to what it was all about.

The first missionaries supported from Scotland had been employed in America by local corresponding committees of the SSPCK. The first missionaries from Scotland were sent by Scottish voluntary societies. The first generation of missionaries from the established Church itself were Chalmers' students. He had been energetic in his support of missionary societies from the time of his conversion, and was keen to harness missionary interest to work for the church at home as well as abroad. From 1823 to 1828, missions were his chief interest outside of his responsibilities as Professor of Moral Philosophy at St Andrews. Although other matters were to the fore after he moved to Edinburgh, the commitment was maintained. During the 1820s and 1830s the locus of missionary support in Scotland shifted from the interdenominational societies to the churches, and in Chalmers can be seen the tensions felt by an Evangelical long committed to the societies and in some ways not entirely convinced about the missionary policies of the Church.

A feature of the missionary movement was the widespread formation of local societies. They had some precedent in praying societies in the past,[5] but these were notable for action as well as prayer. They were also of significance for the ecumenical relationships they cultivated and the way they brought about lay involvement in the mission of the church. During the first half of the 19th century the voluntary religious association became

---

[5]　H. Watt, 'The praying societies of the early eighteenth century', *Original Secession Magazine*, February 1934, 49-53.

a normative feature of church life. In time they became more denominational in character, but as they did so they prepared the way for the ordinary membership of the Church of Scotland to take on a greater financial responsibility once the willingness and ability of successive governments to aid the established Church was eroded.

From the Reformation to the Union of Parliaments

Missionary endeavour towards Scotland if not out from it, can be traced back to Ninian, Columba and Kentigern.[6] However they were more often venerated as saints than emulated as missionaries, and it was many centuries before their precedent was taken as an example. The Reformation in Scotland did not result in mission overseas, but was at least permissive of one taking place. The title page of the *Scots Confession* of 1560 carried the text 'And this glaid tydinges of the kingdom shalbe preached throught the hole world for a witness to all nations and then shall the end cum.'[7] Article 16 stated that the church was 'catholike, that is universal, because it conteinis the Elect of all ages, of all realmes, nations, and tongues'.[8] A prayer at the end included the petition 'Let all Natiouns cleave to thy trew knowledge'.[9]

In the 16th century these texts may have conveyed little more than that Scotland ought to be included among the nations experiencing reformation. At home the task of the church was clear and pressing and feasible openings for missionary work did not exist. For much of the 17th century as well there was reason enough not to seek responsibilities beyond Scotland's shores, yet a missionary purpose was becoming marginally more explicit. In 1644 Scots were among those who called for missionary work in America and the West Indies,[10] and the following year the *Directory of Public Worship* stated that ministers should pray 'for the propagation of the gospel and kingdom of Christ to all nations'.[11] The *Shorter Catechism* did not mention the Great Commission, but the *Larger Catechism* expounded the second petition of the Lord's prayer to include the 'spread of the gospel, the conversion of the Jews' and the 'fulness of the Gentiles'.[12]

---

[6] D. Mackichan, *The missionary ideal in the Scottish churches*, 1927, 16-50.

[7] Matthew 24.14. G. D. Henderson, *Scots Confession, 1560*, 1937, 33.

[8] Ibid., 71.

[9] Ibid., 99.

[10] J. A. Graham, *The missionary expansion of the Reformed Churches*, 1898, 40.

[11] 'Of public prayer before the sermon', *The directory for the public worship of God. The subordinate standards and other authoritative documents of the Free Church of Scotland*, 1850, 366.

[12] *The Larger Catechism*, question 191. *Subordinate standards*, 1850, 272f.

In 1647 there was further expression of concern for the conversion of the Jews,[13] and a letter of encouragement was sent to Scots merchants in Poland, Sweden, Denmark and Hungary noting 'the sad and lamentable condition of many thousands of you our countrymen, who are scattered abroad as sheepe having no shepherd.'[14] The main purpose was to accompany copies of the newly drawn up *Confession* and *Directory of Public Worship*, but it also expressed the desire 'to set forth the Kingdom of our Lord Jesus Christ...not only throughout this nation, but in other parts also, so far as God gave us a call and opportunity'.[15]

However minimal, these were positive steps as far as they went. At least Scotland did not rationalize its situation in its theology and was spared the anti-missionary stances which developed in some other forms of Calvinism and within Lutheranism. If it could not boast a Justinian von Welz[16] (1621-1688) anxious to convert the heathen abroad, neither did it appear to have a Johann Gerhard[17] (1582-1637) arguing that the Great Commission had ceased with the apostles.

With the Revolution Settlement the political situation became in some ways more conducive to missionary enterprise and when the Darien scheme was launched in 1695 the General Assembly was active in its support.[18] The six ministers who sailed with the fleets of settlers to the Isthmus of Panama in 1698 and 1699 were instructed to propagate 'the glorious light of the gospel...among the natives for their instruction and conversion'.[19]

The scheme was a fiasco,[20] but a missionary motive had been stated and generally accepted, even if it was a church and state mission to plant church and state in a foreign land. It is impossible to know how ideas of taking the faith beyond the boundaries of the colony itself would have fared had it been securely established.

---

[13] Graham, *Missionary expansion*, 1898, 17.

[14] *Acts of the General Assembly of the Church of Scotland, 1638–1842*, 1843, 163.

[15] Ibid., 164.

[16] G. Warneck, *Outline of a history of Protestant missions*, 1906, 32-39. J. A. Scherer, *Justinian Welz*, 1969.

[17] Warneck, *Protestant missions*, 1906, 28-31. Boer, *Pentecost and missions*, 1961, 21.

[18] J. Ramsay, 'Scottish Presbyterian foreign missions a century before Carey', *Journal of the Presbyterian Historical Society*, 39(4), 1961, 201-18.

[19] Ibid., 205.

[20] John Prebble, *The Darien disaster*, 1968.

The eighteenth century: promoting Christian knowledge

With the Union of the Scottish and the English parliaments in 1707, itself partly an outcome of the Darien failure, there no longer existed the political situation which enabled Scottish commercial and religious interests to reinforce each other in a colonial scheme. What did remain was a situation where political and religious interests coincided in their attitude towards the Highlands of Scotland. In 1709 the Society in Scotland for Propagating Religious Knowledge[21] (SSPCK) was incorporated by royal letters-patent. It had the objects of

> promoting Christian knowledge and increase of piety and virtue within Scotland, especially in the Highlands, Islands and remote places thereof, where error, idolatry, superstition and ignorance do mostly abound by reason of the largeness of parishes and scarcity of schools, and for propagating the same in popish and infidel parts of the world.[22]

Little time was lost setting up charity schools in the Highlands, and the SSPCK was soon an important agency for extending the influence of Lowland Presbyterian religion and Whig politics. With respect to 'infidel parts of the world', there was not quite the same commitment, but a legacy tied to overseas work[23] became available in 1717 and in the 1720s fresh interest was stimulated by Robert Millar[24] of Paisley (1672-1752) with his publication, *The history of the propagation of Christianity and overthrow of paganism.*[25] It may be no accident that Paisley continued to be a centre of

---

21   The SSPCK, not to be confused with the English SPCK. M. G. Jones, *The charity school movement*, 1938, 176-214; J. MacInnes, *The Evangelical Movement in the Highlands of Scotland, 1688-1800*, 1951, 236-52. D. E. Meek, 'Scottish Highlanders, North American Indians and the SSPCK: some cultural perspectives', *Records of the Scottish Church History Society*, 23(3), 1989, 378-96. G. Robb, 'Popular religion and the Christianization of the Scottish Highlands in the eighteenth and nineteenth centuries', *Journal of Religious History*, 16, 1990, 18-34. H. R. Sefton, 'The Scotch Society in the American Colonies in the eighteenth century', *Records of the Scottish Church History Society*, 17, 1971, 169-84. D. J. Withrington, 'The SSPCK and Highland schools in the mid-eighteenth century', *Scottish Historical Review*, 41, 1962, 89-99.

22   Letters patent, 1709, bound in with SSPCK Records, Minutes of General Meetings, 1, 1709-1718. SRO/GRH GD 95.1.1.

23   *Acts of the General Assembly 1638–1842*, 1843, 617.

24   *Fasti*, 3, 166.

25   A. Fawcett, *The Cambuslang Revival*, 1971, 214f., 229. R. E. Davies, 'Robert Millar – an eighteenth century Scottish Latourette', *Evangelical Quarterly*, 62(2), 1990, 143-56. J. Foster, 'A Scottish contributor to the missionary awakening: Robert Millar of Paisley', *International Review of Missions*, 37, 1948, 138-45.

mission interest. Millar's work was republished in London, read in America, translated into Dutch and extracted into other publications.[26]

In 1730 steps were eventually taken by the SSPCK to establish a mission among North American Indians.[27] In 1732 the Assembly approved taking up a collection in which donors could decide whether to support work in the Highlands and Islands or to help 'subsist missionary ministers or schoolmasters in foreign parts of the world'.[28]

The resulting North American mission was never large and the directors in Scotland and their corresponding committees in America saw themselves as administrators of limited funds rather than propagators of missionary principle. Despite some mixed results their stewardship was not without success. Among those they employed as missionaries was David Brainerd (1718–1747),[29] whose journal became a classic of missionary devotion.

The annual sermons provide an almost continuous record into the 19th century, but overt missionary references from the 18th century are not conspicuous. In 1733 the Edinburgh Divinity Professor James Smith noted the example of the missionary John Eliot (1604-1690).[30] In 1752 John Bonar of Cockpen referred to 'the barbarous regions of Africa, the untutored Indians and the miserate inhabitants of the more distant parts of our own country'.[31] A sermon by Principal Robertson in 1755 was as much as anything an apology for inaction[32] – 'the conversion of distant nations is not the chief care of the SPCK'.[33] However in 1765 James Robertson showed some interest in the Jews and in making the gospel known 'in the dark corners of the earth'.[34]

In 1762 the General Assembly approved a collection specifically for the American work and the following year the Society published an *Account of*

---

26 Davies, 'Robert Millar', 1990, 144ff.

27 *An account of the Society in Scotland for Propagating Christian Knowledge, from its commencement in 1709,* 1774, 7, 13-19.

28 *Acts of the General Assembly 1638–1842,* 1843, 618.

29 J. M. Sherwood, *Memoirs of Rev. David Brainerd,* 1885.

30 James Smith, *The misery of ignorant and unconverted sinners,* SSPCK sermon, January 1, 1733, 20-22.

31 John Bonar, *The nature and necessity of a religious education,* SSPCK sermon, January 6, 1752, 39.

32 D. Mackichan, *The missionary ideal in the Scottish churches,* 1927, 72f.

33 William Robertson, *The situation of the world at the time of Christ's appearance and its connection with the success of his religion, considered,* 6th edition, 1791, 53. Robertson stressed that God worked by gradualism, one is tempted to say moderatism, and believed Christianity was responsible for superior European arts, arms and sciences. The sermon was translated into German and as late as 1817 drew a critical review from the *Edinburgh Christian Instructor,* August 1817, 69-76.

34 James Robertson, *The resemblance of Jesus to Moses considered,* SSPCK sermon February 25, 1865, 73, 81.

some late attempts...to Christianize the North American Indians.[35] Fairly large collections were taken up aided by the visit of William Occum, an American Indian, and 'to all appearances a typical New England divine'.[36] More generally in the eyes of Lowland supporters there was little difference between a pagan Indian and a pagan or Catholic Highlander,[37] and in each case the means of religious salvation and political stabilization were essentially the same.

> The method employed in Scotland was the establishment of schools and the maintenance of schoolmasters and it was not long before the preaching of evangelists was supplemented by the teaching of schoolmasters in America. Evangelization and education however were really inseparable in the view of the Society. Its schoolmasters frequently acted as lay missionaries and the curriculum in both Highland and Indian schools included the study of Scripture and the Westminster Shorter Catechism.[38]

However limited the resources, once established, the commitment of the Church of Scotland through the SSPCK was perfectly real. A consequence was that when the missionary movement arose at the end of the century, whatever else might be said, the principle of missions was not open to serious question. With regard to missionary method, the integration of evangelism and education, known from experience in Scotland, was believed to work equally well among North American Indians. As was later pointed out, the SSPCK was a missionary society, a Bible society and a school society,[39] and not least among its characteristics was that it enjoyed the support of both Moderate and Evangelical. For some time annual sermons were held in London[40] as well as Edinburgh, and among the expatriate Scots strong in its support[41] were many behind the formation of the London Missionary Society in 1795.

---

[35]   *Account of some late attempts by the correspondents of the Society for Propagating Christian Knowledge to Christianize the North American Indians*, 1763.

[36]   Sefton, 'Scotch Society', 1971, 180. Mackichan, *Missionary ideal*, 1927, 71.

[37]   Sefton, 'Scotch Society', 1971, 182.

[38]   Ibid., 184.

[39]   A. Thomson, *The ultimate and universal prevalence of the Christian religion*, SSPCK sermon, 1817, 39. See also Chalmers, *Works*, 11, 221-46.

[40]   The earliest I have reference to is 1789.

[41]   'This nursery of later LMS leaders.' J. A. De Jong, *As the waters cover the sea. Millennial expectations in the rise of Anglo-American missions 1640-1810*, 1970, 168.

The birth of modern missions: 1792-1813

The formation of the Baptist Missionary Society in 1792 owed something to a 'Scottish connection' traceable to a 'concert for prayer' inspired by the Cambuslang Revival of 1741.[42] The Baptist mission was in turn to have influence on Scottish churchmen including Chalmers. However it was the London Missionary Society[43] (LMS) founded in 1795 which first stimulated widespread interest in the conversion of the world.[44] The four ministers of Church of Scotland pulpits in London were all active supporters,[45] as were other expatriate Scots.[46] In Scotland, LMS directors were elected from most denominations. Out of 28 who were Scottish directors sometime during the period 1796-1800, 14 were Church of Scotland, seven Associate Synod, three Independent, one Relief and one from the General Associate Synod of Antiburghers.[47]

---

[42]   R. Pierce Beaver, 'The concert of prayer for mission', *Ecumenical Review*, 10, 1957, 420-27. Fawcett, *Cambuslang Revival*, 1971, 223-35. J. Foster, 'The bicentenary of Jonathan Edwards' "Humble attempt"', *International Review of Missions*, 37, 1948, 375-81. E. A. Payne, 'The evangelical revival and the beginnings of the modern missionary movement', *Congregational Quarterly*, 21, 1943, 223-46.

[43]   I. M. Fletcher, 'The fundamental principle of the London Missionary Society', *Transactions of the Congregational Historical Society*, 19, 1960-1963, 138-46, 192-8, 222-9. C. S. Horne, *The story of the LMS 1795-1895*, 1895, R. Lovett, *The history of the London Missionary Society 1795-1895*, 1899.

[44]   The LMS was inspired by the BMS and able to capitalize on interest generated by the Baptists. It saw itself as national and inter-denominational – hence its designation as 'The Missionary Society' before custom changed it to London Missionary Society.

[45]   Henry Hunter (1741-1802) of London Wall (*Fasti*, 7, 491), William Smith of Camberwell (*Fasti*, 7, 494. R. Lovett, *London Missionary Society*, 1, 1899, 17, 24), James Steven (1761-1824) of Crown Court (*Fasti*, 7, 468; 3, 118) and John Love (1757-1825) of Crispin Street, who was joint secretary of the LMS until he moved to Anderston in 1800 where he became secretary of the Glasgow Missionary Society (*Fasti*, 3, 389. R. Lovett, *London Missionary Society*, 1, 1899, 43).

[46]   Notably David Bogue (1750-1825) of Gosport and Alexander Waugh (1754-1827) of the Associate Synod Congregation, Wells Street, London. Bogue had been assistant to Smith at Camberwell, but left the Church of Scotland for the Independents. A letter of Bogue's in the *Evangelical Magazine*, September 1794, 378-80, was the call to action which led to the formation of the LMS. Waugh was the author of the 'fundamental principle' which sought to ensure an interdenominational constitution. George Jerment (1759-1819), the Antiburgher minister in London, also supported the society. Horne, *Story of the LMS*, 1895, 16. *Fasti*, 7, 494f.

[47]   Appendix 7, table 1. In two cases the denomination is not clear.

In September 1795, just after the inaugural meetings of the LMS, a circular letter was sent out inviting the 'co-operation of ministers and friends in Scotland'.[48] While this communication was still on its way, the then Antiburgher minister of Huntly, George Cowie (1749-1806), was already raising a hundred pounds in his congregation and had begun prayer meetings for missions.[49] The Glasgow Missionary Society[50] and the Edinburgh Missionary Society[51] were formed in February 1796 and later that year other societies were founded in Aberdeen, Dundee, Newton-upon-Ayr, Paisley,[52] Perth and Stirling. By 1800 there were societies in Dumfries, Duns, Greenock and Tain.[53]

All the local societies supported the LMS, many also the Baptists and the Moravians as well as the Edinburgh and Glasgow societies when they

---

[48] R. Lovett, *London Missionary Society,* 1, 1899, 44.

[49] A few years later Cowie was dismissed by the Antiburghers and became an Independent. H. Escott, *A history of Scottish Congregationalism,* 1960, 73, 297. R. Kinniburgh, *Fathers of Independency in Scotland,* 1851, 14, 19.

[50] Early records of the Glasgow Missionary Society are hard to find. The report for 1797 is bound with A. Pirie, *The duties and qualifications of a gospel missionary, a sermon preached before the Glasgow Missionary Society, November 7, 1797,* Glasgow 1797 (copies in NCL and NLS). Some quarterly papers published in the 1820s are bound in with the NCL series of the *Scottish Missionary Register.* See also W. Brown, *History of the propagation of Christianity,* 1854, 2, 450-73.

[51] Ibid., 2, 415-49. Brown was secretary of the society from 1821. In 1819 the name was changed to Scottish Missionary Society. The original regulations and a circular sent out to Scottish ministers in March 1796 were reprinted in R. Heron, *Account of the proceedings and debate in the General Assembly of the Church of Scotland, 27th May 1796,* 66-74. Many of their annual sermons were published together with the reports of the directors. For the first five years the *Missionary Magazine,* published in Edinburgh, is an important source. A complete set is in the Bodleian Library, Oxford. From 1800-1819, annual reports and extracts of correspondence can be found in the *Religious Monitor,* and to a lesser extent from 1810 onwards in the *Edinburgh Christian Instructor.* From 1829 the society published the *Scottish Missionary Register,* for many years a successful periodical which carried information on a wide range of missionary activity at home as well as abroad. See also J. Kilpatrick, 'The records of the Scottish Missionary Society (1796-1848)', *Records of the Scottish Church History Society,* 1950, 196-210. Most of the primary sources referred to by Kilpatrick are in the NLS, MSS 8012-14, 8938-89. For an account of the Scottish Missionary Society Russian mission see M. V. Jones, 'The sad and curious story of Karass, 1802-1835', *Oxford Slavonic papers,* NS 8, 1975, 53-81.

[52] Minutes of procedure of the Paisley London Missionary Society, March 1796 to November 1815, Paisley Public Library, 651.77 REN-IP.

[53] Appendix 6, Scottish missionary societies, 1795-1825.

began sending missionaries in their own right. Interest in missions overseas stimulated concern for the heathen at home, as is evident from the *Missionary Magazine* which began in 1796 under the editorship of Greville Ewing (1767-1841), the secretary of the Edinburgh society. Sermons on the universal claims of Christianity appeared in considerable numbers.[54]

Although many local societies had a bias towards a particular church, their composition often reflected the interdenominational ideals of the LMS. The Edinburgh Missionary Society was supported by Church of Scotland Evangelicals and by Seceders.[55] The first meeting of the Paisley society brought together representatives of most churches, and the monthly meeting of directors functioned as a ministers' fraternal. It was attended by four from the Church of Scotland as well as ministers of the Burgher, Antiburgher and Relief congregations.[56] An efficient band of collectors was organized to canvass subscriptions and together with collections taken at sermons for the cause, large sums of money were raised. Paisley forwarded the LMS £552 in 1797 and £295 in 1799. These figures were not untypical.[57]

Once the possibility of doing so was set before them, people rushed to support world-wide Christian mission. Many factors contributed to this seemingly instantaneous popularity. In England links with the Evangelical Revival are apparent. In Scotland the Evangelical party was a minority which could not yet foresee a change in its fortunes, but some such as its leader John Erskine (1721-1803)[58] had long had international interests and embraced a movement whose moment had now come. The colleague of Principal Robertson at the Greyfriars Church in Edinburgh, Erskine corresponded with the Continent and America, learnt German late in life and republished what he learnt from far afield.[59] He had been a link in the chain between Cambuslang and Carey via Jonathan Edwards, he was close to David Bogue and other Scots involved in the LMS and his defence of missions in the General Assembly in 1796 has gone into history.[60]

Individual Evangelicals who had moved out of the Established church were keen, and some subsequent general support owed a good deal to the activities of James and Robert Haldane.[61] Within the Church of Scotland

---

[54] Bibliography 9, Scottish missionary sermons, 1795-1820.

[55] J. J. Matheson, *A memoir of Greville Ewing*, 1843, 71f.

[56] Minutes, Paisley London Missionary Society.

[57] LMS reports of directors, 1797-1800.

[58] *Fasti*, 1, 47f.

[59] A. L. Drummond, *The Kirk and the Continent*, 1956, 157f. Jong, *As the waters cover the sea,* 1970, 166f., 172.

[60] H. Watt, 'Moderator, Rax me that Bible,' *Records of the Scottish Church History Society*, 10(1) 1948, 54f.

[61] Drummond and Bulloch, *The Scottish Church*, 1973, 152f. Burleigh, *Church history of Scotland*, 1960, 311f. Escott, *Scottish Congregationalism*, 1960, 50ff.

however the association of missions with the Haldanes was at first a liability. The Haldanes were frustrated in their efforts to embark on a large-scale mission to India modelled on Carey[62] and were forced to turn their attention to preaching revival in Scotland. In 1799 the Church of Scotland passed an Act of Assembly and a Pastoral Admonition linking the Haldanes' movement and its 'strange and self-authorized teachers of religion' with the French Revolution.[63]

Groups who had broken from the Church of Scotland during the century might have been an expected seed-bed of support. It was these who were most commonly associated with financial independence and independent thought. However, if individuals were spontaneous, as churches these groups were generally more guarded. While the Associate Synod of Burghers appointed a committee to correspond with the LMS early in 1796, it could not help financially.[64] The Relief responded to LMS enquiries in friendly terms, but their only action was a mission to the Highlands.[65] The General Associate Synod objected to the 'latitudinarian' constitutions of the societies, and to Christians of different convictions mixing together instead of maintaining 'the testimony which each sect was supposed to lift up against the errors of all the rest'. Lay involvement was frowned on,[66] and Reformed Presbyterians joined the Antiburghers in thinking that matters of policy were too important to be compromised by co-operative action.[67]

Missionary activity being dependent on opportunity as much as obligation, improving links of trade and communication were important in giving a sense of being part of a wider world. Factors such as moves for the abolition of the slave trade, the economic advantages of the Industrial Revolution and the facilities and experiences afforded by an emerging empire aided the growth of the movement. The Haldane experience suggested that frontal attack by the wrong people was not going to get very far, but there was nevertheless the possibility of free association despite government suspicions, and the existence of disposable income made action possible outside churches whose administrative machinery had no provision for

---

62   See correspondence including a printed letter from Robert Haldane, David Bogue, William Innes and Greville Ewing of 16 February 1797. EUL La II 500. Some English supporters such as John Newton felt that earlier enthusiasm for events in France and the way the group sought to force the East India Company's hand were counterproductive. A. K. Davidson, *The development and influence of the British Missionary Movement's attitudes towards India, 1786-1830*, University of Aberdeen, PhD thesis, 1973, 102.

63   *Acts of the General Assembly*, 1638–1842, 1843, 868-73.

64   M'Kerrow, *Secession Church*, 1841, 574f. Lovett, *London Missionary Society*, 1, 1899, 75.

65   G. Struthers, *The history of the rise, progress and principles of the Relief Church*, 1843, 394.

66   M'Kerrow, *Secession Church*, 1841, 383.

67   M. Hutchison, *The Reformed Presbyterian Church in Scotland*, 1893, 249.

missionary activity. The French Revolution was an impetus to sermons on prophetic themes, not just to doubts about people's loyalty. If to some, in the troubled decade of the 1790s, any association was suspect and overseas missions never seemed less important, to others in an age of portents they never seemed more. It only needed the later conviction and a feasible situation in which to begin for a missionary movement to emerge.

The most famous debate took place in the General Assembly of the Church of Scotland in May 1796.[68] By 58 to 44, the Moderate majority rejected an Evangelical motion to refer to a committee overtures asking the Assembly to consider 'the most effectual methods by which the Church of Scotland may contribute to the diffusion of the Gospel over the world' and the authorization of 'a general collection throughout the Church to aid the several societies for propagating the Gospel among the heathen nations'.[69]

The second of these overtures was tactically unfortunate and the political climate was sufficiently sensitive to lend plausibility to the suggestion that missionary societies were potentially seditious. The Moderates were the government party and it cannot have been irrelevant that attempts to allow missionaries into British India had failed in 1793. The successful motion gave 'the circumstances of the times' as the reason for not 'adopting any particular measure', but it also expressed an intention 'to embrace with zeal...any favourable opportunity...which Divine Providence may hereafter open'.[70]

Some Moderate speakers provided generations of Evangelicals with ammunition, but what ought to be noted is that the principle of missions was less at issue than the philosophy on which they were to be based and political questions about who was involved. The activity envisaged by the new societies was not specified, and behind comments about people needing to be 'polished and refined in their manners before they can be properly enlightened in religious truths'[71] lay concern whether the LMS and Edinburgh Missionary Society shared the emphasis on education

---

[68]   The only known primary record of the debate is (Robert Heron), *Proceedings and debate in the General Assembly of the Church of Scotland, 27th May 1796*, 1796. This was compiled from memory and checked by some of the speakers. Hill considered it 'incorrect and incomplete, but...as far as it goes, does not appear to me to contain anything false' (G. Hill to R. Dundas, 2 March 1797, EUL IA ii 500). G. White, '"Highly preposterous": origins of Scottish missions', *Records of the Scottish Church History Society*, 19(2), 1976, 111-24 gives some of the intellectual background. Hugh Miller, *The two parties in the Church of Scotland exhibited as missionary and anti-missionary*, 1841, is coloured by Disruption politics.

[69]   (Heron), *Proceedings and Debate*, 1796, 43.

[70]   Ibid., 53. *Acts of the General Assembly,* scroll minutes, 1796. SRO/GRH CH1/4/15.

[71]   Heron, *Proceedings and Debate*, 1796, 18.

characteristic of the SSPCK. An unspoken objection would have been the interdenominational character of the societies. Ecumenical tendencies were a developing Evangelical trait, not a Moderate one.

The decision of the Assembly was less important than it first appeared. The margin and the nature of the defeat still indicated widespread and solid support for the emerging missionary cause. If the vote had gone to the Evangelicals it would have said something about their strength relative to the Moderates, but missions would still have been left in the hands of voluntary societies. Either way, the role of the church itself in missionary activity was a question for the future to decide.

Far more crucial to its immediate fortunes was what happened to the first missionaries the societies actually sent out. The first party of 30 from the LMS were sent to the South Pacific and found, almost but not quite to a man, that they could not cope with what was asked of them. News of this reached the LMS in 1799. On its way with a second contingent their ship, the *Duff*, was captured by the French, and most found their way not to the Pacific but back to Britain.[72] From Scotland six missionaries had been sent to West Africa by the Glasgow Missionary Society and the Edinburgh Missionary Society, but they also met tragedy or failure. No permanent mission was established, never mind any converts made.[73] By 1800 there was practically nothing to show for a very considerable sacrifice of enthusiasm, money and lives. In the beginning the greatest problem of missions was not the failure of the churches, it was the failure of the societies.

Disappointment was obvious,[74] but committees of the local societies tried to rally round.[75] Public support could not be expected to be so resilient and the fall-off in support was dramatic. Meetings were thinly attended,[76] funds slowed to a trickle[77] and recruitment dropped sharply. The Glasgow Missionary Society gave up sending missionaries, and the Edinburgh

---

[72]   Lovett, *London Missionary Society*, 1, 1899, 63-5.
[73]   Brown, *Propagation*, 2, 1854, 419f., 53-456.
[74]   Minutes, Paisley London Missionary Society, 1, 10 September 1799.
[75]   Paisley expressed their 'concern and sorrow' and sent the balance of their funds to the LMS. Societies in Dundee, Kilmarnock, Glasgow and Inverness reacted similarly. LMS home correspondence from M. Colquhoun, 19 September 1799, SOAS LMS 11/6/A; J. V. McKenzie, 2 September 1799, SOAS LMS 11/8/A; J. Mackintyre, 20 September 1799, SOAS LMS 11/8/A; A Fraser, 22 October 1799, SOAS LMS 11/8/; J. Black, 17 September 1799, SOAS LMS 11/8/A.
[76]   Minutes, Paisley London Missionary Society, 5 January 1799.
[77]   The LMS annual reports indicate that in 1798-1800 the Dundee Missionary Society was sending £100 to £150 a year to the LMS. By 1806 this had dropped to £36 and by 1810 to £30. The same pattern can be seen in the figures for Aberdeen, Perth, Glasgow and Paisley.

Missionary Society withdrew from Africa. It was a year or two before it began another mission, this time to Russia.

For the LMS the lesson was salutary and a more considered approach to recruitment and training resulted. Nevertheless for several years the movement tended to drift. Many found the Bible Society an outlet for the interests which had led them to support missionary societies. After the indifferent beginnings of the latter, for Scots as for others, the translation and distribution of Bibles appeared a sounder and more certain strategy – one in which co-operative and missionary ideals could be realized with fewer tensions. At least that is what they believed at the time.

The recovery of the home base was slow. From 1807 the LMS became more active in promoting local societies which helped provide a more stable income. Of immense significance were developments in relation to India. It was the most obvious field for British missionaries, but one where initiatives were blocked by the East India Company's fear of disturbance to their commercial interests. Chaplains appointed by the Company had a broader vision, but by and large they could only plan for another day. The presence of William Carey (1761-1834) as a pioneer who could only be a missionary on Danish territory and who took work as a plantation superintendent to be on British, illustrated frustration and stimulated concern.[78]

In 1793, the year Carey left for Bengal, Wilberforce had failed in an attempt to obtain provision for missionaries in the company's charter when it was renewed by parliament. Twenty years later an evangelical campaign to open India to Christian missions was at length successful.[79] Many forces contributed to this, not least the efforts of one of the chaplains, Cambuslang-born Claudius Buchanan (1766-1815). Through prize essays in the British universities, sermons, contributions to a pamphlet war consequent on the Sepoy rebellion in 1806, and his book *Christian researches in Asia*, published in 1811, Buchanan was instrumental in changing British perception of Indian society.

Many in the 18th century had been impressed by the antiquity and depth of Indian culture, but Buchanan presented a picture of popular Hinduism characterized by *sati*, infanticide and *juggernaut* to the extent that humanitarian considerations alone demanded something be done.[80] Wilberforce wrote that Scotland had done more than England, but still asked if the supporters of missions were asleep.[81] The Associate Synod was

---

[78] A. Christopher Smith, 'The legacy of William Carey', *International Bulletin of Missionary Research*, 16(1) January, 1992, 2-8.

[79] E. H. Howse, *Saints in politics*, 1971, 82-93. J. Pollock, *Wilberforce*, 1977, 235-8.

[80] Davidson, *Attitudes towards India*, 1973, 102. H. Pearson, *Memoirs of the life and writings of the Rev Claudius Buchanan*, 1817.

[81] W. Wilberforce to J. Campbell, 19 March 1813, SRO/GRH GD 50.235.11.

among many who petitioned parliament,[82] and Scottish Evangelicals were active in the campaign.[83] Contrary to subsequent impressions,[84] the General Assembly resisted appeals from Buchanan and Wilberforce.[85] The Assembly had set up a committee on the charter renewal in 1812, but neither its brief nor its report made any mention of missionaries. Their sole concern was obtaining entry for Church of Scotland chaplains.[86]

The passing of the missionary clauses in 1813 opened a new era for the missionary movement from Britain. India provided a non-Christian population, British influence, stability and communications and the societies were in a position to regain support they had earlier enjoyed.

Yet once missions had official sanction it was only a matter of time before churches were likely to decide this was a function which belonged more properly to them than to voluntary organizations. If in Scotland the stage was set for the revival of the societies, in the acceptance of their message was the seed of their demise.

---

[82] M'Kerrow, *Secession Church*, 1841, 633.

[83] Burns, *Stevenson Macgill*, 1842, 55f. *Edinburgh Christian Instructor*, 6, 1813, 1-20, 77-87. Z. Macaulay to R. Paul, 5 June 1813, NLS 5139 f.57.

[84] E. G. K. Hewat, *Vision and achievement 1796-1956*, 1960, 34, says the Church of Scotland was the first to petition for the opening of India to missions, but it asked for chaplains not missionaries. The error is repeated by Drummond and Bulloch, *The Scottish Church*, 1973, 181 and by G. Donaldson, *The faith of the Scots*, 1990, 121. The original culprit is probably R. W. Weir, *A history of the foreign missions of the Church of Scotland*, 1900, 27.

[85] R. I. and S. W. Wilberforce, *The Life of William Wilberforce*, 1838, 4, 14f. H. Pearson, *Claudius Buchanan*, 1817, 278.

[86] *AGA*, 1812, 14; *AGA*, 1813, 13. Acts of the General Assembly, Scroll minutes, 29 May 1813, SRO/GRH CH1/2/141.

Chapter 10

'The utility of missions ascertained by experience'[1]
Chalmers, Bible Societies and overseas missions, 1795-1823

'That gradual progress which the nature of the case requires'[2]

As a student during the 1790s, particularly at the time of the 1796 Assembly debate in which his Principal and Theology Professor George Hill had taken a prominent part, Chalmers was exposed to issues raised by the emerging missionary movement. In his lectures Hill treated the propagation of Christianity[3] in relation to Gibbon's argument[4] that the expansion of the church during the first three centuries could be explained by natural circumstances. He also discussed contemporary prospects for the spread of Christianity and emphasized 'civilization' as a pre-condition for a rational acceptance of the truth and obligations of Christian religion.[5]

> A long intercourse with the nations of Europe, who appear fitted by their character to be the instructors of the rest of the world, may be the means appointed by God for removing the prejudices of idolatry and ignorance; and as the enlightened discoveries of modern times make us acquainted with the manners, the views, and the interests, as well as with the geographical situation of all the inhabitants of the globe, we may – not indeed with the precipitancy of visionary reformers, but in

---

[1] Chalmers' sermon for the SSPCK, 1814. *Works*, 11, 221-46.

[2] G. Hill, *Lectures in divinity*, 1854, 115.

[3] Ibid., 108-112.

[4] *Decline and Fall of the Roman Empire*, 1, 1776, chapter 15.

[5] This was a persistent theme in Moderate speeches during the 1796 debate. The missionary philosophy which lay behind Hill's thinking was W. Robertson's 1755 SSPCK sermon, *The situation of the world at the time of Christ's appearance and its connection with the success of his religion considered*. Robertson's argument was that natural circumstances favouring early Christianity were a sign of providential ordering, not of lack of divine intervention.

that gradual progress which the nature of the case requires – be the instrument of preparing them for embracing our religion; and, by the measure in which they adopt our improvements in art and science, they become qualified to receive, through our communication, the knowledge of the true God and of his Son Jesus Christ.[6]

These issues were also debated in a number of meetings of the Theological Society. In January and December 1797 they considered whether the 'rapid propagation of Christianity' could be 'accounted for from second causes'[7] and in February 1798 asked whether 'the method at present adopted by the Missionary Society in this country for the propagation of Christianity' was 'favourable to its interests'.[8] At a meeting in January 1799 at which Chalmers spoke, the subject was the effect of Christianity on 'the morals of those nations among whom it has been published'.[9]

'We have no right to sit in indolence'[10]

However, it is not until some months after his conversion, that there is evidence of interest from Chalmers. In August 1811 he recorded he was 'much imprest by the worth and utility' of the Baptist mission in India[11] and that December found their work 'most cheering and interesting'.[12] He read Buchanan's *Christian researches* 'with interest and delight'[13] and wrote to his brother-in-law that it demonstrated 'the entire practicality of throwing in Christianity among the half-civilized nations of Asia'.[14]

Missions soon had a place in his prayers,[15] and his support was evident at the opening of the Fife and Kinross Bible Society in July 1812.[16] In September he noted 'a growing interest in this business'[17] which was

---

6   Hill, *Lectures in Divinity*, 1854, 115f.
7   St Andrews Theological Society minutes, 2, 1786-1823, 21 January, 16 December, 1797. StAUL UY 911.
8   Ibid., 17 February 1798.
9   Ibid., 19 January 1799.
10 *Works*, 11, 318.
11 Journal, 14 August 1811. *Edinburgh Christian Instructor*, July 1811, 66ff.
12 Journal, 11 December 1811.
13 Journal, 20 February 1812. He read it to the manse household, 11, 15, and 26 September 1812. He probably first heard of it in the *Edinburgh Christian Instructor*, January 1812, 42-54.
14 T. C. to J. Morton, 29 February 1812, *Memoirs*, 1, 276. He also recommended it to his friend Thomas Duncan. T. Duncan to T. C., 9 March 1812, NCL CHA 4.1.37 (erroneously dated 1811).
15 Journal, 1 June, 7 September, 5 October, 5 November 1812 etc.
16 *Edinburgh Christian Instructor*, 6(1), January 1813, 64-9.
17 Journal, 2 September 1812.

quickened by news of a fire which had destroyed the Baptist printing office in Serampore.[18] Chalmers called a meeting of the Kilmany Bible Association to vote the BMS £25.[19]

At the time he was preparing a sermon for the Dundee Missionary Society which was delivered in October[20] and published in January 1813 as *The two great instruments for the propagation of the gospel.*[21] There was talk of a second edition to help the East India Company charter renewal campaign,[22] and the LMS wrote for copies.[23] It reached its third edition in 1814.[24] It was reviewed in the *Edinburgh Christian Instructor*[25] and extracts printed in the *Evangelical Magazine.*[26] An outcome was Chalmers' election as a director of the LMS, a position he held 16 times during the next 20 years.[27]

In the spring of 1813 the campaign for missionary clauses in the East India Company charter reached its height. With some difficulty Chalmers managed to get petition signatures from some of his heritors. He upset at least one colleague by promoting it outside his own parish. He attended gatherings in Logie and Kirkcaldy, and sought advice how to make the most of the status of signatories.[28]

By this stage he was in correspondence with the Edinburgh Baptist Charles Stuart, who encouraged him with the India petition, kept him supplied with the Baptist *Periodical Accounts*[29] and arranged for deputations to include Kilmany in their itineraries. In March 1813 Chalmers received a

---

[18] *Edinburgh Christian Instructor*, 5(3), September 1812, 214f. Journal, 21, 15 September 1812.

[19] Journal 7, 10, 11 October 1812. *Report of the Bible Society of Fife and Kinross Shires, 24th August 1813*, 1814, 45. Contrary to *Memoirs*, 1, 316, a donation was made by the Kilmany Association and the proceeds of the Dundee sermon went to the LMS not the Baptists. S. W. Tracey to T. C., 23 March 1813, NCL CHA 4.2.49.

[20] Journal, 26 October 1812.

[21] *Works*, 11, 315-44.

[22] S. W. Tracey to T. C., 23 March 1813, NCL CHA 4.2.49.

[23] G. Burder to T. C., 3 March 1813, NCL CHA 4.2.23.

[24] And a fourth in 1817. *Memoirs*, 1, 316.

[25] *Edinburgh Christian Instructor*, December 1813, 394-401.

[26] *Evangelical Magazine*, 21, 1813, 136-8, 178f.

[27] Appendix 7, Scottish Directors of the London Missionary Society.

[28] Journal 5 April to 5 May 1813. *Memoirs*, 1, 328f. T. C. to C. Stuart, 22 April 1813, NCL CHA 3.5.66.

[29] T. C. to C. Stuart, 24 May 1813, NCL CHA 3.5.79. Journal 1 November 1812, 4 March 1813, C. Anderson to T. C., 15 December 1813, StAUL 30385.3.

visit from a 'Mr Dick, missionary from Quebec',[30] and in August Andrew Fuller[31] (1754-1815) of Kettering spent two days in the manse.[32]

This gave him links with Carey and the Baptist mission in India and Baptists remained important for Chalmers.[33] His interests soon included the annual sermons of the Dundee Missionary Society,[34] and the work of Moravians.[35] In June 1814 he preached for the SSPCK in Edinburgh *On the utility of missions ascertained by experience*,[36] having declined to do so the previous year.[37]

The Moravian influence was significant.[38] Their warm piety and active faith spoke to Chalmers' own needs. Their missionary experience provided a

---

[30]   Journal 8 March 1813.

[31]   Fuller's *Gospel worthy of all acceptation*, 1785, marked the theological break with hyper-Calvinism among the Particular Baptists which provided the context for Carey's vision. Fuller was Carey's home secretary, and he toured Scotland in 1799, 1802, 1805, 1808, and 1813. G. Laws, *Andrew Fuller, Pastor, Theologian, Ropeholder*, 1942.

[32]   Journal 4 to 6 August 1813. T. C. to C. Stuart, 17 July 1813, NCL CHA 3.5.86. A. Fuller to T. C., 21 November 1813, NCL CHA 4.2.29. *Memoirs*, 1, 335-9, 369f.

[33]   Chalmers read many of Fuller's works, was influenced by John Foster, and corresponded not only with Charles Stuart, but also with Christopher Anderson, the two John Rylands and Robert Hall.

[34]   Journal, 1 November 1813, 25 April 1814, 1 May 1815.

[35]   'Of all the missionaries who are now at work, I am most in love with the Baptists and the Moravians'. T. C. to C. Stuart, 24 May 1813, NCL CHA 3.5.79.

[36]   It was published in 1815 and reached four British editions and one American by 1825. *Works*, 11, 221-46. Journal 26 April, 7 May 1814.

[37]   T. Fleming to T. C., 9 March 1813, NCL CHA 4.2.27.

[38]   Moravian influence on Methodism is well known, but they also gained the recognition of parliament and the Church of England and in the 19th century became part of the emerging Protestant missionary network. They were episcopal, had links with pre-Reformation reformers, and were a church missionary in its essence. Their activist piety sidestepped the inertia of scholastic theology, they found places where it was possible to go and do something and they learnt from their experience. In Scotland they had a struggling church in Ayr which began in 1765 and did not display the missionary commitment of the movement as a whole. Scottish interest in Moravian missions was considerable and Chalmers was not the only one seeing them as pioneers demonstrating what conversion in another culture actually meant. W. Burns, *Moravian missions illustrated and defended*, Aberdeen, 1814. W. J. Couper, 'The Moravian Brethren in Scotland,' *Records of the Scottish Church History Society*, 5, 1935, 50-72. C. J. Podmore, 'The bishops and the Brethren: Anglican attitudes to the Moravians in the mid-eighteenth century', *Journal of Ecclesiastical History* 41(4) October 1990, 622-46. D. A. Schnattschneider, 'Pioneers in

basis for thinking through what was universal about Christianity and the old debates about civilization and conversion. In May 1813 he read 'almost all'[39] of A. G. Spangenberg, *An exposition of Christian doctrine as taught in the Protestant church of the United Brethren*, and was impressed by their methods.[40] He began to receive their *Periodical Accounts*[41] and arranged for the Kilmany Bible Association to send them £15 in 1814.[42] In August 1814 he worked through Spangenberg again, and inspired by it and annoyed by an article in the *Edinburgh Review* wrote an article for the *Eclectic Review* in defence of their missionary philosophy.[43]

Although he became involved in the movement long after it began, its acceptance was not yet assured. When he preached before the Dundee Missionary Society in 1812 it was to a society founded 16 years previously,[44] but when the Baptist deputation visited the following year he was ashamed to be seen with them in the streets.[45] When he collected signatures for the charter petition close friends referred to its supporters as idiots.[46] With these experiences in mind, he argued before the SSPCK that since it too was a missionary society the newer societies deserved better than they were receiving. There was an

> impetuous and overbearing contempt for everything connected with the name of missionary. The cause has been outraged by a thousand indecencies.... All the epithets of disgrace which a perverted ingenuity could devise have been unsparingly lavished on the noblest benefactors of the species.... A great proportion of our nobility, gentry and clergy, look upon it as a very low and drivelling concern; as a visionary enterprise, and that no good thing can come out of it.[47]

The essence of missionary motivation lay in the Great Commission, yet it was evangelical experience which gave it meaning:

mission: Zinzendorf and the Moravians', *International Bulletin of Missionary Research* 8(2) April 1984, 63ff.

[39] Journal, 16 May 1813.

[40] T. C. to C. Stuart, ibid.

[41] T. C. to T. S. Jones, 17 January 1814, *Correspondence*, 62. Journal, 27 August 1814, 6 January 1815.

[42] C. I. Latrobe to T. C., 13 May 1814, NCL CHA 4.3.33.

[43] *Memoirs*, 1, 389-93. Journal 23 September, 2 October 1814. *Eclectic Review*, 1815, 1-13, 156-73. *Works*, 12, 251-322.

[44] Appendix 6. J. Johnstone, *The pastoral care of Jesus over the heathen*, 1796.

[45] Journal, 9 August 1813.

[46] Ibid., 19 July 1813.

[47] *The utility of missions ascertained by experience*, 1815, *Works*, 11, 232f.

> Those to whom Christ is precious, will long that others should taste of
> that preciousness. Those who have buried all their anxieties and all
> their terrors in the sufficiency of the atonement, will long that the
> knowledge of a remedy so effectual should be carried around the
> globe.... Those who love the honour of the Saviour will long that his
> kingdom be extended till all the nations of the earth be brought under
> his one grand and universal monarchy.[48]

Those who thought it was God's responsibility to convert the heathen were
reminded that while it was 'God alone that worketh' yet 'he worketh by
instruments'.[49]

> We have no right to sit in indolence and wait for the immediate agency
> of heaven if God has told us that it is by the co-operation of human
> beings that the end is to be accomplished.[50]

Like others,[51] he observed that activity on behalf of mission overseas
stimulated work at home.

> So far from there being any interference in the two concerns, they give
> life and energy to one another, and...generally speaking those clergy
> who are most assiduous in the way of vitally christianizing their own
> districts, are ever readiest to give their assistance and their testimony to
> missionary enterprises.[52]

Chalmers had only the vaguest idea of the people among whom
missionaries laboured. They were 'prowling savages',[53] the 'wildest of
nature's children'[54] living 'in the wide and dreary wilderness of paganism',[55]
'myriads who live in guilt and die in darkness'.[56] Nevertheless they were
equal with his countrymen in terms of human potential, though he sought

---

[48]   *The two great instruments appointed for the propagation of the gospel*,
       Works, 11, 343.

[49]   Ibid., 318.

[50]   Ibid., 318f.

[51]   F. S. Piggin, *Making Evangelical Missionairies 1789-1858. The social
       background, motives and training of British Protestant missionaries to
       India*, Sutton Courtenay Press, 1984, 103.

[52]   T. C. to T. S. Jones, 12 February 1813, *Correspondence*, 61.

[53]   *The two great instruments appointed for the propagation of the gospel*,
       1813, *Works*, 11, 336.

[54]   Ibid.

[55]   Ibid., 342.

[56]   Ibid., 343.

evidence to confirm the point.[57] Since they had 'all the essential characteristics of the species',[58] it followed that 'the same moral experiment' was applicable at home and overseas.

> If schools and Bibles have been found…to be the engines of civilization to the people of Britain, it is altogether a fair and direct exercise of induction when these schools and Bibles are counted upon…as equally powerful engines of civilization to the people of other countries.[59]

Although there were the roles of linguist and teacher as well,[60] since 'the same result may be anticipated from the same instrument operating on the same materials',[61] the missionary was essentially a parish minister in another place.[62]

It became axiomatic that voluntary organizations did not suffer by their multiplication, 'there is room for all…there are funds for all',[63] and the principle was the same for Bible societies and missionary societies. The Dundee Auxiliary Bible Society was a relative newcomer[64] and when he preached for the Dundee Missionary Society, he sought to justify the existence of both[65] from the text 'Faith cometh by hearing and hearing by the word of God.'[66] Bibles and preachers were equally necessary parts of missionary enterprise and the same followed for Bible societies and missionary societies:

---

[57] Letter of Chalmers asking for information to be obtained from the Edinburgh African and Asiatic Society, 23 November 1814, NLS 10997, f.63 (name of recipient crossed out).

[58] Speech to the Fife and Kinross Bible Society, July 1812, *Edinburgh Christian Instructor*, January 1813, 66.

[59] Ibid.

[60] *Correspondence*, 267-70. *Works*, 11, 292, 337.

[61] Ibid., 69.

[62] *The utility of missions ascertained by experience*, 1815, *Works*, 11, 228f.

[63] *Works*, 11, 245f.

[64] The Dundee Missionary Society was founded in 1796, the Dundee Auxiliary Bible Society in February 1812. Appendix 6. *Dundee, Perth and Cupar Advertiser*, 21, 28 February 1812.

[65] John Love used the same text and a similar title preaching for the LMS the previous May, and the LMS secretary suggested the topic to one of their preachers the following year. J. Love, *Sermons preached on various occasions*, 1846, 229-57. S. W. Tracey to T. C., 23 March 1813, NCL CHA 4.2.49. See also, 'On the excessive preference of Bible above missionary societies,' *Edinburgh Christian Instructor*, 8(6), June 1814, 377-81.

[66] Romans 10.17.

> Neither…is to be dispensed with. If you have hearing without reading, you lay the church open to all the corruptions of popery…. If you have reading without hearing, you throw away the benefit of a public ministry.[67]

As he read more of the Moravians and Baptists,[68] he was able to use illustrations from Greenland, Labrador and India. The SSPCK also provided a ready example. Here indeed was the 'utility of missions ascertained by experience', and people had to look no further than the Highlands of Scotland and ask 'what would they have been at this moment, had schools and ministers and Bibles been kept back from them?'[69]

Priorities in mission

Like many Evangelicals,[70] Chalmers was sensitive to the priority which should be given to 'christianization' as opposed to 'civilization'. If the antithesis was often false and debate sterile, the difference in attitudes was real enough.

Hill and other Moderates insisted that conversion normally required a prior level of civilization. This was consistent with an understanding of Christian faith as rational assent to propositions believed to be true because of the weight of evidence and the soundness of their philosophical backing. It would be impossible to understand the logic without education.

Evangelicals also valued education, but for them the possibility of faith as an intuitive act of trust was open to any person by virtue of being human, and they were unwilling to support policies which could be construed as denying this.

Each tendency carried its own dangers. Evangelicals could preach a gospel which denied the social relevance of Christian faith. Moderates could be seen as lacking interest in anything spiritual at all. A failure to be

---

67   *Works*, 11, 323, 325.

68   As well as Spangenberg, the Moravian *Periodical Accounts* and the Baptist *Periodical Accounts*, a source of Chalmers' information was W. Brown, *History of the propagation of Christianity*, 1814 edition, 255-64, 310-16.

69   *Works*, 11, 233.

70   There are exceptions. The experience of the LMS at the beginning of its Pacific mission made it doubt the wisdom of rushing in with preaching the gospel. With this in mind the evangelical Anglican Samuel Marsden (1764-1838) proposed to the CMS a mission to New Zealand in which tradesmen would lead the way, since 'nothing in my opinion can pave the way for the introduction of the gospel, but civilization' (S. Marsden to J. Pratt, 7 April 1808, P. Havard-Williams, *Marsden and the New Zealand Mission*, 1961, 15). The CMS agreed, but the first years of the New Zealand mission were also a failure which went to show that leadership and circumstances were often more critical than either priority.

concerned with 'civilization' could hold back genuine benefits of European culture and technology and prevent people from seeing how Christian faith related to their own culture. A commitment to it was transporting more than the gospel and was hardly aware of the distinction. Both sides were seeking to work out what it meant to take Christianity from one culture to another. It would be hard to say who was more prone to cultural imperialism.

In the 18th century the SSPCK included both emphases. However for the first decades of the missionary movement it was not clear whether Scottish Evangelicals, whose focus of support had moved to the newer voluntary societies rather than the SSPCK, were still prepared to accept this.

Chalmers was at first little interested,[71] but noted that those who made 'the civilization of the species' their dream should recognize that Christian missionaries had actually achieved this.[72] He pointed to missionary success in promoting literacy[73] and defended Moravians who preached the gospel before they shared technology.[74]

Given the terms of the debate, there was little doubt Chalmers would come down on the side of christianization. What is ironical is that so many of his concerns were on the other side and in the long run he came to see it as embracing so much of what others intended by civilization. It was an issue which arose out of his own pilgrimage and ministry at Kilmany. For years 'civilization' was the very thing he had tried to achieve.

> I cannot but record the effect of an actual though undesigned experiment, which I prosecuted for upwards of twelve years…. For the greater part of that time I could expatiate on the meanness of dishonesty, on the villany of falsehood, on the despicable arts of calumny, – in a word, upon all those deformities of character, which awaken the natural indignation of the human heart against the pests and disturbers of human society. Now could I, upon the strength of these warm expostulations, have got the thief to give up his stealing, and the evil speaker his censoriousness, and the liar his deviations from the truth, I should have felt all the repose of someone who had gotten his ultimate object. It never occurred to me that all this might have been

---

[71]   T. Duncan wrote that he was 'rather a friend to civilizing people before you convert them.' 9 March 1812, NCL CHA 4.1.37 (erroneously dated 1811).

[72]   *Works*, 11, 336.

[73]   Ibid., 292.

[74]   *Works*, 12, 251-98.

done, and yet every soul of every hearer have remained in full alienation from God.[75]

It was only after his conversion and the change in his preaching that Chalmers heard of any of these 'subordinate reformations' which had been the aim of his earlier ministry. The Moravians in Greenland had made a similar discovery. At first

> they expatiated on the existence, and the unity, and the attributes and the love of God. The poor Greenlanders did not comprehend them; and at the end of many years the missionaries were mortified to find that they had not gained a single proselyte to the faith. On this they resolved to change their measures and…made one great and immediate step to the peculiar doctrines of Christianity…. The effect was instantaneous. When told of sin and of the Saviour, the ears of the savages were constrained to listen to the message, and their understandings opened to receive it.[76]

It was in fact a change in theological focus more than a shift from civilization first, but something communicated which had not before and over a period they had the results of 'civilization' to show for their efforts.[77]

> Go to a Moravian village and you meet not with a few Christian individuals but with a Christian society, where the virtues of the gospel are exemplified in all their primitive simplicity and fulness.[78]

As with poor-relief at Kilmany and St John's, Chalmers was led by the apparent success of particular instances to make unwarranted generalizations. Not for the first or last time he failed to heed his own warning:

---

[75] *The duty of giving an immediate diligence to the business of the Christian life, being an address to the inhabitants of the parish of Kilmany*, 1815, *Works*, 12, 108.

[76] T. C. to the Secretaries of the Fife and Kinross Bible Society, 20 October 1813, *Correspondence*, 268.

[77] This was the burden of Chalmers' article in the *Eclectic Review*. This was a reply to the *Edinburgh Review* which had alleged Moravians were an example to other missionaries (a 'swarm' of whom had injured 'both the happiness and the morals' of one village in Africa) because they began by 'civilizing their pupils' and 'educating them in the useful arts'. Chalmers argued Moravian Missionary policy was the opposite, and the results admired by the *Edinburgh Review* were due to preaching the gospel over a longer period than other missions had had the opportunity of doing. *Memoirs*, 1, 389-93.

[78] Sermon, 3 April 1814. *Posthumous Works*, 6, 207.

The principle of association, however useful in the main, has a blinding and misleading effect in many instances. Give it a wide enough field of induction to work upon, and it will carry you to a right conclusion.... But the evil is, that it often carries you forward with as much confidence upon a limited as upon an enlarged field of experience.[79]

It was left to others to discuss missionary practice in less simplified terms and to point out that if 'civilization' included literacy that was no irrelevant thing – whether the message was rational apologetics or the atonement.[80] Chalmers would hardly have disagreed, but the question in his mind was not whether civilization was useful, but whether it was essential. He remained insistent that it was 'both doctrinally and experimentally untrue that a preparatory civilization is necessary ere the human mind can be in a state of readiness for the reception of the gospel of Jesus Christ'.[81]

When he moved to Glasgow, Chalmers' potential for fund-raising was not lost on missionary societies. He was approached by societies around Scotland[82] and in London, including the Northern Missionary Society,[83] the Scottish Missionary Society,[84] the LMS,[85] the Baptists,[86] Methodists,[87] and Moravians. He preached for the LMS in London in 1817,[88] and in one year raised over £500 for the Moravians.[89]

Few of his missionary addresses from this period were published, but there are signs that he was beginning to give more thought to what it was that made the gospel universal and 'civilization' secondary:

Every faithful missionary and minister of the gospel carried with him that which had always characterized and distinguished it...its discovery

---

[79] *Works*, 11, 223.

[80] For example, J. Douglas, *Hints on missions*, 1822. J. Inglis, *The grounds of Christian hope in the universal prevalence of the gospel*, 1818.

[81] *Posthumous Works*, 9, 155.

[82] For example the Ceres Missionary Society and the Glasgow Society for promoting Christianity among the Jews. W. Bell to T. C., 9 September 1821, NCL CHA 4.51.40. *Memoirs*, 2, 173.

[83] A. MacIntosh to T. C., 20 November 1819, NCL CHA 4.12.28.

[84] Journal, 29 April, 1822.

[85] They had been trying to get him for an anniversary sermon in London since 1814, and in 1821 asked him to preach in Scotland. G. Burder to T. C., 14 October 1814, StAUL 30385.68. *Memoirs*, 2, 62. J. Arundel to T. C., 14 June 1821, NCL CHA 4.17.11.

[86] J. Ryland to T. C., 29 January 1819, NCL CHA 4.13.33.

[87] J. Bunting to T. C., 27 February 1822, StAUL 30385.87. T. C. to J. Butterworth, 12 February 1823, StAUL BX 9225.C4E23.

[88] *Memoirs*, 2, 98f.

[89] Ibid., 95f.

to man of his guilt and misery, and its revelation to him of the only adequate relief and refuge.[90]

This was what he habitually referred to as the 'portable evidence of Christianity'[91] and again his own experience found a parallel in the Moravians. Evangelical literature was being read by members of his congregation long before he saw any value in it.[92] The Moravians showed that 'a clear perception of scriptural truth' could be found 'among men who have just emerged from the rudest and grossest barbarity'.[93] The New Testament suggested a universal principle, 'the manifestation of the truth to the conscience',[94] and in 1823 he asked J. W. Cunningham of Harrow

> What would you think of the universality of the law written in the heart as an invitation to missionary undertakings?.... [I]n all countries you have a ground upon which you can at once enter.[95]

In this his thinking was linked to criticism of his article on Christianity in the *Edinburgh Encyclopedia*[96] for having neglected 'internal' as opposed to 'external' evidences. In time he reversed his preference for the latter and in this his friendship with Thomas Erskine[97] (1788-1870) of

---

[90] *Missionary Register*, 1817, 205.
[91] *Works*, 4, 169-212.
[92] *Memoirs*, 1, 102.
[93] *Works*, 7, 175.
[94] T. C. to C. Stuart, 22 August 1817, NCL CHA 3.8.54. 2 Corinthians 4.2.
[95] T. C. to J. W. Cunningham, 25 March 1823, *Correspondence*, 25. Cunningham (1780-1861) was a member of the Clapham sect and from 1817 corresponded with Chalmers. He was mystified by Scottish theology, and offered friendly criticism, including the suggestion Zachary Macaulay be employed to improve Chalmers' English. J. W. Cunningham to T. C., 2 May 1819, NCL CHA 4.10.54.
[96] *The evidence and authority of the Christian revelation*, 1815, *Memoirs*, 1, 367-72.
[97] They first met in 1818. Chalmers was impressed by Erskine's spirituality, and in 1819 read a draft of his *Internal Evidences*. They shared interests in Moravianism and missions in general, but Erskine did not want to be involved in church politics and after 1838 they drifted apart. Nevertheless in 1843 Chalmers wrote of 'a radical and essential unity between us' (*Correspondence*, 317). He did not agree with Erskine's universalism, but was more at home with Erskine (also Edward Irving and McLeod Campbell) than confessional orthodoxy. This was also true of Chalmers' son-in-law William Hanna who was also Erskine's biographer. W. Hanna, *Letters of Thomas Erskine of Linlathen*, 1878, 17-217. H. H. Williams, *The religious thought of Thomas Erskine of Linlathen: its origin, nature and*

Linlathen was also important.[98]

'*A monthly meeting for missionary information*'[99]

The most interesting aspect of his involvement with the missionary movement while in Glasgow was the St John's Parish Association for Religious Purposes. As noted earlier,[100] each proportion had a group organized from among themselves to distribute missionary literature, collect a penny a week from subscribers and meet quarterly to allocate funds to whatever Bible or missionary society they thought fit.

In December 1821 a circular was sent out in the name of the 'pastor, elders, deacons and Sabbath-school teachers', who had been 'much refreshed and edified' by contact with the missionary movement, concerned that people in the parish should not be ignorant of 'the great work that the Lord is doing among the nations'.[101] It was not simply support for missions Chalmers was after, but stimulus for the faith of his parishioners. Not least of the benefits was acquaintance 'with the moral and political condition of every country under heaven'.

By the time this project was launched Chalmers was making regular visits to a missionary reading room.[102] Missionary meetings were held for the parish as a whole, not just in each proportion,[103] and towards the end of his ministry in Glasgow he wrote:

> I am not aware of a better organization that can be set up in a parish or one that conduces more to the well-being of its people...I have great comfort in a monthly meeting for missionary information. The people assemble in church and from the precentor's desk I read the most important missionary news that has transpired through the preceding month. This simple reading with prayers formed the whole service. It may be done either by a minister or by a layman, and such now is the

---

influence, University of Leeds PhD thesis, 1951, 9f. D. Finlayson, 'Aspects of the life and influence of Thomas Erskine of Linlathen', *Records of the Scottish Church History Society*, 20(1), 1980, 31-45. N. R. Needham, *Thomas Erskine of Linlathen: his life and theology 1788-1837*, Rutherford House, Edinburgh, 1989. J. P. Newell, '"Unworthy of the dignity of the Assembly": the deposition of Alexander John Scott in 1831', *Records of the Scottish Church History Society*, 21, 1983, 258-60.

[98] As was his relationship with Charles Stuart.

[99] T. C. to G. Sinclair, 23 October 1823, SRO/WRH MF RH 5/49, reel 6.

[100] Page 113.

[101] *Scottish Missionary Register*, 3(2), February 1822, 41f.

[102] Journal, 16 January 1822.

[103] Ibid., 4 February.

profusion of monthly sheets and circulars and magazines...the difficulty is to select for an hour's reading.[104]

The St John's Parish Association was a further stage in the development of the local missionary society. In 1807 the LMS had encouraged local societies to bring in donations from poorer people, but it was almost purely a fund-raising exercise.[105] The CMS began a similar programme in 1813, but also wished to promote a 'missionary spirit',[106] and provided newsletters to be circulated through the groups. In St John's the association was organized on a territorial basis and Chalmers was concerned not just that it might support 20 native preachers in India or circulate a thousand Bibles through penny-a-week collections,[107] but that the involvement this entailed would help propagate the gospel in Glasgow.

---

[104] T. C. to G. Sinclair, 23 October 1823, SRO/WRH MF RH 5/49, reel 6.

[105] Lovett, *London Missionary Society*, 1, 1899, 81-3.

[106] *Missionary Register*, 1813, 21-4.

[107] *Scottish Missionary Register*, 3(2), February 1822, 42.

Chapter 11

'To attempt to convert the world without educating it is grasping at the end and neglecting the means'[1]
The Church of Scotland and missions, 1813-1829

In October 1829, Alexander Duff[2] (1806-1879) set sail for India as the first missionary appointed by the Church of Scotland. This was the outcome of an 1824 General Assembly decision which 'unanimously and cordially'[3] agreed to the motion of the Moderate leader John Inglis calling for a committee to investigate the possibility of such a mission.

In 1813 the concern of the Assembly had been that the East India Company charter should provide for Church of Scotland chaplains to Scottish expatriates in India. Appointments had been made to Bengal, Bombay and Madras, and in 1822 the number was increased to six.[4] Oversight was exercised through the Presbytery of Edinburgh, which drew Edinburgh ministers into thinking about India especially when the Bengal chaplain, James Bryce[5] (1785-1866), found himself in situations where his personality and that of the Anglican Bishop[6] made for certain conflict.[7]

Bryce was an extreme Moderate who needs to be better appreciated, but he did not bring out the best in people at home or abroad. He had long had an interest in India,[8] and after several years in Calcutta began to take an

---

[1]   J. Douglas, *Hints on missions*, 1822, 100.

[2]   *Fasti*, 7, 690-92.

[3]   *AGA*, 1824, 37.

[4]   *Fasti*, 7, 568f.

[5]   *Fasti*, 6, 112. Memorial re....India chaplains, SRO/GRH CH1/5/80.

[6]   Thomas Middleton (1769-1822) was the first Bishop appointed to India. He had difficulty with the right of the Church of Scotland to equal treatment as an established church.

[7]   The debates over church steeples, building funds and validity of marriages had their comic side. S. C. Sanial, 'Early history of St Andrew's Kirk, Calcutta', *Bengal Past and Present*, 10, 1915, 195-210.

[8]   J. Bryce, *A sketch of the state of British India with a view of pointing out the best means of civilizing its inhabitants, and diffusing the knowledge of*

interest in the spread of Christianity among Hindus.[9] While in Scotland in 1820 he discussed his ideas with the Moderate leader John Inglis and it was decided that on his return he should gather information on the prospects for a mission.[10] In 1824 the General Assembly had before it a memorial from Bryce, and overtures from the Presbyteries of Edinburgh and Linlithgow and the Synods of Moray and Aberdeen.[11] After what Chalmers described as 'a most Christian discussion',[12] the Assembly accepted Inglis' proposal and in so doing ushered in a new era in the history of the Church of Scotland.[13]

There were no dissenting votes, but the response was neither as unanimous nor as cordial as it appeared. Chalmers' attitude was not shared by all on the Evangelical side and many Moderates were not too sure about the decision for different reasons.

For nearly 30 years Evangelicals had been supporting missions through the societies. Given that the Church's courts were in the hands of their opponents, they were cautious about a mission being organized by the Church of Scotland, the more so since it appeared priority was to be given to 'civilizing'.[14] It did not help that Bryce was instrumental in raising the issue,[15] but Inglis knew that whatever their misgivings, Evangelicals could

---

[9]   *Christianity throughout the Eastern world, being the substance of an essay on these subjects, to which the University of Aberdeen adjudged Dr Buchanan's prize*, 1810.

        The preaching of the gospel, the efficient means of diffusing among mankind a knowledge of the true God. A sermon preached at the opening of the Church of St Andrew, in Calcutta, March 1818, 1818. By 'preaching' Bryce meant the propagation of Christianity generally, and through 'the gentle hand of education' (ibid., 43). He did not mean preaching as opposed to education.

[10]   D. Chambers, 'The Church of Scotland's nineteenth century foreign missions scheme: Evangelical or Moderate revival?' *Journal of Religious History*, 9, 1976, 124.

[11]   Ibid., 122. J. Bryce, Memorial and petition...to the General Assembly of the Church of Scotland anent the establishment of a Presbyterian Missionary College at Calcutta, December 8th, 1823. SRO/GRH CH1/5/81.

[12]   *Memoirs*, 3, 19.

[13]   A. C. Cheyne, '1824: The Kirk votes for a world-wide gospel', *Life and Work*, August 1978, 23.

[14]   Henry Duncan of Ruthwell, was not against the scheme as such, but 'was totally at variance' with the idea that 'it was necessary to civilize men before they could be christianized'. This was the only speech reported by the *Edinburgh Christian Instructor*, 23 June 1824, 484-7. Inglis could afford to offend Evangelicals by such statements; he could not risk losing Moderates by not making them.

[15]   In 1820 he had been responsible for getting the Assembly to censure the *Edinburgh Christian Instructor*; a move which drew equally small-minded reaction from its editor, Andrew Thomson. *Edinburgh Christian Instructor*, 19, 1820, 406-36, 483-505. Chambers, 'Evangelical or Moderate revival?', 1976, 125.

not vote against a missionary scheme. The real problem was to carry the Moderates.

For very different reasons they were also in a predicament. Traditionally they had supported the sort of mission represented by the SSPCK, especially when its political role in the Highlands had been one they identified with, and its more evangelistic role was on the other side of the Atlantic. If they had no particular liking for what was now seen as characteristically Evangelical activity, they could not really bring themselves publicly to oppose what in 1813 had received the sanction of government and more recently that of a Royal letter launching an appeal to build Bishop's College in Calcutta. Glasgow University had awarded honorary doctorates to two LMS missionaries, Robert Morrison in 1817 and William Milne in 1820. It was difficult for respectable opinion to oppose what had become widely acceptable, but a private letter of John Hope (1794-1854) reveals the feelings of some of the older Moderate leaders:

> Dr Inglis has done very great detriment to the Moderate interest during this Assembly…by coming forward with a most preposterous scheme for the Church of Scotland to identify itself with all the missionaries in the two hemispheres and to collect funds by parochial collections etc for sending forth missionaries to all quarters of the world…. We had a doze [*sic*] of fanaticism such as I suppose has not been heard in the General Assembly since the restoration of Charles the 2nd…. Dr Nicoll thought that the best course was to let the storm blow over by…allowing the proposition to go to a committee…. If Dr Inglis should write to your Lordship on the subject I trust that you will throw cold water on his projects.[16]

In tone and vocabulary this is reminiscent of 1796, but such views no longer carried weight and in 1824 were matters for private correspondence. Inglis' task was to carry as many as possible by positive conviction rather than reluctant acceptance.

His thinking about missions stood in that part of the Moderate tradition represented by Principal Robertson's 1755 SSPCK sermon, the teaching of Principal Hill and the concerns raised by their party in the 1796 General Assembly. He believed that the time which had been in the future in 1796 had now arrived, and he was sensitive to points raised in the debate over civilization and Christianization. In a refreshing change from much of the discussion he examined what was involved in some detail.

Preaching for the SSPCK in 1818[17] Inglis asked whether the 'condition of the heathen world' was not important in that on the whole it

---

[16]   5 June 1824, NLS 11, ff.157-60.

[17]   J. Inglis, *The grounds of Christian hope in the universal prevalence of the gospel*, 1818. This was in response to the SSPCK sermon the previous

was the unconverted who were the uncivilized, although 'to what degree this...operates as an obstacle to their reception of the Christian faith, is a question about which wise men will differ':[18]

> It cannot be doubted that a man of an understanding mind, habituated to thought and reflection, has an advantage over others, for estimating both the evidence of Christian doctrine, and its accommodation to human wants.... We should, therefore, do injustice to the hope which we entertain of the universal prevalence of the gospel, if we did not make a fair allowance for the corresponding disadvantage under which others labour. It is obvious that whatever shall tend to remove such an obstruction to the success of the gospel, must have the effect to facilitate its progress in the world.[19]

Education was thus an essential element since it would 'lay a foundation for the success of all other means which may be employed',[20] including the training of a native ministry – upon which long-term progress depended.[21] Bryce took a similar line,[22] but with greater emphasis on seeking to convert the better educated. It was 'too much the exclusive practice of the Christian missionary to address himself to the lower and illiterate classes' and 'desultory harangues' only made a small impression. There was a rising demand for education, and he wished to see the Church of Scotland 'attempt the effect of addressing the better informed natives of this capital, in their own language under the roof of an established Christian temple'[23] – no doubt St Andrew's Church, Calcutta.

In speaking to the 1824 Assembly[24] Inglis called for the redeeming of the pledge of 1796 that opportunity would be taken when more favourable conditions prevailed. Although some might feel the prospects for success were still not great, he believed that if they went about it the right way the situation was promising. It meant taking 'the advantage of improving young minds and teaching the arts of civilization as preliminary steps', but he was far from saying that 'there was no hope in preaching the Gospel to a people in any condition'.[25]

---

year, A. M. Thomson, *The ultimate and universal prevalence of the Christian religion*, 1817.

[18] Inglis, *Grounds of Christian hope*, 1818, 12.

[19] Ibid., 13.

[20] Ibid., 19.

[21] Ibid., 22.

[22] Bryce, Memorial and petition, 1823, SRO/GRH CH1/5/81

[23] Ibid.

[24] *Edinburgh Advertiser*, 28 May 1824.

[25] Ibid.

God forbid that he should limit Divine grace. The reason that he held previous education to be necessary was that a barbarous people were wedded to their superstitious rites; but give them knowledge and information...and it will be found that superstition will not stand before intelligent minds.... He had no view to exclude the preaching of the gospel to all; but he contended it should first be communicated to those most likely to embrace it.[26]

At the following Assembly the committee appointed under Inglis presented their plans. It was intended to begin with 'one central seminary...with branch schools', and the head-master would be an ordained minister who would 'embrace opportunities...to recommend the gospel of Christ to the faith and acceptance of those to whom he finds access'. He would be expected to work especially among those who had already received 'a liberal education' and provide them with 'tracts illustrative of the import, the evidences and the history of our Christian faith'.[27]

The Assembly approved the report, commended the zeal of the committee, and authorized a special collection.[28] In 1826 Inglis published a letter *To the people of Scotland*, setting forth the arguments and proposals brought before the Assembly earlier.[29] It was carefully worded to meet the concerns of both Moderate and Evangelical, each of whom showed greater interest as time went on. A significant development was the insistence that education be in English – not just to equip minds to assess the integrity of Christian evidences, but as in itself a means of destroying idolatry. As in his 1818 sermon Inglis looked to the formation of a native ministry, lest 'the maintenance of the gospel in India...be for ever dependent on such foreign aid as would be very little adequate to the extent of the work'.[30]

The 1824 Assembly is often seen as a reversal of the decision of 1796 not to be directly involved in the missionary movement. However the proposals agreed to in 1824 and 1825 were not those rejected in 1796. If it had been suggested in the 1820s that the Church of Scotland authorize collections for voluntary missionary societies it would have met the same fate as the overtures of 1796. What was agreed to was to send out a head-master to establish a school – the traditional pattern of the SSPCK.

Yet there is no doubt the climate for missions had changed out of recognition. Since the East India Company charter campaign, the

---

[26] Ibid.

[27] *To the people of Scotland, the letter of a committee of the General Assembly of the church, relative to the propagation of the gospel in foreign parts, and, more immediately in the British provinces of India*, 1826, Appendix, Report to the General Assembly (1825).

[28] Ibid.

[29] Ibid.

[30] Cheyne, 'Kirk votes for a world-wide gospel', 1978, 23.

missionary movement had achieved rapid growth evident from the rising income of societies in America and Britain.[31] The campaign had been instrumental in winning support, and in its wake more local societies were formed.[32] In 1813, the CMS launched the *Missionary Register* which carried information on all societies, not just their own. Deputations visited Scotland keeping old support alive[33] and stimulating new. 'Missionary intelligence' was carried in the *Edinburgh Christian Instructor* and the *Religious Monitor,* and more often than not the annual sermons for the Edinburgh Missionary Society found their way into print together with the directors' report.

In 1819 the Edinburgh Missionary Society changed its name to the Scottish Missionary Society, and the year after began to publish a *Scottish Missionary Register.*[34] It covered far more than their own missions, and every month its 40 pages ranged from Russia to the South Seas, with extracts from the major British societies as well as news of local societies in Scotland and items of interest in the life of the churches at home.

At the time the Scottish Missionary Society was at a low ebb. Its mission in Russia was struggling with little to show for patient labours and in March 1820 the society was £1000 in debt.[35] Yet their fortunes steadily improved. Aided by the success of their publication there was further growth in auxiliary societies[36] and by 1821 it was reckoned that 'missionary zeal' was 'assuredly on the increase'.[37] This enabled them to open new fields in Jamaica and Bombay and begin a training scheme for missionary candidates. The Glasgow Society showed signs of fresh life by again becoming a sending society when it began work in South Africa.

These developments were not lost on John Inglis. With its change of name and new lease of life the Scottish Missionary Society was underlining

---

[31]   Between 1812 and 1820 the income of the LMS and the American Board of Commissioners for Foreign Missions increased three-fold and that of the CMS more than twelve-fold. *Scottish Missionary Register,* 11(1), January 1830, 2.

[32]   For example the Fenwick Auxiliary Missionary Society. Minute book, NRA(S), 797.6.

[33]   The visit of an LMS deputation in 1815 served to revive the Aberdeen society founded in 1796. *Aberdeen Auxiliary Missionary Society first annual report,* 1816, 17f.

[34]   First issue, January 1820.

[35]   *Scottish Missionary Register,* 1(3), 1820.

[36]   Six auxiliaries were formed in 1821 and by 1822 the total of new societies reached 19. By 1825 there were 26 societies auxiliary to the Scottish Missionary Society, and the Scottish Missionary Society drive had also brought into existence groups who distributed funds among more than one major society.

[37]   *Quarterly Missionary Paper,* bound with NCL copies of the *Scottish Missionary Register,* n.d. (late 1821).

a claim to become the national missionary society, and almost succeeded. It drew support from both Church and Dissent, including a large number of Evangelicals and a sprinkling of Moderates.[38] The Berwickshire Auxiliary boasted the Earl of Breadalbane as its president.[39]

If the Church of Scotland was to retain its role at the centre of the country's religious life, it could not allow respectable opinion to go elsewhere in search of an outlet for missionary interest. The openings Bryce detected in India provided an obvious remedy.

From 1813 the tide of opinion was running behind supporters of missions, and between then and the Assemblies of 1824 and 1825 it was opponents who shifted to the defensive. Symbolic of the change was a letter of 1820 harking back to the arguments used in the 1796 Assembly. It was written by 'A fellow of the old school' but he died before it was published.[40] Distaste for missions came from a body of opinion which could no longer command the situation. In 1825 a minister from Perth was accused before the Synod that 'having attended a meeting of the missionary society in Cupar and praying therein he did weaken the hands of the minister of the parish and injure the interest of sound religion'. The case was dismissed.[41] The story of the unfortunate missionary to Demerera, John Smith, who died in custody before the news of the remission of his sentence of death for inciting insurrection among the slaves could reach him, was widely reported.[42] Debated in the British parliament, the case could not help but portray opponents of missions as reactionary and pro-slavery.

Objections because of the state of society were archaic by 1824. Plantation owners in the West Indies might view missionaries with suspicion, but nobody in Britain was preoccupied with their seditious potential. People like Chalmers were more likely to argue that missionary societies were an insurance against such tendencies. Some concerns expressed in the 1796 debate were taken into account not only by Inglis in

---

38   At the 1822 annual general meeting of the Scottish Missionary Society John Lee (1779-1859), shortly to be of the Canongate (*Fasti*, 1, 26) and Alexander Brunton (1772-1854), Professor of Oriental Languages at Edinburgh University (*Fasti*, 1, 137) were both speakers to motions. *Scottish Missionary Register*, 3(6), June 1822, 201.

39   *Scottish Missionary Register*, 2(8), August 1821, 288. He was elected president of the Scottish Missionary Society in 1822.

40   He argued that Christianity 'was never meant for man in a state of barbarism' and the gospel could only be propagated 'by means of colonizations'. *Literary and Statistical Magazine for Scotland*, 4, November 1820, 381-98.

41   *Dundee, Perth and Cupar Advertiser*, 13 October 1825.

42   Including: *Blackwood's*, 15, June 1824, 679-90. *Dundee, Perth and Cupar Advertiser*, 10 June 1824. *Scottish Missionary Register*, 5(4), April 1824, 181-9.

his proposals, but also by the Evangelical layman James Douglas of Cavers in his influential *Hints on missions* published in 1822.[43]

From opposite sides of the Assembly Inglis and Douglas represented a further development in the tradition exemplified by the SSPCK. Their insistence on a close relationship between education and missions was instrumental in restoring a consensus between Moderate and Evangelical which enabled both parties again to work together in the overseas mission of the Church.

The degree to which the 1824 Assembly decision was a product of Evangelical renaissance[44] is made pertinent by the extent of Moderate initiative and Evangelical indifference. The key roles of Bryce, Inglis and the ongoing Moderate leadership were hotly disputed by generations of Evangelical writers, beginning with Hugh Miller[45] and Robert Buchanan.[46] Alexander Duff gave John Inglis the credit he deserved,[47] but the debates leading to the Disruption resulted in many[48] saying the 1824 decision was solely a product of the Evangelicals, and that the Moderate party was characteristically anti-missions. There were enough Moderates who fitted this image to give it plausibility, but the problem was less that Moderates were anti-missions than that many of them were anti-Evangelical. If on occasion these amounted to the same thing, it was not the whole story.[49]

The instinctive identification of missions as an Evangelical activity, together with the legacy of Miller and Buchanan, made it possible for a writer such a A. J. Campbell (no uncritical friend of Evangelicals) to say the decision of the 1824 Assembly was made in an atmosphere 'largely created by Thomas Chalmers'.[50] In fact Chalmers had nothing to do with the introduction of the subject and did not take part in the debate. It was Inglis and Bryce, both Moderates, who worked to get the Church of Scotland, as a church, involved in overseas mission. What was true was that their proposals were also born out of a reaction *against* missionary societies as well as from a positive desire to further the mission of the church overseas.

---

[43] Niel Gunson, *Messengers of Grace, Evangelical missions in the South Seas 1797-1860*, 1978, 102f.

[44] D. Chambers, 'The Church of Scotland's nineteenth century foreign mission scheme: Evangelical or Moderate revival?', *Journal of Religious History*, 9, 1976, 115-38.

[45] *The two parties in the Church of Scotland exhibited as missionary and anti-missionary*, 1841.

[46] *The ten years' conflict*, 1, 1849, 320-24.

[47] A. Duff, *India and India missions*, 1839, 481-96.

[48] Another example is in the *Presbyterian Review*, October 1842, 416f.

[49] The question that concerns Chambers, 'Evangelical or Moderate revival', is not who was first, but the validity of the accusation that the Moderate party was characteristically anti-missions.

[50] *Two centuries of the Church of Scotland, 1707-1929*, 1930, 171.

For its part Evangelical revival rode on the back of missionary interest as much as the other way around. From 1796 onwards missionary subjects had become the staple of Evangelical publishing. Local missionary societies drew people together not only in the cause of missions, but also in the cause of Evangelical piety. It was not difficult to attract to both a younger generation who saw no future in the fading domination of the Moderates. Chalmers was one whose overseas mission interest and evangelical commitment grew together.

Inglis could rightly claim continuity with the Moderate commitments of 1796, but it was Evangelical engagement with missions from then onwards and Evangelical agitation over the East India Company charter which created the situation in which it was possible and necessary for Moderates to decide that the Church itself had to be involved.

Chapter 12

'The necessity of uniting prayer with performance for the success of missions'[1]
Chalmers at St Andrews, 1823-1828

His five years at St Andrews in the 1820s were most important for Chalmers' involvement in the missionary movement. Six students[2] set their sights on the mission field, among them Alexander Duff. For much of this period Chalmers was president of the town missionary society and his house was a regular stopping place for missionary deputations visiting Scotland. Requests for fund-raising sermons did not diminish and every year brought its crop of letters from hopeful secretaries – particularly if it was rumoured he might be in London during the summer.

Addresses on missions
Chalmers received requests from the Wesleyan Methodist Missionary Society,[3] the Moravians,[4] the Baptists,[5] and the LMS.[6] He preached for the Scottish Missionary Society on several occasions[7] and for local societies at Perth[8] and elsewhere. At the General Assemblies of 1825 and 1828 he spoke

---

[1] *Works*, 12, 47-68.

[2] For a more detailed account see Stuart Piggin and John Roxborogh, *The St Andrews Seven*, 1985.

[3] J. Bunting to T. C., 16 January 1824, NCL CHA 4.31.26. G. Morley to T. C., 11 December 1827, NCL CHA 4.81.17.

[4] W. Leach to T. C., 10 April 1827, NCL CHA 4.31.26. E. Craig to T. C., 28 May 1824, StAUL 30385.143.

[5] J. Dyer to T. C., 24 December 1824, StAUL 30385.257.

[6] J. Arundel to T. C., 25 April 1827, NCL CHA 4.65.59. J. A. James to T. C., 25 January 1825, NCL CHA 4.45.5. B. Robertson to T. C., 22 November 1826, NCL CHA 4.61.17.

[7] *Memoirs*, 3, 16. *Dundee, Perth and Cupar Advertiser*, 26 August 1824.

[8] *Memoirs*, 3, 28, A. Adamson to T. C., 29 May 1827, NCL CHA 4.65.31. C. J. Murray to T. C., 9 April 1830, NCL CHA 4.144.49.

to the report of the missions committee, and at dinners held during the Assemblies of 1826 and 1827 gave speeches which dealt with the Church of Scotland and missions. His thinking had developed, but these engagements were more an effort of travel than of fresh composition. In 1824 he noted he had delivered 'the same missionary sermon...I have preached in Cupar, Perth, Edinburgh, Lanark and Anstruther. It has...got £300 for the cause.'[9]

While in Edinburgh for the 1824 Assembly he preached for the Scottish Missionary Society.[10] He was mainly concerned about supporters letting trust in God be usurped by 'so many societies...the skilful mechanism of their various offices' and the 'train of auxiliaries all over the land'.[11]

> Christians who flourished in the days of Puritanism...were men of prayer but not men of missionary performance; and the Christians of our present day are men of performance but need perhaps to be humbled by crosses and adversities into men of prayer. It is out of the happy combination of these two habits that the evangelizing of the nations is to come.[12]

As he had often emphasized in the words of the seventeenth-century missionary to the American Indians, John Eliot, it was 'in the power of pains and of prayers to do anything'.[13]

Pedantic minds had been at work in the 1824 Assembly and there had been a question whether overseas mission proposals should be considered before or after a parallel scheme for a new educational mission to the Highlands.[14] In 1825 the point was raised again. Some felt that whoever got to hold a collection first would have an advantage. Since 'Charity did not work by the process of exhaustion, but by fermentation',[15] to Chalmers it was a matter of indifference which had preference.

At the jubilee dinner of the Theological Society in Edinburgh the following year, he was asked to toast 'the universal diffusion of religious

---

[9] *Memoirs*, 3, 45f.

[10] Journal, 21 May 1824. J. Anderson, *Reminiscences of Thomas Chalmers*, 1851, 88-90. *Edinburgh Advertiser*, 25 May 1824. *Works*, 12, 47-68.

[11] *Works*, 12, 59.

[12] *Works*, 12, 59f.

[13] *Works*, 12, 60. The phrase parallels his comment to his daughter Grace, 'I've always been a kind of outlier between the practical and the pious. I have a liking for both.' NCL CHA 2.57.4. quoted by Margot Butt, 'The Chalmers papers,' A. C. Cheyne, ed., *The practical and the pious*, 1985, 189.

[14] Some Evangelicals were prominent in raising this. *Edinburgh Christian Instructor*, June 1824, 449-51.

[15] General Assembly, Monday, May 30 1825, Newspaper cuttings 1816-1831, Charles Watson of Burntisland papers, NCL.

truth'[16] and again emphasized the mutuality of home and overseas mission. They had been launched in the same year and sprang from the same spirit; they were equally signs of life operating on the principle of 'do good unto all men as ye have opportunity'.[17] It was no reproach that these were only recent developments. It was proper that the Church of Scotland act deliberately and build on the experience of others. On May 25 1827 an Assembly dinner again called forth a speech in which the themes were by now familiar, as was the 'long and continued applause'[18] by which it was accompanied.

The 1828 Assembly was the first at which he had spoken to the report of Inglis' committee since 1825. To many it seemed that progress had been negligible. In four years only £2500 had been raised with less than a quarter of congregations contributing and there was no sight of an appointment. Although the country was going through a difficult economic spell, the Scottish Missionary Society was not suffering for want of funds, and by 1826 the Highlands and Islands mission had managed to obtain £5500 from nearly twice the number of parishes.[19]

It was urgent that the India mission get the support of the whole Church and Chalmers directed his efforts to winning his fellow-Evangelicals. Inglis had kept in touch since 1825,[20] and when Chalmers rose in the Assembly it was to defend the committee against charges of inefficiency. The criticism of the 'over-zealous' was not helpful. It was quite proper to take time. The Church was 'like a ponderous machine'. This made it slow to move, but it also meant it was 'effective in motion'.[21]

The St Andrews Missionary Society

From 1827 onwards Chalmers was helping increase Evangelical support for the Church's foreign mission scheme, but at St Andrews it was the local missionary society which provided the main setting for his commitment. In February 1825, he was elected president of the St Andrews Missionary Society, newly formed from an amalgamation of the St Andrews Juvenile Missionary Society and the St Andrews Missionary and School Society.[22]

---

16   *Edinburgh Star*, 23 May 1826.
17   Galatians 6.10.
18   Education in the Highlands, Annual supper, 25 May 1827. Charles Watson papers, NCL.
19   General Assembly Monday, May 22, 1826. Charles Watson papers, NCL.
20   J. Inglis to T. C., 15 April 1825, StAUL 30385.139. J. Inglis to T. C., 1 February 1826, NCL CHA 4.57.74.
21   General Assembly, Thursday May 29, 1828. Charles Watson papers, NCL.
22   Minutes of the St Andrews Juvenile Missionary Society, 7 February 1825, NCL.

He held this position for the remainder of his time in St Andrews, and its monthly meetings became his major interest outside his professorial duties. His method of running meetings was the same as during his last two years at St John's and he culled missionary reports for items of interest. This was not the dull affair it could easily have been. He read reports 'not only for the narratives they contain and the facts they declare...but for the theology and the philosophy and the experimental wisdom included'.[23] As one student observed:

> Dr Chalmers is, in the widest sense of the word a philosopher; and philosophy is his companion wherever he goes.... He seems to regard the history of Christian enterprise as a wide field of observation from whence we may gather by induction some very important truths.[24]

In order to highlight the 'singularities' of different missions, he dealt with one society at a time. The CMS required its missionaries to be 'of the Episcopal persuasion', but this was acceptable as it enabled them to attract the support of 'the most wealthy and influential class...of the British population' and achieve an income of £40,000 a year.[25] Having a number of societies rather than one 'immense and unwieldy association' meant experiments could be 'multiplied and diversified in every conceivable way'.[26] He was impressed by CMS use of catechists, their founding of schools and the practice of appointing 'literary correspondents whose business it is to furnish all the possible information which they can collect in their...territories'.[27]

The CMS was his favourite society next to the Moravians and not least among its merits was its use of penny-a-week schemes. This was also true of the LMS who were more dependent on working-class support and accounted for half their annual income of £20-30,000 by this means.[28] The Baptists were noted for their combination of education, preaching and Bible translation, and their employment of native preachers was 'the likeliest process for a rapid and extensive diffusion of Christianity'.[29] In addition St Andrews could not fail to hear the analysis of Moravian missionary methods he formulated at Kilmany.[30]

---

[23] S. H. Cox, *Interviews memorable and useful from diary and memory reproduced*, 1853, 67.

[24] W. Orme, *Memoirs of John Urquhart*, 1869, 287.

[25] *Memoirs*, 3, 193.

[26] Ibid.

[27] *Memoirs*, 3, 194.

[28] Mss notes, 1f. NCL CHA 6, box 14, fragments.

[29] Ibid.

[30] Orme, *John Urquhart*, 1869, 286-97. Journal, 5 December 1825.

The St Andrews Missionary Society kept close to its aim 'to extend the knowledge of Christianity by aiding the measures which shall seem most conducive to that end'.[31] This meant the usual societies, but they also supported work in Ireland and the General Assembly fund for Gaelic Schools. In November 1827 Chalmers spoke of the ineffectiveness of civil disabilities suffered by Roman Catholics in Ireland. The 'only legitimate and effective instruments of conversion' were the 'circulation of scriptures, the erection of schools and the labours of missionaries'.[32] In his final address he

> combated the prejudices of those who viewed with jealousy the progress of knowledge among the labouring classes – he showed that their souls were of equal value with those of their superiors in rank, and while the cultivation of their minds made them better artisans, it did not unfit them for the humble duties of their calling, and kept them from those gross and dissipating pleasures which they would otherwise have recourse to. The same arguments applied to the instruction of the heathen.[33]

A string of deputations now made a point of including St Andrews on their itineraries. Visitors included Joshua Marshman[34] (1768-1837) and William Yates[35] (1792-1845) from the Baptist mission in India, Henry Townley[36] (1784-1861), formerly with the LMS in India, John Carruthers who had served with the Scottish Missionary Society in Russia[37] and Robert Morrison[38] (1782-1834) from China. The university professors were not conspicuous in their support, but the reputation of Marshman was sufficient to attract Principals Francis Nicoll[39] (1771-1835) and Robert Haldane[40] (1772-1854) together with Professor George Buist[41] (1779-1860) to the meeting and to breakfast with Chalmers.[42] Conversation turned to subjects

---

31   Minutes, NCL, 19 September 1822, 7 February 1825.
32   Ibid., 5 November 1827.
33   Ibid., 19 September 1828.
34   Ibid., 4 January 187. Journal, 4, 5, January 1827.
35   *Memoirs*, 3, 195. Journal, 10 May 1828.
36   Minutes, NCL, 27, 29 June 1827. Journal, 29 June 1827. J. Sibree, *London Missionary Society. A register of missionaries, deputations etc from 1796 to 1923*, 1923, 13.
37   Minutes, NCL, 1 August 1825. Journal, 3, 5 September 1825.
38   *Memoirs*, 3, 195. R. Morrison to T. C., 11 November 1827, NCL CHA 4.81.19. Sibree, *LMS register*, 1923, 7.
39   Ibid., 7, 415.
40   Ibid., 423.
41   Ibid., 432.
42   Journal, 5 January 1827. Minutes, NCL, 4 January 1827.

such as education in India, clerical and lay involvement in missionary societies, and church establishments.[43]

Annual meetings gave opportunity for others to participate and in 1827 the resolution to accept the annual report was moved in 'a speech of much energy and eloquence' exposing 'the fallacy of those objections commonly made against the cause of missions'. This was seconded by Alexander Duff 'who forcibly illustrated the adaptation of the gospel scheme to the moral condition of man'.[44]

The membership was varied. Students had their own society, but often attended meetings of both, and after Chalmers' departure took the prayers. The president of the society before and after Chalmers' four years in office was a local banker, but the status of the membership is illustrated by the fact that the annual meeting could be rearranged at short notice to suit Thomas Erskine of Linlathen.[45] In 1832 the society gained the support of the Liberal MP, Andrew Johnston, and in 1834 the Provost of St Andrews became president. Chalmers apart, the society was never really accepted by the University or by the parish ministers who were its professors and there was a history of frustrated attempts to gain the use of a parish church for deputations. In 1831 Haldane and Buist cautiously consented to subscribe to the society, but that was as far as they were prepared to go; Buist declined honorary office.[46]

Seceders and Independents predominated, which helps explain the coldness of the established ministers. The secretary for many years was William Lothian, minister of the Independent Chapel.[47] Secession ministers were consistent in their support and attended meetings from far afield. After Chalmers' time the only Church of Scotland minister who showed any interest was Thomas Gillespie[48] (1778-1844), although there were a few Church of Scotland lay members on the committee.

The society took weekly collections around the town, which brought the predictable complaint of robbing the poor and Chalmers was ready with his reply.[49] The sums raised were tiny compared with those collected in Scotland when the missionary movement first arose, but they were not out

---

[43]   *Memoirs*, 3, 195.

[44]   Minutes, NCL, 29 January 1927.

[45]   Minutes, NCL, 18, 19 September 1828.

[46]   Haldane objected to their method of raising funds and did not like students speaking at public meetings. Buist did not like meetings at all. Minutes, NCL, 18, 21 July, 1 August 1831.

[47]   Faced with Moderate preachers he could not decently avoid on Sundays, Chalmers attended Lothian's mid-week services from February 1826. Journal, 2 February to 9 March 1826.

[48]   Minutes, NCL, 25 September 1832, *Fasti*, 5, 140.

[49]   Minutes, NCL, 4 July 1825. Journal, 30 June, 4 July 1825. *Memoirs*, 3, 83-5, 491-3.

of line with other societies in this period. Of the £150 allocated during Chalmers' period as president, the LMS received the largest amount, followed by the Baptists and the Moravians, then the Scottish Missionary Society. Lesser donations were made to Irish school societies and the General Assembly's Indian and Highland missions. This pattern was not untypical of other societies.

After his move to Edinburgh late in 1828, the society felt his absence at the monthly gatherings, but the annual meetings and those held for visiting deputations could still draw good crowds. Chalmers' prestige and continuous interest helped set the society on its feet and it had a support base which was not dependent on him.[50] Whereas in St Andrews his interest contrasted with other Church of Scotland ministers, in Edinburgh the difference would have been less marked. Although the importance of his involvement in the St Andrews' Missionary Society ought not to be underestimated, this was the period when missions gained general acceptance, including by the General Assembly.

The St Andrews Students' Missionary Society

The student missionary society had its beginnings in February 1824 with meetings of a small group of divinity students at St Mary's College. At the start of the following session in December that year a number in the United College also met together and the two groups decided to amalgamate as 'An association among the students of the University of St Andrews for the review and support of missions'.[51] Similar societies had been formed in Aberdeen in January 1820[52] and in Glasgow in December 1821.[53] Edinburgh followed in December 1825[54] and in 1827 the United Secession and Relief theological students did likewise.[55] Student societies were another sign of quickening missionary interest and of great significance in providing a new generation of missionaries. Their role in the development of university student Christian movements also needs to be recognized.

---

50   Duff's remark that Chalmers was 'seen to be the sole reviver of an all but defunct missionary society' is unfair to its other office-bearers. There was never any question of the viability of the society, but they were understandably keen to have the prestige of Chalmers' involvement. *Memoirs*, 3, 202.

51   Minutes of the Students' Missionary Society of St Andrews, 1824-1846, StAUL UY 911. This is variously referred to as the 'university society', the 'students' society' or the 'combined society'.

52   *Scottish Missionary Register*, 3(5), May 1822, 173.

53   *Scottish Missionary Register*, January 1822, 3.

54   *Scottish Missionary Register*, January 1826, 15.

55   *Scottish Missionary Register*, December 1827, 550. M'Kerrow, *Secession Church*, 1841, 794.

Despite being a difficult environment, there was a good response among students at St Andrews. Within two weeks of their first meeting the society had 40 names,[56] and by the end of the 1824-25 session the total reached 70[57] out of a student population of about 320.[58] Initially they were regarded as 'thoroughly unacademical...too Puritanical and Methodistical',[59] and there was difficulty finding a room for meetings, but gradually they proved their worth.

At the end of the first year Principal Nicoll declined to be patron, but did so 'politely...requesting such information as we could afford him'.[60] So wrote the secretary, Henry Craik (1805-1866), who found himself approached by Principal Haldane to take on some of the town Sunday schools[61] – an indication that relationships cannot have been too bad. By the following session Haldane offered the Divinity Hall for meetings.[62] An 'Appeal to the students of St Andrews'[63] was followed up in December 1825 with a fortnightly publication the *St Andrews University Magazine*.[64] It was an ambitious and spirited project which soon produced a rival, *The Argus*.[65]

There was undoubtedly a change in atmosphere from the year before, but it is misleading to suggest (as Alexander Duff did in the account used in the *Memoirs*[66]) that Chalmers was chiefly responsible. His presidency of the town society was a boost to morale, but students themselves were largely responsible for improvement in their own situation. Chalmers advised members of the university missionary society when they approached him,[67] but his main role was attracting students likely to be interested in such things.[68]

---

56 Orme, *John Urquhart*, 1869, 70.

57 W. E. Tayler, *Passages from the diary and letters of Henry Craik of Bristol*, 1866, 318.

58 Not including irregular students. *Evidence, oral and documentary taken and received by the Commissioners for visiting the universities of Scotland, 3, University of St Andrews*, 1837, 38, 400.

59 *Memoirs*, 3, 198f.

60 Tayler, *Henry Craik*, 1866, 318.

61 Ibid., 318f.

62 *Memoirs*, 3, 200.

63 Tayler, Minutes, *Henry Craik*, 1866, 25 April 1825. *Scottish Missionary Register*, 7(3), March 1826, 108-10.

64 P. R. S Lang, *Duncan Dewar. A student of St Andrews 100 years ago*, 1926, 105.

65 Ibid., 106.

66 *Memoirs*, 3, 196-202. Duff was prone to exaggeration.

67 H. Craik to T. C., 17 December 1825, NCL CHA 4.104.37.

68 Orme, *John Urquhart*, 1869, 38f.

It had been the hope of the University that Chalmers would literally improve their fortunes by increasing the student population,[69] and in this at least they were not disappointed. Those who transferred from other universities comprised about 40% of his moral philosophy class during his first four years,[70] and his second session, 1824-25, brought the largest number of matriculations and the largest total roll during the 18th and 19th centuries.[71] It might not have been anticipated that so much of the influx was to be evangelical; but it was, and given that student missionary societies were being founded in the other Scottish universities, it would have been surprising if St Andrews had not followed suit.

Chalmers' role in stimulating other religious activity was also less direct than the *Memoirs* imply. He started a Sunday school in his house during the 1824-25 session and later handed it over to students to run, yet when those such as John Urquhart and his close companion John Adam (1803-1831) got involved in Sunday schools and preached in services in various chapels, it was primarily because they were active members of churches for whom this was the natural thing to do. This was also the case with James Hoby[72] (1788-1871), a Baptist minister from London who came to study under Chalmers. By and large they brought their missionary and evangelistic interests with them, and as well as by Chalmers' example, lectures and friendship, these were encouraged by the ministry of William Lothian in the Independent chapel.[73] A number of the Church of Scotland students such as John Lorimer[74] (1804-1868) and Duff himself also had an interest in missions as part of their background.

The regular meetings with one another were central to the development of student commitment to missions. Although they also attended Chalmers'

---

[69]   F. Nicoll to Lord Melville, 25 October 1822; reply, 29 October 1822, StAUL MSS 4644.

[70]   *Evidence, University of St Andrews*, 1837, 76.

[71]   J. M. Anderson, *The matriculation roll of the University of St Andrews 1747-1897*, 1905, lxviif.

[72]   *Memoirs*, 3, 191. Information on Hoby is scanty, but he was later the biographer of the BMS missionary, William Yates.

[73]   Lothian was also secretary of the town missionary society and the inspiration behind the decision of James Paterson (1807-1854) to become a LMS missionary. Paterson was a student at St Andrews from 1821 to 1824 and went to India in 1832. *Address by Mr James Paterson, of the University of St Andrews and afterwards of Highbury College, London, at his public designation as a missionary to India: which took place in the Congregational Chapel, St Andrews, 21 December 1831. With the substance of the charge delivered to him by Mr Lothian*, 1832, 10. J. Sibree, *LMS Register*, 1923, 31.

[74]   *Fasti*, 3, 439. Lorimer's father was a foundation supporter of the Edinburgh Missionary Society in 1796. *Scottish Missionary Register*, 46(4), April 1845, 49.

monthly meetings of the town society, it was in the university missionary society that they came together as an intense and well-informed small group to pray, read papers on missionary subjects, and encourage one another. Subscriptions were spent not only on the usual donations to missionary societies, but also to establish a library.

Despite nearly a third of students at St Andrews becoming subscribers, there was a sense of being a small group against a hostile world. One paper sought to demonstrate

> the pernicious folly of those who persist in pouring forth their sarcasm on those who are engaged in an employment so sacred and so glorious as that of a Christian missionary.[75]

Objections to missions were a common theme, and obviously a challenge; but they also considered issues such as missionary methods and the fate of those who died without hearing the gospel. Significantly there also came a point in defending the cause when the question they had to face was 'whether the advocate for the general principle is not inconsistent…if whilst exhorting others…he draw back from the work himself'.[76]

Of the more than three hundred students who passed through Chalmers' hands at St Andrews[77] six offered for missionary services overseas. The most notable was Alexander Duff,[78] but the six also included the next two missionaries appointed to join him in Calcutta; William Sinclair Mackay[79] (1807-1865) and David Ewart[80] (1806-1860). Robert Nesbit[81] (1803-1855) went to India with the Scottish Missionary Society in 1826. John Adam[82] also went to India, but with the LMS. John Urquhart[83] had his heart set on going to China with the LMS, but died suddenly in January 1827.

These young men studied under Chalmers at the peak of his popularity and as part of a remarkable generation of students. With others they looked back to their time at St Andrews with fond memories, particularly of the 1824-25 session:

---

75 Minutes, NCL, 19 November 1825.

76 J. Adam to LMS secretary, 9 November 1827, Candidates papers, SOAS. Quoted by F. S. Piggin, *Making evangelical missionaries*, 1984, 308.

77 *Evidence, University of St Andrews*, 1837, 338.

78 M. A. Laird, 'The legacy of Alexander Duff', *Occasional Bulletin of Missionary Research*, 3(4) October 1979, 146-9. O. G. Myklebust, *The study of missions in theological education*, 1955.

79 *Fasti*, 7, 699.

80 *Fasti*, 7, 693.

81 *Fasti*, 7, 703. J. M. Mitchell, *Memoir of the Rev Robert Nesbit missionary of the Free Church of Scotland*, Bombay, 1858.

82 *Memoir of John Adam, late missionary at Calcutta*, 1833. Sibree, *LMS Register*, 1923, 29.

83 Orme, *John Urquhart*, 1869.

It would not be easy...to convey to a stranger the effect of Dr Chalmers' lectures on the young men who attended his class during this year.... The students were moved...both to investigate the whole system of the philosophy of duty and to exemplify its practical details in their ordinary conduct.... I remember well the aspect of the Old College of St Andrews during this session. It has never had such a session before, and it may be that it will never have another again.[84]

There are many accounts of the crowded lecture room, the forbidden applause and the 'enthusiasm, moral and intellectual'[85] which pervaded Chalmers' class, where his oratory – little attenuated for its change of situation – produced the same effects as from the pulpit. In his moral philosophy Chalmers excluded epistemology and concentrated on ethics, and this removal of associations with scepticism was appreciated by Evangelicals. A sense of high adventure developed as these young men felt they were witnessing the world being set to rights by the hero at whose feet they sat, and it is to this atmosphere that some of the subsequent exaggeration must be attributed.

For many students their relationship with Chalmers was personal. Groups were invited to meals[86] and on Sunday evenings a growing number went to his home for religious instruction.[87] John Adam wrote home about Chalmers' kindness,[88] and to Urquhart it was at times almost oppressive.[89] Nesbit felt free to send Chalmers an epic poem.[90] Some recalled being invited to accompany 'the Doctor' on pastoral visits.[91]

Given this involvement with students and his interest in missions, it is right to ask how much he was responsible for the decision made by the six that they would become missionaries. An examination of Chalmers' relationship with each highlights the complexity of the missionary call, and confirms that while his part in their vocation may not always have been direct, it was nonetheless important.[92]

The first to leave as a missionary was Robert Nesbit. He had matriculated in 1816 and became a regular student in 1823-24 in order to repeat moral philosophy under Chalmers.[93] He was treasurer of the missionary society formed among the divinity students in February 1824,

---

84　*Edinburgh Christian Instructor*, NS 3, October 1834, 690.

85　Ibid.

86　There are frequent references in Chalmers' Journals.

87　*Memoirs*, 3, 187f.

88　Memoir of John Adam, 48f.

89　Orme, *John Urquhart*, 1869, 131.

90　R. Nesbit to T. C., 31 January 1824, NCL CHA 4.37.13.

91　(J. Ross), *W. Lindsay Alexander, his life and work*, 1877, 11-15, 145.

92　*Memoirs*, 3, 201-3. G. Smith, *Life of Alexander Duff*, 1, 26.

93　Mitchell, *Robert Nesbit*, 1858, 12.

and secretary of the combined society until his departure from St Andrews in April 1825.[94] That summer was spent in a tutoring position obtained by Chalmers,[95] who also helped him obtain a second position, this time in Exeter with Anthony Norris Groves[96] (1795-1853). It was there that his earlier promptings towards the mission field came into focus, aided by Groves' chiding remark that 'the high Calvinistic tenets of the Scottish Church were unfavourable to a missionary spirit'.[97]

Nesbit corresponded with Urquhart and Chalmers[98] but rejected Chalmers' proposal that he take the Scotch Church in Buenos Aires.[99] In July 1826 he applied to the Scottish Missionary Society naming Chalmers as referee.[100] In December he returned north for ordination[101] and spoke at the university missionary societies in Edinburgh and St Andrews,[102] where his example was made a matter of 'personal concern'.[103] Before Nesbit left, he and Chalmers had tea and 'a congenial walk'[104] and in May 1827 he sailed for Bombay.[105]

The central figure in the formation of the combined society in December 1824 was John Urquhart. He had been a friend of Duff's at Perth Grammar School and they roomed together during Urquhart's first year at St Andrews, 1822-23.[106] An essay on the divisions of philosophy attracted Chalmers' attention early in the 1824-25 session,[107] and from then on Chalmers took a close interest. This session brought the first thoughts of becoming a missionary, though during the summer they were discouraged[108] by William Orme, minister of the Independent Congregation at Perth.[109] In September Urquhart stayed with John Adam in London and developed an

---

94   Minutes, NCL, 2 February 1824, 25 April 1825.

95   R. Nesbit to T. C., 27 September 1825, NCL CHA 4.48.4.

96   Later a leading member of the Plymouth Brethren and a missionary to India.

97   Mitchell, *Robert Nesbit*, 1858, 28.

98   R. Nesbit to T. C., 17 February 1826, NCL CHA 4.60.5.

99   R. Nesbit to T. C., 13 March 1826, NCL CHA 4.60.7. Mitchell, *Robert Nesbit*, 1858, 32f.

100   W. Brown to T. C., 2 August 1826, NCL CHA 4.52.42. Mitchell, *Robert Nesbit*, 1858, 33-8.

101   Mitchell, *Robert Nesbit*, 1858, 40f. Journal, 15 December 1826.

102   Minutes, NCL, 22 September 1826.

103   Mitchell, *Robert Nesbit*, 1858, 36f.

104   Journal, 14, 16, December 1826.

105   With others of the Scottish Missionary Society mission in Western India, in 1835 Nesbit transferred to the Church of Scotland and in 1843 to the Free Church.

106   Orme, *John Urquhart*, 1869, 34, 50.

107   Ibid., 67.

108   Ibid., 106.

109   Later Urquhart's biographer, in 1828 Orme moved to London as LMS foreign secretary.

acquaintance with Robert Morrison, then on furlough from China.[110] When he returned to St Andrews for the winter it was with the intention of returning to London the following year and training for the LMS as a missionary to China.

During the 1825-26 session Urquhart was joint-president of the university society along with Duff,[111] and with Adam began an intensive study of all the missionary literature they could lay their hands on.[112] Chalmers invited him to take over his Sunday school, and frequently had him to tea, including regularly on Sunday evenings.[113]

Chalmers was no happier with Urquhart's desire to be a missionary than Orme and did his best to talk him out of it. While the opposition of his family was something Urquhart anticipated, that of his spiritual mentors was harder to take. At length he was prevailed on to delay entering LMS training at Homerton in London and became another who took a tutoring position obtained by Chalmers. Although brilliant, his health as well as his youth told against rushing off to China,[114] and the worst fears of his friends were realized in January 1827 when he took sick and died while staying with Greville Ewing in Glasgow.[115]

Urquhart's death had a profound effect.[116] He had been an assiduous correspondent, particularly with Adam, Nesbit and Duff, and also with others such as W. L. Alexander[117] and Henry Craik.[118] In April 1826 he had addressed the university society on 'the duty of personally engaging in the work of missions'. Craik minuted it was 'most eloquent, most solemn, most affecting' and his feelings afterwards 'were too strong for utterance'.[119] Urquhart's death imprinted this call on the minds of his fellows and John Tod Brown spoke for many when he wrote to Chalmers, 'We have all received a most impressive summons to vigilance at our several posts.'[120] William Orme lost no time collecting reminiscences, essays and letters, and

---

[110] Orme, *John Urquhart*, 1869, 126-30.

[111] Minutes, NCL, 5 December 1825.

[112] Orme, *John Urquhart*, 1869, 126-30.

[113] Ibid., 131f. Journal, 13 November 1825 to 30 April 1826.

[114] Orme, *John Urquhart*, 1869, 139, 154, 158f.

[115] G. Ewing to T. C., 10 January 1827, NCL CHA 4.73.21.

[116] Including on those at Glasgow, *Scottish Missionary Register*, 8(4), April 1827, 184.

[117] Later a leading figure in the Congregational Union in Scotland.

[118] Craik followed Nesbit as tutor for the Groves family, and together with Groves adopted Brethren principles. Groves later went to India and Craik developed a partnership with George Muller (1805-1898) of Bristol.

[119] Tayler, *Henry Craik*, 1866, 40. Duff was another who was moved by this paper, Orme, *John Urquhart*, 1869, 15-17.

[120] J. T. Brown to T. C., 2 April 1827. NCL CHA 4.67.13.

to some embarrassment printed a two-volume memoir.[121] Despite its length and absence of chapter divisions it became a missionary classic and a better edited version was brought out with Duff's assistance in 1869.

The closest among Urquhart's circle was John Adam, who had been converted in Geneva[122] and spent the 1823-24 academic year at the Glasgow Theological Academy before going to St Andrews to sit under Chalmers.[123] Like Urquhart, he attended William Lothian's chapel and preached in chapels around East Fife. Adam was impressed by Chalmers' use of moral philosophy as a 'stepping stone to revelation'[124] but lectures in political economy were too much like 'newspaper discussions' to be inspiring. His interest in missions derived from his time in Switzerland and he was treasurer of the combined student society when it was founded in December 1824. While Urquhart was staying with him in London in the autumn of 1825 this turned into a resolve to become a missionary, and in 1826 he left St Andrews to spend two years at Homerton before going to Calcutta with the LMS in 1828.

Adam was on friendly terms with Chalmers and met him informally on several occasions,[125] including having breakfast with Erskine of Linlathen.[126] No correspondence has survived and Urquhart and Pye Smith (at Homerton) would appear to have been more formative influences. In India Adam met up with Duff, for whom he had once wished that 'classical enthusiasm' would be turned 'towards the Bible and the great concerns of religion'.[127] He died in Calcutta in 1831.

Duff was the next of the six to leave for the mission-field. Adam's opinion notwithstanding, Duff's missionary interest had its origin in his childhood and developed through friendship with Urquhart[128] and five years in the student missionary society from its inception as a combined society until he left St Andrews in April 1829.[129] In 1824 he was one of four vice-presidents, and thereafter one of the two joint-presidents.[130] For several years he was librarian, and by the time he left he had become so much the

---

[121] W. Orme, *Memoirs including letters and select remains of John Urquhart*, 1828. J. Hoby to T. C. 19 July 1827, NCL CHA 4.76.18. *Edinburgh Christian Instructor*. NS 3, October 1834, 672-92.

[122] *Memoir of John Adam*, 1833, 15.

[123] Ibid., 47.

[124] Ibid., 52.

[125] Journal, 19, 21, 23 July 1825, 19 April 1826.

[126] *Memoir of John Adam*, 1833, 91f.

[127] Ibid., 84.

[128] Orme, *John Urquhart*, 1869, 15-17.

[129] 'Well can I trace the dawn, the rise, and progress of any feeble missionary spirit I possess to the readings, conversations, and essays called for by (the) university association at St Andrews.' A. Duff to G. Knight, 19 March 1831. F. S. Piggin, *Making evangelical missionaries*, 1984, 308.

[130] There was one each from St Mary's and the United College.

grand old man of the place it was impossible for anything to happen without him.

There is no reason to disbelieve that Urquhart's death led Duff to suggest to his parents he might be the one to take his place as a prospective missionary,[131] but when approached on behalf of the General Assembly committee during the 1827-28 session he declined. The following year he considered it more seriously[132] and early in March 1829 wrote to Chalmers that he intended to accept.[133]

It is difficult to say how much Chalmers was an influence in this. Given the interest they took in one another in later years there is surprisingly little correspondence,[134] and in personality Duff was as independently-minded as Chalmers. However, he did use a familiar tone in letters to Chalmers[135] whose journal records the occasional 'long conversation'[136] and Duff as another who taught his Sunday school.[137] When Chalmers went to Edinburgh it is possible he had a hand in renewing the missions committee's invitation to Duff,[138] but the first positive evidence[139] of involvement came after Duff's decision to accept. On 16 March 1829 Duff called on Chalmers in Edinburgh[140] and four days later Chalmers attended the meeting of the missions committee to consider his appointment.[141] In August Chalmers preached at Duff's ordination.[142]

Within two years of his arrival in India Duff was joined by W. S. Mackay who had attended Chalmers' classes from 1823 to 1825, but became

---

[131] Smith, *Alexander Duff*, 1, 1879, 44.

[132] Ibid., 45.

[133] A. Duff to T. C., 12 March 1829, ibid., 46-9.

[134] There are seven letters whose contents are known; all from Duff to Chalmers and all except one known only through Smith's *Life of Alexander Duff*. Three date from 1829, two from 1830 and one each from 1834 and 1839. That written in 1834 can be found in the NLS 7530 f.224. Apart from the missing letters from Chalmers to Duff, there is no indication their correspondence was much more extensive.

[135] A. Duff to T. C., 20 January 1829, contains familiar greetings to the Chalmers' family, candid comments about the town missionary society and the inadequacies of his successor in the chair of moral philosophy. Smith, *Alexander Duff*, 1, 1869, 27-32.

[136] Ibid., 15 March, 6 April 1828.

[137] Journal, 21 October 1827 to 6 April 1828.

[138] On his arrival in Edinburgh Chalmers was again invited to join the foreign missions sub-committee. J. Inglis to T. C., 1 December 1828, NCL CHA 4.103.2.

[139] The minutes for the meetings for this period are not among the rest of the committee records held in the NLS.

[140] Journal, 16 March 1829.

[141] Ibid., 18 March 1829.

[142] *Scottish Missionary Register*, September 1829, 436-9.

an irregular student at Edinburgh because of financial difficulties.[143] There is no evidence of his involvement in the student missionary society, but Mackay was another who through Chalmers' patronage obtained a tutoring position near Exeter and while there was in contact with Craik and corresponded with Nesbit.[144] On reading Orme's biography of Urquhart he resolved to take Urquhart's missionary ambition for his own,[145] but it was some years before this showed signs of fruition.

In 1828 he wrote to Chalmers about assisting Marshman in translation work at Serampore, and hoped the state of his soul might be improved by missionary company.[146] The project came to nought and two years later he again approached Chalmers, this time about going out with the Scottish Missionary Society.[147] Chalmers suggested he join Duff, a proposal Mackay was quick to accept.[148] He was ordained in May 1831[149] and sailed to Calcutta the following month where be became a valuable member of the Church of Scotland mission, taking on its leadership during the years Duff was back in Scotland.

The last of this St Andrews' generation to become a missionary was David Ewart. Ewart matriculated in 1821 at the same time as Duff, with whom he formed a close friendship.[150] Apart from this and the fact that he was a member of the university missionary society from 1825 and a vice-president in 1826-27, little is known of Ewart before his ordination to the Church of Scotland mission in July 1834,[151] news of which Duff was delighted to hear.[152] Mackay recalled that Ewart was attracted to India by the presence of two fellow-students from St Andrews, and as for others the paucity of openings for licentiates in Scotland was a consideration.[153]

Many active in the university missionary society during Chalmers' time had notable careers. W. L. Alexander and Henry Craik have been mentioned. Others include John Tod Brown[154] (1805-1873), John G.

---

[143]   G. Sinclair to T. C., 31 December 1824, NCL CHA 4.38.31. W. S. Mackay to T. C., 30 September 1826, NCL CHA 4.58.26.
[144]   W. S. Mackay to T. C., 8 April 1827, NCL CHA.4.79.51.
[145]   W. S. Mackay, 'The late Dr Ewart', *Oriental Christian Spectator*, November 1860, 437.
[146]   W. S. Mackay to T. C., 13 September 1828, NCL CHA.4.95.51.
[147]   W. S. Mackay to T. C., 9 July 1830, NCL CHA.4.143.13.
[148]   W. S. Mackay to T. C., 12 September 1830, NCL CHA.4.143.14.
[149]   *Fasti*, 7, 699.
[150]   W. S. Mackay, 'The late Dr Ewart,' *Oriental Christian Spectator*, November 1860, 436.
[151]   *Fasti*. 7, 693.
[152]   A. Duff to D. Ewart, 20 May 1835, Smith, *Alexander Duff*, 1, 1869, 287.
[153]   Mackay, 'The late Dr Ewart', 1860, 437.
[154]   *Fasti*, 5, 35.

Lorimer[155] (1804-1868), George Lewis[156] (1804-1868), William Tait[157] (b.1807) and W. K. Tweedie[158] (1803-1863). The last of these was for 15 years convener of the Free Church Foreign Missions Committee.

The denominational spread was quite wide. Alexander was from a Baptist family and became a noted Congregationalist. James Hoby was a Baptist minister before he went to St Andrews. Craik left the Church of Scotland for the Brethren, and Brown and Tait both became ministers in the Church of England, Tait having first spent several years in the Catholic Apostolic Church. All these corresponded with Chalmers and never lost contact, no matter how far their paths diverged.

For those who became missionaries as well as those who did not, a relationship with Chalmers did not stop in the lecture room nor end when they left St Andrews. He took a keen interest in all their careers. That in six cases their ambition became the mission-field was due to their interaction as much with one another, and especially with Urquhart, as with him. But Chalmers was all along a welcome guide, and the example of his idealism and the atmosphere he helped create were important, as was his role in attracting them to St Andrews. As Mackay observed of Chalmers 30 years later, 'It was not so much his words, as the virtue that went out of him, that turned our hearts to the heathen.'[159]

---

[155] *Fasti*, 3, 439.
[156] *Fasti*, 5, 326.
[157] *Fasti*, 1, 128f.
[158] *Fasti*, 1, 121. Mackay, 'The late Dr Ewart', 1860.
[159] Ibid., 437.

Chapter 13

'Commending ourselves to every man's conscience in the sight of God'[1]
Chalmers and missions, 1828-1847

At St Andrews Chalmers consolidated his thinking on missions and made it a topic of study through preparation for the monthly meetings of the town missionary society. He now had personal acquaintance with a number of missionaries, and by the time he left for Edinburgh in the first week of November 1828, two of his students were serving in India with others to follow.

Once resident in Edinburgh he was an obvious person to be involved in the Foreign Missions Committee. Although he had kept in touch with Inglis while in St Andrews, now he was able to attend meetings handling the day to day business of the mission. This accompanied a shift in interest away from the societies – with the exception of presidency of the Edinburgh Association in aid of Moravian Missions which he held until his death in 1847. He was also patron of the Edinburgh University Missionary Association and accepted honorary positions with the New York Board of Foreign Missions of the Presbyterian Church[2] and the American Board of Commissioners for Foreign Missions.[3]

---

[1] 2 Corinthians 4.2. Chalmers' sermon at the ordination of Alexander Duff, 12 August 1829. Chalmers, *Select Sermons*, 1881, 193-221.

[2] An impressive but undated certificate is in New College Library. It arose out of a donation by Chalmers' American publisher, Robert Carter of New York.

[3] Chalmers was made an honorary member in 1829. J. Evarts to T. C., 6 February 1829, NCL CHA 4.121.14. In 1841 he was elected a corresponding member. R. Anderson to T. C., 30 October 1841, NCL CHA 4. S. H. Cox to T. C., 22 November 1841, NCL CHA 4.

Invitations to preach for missionary societies continued for a time. The SMS,[4] the Perthshire Missionary Society,[5] the Edinburgh auxiliary of the LMS,[6] the London committee of the SSPCK[7] and the St Andrews Missionary Society[8] sought his services during his first two years in Edinburgh. He declined the invitation to St Andrews and conveyed the impression there would be no point in its being renewed.[9] It is not known if he acceded to any other requests either, but he preached on many occasions for the General Assembly scheme,[10] and the flow of other invitations dried up. In 1831 he asked not to be re-elected as a director of the LMS,[11] although his name continued to be listed until 1834.[12]

From May 1834 his convenership of the Assembly's Church Accommodation Committee made it unlikely that foreign missions would regain the attention it had held in St Andrews, though his basic commitment was undiminished. In 1838 he lent his signature to an essay competition on missions[13] and the following year preached the farewell sermon marking Duff's return to India after four years back in Scotland. After the Disruption his former students in India were pleased to find a personal note from their old teacher appended to the letter inviting them to join the Free Church.[14]

From missionary society to missionary church

Although he never denigrated the voluntary missionary societies, Chalmers' shift in allegiance to the missions scheme of the Church of Scotland reflected a general change in Scottish missionary support during the 1830s and 1840s. In the previous decade the SMS had been financially comfortable while the Church of Scotland's India mission remained a Cinderella. From about 1830 there was a change in both their fortunes. In that year the SMS

---

4   W. Brown to T. C., 17 February 1829, NCL CHA 4.117.22. W. Brown to T. C., 1 March 1830, NCL CHA 4.133.18.

5   J. Murray to T. C., 9 April 1830, NCL CHA 4.144.49.

6   W. Manuel to T. C., 24 February 1829, NCL CHA 4.125.3.

7   J. Tawse to T. C., 4 October 1830, NCL CHA 4.149.12.

8   W. Lothian to T. C., 15 December 1830, NCL CHA 4.124.15.

9   Minutes of the St Andrews Juvenile Missionary Society, 21 September 1832, NCL.

10   For example in London on 15 July 1833 and in June 1835, and in Liberton on 6 October 1833. *Oriental Christian Spectator*, 1834, 249-51. Chalmers, *Select sermons*, 1881, 193. Anderson, *Reminiscences*, 1851, 207-11. See also Journal, 22 May, 10 July 1831.

11   J. Arundel to T. C., 4 July 1831, NCL CHA 4.151.64.

12   See Appendix 7.

13   R. W. Hamilton, *Missions: their authority, scope and encouragement*, 1842, vii.

14   R. Nesbit to T. C., 17 June 1843, NCL CHA 4.

secretary felt missionary interest was in decline,[15] and the *Scottish Missionary Register* carried frequent references to financial problems.[16] The LMS also found things difficult and in 1829 considered closing some of its missions.[17] By contrast, support for the India mission of the Church of Scotland steadily improved, and by 1835 the Church was able to relieve the ailing SMS of responsibility for its mission in Western India.

The most important single factor in this change in the Scottish base of the missionary movement was the Voluntary Controversy. The efficiency as well as the validity of established churches had been challenged, and Chalmers was one who saw the necessity of a successful foreign mission if the first of these arguments at least was to be disproved.[18] As with the church extension movement the Voluntary Controversy divided Evangelical and Dissenter and brought Moderate and Evangelical together to demonstrate the vitality of their church. Argument over who made the greatest contributions to overseas missions, not to mention city missions, church building and Sunday schools, became a sorry feature of the debate.[19]

It was soon evident that Church of Scotland members were withdrawing from local missionary societies. In 1833 the *Edinburgh Christian Instructor* answered the question 'Shall I continue to support the SMS?' in the affirmative,[20] but such hopes could not be realized for long. In Fenwick the local society struggled to maintain the good relationship between Church of Scotland and Secession members it had nurtured for 20 years, but by 1839 all but two of the Established Church members had withdrawn and the Society renamed itself the Fenwick United Associate Congregational Missionary Society.[21] In St Andrews Duff refused to speak at the town society meeting, hurting the feelings of the committee who nevertheless voted him £10 to send with their expressions of distress.[22]

Although the sense of novelty was passing, underlying public interest in missions was still real and special occasions could still draw enthusiastic crowds. In the summer of 1837 an LMS deputation including an articulate African chief was well received in St Andrews[23] and spoke to tumultuous

---

15   W. Brown to T. C., 1 March 1830, NCL CHA 4.133.18.

16   For example, *Scottish Missionary Register*, 33(7), July 1832, 329.

17   W. Orme and J. Arundel to T. C., 4 January 1830, NCL CHA 4.145.28.

18   Presbytery of Edinburgh, India mission, 24 February 1830, Newspaper cuttings 1816-1831, Watson of Burntisland papers, NCL.

19   *Church of Scotland Magazine*, 2, 1835, 29-33, 45-50, 146-52.

20   The article was reprinted in the *Scottish Missionary Register*, 35(1), January 1834, 45-58.

21   Fenwick Auxiliary Missionary Society minute book, 30 May, 3 June 1839. NRA(S) 797.

22   Minutes of the St Andrews Juvenile Missionary Society, 4 March, 29 April 1835, NCL.

23   Minutes, NCL, 23 January 1837.

audiences in Aberdeen.[24] Nevertheless support for local interdenominational societies was diminishing. In 1838 the St Andrews society attributed small attendances to 'the present differences between Churchmen and Dissenters'.[25] The Glasgow Missionary Society split into two, one group supporting establishment principles, the other voluntary.[26]

The effect was the break-down of missions as an interdenominational activity,[27] though the conflict did serve to make missions part of the function of each church as such and encouraged the idea that the evangelization of the world should be part of the life of a church as a whole, not just an activity for enthusiasts. After the Disruption the move from missionary society to missionary church was complete. In 1844 the Glasgow Missionary Society, adhering to the principles of the Church of Scotland, became part of the Free Church. In 1847 the Voluntary section of the old Glasgow Missionary Society became part of the United Presbyterian Church[28] and the remaining work of the SMS was handed over to the Free Church. The Church of Scotland was left bereft of missionaries in 1843, but did not waver in its resolve to continue their work and appointed replacements as soon as it was able.

The India mission of the Church of Scotland

Chalmers' most active involvement in the India mission took place between late 1828 and the death of the Foreign Missions Committee[29] convener, John Inglis, five years later. He enjoyed a good relationship with Inglis, and worked closely with him after Andrew Thomson died in February 1831. Thomson had been the leader of the Evangelicals since 1827, and despite petty criticism of Inglis' proposals in 1824, had become a valued member of

---

[24]   They addressed the Aberdeen Missionary Society, the Aberdeen Female Missionary Society, the Juvenile Missionary Society, and a public breakfast, *Aberdeen Herald*, 8 July 1837.

[25]   Minutes, NCL, 20 December 1838.

[26]   Hewat, *Vision and achievement*, 1860, 180.

[27]   The movement of the LMS towards the denominational society of the Congregational churches can be seen in the proportion of Independents elected as Scottish directors. By 1841-42 they were 44% of the total compared with 13% in 1821-25. Appendix 7, table 1.

[28]   The United Presbyterians were formed by a union of the United Secession and the Relief churches earlier in 1847.

[29]   This committee was rarely called by its full title and descriptive terms have generally been used. It was originally known as the 'General Assembly Committee on the Propagation of the Gospel Abroad', later changed to 'The Committee of the General Assembly of the Church of Scotland for the Propagation of the Gospel in Foreign Parts'.

the committee.[30] Thomson's position in the Evangelical party was taken by Chalmers, ensuring that the foreign mission of the Church continued to involve the leaders of the two parties in the Church, at least until 1834 when church extension became his priority.

In December 1834 Duff returned to Scotland. His four years in India had been outstanding, but the effort had taken its toll. The voyage home wrought a transformation, and in a Scotland divided by the Voluntary Controversy and facing greater divisions still, Duff was able to capture the imagination of all sections of the Church and achieve unprecedented commitment to its missionary programme and the policy he had implemented in Calcutta.

Duff was an Evangelical, yet he was an exponent of Inglis' ideas. In Chalmers' relationships with Duff and Inglis, and through the missionary statements he produced while in Edinburgh, can be seen some of the tensions of one who despite a common commitment often spoke a different language. Duff had been inspired by Chalmers' energy and vision, but his models were also educational reformers like David Stow and John Wood.[31]

Chalmers preached to the large congregation at Duff's ordination on 12 August 1829 in St George's Edinburgh on the text, 'By manifestation of the truth, commending ourselves to every man's conscience in the sight of God'.[32] This became his standard statement on missions and one he pulled out regularly to raise funds for the General Assembly scheme.[33] Few of the arguments were new, but it represented a more consolidated missionary philosophy than hitherto. Methods which were known to work in Scotland had been shown to work overseas. Conscience was a universal phenomenon, and an awareness of right and wrong made the Bible's language of sin and salvation comprehensible to any man. Results came from the 'simple preaching of Christ crucified' not discourses on the being and attributes of God.

---

[30] Following Thomson's death, Inglis paid tribute to his 'sound judgement and discerning mind' which had often extricated them 'from difficulties of no small importance' and made it clear that Thomson had been important in winning Evangelical support for the mission. Presbytery of Edinburgh, 23 February 1831, India mission, the late Dr Thomson. Charles Watson papers, NCL.

[31] M. A. Laird, 'The legacy of Alexander Duff', *Occasional Bulletin of Missionary Research*, 3(4) October 1979, 147.

[32] 2 Corinthians 4.2.

[33] He used it at least six times up to October 1833. The fullest known text is in *Select Sermons*, 1881, 193-221, and part of it is in the *Oriental Christian Spectator*, 5(8), August 1834, 249-64, and *The Pulpit*, 562. It was preached in London in July 1833, and appears to be virtually identical to that used at Duff's ordination, a summary of which is in the *Scottish Missionary Register*, September 1829, 436-9. See also J. Anderson, *Reminiscences of Thomas Chalmers*, 1851, 151-4, 207-11.

Oblivious to more considered statements, he again emphasized the priority of christianization over civilization and the confirmation of this approach in the experience of the Moravians and the LMS. He appealed to those 'careless of the souls of others because they were careless of their own' to 'come to Christ for themselves' and do so 'without delay as death was at their doors and judgement before their eyes'.[34]

Duff was charged to keep records of the progress of conversion, to be watchful in prayer, to be prepared to learn from the experience of others as well as his own, and not to get involved in the politics of India. The congregation were to play their part by their support, and were reminded that there was sufficient means available for both the Assembly's mission and the work of the societies.

With Duff on his way the committee turned attention towards finding two more missionaries to assist him and the income for their support. Inglis prepared an annual statement to be read from pulpits when collections were made and he and Chalmers frequently spoke in the Edinburgh presbytery to report progress at home and overseas.

Inglis' style was not likely to set the world on fire, but he laid a solid foundation with his careful setting forth of the philosophy of the mission and the motives the Church should have in supporting it. It was not only a matter of Christian duty and gratitude, and a due sense of the honour of Christ, but also that Britain had derived 'wealth and prosperity' from India, for which the benefits of Christianity were the least that could be done in return.[35] As Duff sent back favourable reports of his school including news of conversions, Inglis displayed a profound sense of the missionary obligations of the Church of Scotland and its responsibility if it should fail to exploit opportunities presented to it.[36]

Duff's intention had been to establish an English medium secondary-school, but once in Calcutta he decided that of the potential students 'none who were willing were found qualified' and 'none who were qualified were found willing',[37] and he began instead at a more elementary level and concentrated on building up the one institution.

It was not long before there were over 200 enrolled and he was turning children away. Duff was able to capitalize on a rising demand for English education and in a position to carry his resolve that the school have a positive Christian character including prayers and Bible readings. For an older audience he began lectures on the attributes of God and the evidences of Christianity. Notwithstanding Chalmers' questioning of the value of the

---

34   All quotations from *Scottish Missionary Register*, September 1829, 436-9.

35   John Inglis, *East India missions*, 22 March 1830, Charles Watson papers, NCL.

36   *Scottish Missionary Register*, 34(4), April 1833, 137-41.

37   A. Duff, *India and India missions*, 1839, 507.

first of these at least, they were the means of winning the mission's first converts.

During Duff's second year in India, it was agreed between himself, the Calcutta Baptists, the LMS and the Methodists, subject to consent from their respective societies, that higher education be provided on an interdenominational basis. Duff was appointed secretary of a committee, with the idea that a College be set up by the Church of Scotland on behalf of all the missions.[38] His letter reached Edinburgh just after the 1832 Assembly, and Inglis was in contact with Chalmers over what they should do. They agreed not to discourage Duff, and the following Assembly approved the scheme, only to have it turned down by the other parties.

Behind the apparent unanimity between Chalmers and Inglis, and the undoubted cordiality and respect, differences of missionary philosophy remained. To Inglis the provision of higher education which would also serve to train native clergy was central, and he was 'inclined to rely upon it more than any other means that can be in the first instance employed for Christianizing the Eastern World'.[39] Chalmers could not disagree, but was worried about Duff's commitment to preaching, necessary not only from principle, but also to 'maintain the popularity of the cause' in Scotland.[40]

Mackay left for Calcutta in June 1831 and Ewart followed in 1834 without realizing that Duff was on his way back to Scotland. Duff began to see that his return could be of value,[41] and so it proved to be. He was naturally enthusiastic and compelling if verbose, and addressed the Assembly to great effect.[42] He toured Scotland visiting presbyteries and congregations to set up local associations in aid of the India mission. As the first official missionary of the Church he spoke with authority and with first-hand experience. It was no disadvantage that he presented his appeal in terms of a coherent missionary philosophy rooted in Scottish educational ideals and illustrated by concrete examples in demonstration of its success.

The by then traditional annual appeal letter was in 1835 written by Duff who produced a masterly if breathless account of the policy and practice of the mission.[43] Duff claimed that their activities embraced 'all the departments of labour that have been resorted to...in reclaiming the wastes of heathenism' including 'the Christian education of the young, the teaching and preaching of the gospel, the translation and distribution of the sacred

---

38 M. A. Laird, *Missionaries and education in Bengal 1793-1837*, 1972, 249-52.

39 J. Inglis to T. C., 5 June 1832, NCL CHA 4.181.55.

40 T. C. to J. Inglis, 8 June 1832, NCL CHA 3.14.21.

41 A. Duff to T. C., 26 December 1834, NCL CHA 7530 f.224.

42 In 1835, 1837 and 1839.

43 An original copy of the appeal circular is at NLS 7530 f.236. The text was reprinted in the *Calcutta Christian Observer*, December 1835, 651-6. It is by far the most succinct of Duff's missionary statements.

scriptures and religious tracts'. However, one did not have to read far to see that education occupied almost the entire attention of the missionaries.

Attempting to convert the millions of India by 'the direct…exertions of a few foreign agents labouring…under numberless disadvantages' was doomed to failure, and the only workable scheme was the preparation of a native ministry. English was 'the key of all knowledge' and the higher department of the school gave English-medium instruction in a wide range of subjects. Its pupils were expected to form an educated elite able to pass on their new learning in the vernacular languages.

Duff overestimated the extent of downward filtration in a caste society and underestimated the capacity of Hinduism to cope with the intellectual challenge of western science. However, he had seen western science destroy faith in Hinduism and prepare the way for the gospel. 'Almost all the youths in the two senior classes have become thorough unbelievers in Hinduism and at the same time as thorough believers in Christianity so far as the understanding…is concerned.'[44] One of the class had been baptized together with several 'young men of good families' converted through the lectures on Christian evidences.[45]

The connection with Chalmers at St Andrews is not obvious, and other influences on Duff have been noted. However, Chalmers took all knowledge very seriously and had a reputation as a competent scientist. He was an Evangelical who, despite his repeated comments about christianization and civilization, regarded Christian evidences and natural theology as valid forms of religious enquiry as far as they went, and he justified teaching moral philosophy because he could give it a definite if subordinate relationship to revelation.

In India Duff saw Christianity and western science as a unity in conflict with an equally coherent system of beliefs and theories. His sense of truth as a unified whole may have owed something to Chalmers, but it was intrinsic to the philosophical bias of Scottish tertiary education generally.[46] Chalmers was not alone in demanding of his students that they examine the relationships between disciplines, and for whom the classification of subjects was an important topic in itself. At other levels the influence was more direct. Duff lectured on political economy on the basis of what Chalmers had taught, and like others faced with the vastness of India, benefited from the wisdom of Chalmers' 'territorial principle'.[47]

---

[44]   *Calcutta Christian Observer*, December 1835, 651–6.

[45]   Ibid.

[46]   G. E. Davie, *The democratic intellect. Scotland and her universities in the nineteenth century*, 1964.

[47]   The Scottish Missionary Society advised their missionaries: 'It is particular labours that are productive of substantial and permanent good. The principle of locality is applicable to Heathen no less than to Christian countries.' *Letter of instructions from the directors of the Scottish*

The most obvious source of Duff's missionary policy was John Inglis, and there is no difficulty tracing this from Inglis' many pronouncements, including his SSPCK sermon in 1818, the letter *To the people of Scotland* in 1826 and the annual appeals and reports he wrote until his death at the end of 1833. Earlier sources of this tradition have already been mentioned, but it might be added that there were other features of Scottish life besides 'a school in every parish' and the experience gained through the SSPCK which reinforced a bias towards education as an instrument of missions.

The place held by the Westminster Confession and its catechisms was testimony to a conviction that 'the mind must have certain basic information before it can think correctly about matters divine'.[48] The 'Epistle to the reader' which prefaced the Confession expounded a strong bond between sin and ignorance. It was a logical consequence of emphasizing texts saying that 'without knowledge the mind cannot be good'[49] and 'people are destroyed for lack of knowledge'[50] that education and salvation were held to be closely related.

Given the open entry to Scotland's universities which provided many of those who became missionaries with a road to salvation in another sense, it was only to be expected that Duff was not the only Scot to make education a central feature of his missionary programme. The fact that the medium of this instruction was English also owed something to Scottish experience. As a Highlander Duff learnt English as a second language, and knew first-hand its utility.[51] The policy he adopted towards the vernacular languages of India had been that of the SSPCK towards Gaelic.

Many got the impression that Duff's success in Calcutta was the result of a scheme which redressed all the errors of his missionary predecessors. This may have been precisely the message he wished to convey; however other societies

with the possible exception of the LMS...had all recognized the importance of English education and had started English schools: they all recognized the importance of training Indian missionaries and teachers.... They did not need Duff to articulate a 'downward filtration' policy...and they were all giving Christian as well as secular teaching in their schools.[52]

Missionary Society to their missionaries among the heathen, 22. See also R. Nesbit to T. C., 17 June 1843, NCL CHA 4.

48   I. Breward, *The work of William Perkins*, 1970, 139.

49   Proverbs 19.2.

50   Hosea 4.6.

51   Laird, *Missionaries and education in Bengal*, 1972, 208f.

52   Ibid., 257.

Duff's contribution, very like Chalmers', lay more in the energetic application of ideas than their creation:

> Although none...were original, he was far more successful at putting them into practice than his predecessors.... Within a few years of its foundation his school had developed into the best missionary institution in Bengal.[53]

In a manner reminiscent of St John's, a factor in Duff's success was his ability to inspire others and present them with a plan of action where they could see their own role fitting in with others and contributing to the purpose of the whole. No one who has read Lal Behari Day's account of Duff's teaching methods can doubt Duff's genius as a teacher.[54] He was professional however, not just inspired, and strove to make one school work really well before he spread his energies further. He was systematic in training assistant teachers and established an integrated religious and secular curriculum. Not surprisingly the morale of his fellow-missionaries and other staff was high.

It also has to be said that the success of Duff was not unqualified, and some others in the missionary community were more aware of the cultural sensitivities and complexities inherent in their task. The value of English education was one thing, the undifferentiated condemnation of Indian language, religion and culture another. His own Highland experience reinforced a policy which supported the conquest of one culture over another more than giving him sympathy for finding a route to a Christianity which respected its host culture. Yet it may have been that the quality of what was done in its own terms did provide a basis for others to achieve what he did not attempt.

While elements of the Church of Scotland missionary policy can be found elsewhere, its presentation as a coherent missionary philosophy appears unique.[55] In contrast to others, the emphasis was far more on the plan of action for the mission than on the piety of the missionary, which rightly or wrongly was taken for granted. The SMS and the LMS were little less involved in education, but they often displayed quite deep uncertainty whether teaching was fit employment for someone sent out to preach the gospel. The SMS warned against the notion that education was 'the grand engine for ameliorating the condition of mankind',[56] and James Paterson is one who reflected the views of many others when he made it clear that he did not consider

---

53 Ibid.
54 Lal Behari Day, *Recollections of Alexander Duff*, 1879, 49-51, 118-25.
55 The *Letter of instructions from the directors of the Scottish Missionary Society* provides an interesting comparison.
56 Ibid., 73.

attention to the physical wants of the heathen and exertions to improve
their temporal concerns to form any necessary part of direct missionary
work; still the feelings of common humanity would urge such conduct
as duty, and reasons would lead us to consider it as the best means of
gaining their affections, and predisposing them to listen to Christian
instruction.[57]

Duff was well aware that the education he was offering was attractive and
brought people within the hearing of the gospel. However its purpose was
not just to serve as bait, but to be itself a part of the presentation of the
Christian faith. The Church of Scotland mission in India enjoyed good
relationships among its missionaries and between them and the Assembly
committee, and it must have been a considerable help in achieving this that
they operated with an agreed policy, and one which did not leave the
missionaries thinking that they really ought to be doing something else.

Nevertheless, among supporters at home at least, there were important
differences. Many such as Chalmers had similar attitudes towards education
as were common in the LMS and SMS. There was a tension within
Chalmers which he never resolved. He did not undervalue education – as his
own career illustrated. He was a central figure in moves to raise the standard
of theological education, as education – as high as possible – was what
equipped apologists for the gospel. For Duff, education was in itself an
apologetic.

At Duff's request,[58] Chalmers preached at his farewell service in
October 1839 prior to his return to India. Chalmers was worried that Duff
had become secular in his approach, but was reassured to learn that he was

> fully and feelingly aware…that unless a blessing, to be evoked only by
> prayer, shall descend from the sanctuary above upon your enterprise, all
> the labour you have bestowed upon it will prove but a vain and empty
> parade.[59]

Perhaps for the first time Chalmers made a real effort to relate his own
missionary thinking to the concepts Duff had been making familiar
throughout Scotland. While he was strangely unable to comprehend Duff's
emphasis on education within the categories of civilization and
christianization, he found scope in his favourite saying of John Eliot. Since
it was 'in the power of pains and of prayer to achieve anything', education
could be construed as the 'pains' of Duff's mission. Thus Chalmers advised
Duff to ignore critics on the right hand and on the left. He was to beware
those of 'shrewd, but withal of secular intelligence' who sought to divert

---

[57]   *Address by Mr James Paterson*, 1832, 18.
[58]   Smith, *Alexander Duff*, 1, 1879, 370.
[59]   *Posthumous Works*, 6, 4.

him from his prayer, and also those 'of serious, but withal of weak and drivelling piety' who despised Duff's science, geometry and economics as 'heathenish innovation'.[60]

When the mission began, the challenge of the Voluntary Controversy required Evangelicals and Moderates to ignore differences of emphasis in missionary philosophy and embark on a practical plan of action. The fact that Duff proved the Moderate policy to have Evangelical results and succeeded in changing the missionary vocabulary of the country meant that Chalmers was at length obliged to come to terms with it. When in 1832 he had been worried about the mission neglecting preaching by its attention to education, he had been able to claim public opinion was on his side. By 1839 it was possible for Duff to say that it was a diminution in the education programme which would place the public support of the mission at risk.[61]

Despite its patchy nature and the mixed motives which brought it about, the unity of Moderate and Evangelical support for the Church of Scotland mission was a considerable achievement. The Moderates were in the end gratified that it was they who provided the leadership in the Assembly committee, and that it was their policy whose value was proved in practice. Evangelicals had the satisfaction that they staffed the mission and made the policies work. In the face of success overseas and need for unity at home any differences of theory could be forgotten – for a time at least. In any case the missionary philosophy which Inglis had articulated and Duff implemented had deeper roots in Scottish culture than the vocabulary which one generation of Evangelicals had learnt through the missionary societies.

---

60 Ibid.
61 Smith, *Alexander Duff*, 1, 1879, 370.

PART THREE

THEOLOGY AND THE THEOLOGY OF MISSION

God has good will towards each and towards all. There is no limitation with him; and be not you limited by your own narrow and fearful and superstitious conceptions of him.

Chalmers[1]

It was called theology...but really it was a course of Chalmers himself, and of Chalmers in all his characters.... Merely to look at him day after day was a liberal education.

David Masson[2]

---

[1] 'On the universality of the Gospel offer,' *Works*, 10, 395.

[2] 'Dead men whom I have known; or, recollections of three cities,' *Macmillan's Magazine*, 11, 1865, 127.

Chapter 14

'Jesus Christ died, the just for the unjust, to bring us to God.'[3]

Theology and the theology of mission

Introduction[4]

Although Chalmers lectured for twenty years in divinity and edited much of his class material for publication, he is little remembered as a theologian, and a systematic 'theology of mission' is not to be found in so many words in his *Institutes of theology*.[5] However his sermons, letters, and journals, what he did as well as what he said, provide elements of what we are looking for and have the merit of being closer to the place where theology is actually done.[6]

It has been said that if his *Institutes* had been 'less orthodox in content or more orthodox in system' they might have better survived the passage of time.[7] This is to overstate their orthodoxy and mistake the novelty of their structure. The continuities of theological viewpoint between those later

---

3   *Works*, 6, 261. 1 Peter 3.18.

4   Other versions of this chapter have appeared in the 1980 annual lecture of the Presbyterian Historical Society of New Zealand and in A. C. Cheyne, ed., *The practical and the pious*, 1985, 174-85.

5   *Posthumous Works*, 7, 8.

6   For treatment of Chalmers' theology in traditional categories, see W. P. Huie, *The theology of Thomas Chalmers*, University of Edinburgh PhD thesis, 1949. H. P. Philips, *The development of demonstrative theism in the Scottish thought of the nineteenth century*, University of Edinburgh PhD thesis, 1951, 89-126. D. F. Rice, *The theology of Thomas Chalmers*, Drew University PhD thesis, 1966. Daniel F. Rice, 'An attempt at systematic reconstruction in the theology of Thomas Chalmers', *Church History*, 48, 1979, 174-88.

7   H. Watt, *Thomas Chalmers and the Disruption*, 1943, 84.

divided by the Disruption has been noted,[8] and it is not necessary to go further than the *Lectures in divinity* of his teacher, George Hill, to find the model for the *Institutes*. However orthodoxy did not mean agreeing with every detail of the Westminster Confession nor did it prevent Chalmers having sympathy with those the Church judged heretical.

The most basic reason for the general neglect of Chalmers' theology is that people then and now have not seen him as a theologian, even if he was a lecturer in divinity. He was a preacher and social reformer with strong interests in political economy. In these areas his ideas have been studied in detail. His natural theology has attracted attention, but not his systematic.

The Disruption conflicts also meant that generations of Evangelicals could not admit their leader was other than solidly behind the theology they believed was central to their identity and cause. The tradition that he was a key representative of the scholastic Calvinism[9] typified by William Cunningham[10] (1805-1861), George Smeaton[11] (1814-1889) and James Bannerman[12] (1807-1868) is understandable, but reflects later conflicts. It mistakes altogether the temper, thrust and emphasis of Chalmers' concerns and also his teaching. It may also be a factor that the tendency of Chalmers' thinking was quite apparent at the time. He was too important to disown, and silence masked doubts about how much he really fitted the mould. Both friends and detractors had reasons for not drawing too much attention to ways in which he was more liberal theologically than was commonly perceived.

His ideas were rooted in his personal hobby-horses, history and times. If to some this is part of what makes him interesting, it may not appeal to those concerned for traditional theological questions in the abstract. If theology is mostly about dialogue with those exercised by a set of classic questions, then Cunningham[13] in particular had abilities Chalmers never developed – or it might be better to say that Cunningham was interested in things Chalmers believed were a waste of time. However, if authentic theology arises out of engagement with one's environment as well as one's past, Chalmers has merits which need to be better appreciated.

At the same time it has to be admitted that there were and are mixed opinions about his abilities outside the areas for which he is better remembered. James M'Cosh could refer to his 'genius as a deep and original

---

8   F. Voges, 'Moderate and Evangelical thinking in the later eighteenth century: differences and shared attitudes', *Records of the Scottish Church History Society*, 22(2), 1985, 141-57.

9   R. A. Riesen, 'Higher criticism in the Free Church Fathers,' *Records of the Scottish Church History Society*, 20(2), 1979, 119-42.

10 *Fasti*, 1, 129.

11 *Fasti*, 5, 154.

12 *Fasti*, 1, 342.

13 W. Cunningham, *Historical theology*, 1862, 1960.

thinker'.[14] Others referred to 'deficiencies in his knowledge of theology which would have sunk any other man' and said he was a 'theological amateur' with no critical acquaintance with classical languages or writers.[15] Certainly his reasoning often lacked precision and was related to gifts as a speaker rather than as a writer. Despite a concern to work from facts, he characteristically operated with ideas which were applied and illustrated in all directions. He was better equipped as a philosopher than as a theologian, but even here he had his limitations.

> Of Greek he knew little more than of German, and he had dim ideas of what had been done by Plato and Aristotle, and the schoolmen of the middle ages. For him the history of true philosophy began with Bacon: to be a Baconian was to be sound. After Bacon, Samuel Clarke and Butler were great names in his books.[16]

The ease with which students could eclipse Chalmers in classical languages or historical theology was proverbial. However, those who saw his failings were seldom deterred from admiration. The writer who called him a theological amateur also noted his 'influence over public opinion which no other Divine of his day in any country possessed'.[17]

The form of his theology, in language and structure, was deliberate and it was missionary. As in preaching, he believed he should speak to communicate, and it was not ignorance or lack of ability which inhibited him from delving into disputes over Christology or election. He found Hill's structure congenial because by beginning with natural theology and moving through 'the disease for which the gospel is provided' to the nature and extent of the remedy, before dealing with the Trinity, the person of Christ and the doctrine of the Holy Spirit, he was following a chronology of spiritual pilgrimage which matched his own as well as his reading of missionary experience.[18] It was something he had come to believe was universal.

The possibility of theological change was risky. Chalmers knew he believed in the things that mattered and that there were some fights not worth fighting. It was one thing for students to debate issues, as he himself had once done, but the Westminster Confession was entrenched. He was not the only one for whom it inhibited theological innovation. A number of his friends were forced out of the Church when they tried to appeal to the Bible over the Confession. Chalmers said nothing when the Assembly dealt with

---

[14] A *tribute to the memory of Dr Chalmers*, 1847, 4.
[15] 'The late Rev Dr Chalmers,' *Macphail's Edinburgh Ecclesiastical Journal*, 3(18), July 1847, 481.
[16] D. Masson, *Memoirs of two cities, Edinburgh and Aberdeen*, 1911, 75.
[17] 'The late Rev Dr Chalmers', 1847, 481.
[18] On the right order of a theological course, *Posthumous Works*, 7, ix-xx.

Edward Irving, John McLeod Campbell and Alexander Scott.[19] His silence was significant, but his support could only have been qualified and would have done neither them nor him any good.

However, his approach was not simply to accept the *status quo*. As will be noted, it was to affirm the Confession at the same time as he re-interpreted it and put it in its place as a historical document. As he explained in an introductory lecture:

> Although the subject-matter of theology is unalterably fixed...is there not a constant necessity for accommodating both the vindication of this authority and the illustration of this subject-matter to the ever-varying spirit and philosophy of the times? ... In theology, as well as in all the other sciences, there is indefinite room for novelties both of thought and of illustration.[20]

Interaction with the issues of the day was a deliberate product of his understanding of the task of theology. In a speech on theological education while still at St John's, he said that, were theology to occupy its right place,

> it would be found to touch at almost every point on the nature of man, and to bear with decisive effect on the whole frame and economy of civil society.[21]

It is in this sense that the claim of James M'Cosh[22] (1811-1891) and others[23] that Chalmers was the reconciler of the theology and the philosophy of Scotland[24] is to be understood. Chalmers believed 'a sound faith and a sound philosophy are one'[25] and conveyed to his students that the two were compatible pursuits.[26]

---

19   Formerly Irving's assistant in London and the immediate source of his charismatic beliefs. *Fasti*, 7, 502f. See also J. Philip Newell, '"Unworthy of the dignity of the Assembly": the deposition of Alexander John Scott in 1831', *Records of the Scottish Church History Society*, 21(3), 1983, 249-62.

20   *Posthumous Works*, 9, xv.

21   *Memoirs*, 2, 535.

22   *Fasti*, 5, 377f.

23   G. L. Craik, *Lowe's Edinburgh Magazine*, 9, 1864, 381f.

24   J. M'Cosh, *The Scottish Philosophy*, 1875, 87, 337, 393-406.

25   T. C. to James Thomson, 12 February 1847, Cambridge University Library.

26   This has been examined by D. F. Rice, who seems to mistake M'Cosh's intention by confining himself to how far Chalmers reconciled Scottish common-sense philosophy with orthodox theology. D. F. Rice, 'Natural theology and the Scottish philosophy in the thought of Thomas

His theological reading was wider than his published writings might suggest. The last years in Kilmany had been industrious, and at St Andrews, particularly in his final year, he also applied himself to serious study. There was the incentive of his new position in Edinburgh for which he needed to prepare, but the notes in his common-place books[27] indicate a considerable breadth of interest. He grappled with Turretin,[28] and Ernesti,[29] and read on topics such as Hume on miracles, the problem of evil, and questions of eschatology.[30] He knew nothing of Schleiermacher or of developments in biblical criticism,[31] but was concerned that German theology be known about, even if its debates proved to be self-cancelling.[32]

In the theology lecture-room the set books were Hill, Paley and Butler.[33] Butler was the 'Bacon of theology' and Chalmers shared the conviction that inductive reasoning was the only sound approach, as well as a tendency to go no further with challenges to belief than necessary to keep orthodoxy as a reasonable option. Paley's argument from design fascinated him, and he was always impressed by discoveries of man's needs and nature's provisions and by correlations between scientific and theological orthodoxy.[34]

The Bible was the all-important source book of Christian belief. Although he believed in its 'plenary inspiration', that was 'responsible not for the thing recorded, but the truth of it'.[35] Chalmers leaned towards Paul, and made relatively little use of the Old Testament.[36] A simple outline of his theology is conveyed by questions he used for catechizing children,[37] and

---

27 Chalmers', *Scottish Journal of Theology*, 21, 1971, 23-46. D. F. Rice, *The theology of Thomas Chalmers*, Drew University, PhD thesis, 1966, 56-91. NCL.

28 Francis Turretin (1623-1687), *Institutio theologiae elencticae*, T. C. to G. H. Baird, 20 June 1829, NLS 3437 f.229.

29 Johann August Ernesti (1707-1781), *Institutio Interpretis Novi Testamenti*, ET 1832, *Memoirs*, 3, 437.

30 Theological commonplace books, NCL.

31 By 'biblical criticism' Chalmers meant textual criticism, which was dealt with in lectures.

32 T. C. to D. Welsh, 18 July 1834, *Memoirs*, 3, 436-41. See also Chalmers' review of Morell's *Modern philosophy, North British Review*, February 1847, 271-331.

33 *Posthumous Works*, 9, ix-xxi.

34 See for example Chalmers' contribution to the Bridgewater treatises, *On the power, wisdom and goodness of God as manifested in the adaptation of external nature to the moral and intellectual constitution of man*, 1833. *Works*, 1-2.

35 T. C. to A. J. Scott, 22 March 1845, W. Hanna, *Letters of Thomas Erskine of Linlathen*, 1878, 569f.

36 Appendix 9.

37 Appendix 8.

his understanding of the essentials of the Christian faith is also revealed by his summary of beliefs held in common with Evangelicals in general.

> We are all agreed on the precious doctrine of the atonement, and on the no less precious doctrine of regeneration. We all hold that when a man is justified by faith he is judged by works and that he must have an interest in the Spirit which sanctifies as well as in the Saviour that died for us. We all hold the Bible to be the only rule of faith and manners.[38]

Doctrine of man[39]

Chalmers stood within the tradition of Scottish common-sense philosophy, and this had its theological counterpart in the *imago Dei*. After reading Genesis 1.26-31, he noted:

> Let me make this use of the information that God made man in his own image. Let it cure me of the scepticism which distrusts man's instinctive beliefs or perceptions. Let me recollect that in knowledge or understanding we are like unto God – and that in this light we see light. He would not practise a mockery upon us by giving us constitutional beliefs at variance with the objective reality of things.... We were formed in his image intellectually as well as morally.[40]

The Fall did not obliterate the image of God as far as human relationships were concerned. While there was sin and evil in the world, there was also virtue which a preacher was bound to acknowledge as of value in this world, if not in the next. Paul asked the Philippians to think on 'whatsoever things are true, whatsoever things are honest, whatsoever things are just'[41] without regard to whether these qualities were found before or after the exercise of saving faith. Chalmers disliked 'injudicious defenders of orthodoxy' who proclaimed

> the utter depravity of our nature...in such a style of sweeping and vehement asseveration as to render it not merely obnoxious to the taste but obnoxious to the understanding. Let the nature of man be a ruin, as it certainly is; it is obvious to the most common discernment that it does not offer one unvaried and unalleviated mass of deformity.[42]

---

38   J. Anderson, *Reminiscences of Thomas Chalmers*, 1851, 289.

39   See also *Posthumous Works*, 7, 363-512.

40   *Posthumous Works*, 1, 2f.

41   Philippians 4.8.

42   *Works*, 6, 15f.

The character of men in classical antiquity or in the contemporary commercial world could be perfectly moral, and should be applauded.[43] Depravity did not lie 'in the utter destitution of all that is amiable in feeling.... It lies in ungodliness.'[44]

Chalmers was caught between those who objected to talking of sin at all, and those who felt he was lenient and less than orthodox. William Cunningham succeeded him as Principal of New College and took exception to Chalmers' praise of natural virtue. 'Works done before justification...are truly sins and deserve the displeasure and condemnation of God.'[45] Referring to Chalmers, he disputed the 'propriety of calling anything in the character of unrenewed men *good*, absolutely or without explanation'.[46]

For Cunningham what was at stake was the danger of compromising orthodox Calvinism. For Chalmers Calvinism was historically conditioned and what mattered was communicating a gospel which could not be imprisoned in theological systems. His was a hermeneutic of mission, and he did not believe he could do what he was called to do if he ignored people's use of language and their best aspirations. Creeds and confessions were 'out of their place...as magazines of truth'. They had generally come into existence as 'mere landmarks against heresy',[47] and he lamented their use as 'insignia' for different denominations.[48]

The *imago Dei* also carried the implication that all were equal in the sight of God. While he accepted a stratified society, was no lover of democracy and looked to the civilization of the heathen, this was a principle he constantly reiterated. As he declared at the laying of the New College foundation stone in 1846, this was the 'one equality of man' which was to be 'strenuously taught',[49] and it was because this applied to the poor that one worked to convert and educate them. They have

> all the capacities of human spirits...they have talents...they have imperishable souls...they are on a full level of equality with ourselves in all that is essential to man.[50]

---

43 Chalmers probably had in mind his friend from student days, Thomas Duncan, whom he described as 'the best specimen of the natural man he had ever known'. M. F. Connolly, *Eminent Men of Fife*, 1866, 154.

44 *Works*, 8, 174.

45 *Historical theology*, 1, 1960, 553.

46 Ibid., 554.

47 *Memoirs*, 4, 456.

48 T. Chalmers, *On the Evangelical Alliance*, 1846, 9-17.

49 H. Watt, *New College Edinburgh. A centenary history*, 1946, 3f.

50 T. Chalmers, *Churches and schools for the working classes*, 1846, 11.

However equality applied to judgement as well as to salvation, and while he preferred to strike a more positive note, he did not shrink from what he regarded as the facts of life:

> Even to the most remote and unlettered tribes, men are everywhere the fit subjects for a judgement day. Their belief, scanty though it be, hath a correspondent morality which they may either observe or be deficient in, and so be reckoned with accordingly.[51]

The theme of his favourite sermon, 'Fury not in God',[52] was God's mercy to all who would receive it, yet the consequences of refusal were not to be ignored:

> It makes one shudder seriously to think that there may be some here present whom this devouring torrent of wrath shall sweep away; some here present who will be drawn into the whirl of destruction, and forced to take their descending way through the mouth of that pit where the worm dieth not, and the fire is not quenched.[53]

He was sympathetic to the reasons which led his friend Erskine of Linlathen into universalism,[54] and said it did not detract from his book.[55] Not surprisingly he was accused of the same opinions.[56] Not all Evangelicals were confident about eternal torments,[57] and Chalmers preferred to avoid speculations.[58] He did not want to appear a 'stern dogmatist' but he was mindful of people putting off repentance until it was too late. The Bible gave no warrant for believing that 'our all is not staked, and irrevocably staked, on the faith and obedience of the present life'.[59]

Judgement raised the problem of being accountable for ignorance. Byron had asserted that people were not responsible for what they believed. Asked for his opinion, Chalmers replied:

---

[51] *Works*, 1, 76.

[52] Isaiah 27.3.

[53] *Posthumous Works*, 6, 425.

[54] *Works*, 3, 247. T. C. to Lady Elgin, 6 March 1830, *Correspondence*, 348.

[55] *The unconditional freeness of the gospel*, while 'exceptionable in regard to the wording of some things...in respect of principle and substance', was 'unspeakably precious' and made 'a great and...salutary impression on Mrs Chalmers', T. C. to J. Morton, 29 November 1828, *Correspondence*, 213.

[56] Anon to T. C., n.d., NCL CHA 4.102.13.

[57] Hannah More wrote to Wilberforce of the 'impenetrable veil' drawn over 'the awful mysteries of judgement'. 2 September 1823, PLDU.

[58] *Posthumous Works*, 9, 416. See also *Works*, 8, 310-31.

[59] *Posthumous Works*, 6, 417. See also *Posthumous Works*, 5, 9.

You are not to blame if you have not found some valuable article that you had lost in an apartment of thickest darkness: but you are to blame if you might have opened the shutters or lighted a candle…. Neither are you to blame if you find not the hidden treasure of the gospel provided that it is placed beyond the reach of all your strenuousness…but you are to blame if you have not gone in quest of it, or if you have wilfully and determinedly shut your eyes against it.[60]

He believed that

there was a sufficient difference between the future prospects of the heathen and those of Christian believers to justify the utmost extent and ardency of missionary exertions.[61]

Nevertheless the heathen would be judged less severely. 'The nations of Christendom who have been plied with the offers of the gospel'

incur a darker doom throughout eternity than the native of China, whose remoteness, while it shelters him from the light of the New Testament in this world, shelters him from the pain of its fulfilled denunciations in the next.[62]

He was flying in the face of the Westminster Confession[63] and when he read of the centurion whose alms and prayers had been accepted by God before be became a Christian,[64] he prayed that 'a factitious and freezing orthodoxy' would not 'shut him up' against the lesson of the passage.[65]

---

[60] Recipient unknown, 15 March 1826, *Correspondence*, 299f. There are manuscript copies at NLS 10997 f.68 and StAUL MS 2032. See also *Works*, 1, 72.

[61] *Memoirs*, 3, 392.

[62] *Works*, 22, 141. Part of a sermon examining the converse implication of the text that 'to whom much is given, of them much will be required'. See also *Works*, 10, 380 and *Works*, 13, 142f.

[63] Chapter 10.4, 'Of effectual calling' states that there is no prospect of non-Christians being saved 'be they ever so diligent to frame their lives according to the light of nature…and to assert that they may, is very pernicious and to be detested'.

[64] Acts 10.

[65] *Posthumous Works*, 4, 161. Chalmers made a similar observation when reading of the Queen of Sheba's visit to Solomon; 'even at great distances from Judea, the true God was not altogether unknown'. *Posthumous Works*, 5, 469.

The duty of the Christian was to be preparing for heaven.[66] This was not to cultivate other-worldliness so much as to demonstrate the reality of faith by conduct, and 'the business of...sanctification' was a 'daily and hourly and ever-doing business'.[67] He was well aware of his own shortcomings, but since heaven was 'no heaven at all but to the holy',[68] it was the more necessary to remember that 'the great end and object...of the Christian doctrine is not that I should believe as a Christian but that I should do as a Christian'.[69] 'The great object of the economy under which we sit' was to be restored to the image of God.[70]

Calvinism and the universality of the gospel offer[71]

That a high doctrine of election, such as the theology of the Westminster Confession, can be compatible with evangelism, has often been more of a problem outside the tradition than within. Logical possibilities are not always logical necessities, and the morbid doubts of William Cowper, and the antinomianism of James Hogg,[72] are possible rather than typical outworkings of Calvinistic faith. Sluggishness in Calvinistic missions has more to do with apathy than theology.

During Chalmers' life-time, examples of 'hyper-Calvinism' were to be found in Scotland, but it was unheard of in the established Church. It was among Scottish Baptists that there was most concern about whether it was presumptuous or necessary to preach the gospel to the unconverted.[73] Those for whom the Westminster Confession was their own creed knew that whatever else it said, it noted that God in his ordinary providence used means for the achievement of his ends, however foreordained.[74] Thomas Boston[75] (1676-1732) was among those who taught that 'calls and

---

66 See Chalmers' sermons, 'The necessity of a personal meetness for heaven', *Works*, 10, 122-32, and 'Heaven a character and not a locality', *Works*, 7, 320-38.

67 *Works*, 11, 367.

68 T. C. to R. Edie. 3 April 1819, J. Baillie, *The missionary of Kilmany*, 1854, 35.

69 *Posthumous Works*, 4, 52.

70 *Posthumous Works*, 6, 2.

71 *Posthumous Works*, 8, 403-13.

72 J. Hogg, *The private memoirs and confessions of a justified sinner*, 1824, 1970. Drummond and Bulloch, *The Scottish Church*, 1973, 217f.

73 See, for example, (A. Maclean), *Thoughts on the calls and invitations of the gospel*, Edinburgh, 1797.

74 Westminster Confession, chapter 5.3.

75 *Fasti*, 2, 174f.

exhortations' were necessary since they were 'the means that God is pleased to make use of for converting his elect'.[76]

While Chalmers was not inhibited by a Calvinistic heritage when it came to preaching salvation as a free gift open to any who would receive it, he was sensitive to theological barriers between God's offer and the possibility of response. When a tract by Horatius Bonar[77] (1808-1889) was treated with suspicion because it was too 'free', he would have none of it.[78] If the gospel was not freely offered it was no good to himself and little use to others. Almost the last sermon he preached was entitled 'the fulness and freeness of the gospel message'[79] and the evening before his death he complained of those who restricted 'the word *world* as applied in scripture to the sacrifice of Christ'.

> The common way of explaining it is that it simply includes Gentiles as well as Jews. I do not like that interpretation and I think that there is one text that puts that interpretation entirely aside...God commandeth *all men, everywhere* to repent.... In the offer of the gospel we must make no limitation whatever.[80]

The problem with predestination lay not in philosophical and theological difficulties, which he ignored, but in keeping it out of the way of a message which had worked in his own experience. If Paul found no difficulty preaching the gospel and believing in election, Chalmers saw no reason to quibble with apostolic precedent.[81] As far as predestination was concerned (and the related question of the extent of the atonement), he was happy to be agnostic. It was irrelevant to practical Christian life,[82] and in a conversation with the Quaker, J. J. Gurney, he was reported as saying

> I believe the doctrine to be true; nevertheless, the Christian's course of duty is precisely the same as it would be if the doctrine was not true.[83]

---

[76] *Human nature in its four-fold state*, 1769, 147. See also J. Walker, *The theology and theologians of Scotland*, 1872, 60.

[77] *Fasti*, 2, 74f. The tract was entitled *Believe and live*.

[78] T. C. to Mrs Dunlop, 22 September 1844, *Correspondence*, 514-16.

[79] *The fulness and freeness of the gospel message. A sermon, preached in Hanover Presbyterian Church, Brighton, on Sunday, May 16, 1847*, 1847. *Memoirs*, 4, 508.

[80] *Memoirs*, 4, 512. See also *Works*, 13, 387f.

[81] T. C. to E. Morgan, 1 March 1827, *Memoirs*, 3, 528f. On the doctrine of predestination, *Works*, 9, 151-75. R. Watson, *Works*, 7, 240-57.

[82] *Posthumous Works*, 8, 345-413. T. Chalmers, *A course of five lectures on predestination*, 1837.

[83] A. Philip, *Thomas Chalmers apostle of union*, 1929, 223. See also T. C. to Mrs Glasgow, 12 October 1825, *Correspondence*, 126.

As one of his students took down in his notes, the subject of predestination could only be 'cautiously introduced into the pulpit'.[84]

> Calvinism is not to influence you...you have nothing to do except with what is revealed. Repent else you perish, believe in the Lord Jesus – Seek the Lord while he may be found. Cease to do evil.[85]

Chalmers' sense of distance from the Westminster Confession has been noted. He could eulogize it, but his summary of its teaching is revealing.

> The natural depravity of man; his need both of regeneration and of an atonement; the accomplishment of the one by the efficacy of a divine sacrifice, and of the other by the operation of a sanctifying Spirit; the doctrine that a sinner is justified by faith, followed up...by the doctrine that he is judged by works; the righteousness of Christ as the alone foundation of his meritorious claim to heaven, but this followed up by his own personal righteousness as the indispensable preparation for heaven's exercises and heaven's joys; the free offer of pardon even to the chief of sinners, but this followed up by the practical calls of repentance, without which no orthodoxy can save him; the amplitude of the gospel invitations, and, in despite of all that has been unintelligently said about our gloomy and relentless Calvinism, the wide and unexpected amnesty that is held forth to every creature under heaven.[86]

These emphases were indicative of what was to become more widespread. The attitudes of Scottish Presbyterians towards the Confession shifted considerably during the course of the century, and when the United Presbyterians passed a declaratory act in 1879 to modify the terms of subscription to the Confession, there was hardly a point discussed which can not be found in Chalmers' lectures from 50 years previously.[87] The Free Church followed with a similar act in 1892[88] and the Church of Scotland in 1910.[89] Chalmers may have refrained from drawing attention to the way in which he moved away from the Confession, but the correlation between

---

84　Notes from Dr Chalmers' lectures on theology, n.d. (c.1831) EUL Dc.7. 115, 23.

85　Ibid., 21.

86　*Works*, 11, 155. Sermon preached 11 May 1827, at the opening of the National Scotch Church, Regent Square, London.

87　J. T. Cox and D. F. M. Macdonald, eds., *Practice and procedure in the Church of Scotland*, 1976, 435f.

88　Ibid, 436f.

89　Ibid, 434.

these acts and Chalmers' teaching indicates he is more representative of mainstream 19th-century Scottish theology than has been recognized.

The Church in the world

In common with Geneva, the Scottish Reformers took, as the 'notes' of a true church, the preaching of the Word of God and the right administration of the sacraments, and added the proper exercise of discipline.[90] As a result of the Voluntary Controversy, in the Scotland of the 1830s a true church was one which had control of its own spiritual affairs and proved itself by evangelistic activity at home and overseas.[91] It is not difficult to see the Disruption as a move to preserve these *notae ecclesiae*.

For Chalmers the organization of the church, like the organization of theology, was subservient to proclaiming the gospel. On reading a sermon which argued that the church was free in different times and circumstances to alter its government, worship, and discipline, since its 'institutions stand not on the strength of statute, but in that of their fitness to fulfil the great objects of her mission',[92] he felt moved to write to the author:

> Yours is no every-day pamphlet; and I have read it with the most entire and cordial satisfaction.... The saying of Paul that 'I speak as a man', teaches in my opinion, your very lesson, by letting posterity know...that it was competent on mere human discretion to decide on questions of ecclesiastical regulations and polity.[93]

His divinity lectures never got as far as the nature of the church, although he always found time for the principles of parochial organization and defending the utility of established churches. He was a supporter of 'the sole headship of Christ over his church' but was irritated by the phrase 'the crown rights of the Redeemer' and did not make use of 'the body of Christ' as a model of the church.

Church government was a matter of expediency because the missionary purpose of the church underlay all his thinking concerning polity, independence and unity. His interests in pauperism and political economics arose out of a vision of community and his conviction that Christianity ought to be applied to the whole of society.

---

90 G. D. Henderson, *Scots Confession, 1560*, 1937, 75.

91 See also Alexander Duff's address, *Missions the chief end of the Christian church*, 1839.

92 W. Hanna, *Letters of Thomas Erskine of Linlathen*, 1878, 569.

93 T. C. to A. J. Scott, 22 March 1845, *Correspondence*, 569f. In 1829 Chalmers rejected attempts to use Israel in the Old Testament as a model for the relationship of church and state. Presbytery of Edinburgh, the Catholic claims, 1 April 1829. Charles Watson papers, NCL.

It would be well if religion was to pervade the corporate as well as the individual body, that the day might arrive when corporate bodies were as much under the influence of religion in all their operations as pious individuals are.[94]

Here is the meeting point of his social and evangelistic concerns, but he did not resolve his claim to 'count the salvation of a single soul of more value than the deliverance of a whole empire from pauperism' with spending so much time attempting to achieve the latter.[95]

In his heavily worked phrase, 'the Christian good of Scotland',[96] Chalmers sought to convey the wholeness of the Christian enterprise. He held that 'every part and every function of a commonwealth should be leavened with Christianity'[97] and prayed that 'rulers might christianize their legislation and philosophers their systems'.[98] The church as an organization and Christians as individuals were called to apply themselves not only to evangelism, but to pastoral work, the problems of working-class society, the ethics of the business world, famine relief and prevention, issues of science and religion and questions raised by philosophy. Environment must influence the church as well as the church its environment.

He was often impressed by the piety of those interested in prophecy though he frequently doubted their judgement. Perhaps the most consistent theme in his fluid convictions about eschatology was the belief that

The kingdoms of the earth may become the kingdom of God and of his Christ with the external framework of these present governments.... There must therefore be a way in which Christianity can accommodate itself to this framework – a mode by which it can animate all the parts and all the members of it.[99]

The centrality of Chalmers' missionary vision and theology is illustrated by the continuities which run through the varied events of his life, but they also show in the causes he did not get involved in. The acrimony of the Apocrypha controversy was something he left to one side, and beyond the benefits of worshipful and peaceful Sundays, Sabbatarianism held few attractions. Temperance never interested him for more than a day or two at a time. The breadth of his sympathies is shown not only by the involvements

---

94 Notes from Dr Chalmers' lectures on theology, n.d. [c.1831], EUL Dc.7.115, 123.
95 T. C. to James Brown, 30 January 1819, *Memoirs*, 2, 341f.
96 *Memoirs*, 4, 394 and elsewhere.
97 T. Chalmers, *The addresses delivered at the commencement and conclusion of the first General Assembly of the Free Church of Scotland*, 1843.
98 *Posthumous Works*, 5, 417.
99 *Memoirs*, 3, 203. See also *Memoirs*, 4, 496f.

of an extraordinary lifetime, but by the encouragement he gave to others. Many looked to him from both sides of the divide created by the Ten Years' Conflict and the events of May 1843. In the town of Chalmers' birth Hew Scott had not 'gone out' at the Disruption and laboured on a seemingly thankless task, compiling the monumental record of the ministers of the church, the *Fasti Ecclesiae Scoticanae*. It was Chalmers who said to him 'Go on, Mr Scott, go on; the unborn will bless you, sir. It is the work I would so like to do.'[100]

There was great diversity in Chalmers' life and thought, but there was also a particular focus, a well-spring he had discovered for himself in Kilmany in 1811:

> Jesus Christ died, the just for the unjust, to bring us unto God. This is a truth, which, when all the world shall receive it, all the world will be renovated.... It is this doctrine which is the alone instrument of God for the moral transformation of our species.[101]

Therein lies 'the Christian good', not only of Scotland, but also of the world.

---

[100] *Fasti*, 1, xvi.
[101] *Works*, 6, 261.

APPENDIX 1

Kilmany church attendance 1801-1815[1]

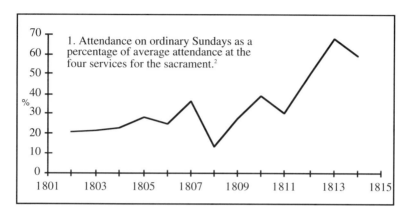

1. Attendance on ordinary Sundays as a percentage of average attendance at the four services for the sacrament.[2]

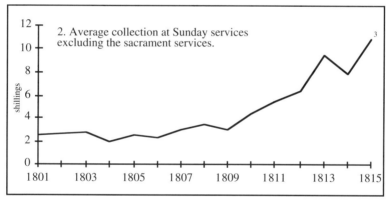

2. Average collection at Sunday services excluding the sacrament services.[3]

---

[1] These graphs are derived from the weekly collections recorded in the Kilmany kirk-session account book, SRO/GRO OPR 437/1.

[2] Based on the assumption that the collections are a reasonable guide to attendance, particularly since as a ratio for each year the percentage is independent of inflation. Attendance at ordinary Sunday services would be more sensitive to the popularity of the minister than attendance at the annual communion sacrament. In 1803 and 1809 the sacrament was not celebrated.

[3] Chalmers' successor had a difficult time retaining the enlarged congregation and the collections fell back sharply after Chalmers' departure.

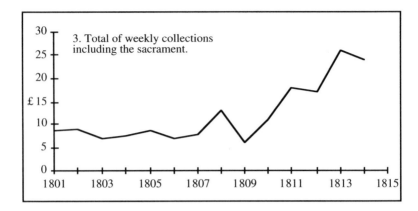

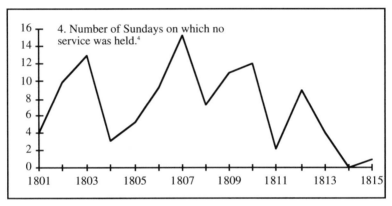

5. Sacraments 1810-1815[5]

	1810	1811	1812	1813	1814	1815
Communion tokens issued	270	457[6]	—	334	386	371
New Communicants	11	15	10	4	7	13

---

[4]   While this does give some indication of Chalmers' interest in the parish it
      is a far from infallible guide to his commitment as absence could result from
      quite innocent circumstances, e.g. in the last months of 1809 services were
      only held fortnightly because of Chalmers' illness.
[5]   MSS Communicants 1810-1815, NCL.
[6]   This probably included the Balmerino congregation. *Memoirs*, 1, 227.

APPENDIX 2

Glasgow population 1780-1851

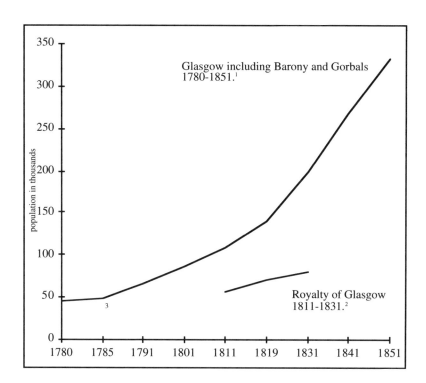

Glasgow including Barony and Gorbals 1780-1851.[1]

population in thousands

Royalty of Glasgow 1811-1831.[2]

350 300 250 200 150 100 50 0

1780 1785 1791 1801 1811 1819 1831 1841 1851

---

[1]   The area over which the census was taken changed frequently, but was approximately constant for the years 1801-1831. For a discussion of the problem of Glasgow's population statistics, and the source of these figures, see J. Cunnison and J.B.S. Gilfillan, eds., *The third statistical account of Scotland, Glasgow*, 1958, 54, 58, 787.

[2]   Figures from: *Accounts of the population of certain parishes in Scotland*, 1819, 4. J. Cleland, *Statistical tables relative to the city of Glasgow*, 1823, 7. J. Cleland, *Enumeration of the inhabitants of the city of Glasgow*, 1831, 30.

[3]   The 1785 figure is from J. Cleland, *Statistical tables relative to the city of Glasgow*, 1823, 3.

APPENDIX 3

Glasgow churches to 1834[1]

Table 1

Royalty parishes	Date founded
Cathedral (St Mungo's, Inner High)	1123
Tron (St Mary's)	1528
Blackfriars (College)	1622
Outer High (East, after 1836 St Paul's)	1648
St Andrews (before 1761 the Wynd)	1691
Ramshorn (Northwest, after 1825 St David's)	1720
St George's (Wynd or West)	1761
St Enoch's	1780
St John's	1819
St James'	1820

Table 2

Royalty chapels-of-ease	Date founded
Ingram Street Gaelic (later St Columba's)	1770
North Albion Street (Canon Street)	1774
Duke Street Gaelic	1798
St John's chapel-of-ease (later St Thomas')	1823
Hope Street Gaelic	1824
St George's-in-the-fields	1824
St Anne's	1831

[1] J. Cleland, *Statistical tables relative to the city of Glasgow*, 1823, 29-33. H. Escott, *A history of Scottish Congregationalism*, 1960, 26, 355f. M. Lochhead, *Episcopal Scotland in the 19th century*, 1966, 104f. *Second report of the Commissioners of Religious Instruction*, Scotland, 1837, 36, H. Scott, *Fasti*, 3, 1920. R. Small, *History of the congregations of the United Presbyterian Church*, 2, 1904. G. Yuille, *History of the Baptists in Scotland*, 1926, 169, 178-180, 281f.

Table 3

	Date founded
Barony parish church	1595

Table 4

Barony chapels-of-ease	Date founded
Shettleston	1750
Calton	1793
Anderston	1799

Table 5

	Date founded
Gorbals parish church	1771

Table 6

Gorbals chapel-of-ease	Date founded
Kirkfield Gaelic	1814

Table 7

United Secession	Date founded
Greyfriars	1739
Duke Street	1750
Campbell Street	1789
Wellington Street (Anderston)	1792
Regent Place	1819
Nicholson Street (Laurieston)	1821
Gordon Street	1823
Eglington Street	1824

Table 8

Relief	Date founded
Anderston	1770
Dovehill	1774
Campbell Street	1792
John Street	1800
Hutchisontown	1800
Bridgeton	1805
Tollcross	1806
Calton	1821
Great Hamilton Street (Independent Relief)	1823[2]

Table 9

Original Burghers[3]	Date founded
Campbell Street	1799
Renfield Street	1819

Table 10

Independent	Date founded
Old Scottish Independents (Greyfriars Wynd)	1768
Nile Street	1800
George Street	1803

---

[2] Known to be active at this date.

[3] Before 1820 these were part of the Associate Synod of Burghers, but they declined to join the United Secession.

Table 11

Methodist	Date founded
John Street	1787
Tradeston	1812
Green Street	1820
Calton	1823[4]
Anderston	1823[4]

Table 12

Baptist	Date founded
George Street	1769
Morrison's Court	1810
Albion Street	1820
Adelaide Place	1829

Table 13

Other denominations	Date founded
Society of Friends	1716
Reformed Presbyterian	1733
Episcopal	1750
Berean	1780
Roman Catholic	1792
Unitarian	1812
New Jerusalem	1817
Jewish Synagogue	1821
Christian Congregation (John McLeod Campbell)	1832

---

[4] Known to be active at this date.

APPENDIX 4

Tron and St John's parish boundaries 1815-1823[1]

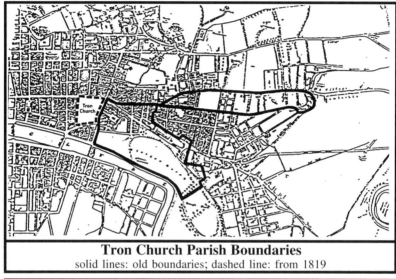

Tron Church Parish Boundaries
solid lines: old boundaries; dashed line: from 1819

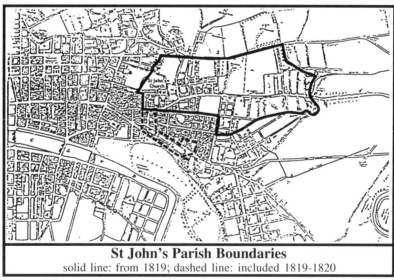

St John's Parish Boundaries
solid line: from 1819; dashed line: included 1819-1820

---

[1] Boundaries derived from maps in Mitchell Library Glasgow and Strathclyde Regional Archives as well as from information in SRA A2/1/3.157, 186, 18 February 1818. Base map, 1832, in R. Rendwick, *Extracts from the records of the Burgh of Glasgow*, 11, 1823-1832, Glasgow, 1906.

APPENDIX 5

St John's statistics[1]

1. Population of Glasgow parishes

2. Nominal Church of Scotland membership

3. Church sittings held by St John's population 1819-1836

4. Relative strength of the Church of Scotland and Dissent among seatholders resident in St John's parish

5. Church sittings held by St John's population, 1825-1836

6. Church sittings held by St John's households

7. Church sittings in St John's church or chapel held by parishioners

8. Seatholders residing in proportion 7 of St John's parish

9. Occasional worshippers residing in proportion 7

10. Churches where seats were held by residents in proportion 7

11. Churches attended by residents in proportion 7 without holding seats

12. Religious commitment of St John's population and households

13. Occupations of householders in proportion 7 in 1823

14. Sessional poor in Glasgow city parishes

15. Sessional poor per thousand population in Glasgow city parishes

16. New paupers admitted to Glasgow Town Hospital

17. Glasgow Town Hospital: total paupers and annual assessment

---

[1] Sources used in the compilation of these tables:

Abstract of the survey of St John's Parish, Glasgow, June 1825, NCL. *Works*, 16.

J. Cleland, *Enumeration of the inhabitants of the City of Glasgow and County of Lanark for the government census of 1831*, 1831, 30, 96.

J. Cleland, *Statistical tables relative to the city of Glasgow*, 1823.

Matthew Montgomery, William Mathieson and John Cunninghame, St John's survey notebook (proportion 7, 1823), NCL.

A. Ranken, *A letter addressed to Dr Chalmers on the subject of the pauperism of Glasgow*, 1830.

Second report of the Commissioners of Religious Instruction, Scotland, 1837.

Statistical, moral and educational survey of St John's parish, Glasgow, for the year 1819. NCL.

Table 1
Population of Glasgow parishes

	1819	1820[2]	1825	1831	1836
Cathedral		7,794		10,295	
Blackfriar's		6,913		7,569	
Tron		7,117		7,529	
St Andrew's		5,815		5,923	
Outer High		7,685		9,137	
St George's		9,641		15,242	
St Enoch's		7,256		7,921	
Ramshorn		6,289		6,268	
St John's	10,304	8,366[3]	10,231	11,746	12,003[4]
St James'		6,920		8,217	
Total		**73,796**		**89,847**	
St John's households	2,161	1,774	2,255	2,489	2,797

Table 2
Nominal Church of Scotland membership (% of population)

	1819	1831	1836
St John's parish	53%	56%	—[5]
Glasgow city	60%	56%	48%
Glasgow, Gorbals and Barony	55%	51%	46%

[2] Strictly 1819, but Cleland, *Statistical tables*, 1823, 6f. uses the 1820 parish boundaries for his 1819 figures.

[3] Five proportions, containing a population of 2000, were transferred from St John's to the new parish of St James' in 1820.

[4] In 1834 the St John's chapel-of-ease was erected into a parish as St Thomas', but the figures for population and number of households here include that part of St John's which was transferred to the new parish.

[5] The figure for St John's in *the Second report of the Commissioners of Religious Instruction* is not used as it refers to seatholders, not nominal members.

Table 3
Church sittings held by St John's population 1819-1836

	1819	1822	1825	1836	1836[6]
Church of Scotland	8%	10%	12%	11%	12%
Dissent	20%	18%	16%	14%	14%
No seats held	72%	72%	72%	75%	74%

Table 4
Relative strength of the Church of Scotland and Dissent among seatholders resident in St John's parish

	1819	1822	1825	1836	1836
Church of Scotland	29%	36%	44%	43%	47%
Dissent	71%	64%	56%	57%	53%

Table 5
Church sittings held by St John's parishioners 1825-1836

	1825	1836
St John's Church or Chapel	650	374
Other Church of Scotland	611	909
Relief	646	570
Secession	584	348
Burgher		149
Reformed	46	26
Independent		65
Methodist	213	117
Baptist		10
Roman Catholic	94	344
Episcopal	30	43
Quaker		4
Persons without sittings	7357	9043
Total population	**10,231**	**12,002**

---

[6]   Figures for Glasgow, Gorbals and Barony, *Second report*, 1837, 19, 21.

Table 6
Church sittings held by St John's households (% of households)

	1819	1836
Church of Scotland	24%	
Dissent	37%	
None	39%	41%

Table 7
Church sittings in St John's church or chapel held by parishioners

	1819	1825	1836
Number of sittings	c.100	650	374
Percentage of total let	1%	—	18%
Percentage of population	1%	6%	3%

Table 8
Seatholders residing in proportion 7 of St John's parish

Number of seats held in:	1819		1823		1825	
St John's church or chapel			5	9%	18	28%
Other Church of Scotland	25	41%	23	43%	15	24%
Secession	25	41%	22	42%	25	40%
Other Dissent	11	18%	3	6%	5	8%
Total Church of Scotland	25	41%	28	52%	33	52%
Total Dissent	36	59%	25	48%	30	48%
Population	290		275		305	

Table 9
Occasional worshippers residing in proportion 7

Householders who had an attachment to a specific congregation without necessarily holding a seat. (% of total households)

	1823	
St John's	8	12%
Other Church of Scotland	14	20%
Relief	12	17%
Secession	6	9%
Other Dissent	8	12%
Total Church of Scotland	22	32%
Total Dissent	26	38%
No seat or attachment	21	30%
Total	**6 9**	

Table 10
Churches where seats were held by residents in proportion 7

	1819	1823
Church of Scotland	9	10
United Secession	3	3
Relief	4	4
Reformed	1	
Independent	1	1
Episcopal	1	
Roman Catholic	1	1
Unidentified	2	
Total	**2 2**	**1 9**

Table 11
Churches attended by residents in proportion 7 without holding seats

	1823
Church of Scotland	2
United Secession	1
Independent	1
Methodist	1

Table 12
Religious commitment of St John's population and households

	1819	1822/3	1825	1836
Percentage of householders without either a seat or attachment to a specific congregation (Proportion 7)		30%		
Percentage of householders with no seats	39%			41%
Percentage of population holding no seats	72%	72%	72%	76%

Table 13
Occupations of householders in proportion 7 in 1823

widow	17	clothcapper	1
carter	5	copper-smith	1
labourer	4	engraver	1
stocking-weaver	4	grocer	1
shoemaker	3	hosier	1
warper	3	merchant	1
weaver	3	messenger	1
bricklayer	2	porter	1
sawyer	2	soldier	1
baker	1	victualler	1
broker	1	vinter	1
brushmaker	1	wire-worker	1
clerk	1	wright	1
clipper	1	not specified	4

Table 14
Sessional poor in Glasgow city parishes

	1818		July 1819		Feb. 1821		Nov. 1822	
Cathedral	199	17%	148	12%	143	11%	132	11%
Blackfriar's	182	15%	218	17%	258	19%	251	20%
Tron	194	16%	271	21%	187	14%	148	12%
St Andrew's	180	15%	141	11%	162	12%	130	10%
Outer High	149	13%	122	10%	105	8%	97	8%
St George's	125	10%	47	4%	59	4%	73	6%
St Enoch's	97	8%	156	12%	148	11%	153	12%
Ramshorn	56	5%	31	2%	31	2%	38	3%
St John's			125	10%	108	8%	89	7%
St James'					126	9%	133	11%
Total	**1182**[7]		**1259**		**1327**		**1244**	
Expenditure			£2,266				£2,370	

Table 15
Sessional poor per thousand population in Glasgow city parishes[8]

	1818	July 1819	Feb. 1821	Nov. 1822
Cathedral	25	19	18	17
Blackfriar's	24	32	37	36
Tron	23	38	26	21
St Andrew's	23	24	28	22
Outer High	19	16	14	13
St George	15	5	6	8
St Enoch's	14	21	20	21
Ramshorn	6	5	5	6
St John's		15	13	11

---

[7] The total of the sessional poor was 1350, but 168 did not appear before the committee which surveyed the poor in 1818. J. Cleland, *Statistical tables relative to the city of Glasgow*, 1823, 109.

[8] Population taken as for 1819, with the 1820 parish boundaries.

Table 16
New paupers admitted to Glasgow Town Hospital

	1821	1822	1823
Cathedral	14	12	20
Blackfriar's	31	22	16
Tron	21	18	21
St Andrew's	10	15	9
Outer High	8	4	0
St George's	11	2	4
St Enoch's	17	14	12
Ramshorn	4	0	0
St John's	0	0	0
St James'	4	12	11
Total	**120**	**99**	**93**

Table 17
Glasgow Town Hospital: total paupers and annual assessment

Year	Paupers	Assessment
1810	1228	£5,770
1811	1352	£5,740
1812	1604	£7,480
1813	2017	£10,273
1814	1798	£10,709
1815	1644	£9,940
1816	1617	£9,063
1817	1623	£10,535
1818	1587	£11,864
1819	1529	£10,303
1820	1440	£13,136
1821	1355	£12,560
1822	1356	£9,213
1823	1327	£8,561
1824	1321	£8,305
1825	1226	£8,747
1826	1205	£9,500
1827	1084	£7,130
1828	1004	£6,403
1829	1034	£8,007
1830	1057	£7,866

APPENDIX 6

Scottish missionary societies 1795-1825

Although this list attempts to be as complete as possible, it is not exhaustive, and does not include societies which were only congregational, nor many which also functioned as Bible societies. Where several titles were used for the same society the main variant is given in brackets. The first date refers to when the society was founded. Where this is not known a bracketed date indicates a year in which the society was known to be active. A second unbracketed date refers to a revival of the society.

Sources used include published sermons, annual reports, subscription lists, and references in correspondence, periodicals, newspapers and directories.

Aberdeen (Auxiliary) Missionary Society, 1796, 1816.
Aberdeen Female Missionary Society, 1811.
Aberdeen Methodist Missionary Society, 1816.
Aberdeen University Missionary Society, 1820.
Association of Theological Students in the University of Glasgow in aid of Missionary Exertions, 1821.
Berwickshire Missionary Society, (1822).
Brechin and Montrose Missionary Society, (1818).
Ceres Missionary Society, (1821).
Cupar-Fife Missionary Association, (1822).
Dumfries and Galloway branch of the Scottish Missionary Society, (1822).
Dumfries Missionary Society, (1797).
Dundee Auxiliary Society for the Promoting of Christianity among the Jews, (1811).
Dundee Missionary Society (Dundee Society for Propagating the Gospel among the Heathen), 1796.
Duns Missionary Society, (1797).
East Lothian Society for Propagating Christian Knowledge, (1822).
Edinburgh Association in aid of Missions of the United (Moravian) Brethren, (1822).
Edinburgh Auxiliary Church of England Missionary Society, 1818.
Edinburgh Auxiliary to the London Missionary Society, 1813.
Edinburgh Juvenile Auxiliary Scottish Missionary Society, (1822).
Edinburgh Missionary Society, 1796.
Edinburgh University Missionary Association, 1825.
Elgin and Morayshire Missionary Association, (1822).
Falkirk Auxiliary Bible and Missionary Society, (1822).

Fenwick Auxiliary Missionary Society, 1813.

Fife Auxiliary Missionary Society, 1814.

Gala-water Missionary Society, (1822).

Glasgow Association in aid of the Moravian Missions, (1821).

Glasgow Auxiliary Society for Promoting Christianity among the Jews, (1812).

Glasgow Branch (Committee) of the Missionary Society, (1797).

Glasgow Missionary Society, 1796.

Greenock Branch of the Missionary Society, (1798).

Greenock Auxiliary Missionary Association, (1822).

Haddington Auxiliary Society for Promoting Christianity among the Jews, 1811.

Haddington Juvenile Missionary Society, (1822).

Haddington Ladies Association for Promoting Christianity, (1822).

Huntly Missionary Society, 1795.

Kelso Corresponding Branch of the London Missionary Society, (1801).

Kilmarnock Auxiliary Society in aid of the London Society for Promoting Christianity among the Jews, 1810.

Kilmarnock Missionary Society, (1803).

Leith Auxiliary Missionary Society, 1815.

Lerwick Penny-a-week Society, (1822).

Markinch Missionary Association, (1822).

Nairnshire Society for Propagating the Gospel, (1822).

New Greeholm Orkney Scottish Missionary Association, (1822).

Newton-upon-Ayr Missionary Society, 1796.

Northern (Tain) Missionary Society, 1800.

Paisley London Missionary Society, 1796.

Panbridge Bible and Missionary Society, (1822).

Perth Auxiliary Society for Converting Jews, 1810.

Perth Society for Propagating the Gospel among Heathen and Unenlightened Nations (Perth Missionary Society), 1796.

Perthshire Juvenile Missionary Society, 1816.

Prestonpans Bible and Missionary Society, (1822).

St Andrews (Juvenile Auxiliary) Missionary Society, 1822.

St Andrews Ladies Association in aid of Missions and Schools, (1823).

St Andrews Students (University) Missionary Society, 1824.

Stirling Society for Promoting the Spread of the Gospel among the Heathen, 1796.

Tarvas and Old Meldrum Female Missionary Society, (1822).

APPENDIX 7

London Missionary Society Scottish directors 1796-1842[1]

Name	Location[2]	Denomination[3]	Years elected director	Total
Aikman, J.	Edinburgh	I	1816-1819, 1824-1827, 1830-1833	12
Alexander, W. L.	Edinburgh	I	1832-1835 1836-1839, 1840-1842	11
Angus, H.	Aberdeen	US	1826-1829	4
Balfour, R.	Glasgow	CS	1807-1810, 1814-1817	8
Balmer, R.	Berwick	AS	1822-1825	4
Barr, J.	Port Glasgow	CS	1816-1819, 1828-1831	8
Bayne, K.	Greenock	CS	1797-1798	2
Beattie, A. O.	Glasgow	US	1833-1836, 1839-1842	8
Belfrage, H.	Falkirk	AS/US	1802-1805, 1807-1810, 1816-1819, 1824-1827, 1831-1834	20
Bennie, A.	Edinburgh	CS	1839-1842	4

[1] Derived from the lists of directors in the LMS annual reports, 1796-1842.
[2] Location and denomination have been determined from: H. Escott, *A history of Scottish Congregationalism*, 1960. H. Scott, *Fasti Ecclesiae Scoticanae*, 1915-1928. R. Small, *History of the congregations of the United Presbyterian Church from 1733 to 1900*, 1904.
[3] Abbreviations:
  *   Layman
  I   Independent (Congregational)
  AS   Associate Synod of Burghers
  CS   Church of Scotland
  OB   Original Burgher
  GAS   General Associate Synod of Anti-Burghers
  US   United Secession
  DU   Denomination unknown

Black, A.	Edinburgh	I*	1842	1
Black, J.	Dundee	AS	1798-1806	9
Black, J.	Dunkeld	I	1833-1841	9
Blackhall, J.	Berwick	AS	1797	1
Brotherston, P.	Dysart	CS	1815, 1824-1827	5
Brown, E.	Inverkeithing	AS/US	1799, 1823-1826	5
Brown, J.	Whitburn	AS/US	1800-1803, 1820-1823	8
Brown, J.	Biggar, Edinburgh	US	1821-1839, 1841-1842	21
Buchan, G.		DU*	1835-1838, 1840-1842	7
Burns, R.	Paisley	CS	1820-1823, 1832-1835	8
Burns, W.	Paisley	DU*	1810-1813	4
Campbell, J.	Edinburgh	CS	1805-1808, 1814-1817	8
Campbell, J.	Stirling	DU	1797, 1801-1802	3
Carlile, W.	Paisley	DU*	1806-1809, 1820-1827	12
Carlisle, J.	Paisley	DU	1806-1809, 1816-1819	8
Chalmers, T.	Kilmany	CS	1813-1816, 1818-1821, 1826-1829, 1831-1834	16
Clyde, J.	Dumfries	US	1835-1838	4
Cowie, G.	Huntly	GAS/I	1798-1801, 1804-1805	6
Cruden, D.	Nigg	CS	1816-1819	4
Cullen, G. D.	Leith	I	1828-1831, 1837-1840, 1842	9
Cupples, G.	Stirling	CS	1834-1837	4
Dalzell, Major		DU*	1835-1838, 1840-1842	7
Dewar, D.	Glasgow	CS	1816-1818, 1820-1823, 1828-1831	11

Dick, J.	Glasgow	AS/US	1810-1813, 1816-1819, 1830-1832	11
Dickson, D. Snr	Edinburgh	CS	1804-1811, 1812-1820	17
Dickson, D. Jnr	Edinburgh	CS	1818-1821, 1824-1827, 1829, 1833-1836, 1838-1841	17
Douglas, J.	Cavers	CS*	1824-1827, 1829-1832, 1834-1837, 1839-1842	16
Dugid, P.	Aberdeen	DU*	1826-1829	4
Duncan, A.	Mid-Calder	US	1824-1827	4
Duncanson, A.	Airdrie	AS	1798	1
Ellis, J.	Saltcoats	AS	1816-1819	4
Erskine, T.	Linlathen	Episcopal*	1819-1822	4
Ewing, G.	Glasgow	I	1800-1803, 1812-1815, 1820-1823, 1827-1830, 1832-1835, 1838-1841	24
Ferrier, W.	Paisley	GAS/US	1820	1
Findlay, J.	Paisley	CS	1799-1802, 1805-1808, 1816-1819	12
Fleming, T.	Kirkcaldy	CS	1797-1798	2
Foote, J.	Logie-Pert	CS	1819-1822	4
Fraser, A.	Kirkhill	CS	1800-1803	4
Fraser, D.	Inverness	CS	1826-1829	4
Fraser, M.	Dundee	US	1828-1831	4
French, J.	Edinburgh	Relief	1841-1842	2
Fullarton, J. A.	Glasgow	DU*	1839-1841	3
Gibb, J.	Banff	I	1825-1828	4
Gilfillan, J.	Stirling	US	1836-1839	4
Gillies, C.	Paisley	CS	1797-1800	4
Gordon, R.	Edinburgh	CS	1825-1828	4

Grey, H.	Edinburgh	CS	1816-1819, 1821-1824, 1826-1829, 1836-1840, 1842	18
Haldane, R.	Edinburgh	I*	1796-1800, 1802-1805	9
Hall, J.	Edinburgh	AS	1806-1809	4
Hall, R.	Berwick	Relief	1825-1829	5
Hall, R.	Kelso	AS	1796, 1798-1800, 1802, 1818-1821	9
Harper, J.	Leith	US	1828-1831	4
Hay, J.	Kinross	AS/US	1811-1814, 1828-1831	8
Henderson, G.	Lauder	AS	1811-1814	4
Henderson, J.	Hawick	AS	1797	1
Hepburn, D.	Newburgh	AS	1808-1811	4
Heugh, H.	Glasgow	US	1827-1830, 1832-1835, 1837-1840, 1842	13
Husband, J.	Dunfermline	AS/US	1806-1808, 1819-1822	7
Innes, W.	Dundee	I	1799-1802	4
Jaffray, R.	Kilmarnock	AS	1807-1811	5
Jamieson, H.	East Linton	US	1824-1827	4
Johnston, J.	Edinburgh	Relief	1825-1828	4
Kennedy, J.	Inverness	I	1842	1
Ker, A.	Greenock	DU*	1820-1839	20
Kidston, W.	Glasgow	AS/US	1820-1823, 1825-1828, 1829-1833	13
King, D.	Glasgow	US	1840-1841	2
Kirkcaldy, W.	Dundee	DU*	1826-1829	4
Kirkwood, J.	Edinburgh	Relief	1824, 1829-1832	5
Laird, J.	Greenock	DU*	1810-1813, 1816-1819	8
Lawson, G.	Selkirk	AS	1801-1802, 1807-1810	6
Letham, P.	Glasgow	DU*	1837-1838	2
Lockhart, J.	Glasgow	CS	1803-1806	4

Logan, G.	Eastwood	CS	1810-1813	4
Lothian, A.	Edinburgh	AS/US	1810-1813, 1820-1823	8
Love, J.	Anderston	CS	1812-1815, 1817-1820	8
Lowrie, A.	EastCalder	US	1828-1831	4
M'Dermid, J.	Paisley	Relief	1816-1819	4
M'Donald, J.	Urquhart		1820-1823	4
M'Gavin, W.	Glasgow	I*	1823-1826, 1828-1831	8
Macgill, S.	Glasgow	CS	1824-1827	4
Machray, R.	Perth/ Dumfries	I	1833-1834, 1838-1841	6
MacIntosh, A.	Tain	CS	1797-1800, 1804-1807, 1812-1815	12
MacKenzie, J.	Glasgow	DU	1796-1800	5
MacKinlay, J.	Kilmarnock	CS	1798-1801, 1805-1806	6
MacNaughton, J.	Paisley	CS	1836-1839	4
M'Neil, N.	Elgin	I	1829-1832, 1834-1837, 1839-1842	12
Marshall, J.	Stirling	CS	1826, 1828-1831	5
Martin, J.	Kirkcaldy	CS	1809-1812	4
Mason, A.	Wishawtown	DU	1830-1833	4
Mill, J.	Shetland	CS	1797	1
Mitchell, A.	Glasgow	DU*	1824-1831, 1833-1836, 1838-1841	16
Mitchell, J.	Glasgow	US	1822-1825, 1827-1830, 1832-1835	12
Molleson, A.	Montrose		1815-1819	5
Morrison, D.	Perth	DU*	1817-1820	4
Murray, A.	Ayton	DU*	1818-1821	4
Muter, R.	Glasgow	US	1824-1827	4
Orme, W.	Perth	I	1820-1822	3
Payne, G.	Edinburgh	I	1820-1821	2
Paterson, J.	Edinburgh	DU	1831-1834, 1837-1840, 1842	9
Paton, W. P.	Glasgow	DU*	1841-1842	2

Peddie, J.	Edinburgh	AS/US	1809-1812, 1816-1819, 1821-1824, 1830-1833	16
Peebles, W.	Newton-upon-Ayr	CS	1800-1803	4
Penman, R.	Aberdeen	I	1828-1831, 1835-1838	8
Philip, J.	Aberdeen	I	1812-1814	3
Pitcairn, J.	Dundee	DU*	1812-1815	4
Pitcairn, J.	Kelso	Relief	1797	1
Ranken, J.	Paisley	CS	1801-1804	4
Rennie, R.	Borrow-stowness	CS	1820-1823	4
Reston, J.	Edinburgh	Relief	1802-1805	4
Richardson, J.	Perth	DU	1813-1816	4
Risk, J.	Glasgow	DU*	1837-1840, 1842	5
Ritchie, W.	Haddington	I	1828-1831	4
Ross, J.	Aberdeen	CS	1797-1798, 1811-1815	7
Russell, D.	Dundee	I	1824-1827, 1831-1834, 1841-1842	10
Russell, J.	Stirling	CS	1797, 1801-1803, 1815-1818	8
Sanderson, J.	Berwick	DU*	1822	1
Scott, W.	Greenock	DU	1816-1819	4
Small, A.	Stirling	CS	1821-1824	4
Smart, J.	Leith	US	1833-1836, 1838-1841	8
Smart, J.	Stirling	AS/US	1798-1801, 1814-1815, 1824-1827, 1832-1835	14
Smart, W.	Paisley	AS/US	1810-1813, 1818-1821, 1828-1831, 1835-1836	14
Smith, J.	Edinburgh	Relief	1816-1820	5
Snodgrass, J.	Paisley	CS	1796	1
Somerville, J.	Stirling	CS	1796-1798	3

Stark, J.	Dennyloan-head	US	1828-1831	4
Stark, T.	Forres	US	1835-1838	4
Steven, J.	Kilwinning	CS	1803-1804, 1806-1810, 1820-1823	11
Stewart, A.	Moulin	CS	1801-1804, 1816-1819	8
Stewart, D.	Stirling	OB	1828-1831	4
Tait, W.	Lundie/ Edinburgh	CS	1797-1798, 1820-1823, 1828-1831	10
Thomson, A.	Coldstream	AS	1811-1814, 1828-1831	8
Thomson, A.	Aberdeen	I	1832-1835	4
Thomson, J.	Dundee	CS	1824-1827	4
Thomson, J.	Paisley	Relief	1832-1836, 1838-1840	8
Thomson, J.	Glasgow	DU*	1819-1822	4
Thomson, W. A.	Perth	CS	1808-1811, 1820-1823	8
Wardlaw, G.	Edinburgh	I	1828-1829	2
Wardlaw, R.	Glasgow	I	1816-1819, 1823-1831, 1835-1838, 1840-1842	20
Watson, J.	Musselburgh	I	1828-1831, 1835-1838, 1840-1842	11
Wilkes, H.	Edinburgh	I	1834-1835	2
Willison, J.	Forgandenny	CS	1812-1815, 1817-1820, 1823-1826	12
Wilson, W.	Greenock	DU*	1824-1838	15
Wright, G.	Markinch	CS	1815-1818, 1819-1823, 1825-1828	13
Young, P.	Jedburgh	AS	1802-1805, 1814-1817	8
Yule, G.	Edinburgh	DU*	1826-1829, 1831-1834, 1837-1840	12

Table 1

Denominational allegiance of Scottish directors of the London Missionary Society 1796-1842

	1796-1800	1801-1805	1806-1810	1811-1815	1816-1820	1821-1825	1826-1830	1831-1835	1836-1840	1841-1842
Church of Scotland	50%	48%	43%	47%	44%	34%	27%	17%	19%	15%
Original Burgher							2%	2%		
Associate Synod of Burghers	25%	28%	38%	33%	20%	7%				
General Associate Synod of anti-Burghers	3%				2%					
United Secession						28%	31%	34%	25%	15%
Independent	11%	16%		7%	10%	19%	27%	36%	25%	44%
Episcopal					2%	2%				
Relief	4%	4%			4%	6%	5%	4%	3%	4%
Denomination unknown	7%	4%	19%	13%	18%	4%	8%	7%	28%	22%
Total number of Scottish directors in each five-year period	28	25	26	30	50	53	60	53	32	27

APPENDIX 8

Chalmers' catechism for children[1]

1. Who made you?

2. Is God your master?

3. Does not he order you to do what is good?

4. Does not he forbid you to do what is bad?

5. Does he at all times know what you are doing?

6. Where do the good go to?

7. Where do the bad go to?

8. Have you ever sinned against God?

9. How shall God ever take you into favour when you are a sinner?

10. Who redeemed you?

11. What did he do to save you?

12. And what must you do to be saved?

13. Will you be saved if you do not have Christ?

14. Will you be saved if you do not obey him?

15. Are you able in your own strength to obey him?

16. Who sanctifies you?

17. What must you do to get the Holy Spirit?

18. Whither does anger come from, your own spirit or the Spirit of God?

19. Would you like to know more about Christ and the way of Salvation?

20. What book should you principally read for this purpose?

21. Are you able in your own wisdom to understand it?

22. Who makes you able?

---

[1] Tron Church examinations. NCL.

APPENDIX 9

Sermon texts

Table 1
Chalmers' sermon texts 1798-1847[1]

	times text used	percentage
Genesis	9	0.9
Exodus	13	1.3
Leviticus	7	0.7
Numbers	7	0.7
Deuteronomy	10	1.0
Torah	**46**	**4.4**
Judges	4	0.4
Chronicles	2	0.2
Nehemiah	1	0.1
Historical	**7**	**0.7**
Job	8	0.8
Psalms	52	5.0
Proverbs	19	1.8
Ecclesiastes	8	0.8
Wisdom	**87**	**8.4**

---

[1] This analysis is based on 1035 of Chalmers' sermon texts wherever they could be found and covering the whole of his preaching life. Besides the 160 or so published sermons, the main sources used were J. Anderson, *Reminiscences of Thomas Chalmers*, 1851, the *Memoirs*, and for the years 1822-1824 the diary of a student in the St John's congregation (C. H. Hutcheson, NLS MSS 2773). Chalmers kept a record for the years 1812-1816 (Record of preaching, NCL), 1822 (Journal 6, NCL), 1824-1826 (Journal 6, NCL), and 1827-1832 (Journal 7, NCL). The apparent errors in addition are due to rounding.

Isaiah	32	3.1
Jeremiah	24	2.3
Lamentations	4	0.4
Ezekiel	2	0.2
Daniel	2	0.2
Hosea	5	0.5
Jonah	1	0.1
Micah	1	0.1
Zechariah	1	0.1
Prophets	**72**	**7.0**
Old Testament	**212**	**20.5**
Matthew	71	6.9
Mark	30	2.9
Luke	77	7.4
John	53	5.1
Acts	82	7.9
Gospels & Acts	**313**	**30.2**
Romans	202	19.5
Corinthians	91	8.8
Galatians	18	1.7
Ephesians	23	2.2
Philippians	15	1.4
Colossians	15	1.4
Thessalonians	10	1.0
Timothy	31	3.0
Titus	6	0.6
Pauline	**411**	**39.7**
Hebrews	32	3.1
James	11	1.1
Peter	34	3.3
John	16	1.5
Jude	1	0.1
Non-Pauline	**94**	**9.1**

Revelation	5	0.5

New Testament 8 2 3		**7 9 . 5**

Total   1 0 3 5

Table 2
Comparative use of sermon texts[2]

	Chalmers	Wright[3]	Macfarlan[4]	Evangelicals[5]	Moderates[5]
Torah	4	2	8	6	5
History	1	0	3	2	3
Psalms	5	15	15	10	10
Wisdom	3	4	5	4	5
Prophets	7	11	15	11	8
Old Test.	**2 0**	**3 2**	**4 6**	**3 3**	**31**
Gospels & Acts	30	27	21	31	34
Pauline	40	29	19	23	20
Non-Pauline	9	8	11	10	12
Revelation	1	4	3	3	2
New Test.	**8 0**	**6 8**	**5 4**	**6 7**	**6 8**

---

[2]   All figures are percentages.

[3]   Taken from a record of 351 sermons preached or heard by the Evangelical
George Wright of Stirling during 1818-1819. George Wright misc. Vol.
23, NCL.

[4]   Taken from a catalogue of 200 of the sermons of the leading Moderate,
Principal D. Macfarlan of Glasgow University. GUA P/CN/Macfarlan.

[5]   Derived from G. B. Robertson, Spiritual awakening in the North-east of
Scotland, University of Aberdeen PhD thesis, 1970, 203, table B.
Robertson analysed some 8000 sermon texts from Church of Scotland
ministers in the Synod of Aberdeen. Those here relate to 1811-1843.

BIBLIOGRAPHY 1

Newspapers

Aberdeen Herald, 1834, 1837.
Aberdeen Observer, 1832-1834.
Dundee, Perth and Cupar Advertiser, 1807-1828.
Edinburgh Advertiser, 1824.
Edinburgh Star, 1826.
Glasgow Chronicle, 1817.
Glasgow Courier, 1815-1823.
Glasgow Herald, 1808, 1815-1817, 1820, 1915.
Glasgow Sentinel, 1822.
Montrose Standard and Angus and Mearns Register, 1842-1843.
Paisley Advertiser, 1838.
People's Journal, 1847.
Scotsman, 1819, 1823-1824.
Stirling Observer, 1837.
Stirling Journal, 1820-1828.
Times, 1811-1828.
Witness, 1840-1847.

BIBLIOGRAPHY 2

Periodicals and annual reports, pre-1920

Acts of the General Assembly of the Church of Scotland, 1796-1843.
Baptist Magazine, 1814, 1821.
Baptist Missionary Society Periodical Accounts, 1800, 1813.
Bengal Past and Present, 1915.
Blackwood's Edinburgh Magazine, 1817-1824, 1847.
British and Foreign Bible Society Annual Reports, 1805-1815.
British and Foreign Evangelical Review, 1854-1855, 1884.
British Critic and Quarterly Theological Review, 1831-1840.
Calcutta Christian Observer, 1835.
Christian Guardian and Church of England Magazine, 1824.
Christian Observer, 1802-1831.
Christian Recorder, 1821.
Church of England Preacher, 1837.
Church of Scotland Magazine, 1834.
Church Review and Scottish Ecclesiastical Magazine, 1836-1838.
Eclectic Review, 1808, 1815-1826, 1840.
Edinburgh Almanack or Universal Scots and Imperial Register, 1813-1830.
Edinburgh Bible Society Reports, 1810-1850.
Edinburgh Christian Instructor, 1810-1834.
Edinburgh Magazine and Literary Miscellany (a new series of the *Scots Magazine*), 1817-1823.
Edinburgh Review, 1807-1809, 1812, 1817-1818, 1824, 1828.
Evangelical Magazine and Missionary Chronicle, 1794, 1811-1826.
Fraser's Magazine for Town and Country, 1830, 1841.
Free Church Magazine, 1844-1850.
Good Words, 1860.
Home and Foreign Missionary Record for the Church of Scotland, 1838.
Literary and Statistical Magazine for Scotland, 1820.
London Missionary Society, Annual Report of Directors, 1796-1842.
Lowe's Edinburgh Magazine, 1846-1848.
Macmillan's Magazine, 1864-1865.
Macphail's Edinburgh Ecclesiastical Journal and Literary Review, 1846-1851.
Missionary Magazine, 1796-1800, 1812-1813.
Missionary Register, 1813-1819.
North British Review, 1844-1847, 1856.
Oliver and Boyd's New Edinburgh Almanac and National Repository, 1840-1847.
Oriental Christian Spectator, 1834.

Original Secession Magazine, 1847.
Presbyterian Review, 1831-1834, 1837-1844.
Proceedings of the Royal Society of Edinburgh, 1832-1834.
Pulpit, 1834-1835.
Quarterly Review, 1815-1839.
Religious Monitor or Scots Presbyterian Magazine, 1803-1812.
Saturday Magazine, 1838.
Scots Magazine, 1817.
Scottish Missionary Register, 1820-1846.
Wesleyan Methodist Magazine, 1808, 1821-1822, 1832, 1837.

BIBLIOGRAPHY 3

Archives and manuscript sources

Bodleian Library, Oxford

Eleven letters from Chalmers in various collections including the Wilberforce papers.

British Library Reference Division, Department of Manuscripts, London

Sixty-eight letters from or relating to Chalmers in various collections including the following:

Aberdeen papers
Egerton manuscripts
Gladstone papers
Macvey Napier papers
Peel papers
Sherborn autographs

Cambridge University Library

Five letters of Chalmers.

Cambridge University Library. Bible Society Archives

Information supplied by Miss K. J. Cann concerning Chalmers, including a copy of a letter from James Anderson to John Owen, 1812.

City of Edinburgh District Council Archives

Index to Council records, 1818-1836.

Duke University, William R. Perkins Library, Durham, North Carolina

Seventeen letters of Chalmers, Hannah More and Marianne Thornton, from the Wilberforce papers.

Gloucestershire County Council County Record Office

Four letters from or relating to Chalmers.

Sir Roderick Inglis of Glencorse

Papers of John Inglis.

Miss K. F. Lambert

Fenwick Auxiliary Missionary Society, minute book 1813-1839.
Fenwick Female Association for Religious Purposes, account book 1823-1846.

James C. Macnab of Macnab

Letters of John McLeod Campbell

National Bible Society of Scotland

G. A. F. Knight, The history of the National Bible Society of Scotland, 1809-1900. Typescript. n.d.

National Library of Scotland

Next to New College Library, the major depository of material relating to Chalmers and his period. Collections utilised include the following:

Adam Black papers
Blaikie letters
Buchanan autographs
Thomas Carlyle papers
Church of Scotland India mission
George Combe papers
C. H. Hutcheson diary
John Lee papers
Lundie papers
Melville papers
Hugh Miller papers
Minto papers
Paul papers
Rose papers
Rutherford papers
Scott of Raeburn papers
Scottish Missionary Society
William Wilson letters

National Library of Wales

Two letters of Thomas Chalmers in the Verney manuscripts

National Register of Archives (Scotland), Scottish Record Office, West Register House, Edinburgh

The Register was consulted to locate material in private hands and in archives outside Edinburgh.

Paisley Public Library

Minutes of procedure of the Paisley London Missionary Society, March 1796-November 1815.

Princeton University Library

Two letters from Chalmers to James M'Cosh.

School of Oriental and African Studies, University of London

Correspondence of the London Missionary Society in the archives of the Council for World Mission.

Scottish Record Office, General Register House

Materials consulted include:

Thomas Chalmers' will
Sir George Clerk of Penicuik papers
Dalhousie muniments
Dundas papers
General Assembly of the Church of Scotland, papers relating to missions and church extension.
General Assembly of the Church of Scotland, petitions anent chapels of ease and patronage 1828-1834.
General Assembly of the Church of Scotland, scroll minutes.
Glasgow Presbytery minutes, 1808-1819.
St John's Chapel-of-ease, minutes of managers, 1822-1840.
St John's Kirk-session minute book, 1819-1836.
Seaforth muniments
Society in Scotland for the Propagation of Christian Knowledge, records, minutes of general meetings, 1, 1709-1718.

Scottish Record Office, General Register Office

Kilmany Old Parochial Register, 1706-1819.

Scottish Record Office, West Register House

Sinclair of Ulbster papers.

Strathclyde Regional Archives, Glasgow

Materials consulted include:

> Glasgow Town Council records, 1814-1823.
> Sir John Maxwell of Pollock papers.

University College London, Manuscript Library

Nine letters of Chalmers from the Brougham papers.

University of Edinburgh, Library

Twenty-three letters from or relating to Chalmers together with a number of letters relating to the rise of the missionary movement in Scotland.

University of Edinburgh. New College Library

The location of most of the published and manuscript material consulted. The Chalmers Papers comprise some 15,000 letters including about 700 from Chalmers, and many other papers including his manuscript journals. The final cataloguing of the collection was completed after the bulk of my research was carried out.[1]

Other collections used include:

> R. M. McCheyne papers
> A. L. Simpson papers
> St Andrews Juvenile Missionary Society minute book 1822-1857
> Boog Watson, Chalmers' family tree.
> Charles Watson of Burntisland diaries and papers
> George Wright of Stirling, papers and correspondence

University of Glasgow Archives

Principal Macfarlan papers.

University of Glasgow Library

Forty-three letters of Thomas Chalmers to William Buchanan of Glasgow, 1820-1847.

---

[1] Margot Butt, 'The Chalmers Papers', A. C. Cheyne, ed., *The practical and the pious*, 1985, 186-94.

University of St Andrews Library, Manuscripts Department

Materials consulted include:

Thomas Chalmers letters, 1810-1825 (a volume of 438 letters
originally part of the collection now in New College Library).
J. D. Forbes papers.
Melville papers.
St Andrews University Library receipt book, Chalmers' borrowing
record, 1795-1828.
Students Missionary Society of St Andrews, minute book, 1824-
1846.

BIBLIOGRAPHY 4

Parliamentary papers

A digest of parochial returns made to the select committee appointed to inquire into the education of the poor, 1818, 1 April 1819.

Accounts of the population of certain parishes in Scotland with the capacity of their churches and chapels. Prepared and certified by a committee of the General Assembly of the Church of Scotland, 1819, 21 April 1819.

Census of Great Britain, 1851. Religious worship. England and Wales. Report and tables, London, HMSO, 1853.

Comparative account of the population of Great Britain in the years 1801, 1811, 1821, and 1831, 19 October 1831.

Evidence, oral and documentary, taken and received by the commissioners appointed by His Majesty George IV., July 23d, 1826; and reappointed by His Majesty William IV., October 12th, 1830; for visiting the Universities of Scotland. Volume III. University of St Andrews, London, HMSO, 1837.

First report of the commissioners of religious instruction, Scotland, 18 April 1837.

General report of the commissioners appointed to inquire into the state of municipal corporations in Scotland, London, HMSO, 1835.

Report from Her Majesty's commissioners for inquiring into the administration and practical operation of the poor laws in Scotland, Edinburgh, HMSO, 1844.

Report from select committee on Church patronage, (Scotland;) with the minutes of evidence, 23 July 1834.

Report from the select committee on inquiry into drunkenness, 1834.

Report relative to the University and Colleges of St Andrews, 1830.

Second report of the commissioners of religious instruction, Scotland, Edinburgh, W. & A. K. Johnston, 1837.

Third report of the commissioners of religious instruction, Scotland, Edinburgh, 1837.

Third report from the select committee on the poor laws (1818), with an appendix containing returns from the General Assembly of the Church of Scotland, 26 May 1818.

BIBLIOGRAPHY 5

Chalmers' publications

Collections

Posthumous Works of the Rev Thomas Chalmers, edited by the Revd William Hanna, 9 vols, Edinburgh, Sutherland and Knox, 1847-1849.
Select Sermons, Edinburgh, James Gemmell, 1881.
Select Works of Thomas Chalmers, edited by his son-in-law, the Revd William Hanna, 12 vols, Edinburgh, Thomas Constable, 1856.
Sermons and Discourses, 2 vols, New York, Robert Carter, 1854.
The Works of Thomas Chalmers [various series titles], 25 vols, Glasgow, William Collins, 1836-1842.

Correspondence

The correspondence between Dr Chalmers and the Earl of Aberdeen in the years 1839 and 1840, Edinburgh, David Douglas, 1893.
A selection from the correspondence of the late Thomas Chalmers, edited by his son-in-law, the Revd William Hanna, Edinburgh, Thomas Constable, 1853.

Periodical articles

'An historical and critical view of the speculative philosophy of Europe in the nineteenth century by J. D. Morell', North British Review, 6, February 1847, 271-331.
'Causes and cure of pauperism. Review of *Minutes of the evidence taken before the committee appointed by the House of Commons to inquire into the state of mendicity and vagrancy in the metropolis...General report, 28 May 1816*', *Edinburgh Review*, 28(55), March 1817, 1-31.
'Dr Chalmers on prophecy', *The Church of England Preacher*, 1837, 86-9, 131-5.
'Political economy of a famine', *North British Review*, 7, May 1847, 247-90.
'Report on the poor laws of Scotland', *North British Review*, 2, February 1845, 471-514.
'Reports on the state of the poor. Review of *Report from the select committee on the poor-laws, 4 July 1817*', *Edinburgh Review*, 29(58), 1818, 261-302.

'Review of *Essay on the theory of the earth*, translated from the French of M Cuvier', *Edinburgh Christian Instructor*, 8, April 1814, 261-74

'Review of *Hints on toleration* by Philagatharches', *Edinburgh Christian Instructor*, May 1811, 311-20.

'Review of *Journal of a voyage from Okkak*, by Benjamin Kohlmeister and George Kmoch, missionaries of the Church of the Unitas Fratrum or United Brethren', *Eclectic Review*, 1815, 1-13, 156-73.

'Review of *Sermons* by Samuel Charters', *Edinburgh Christian Instructor*, 3, July 1811, 43-53.

'Review of *Sermons* by Thomas Snell Jones', *Eclectic Review*, 1816, 238-51.

'Saving banks', *North British Review*, 3, August 1845, 318-44.

'State and prospects of manufacturers. Review of James Cleland, *The rise and progress of the city of Glasgow*, 1820', *Edinburgh Review*, 33, May 1820, 382-95.

'The geological argument for a God, 1', *The Pulpit*, 25(636), 26 December 1934, 158-62.

'The geological argument for a God, 2', *The Pulpit*, 25(639), 15 January 1935, 215-20.

'*The philosophy of trade* by P. J. Stirling', *North British Review*, 6, November 1846, 87-116.

'The political economy of the Bible', *North British Review*, 2, November 1844, 1-52.

'Tracts on the corn trade', *North British Review*, 1, May 1844, 67-98.

Single Works

A conference with certain ministers and elders of the Church of Scotland, on the subject of the moderatorship of the next General Assembly: to which is added an address on the same subject, to the church at large, Glasgow, William Collins, 1837.

A course of five lectures on predestination selected from the Pulpit, London, Sherwood, Gilbert and Piper, 1837.

A series of discourses on the Christian revelation viewed in connection with the modern astronomy, Glasgow, John Smith, 1817.

Address delivered by Dr Chalmers to the Tradesmen's Association for promoting the interests of the Church of Scotland at a meeting held in Roxburgh church, Edinburgh on Thursday 16 February, 1843. Extracted from the *Witness* newspaper. n.d. n.p.

An enquiry into the extent and stability of national resources, Edinburgh, Oliphant and Brown, 1808.

Churches and schools for the working classes, Edinburgh, John D. Lowe, 1846.

Earnest appeal to the Free Church of Scotland on the subject of its economics, Edinburgh, John D. Lowe, 1846.

Fourth report of the committee of the General Assembly of the Church of Scotland on church extension. Given in and read on the 22nd of May 1838 by Thomas Chalmers, convener, Edinburgh, William Whyte, 1838.

Lectures on the establishment and extension of national churches, Glasgow, William Collins, 1838.

Letter to the Royal Commissioners for the visitation of colleges in Scotland, Glasgow, William Collins, 1832.

Observations on a passage in Mr Playfair's letter to the Lord Provost of Edinburgh relative to the mathematical pretensions of the Scottish clergy, Cupar-Fife, R. Tullis, 1805.

On the Evangelical Alliance; its design, its difficulties, its proceedings, and its prospects: with practical suggestions, Edinburgh, Oliver and Boyd, 1846.

On the power, wisdom and goodness of God as manifested in the adaptation of external nature to the moral and intellectual nature of man, with the author's last corrections. To which is prefixed a biographical preface by the Rev John Cumming, London, Henry G. Bohn, 1853.

Remarks on the present position of the Church of Scotland. Occasioned by the publication of a letter from the Dean of Faculty to the Lord Chancellor, Glasgow, William Collins, 1839.

Replies to queries regarding the city churches, proposed by the committee of the Town Council to the Presbytery of Edinburgh, Edinburgh, A. Balfour, 1834.

Reply to the attempt to connect the cause of church accommodation with party politics, Glasgow, W. Collins, 1835.

Report of the Committee of the General Assembly of the Church of Scotland on church extension, being formerly the committee on church accommodation. Given in and read on the 28 of May, 1835, by Thomas Chalmers, convener, Edinburgh, John Waugh, 1835.

Report of the Committee of the General Assembly of the Church of Scotland on church extension. Given in and read on the 23 of May, 1836 by Thomas Chalmers, convener, Edinburgh, Balfour and Jack, 1836.

Report of the Committee of the General Assembly of the Church of Scotland on church extension. Given in and read on the 25 of May 1837, by Thomas Chalmers, convener, Edinburgh, Balfour and Jack, 1837.

Scripture references; designed for the use of parents, teachers, and private Christians, Glasgow, John Smith, 1818.

Sermon preached before the convocation of ministers in St George's Church, Edinburgh, on Thursday the 17 of November, 1842, Glasgow, William Collins, 1842.

Sermons preached in St John's church, Glasgow, Chalmers and Collins, 1823.

Sermons preached in the Tron church, Glasgow, Glasgow, John Smith, 1819.

Specimens of the ecclesiastical destitution of Scotland, in various parts of the country: being extracts of correspondence and results of statistical surveys in 1834-5. Printed for the use of the church-extension committees of the General Assembly, Edinburgh, John Waugh, 1835.

Substance of a speech delivered in the General Assembly on Wednesday the twenty-second of May, 1839. Respecting the decision of the House of Lords on the case of Auchterarder, Glasgow, William Collins, 1839.

The application of Christianity to the commercial and ordinary affairs of life, in a series of discourses, Glasgow, Chalmers and Collins, 1820.

The evidence and authority of the Christian revelation, Edinburgh, William Blackwood, 1814.

The fulness and freeness of the gospel message. A sermon preached in Hanover Presbyterian Church, Brighton, on Sunday May 16, 1847, Brighton, Robert Folthorp, 1847.

The speech of Dr Chalmers on the Catholic Question at the pro-Catholic meeting, Edinburgh, March 14th, 1829, London, H. Arliss, 1829.

The substance of a speech delivered in the General Assembly on Thursday May 25th inst. respecting the merits of the late bill for the augmentation of stipends to the clergy of Scotland, Edinburgh, Oliphant and Balfour, 1809.

What ought the church and the people of Scotland to do now? Being a pamphlet on the principles of the church question: with an appendix on the politics and personalities of the church question, Glasgow, William Collins, 1840.

Works containing contributions by Chalmers

Brown, Thomas. *Lectures on ethics...with a preface by Thomas Chalmers*, Edinburgh, William Tait, 1846.

Cochrane, James. *The manual of family and private devotion...with a preface by Thomas Chalmers*, Edinburgh, William Whyte, 1848.

Essays on Christian Union, by Thomas Chalmers, R. Balmer, R. S. Candlish, J. A. James, D. King, R. Wardlaw, G. Struthers and A. Symington, Edinburgh, William Oliphant, 1845.

Sermons by the late Rev Robert Coutts, Brechin, with a preface by Thomas Chalmers and a memoir by the Rev Thomas Guthrie, Edinburgh, John Johnstone, 1847.

The Church of Scotland's claim of right. To which are prefixed the speeches of Dr Chalmers, Dr Gordon, and Mr Dunlop in the General Assembly in support of the same, May 24, 1842, Edinburgh, John Johnstone, 1842.

BIBLIOGRAPHY 6

Books, pamphlets and periodical articles, pre-1920

An account of the Society in Scotland for Propagating Christian Knowledge, from its commencement in 1709, Edinburgh, Murray and Cochrane, 1774.

Alexander, William Lindsay. *Memoirs of the life and writings of Ralph Wardlaw*, Edinburgh, A. & C. Black, 1856.

Alison, William Pulteney. *Observations on the management of the poor in Scotland and its effects on the health of great towns*, Edinburgh, William Blackwood, 1840.

Alison, William Pulteney. *Reply to Dr Chalmers' objections to an improvement of the legal provision for the poor in Scotland*, Edinburgh, William Blackwood, 1841.

Anderson, James Maitland. *The matriculation roll of the University of St Andrews 1747-1897*, Edinburgh, William Blackwood, 1905.

Anderson, John. *Reminiscences of Thomas Chalmers*, Edinburgh, James Nichol, 1851.

(Anderson, John.) *Sketches of the Edinburgh clergy of the Established Church of Scotland*, Edinburgh, John Anderson, 1832.

Baillie, John. *The missionary of Kilmany: being a memoir of Alexander Paterson with notices of Robert Edie*, Edinburgh, Thomas Constable, 1854.

Baxter, Richard. *A call to the unconverted to turn and live and accept of mercy while mercy may be had*, Edinburgh, Oliphant, Anderson & Ferrier, n.d.

Begbie, James. *Contributions to practical medicine*, Edinburgh, A. & C. Black, 1862.

Begg, James. *The antiquity of church extension; with the methods by which it was promoted by the Church of Scotland nearly two hundred years ago*, Edinburgh, John Johnstone, 1838.

Bickersteth, E. *The Christian student: designed to assist Christians in general in acquiring religious knowledge*, London, Seeley, Burnside and Seeley, 1844.

Blaikie, William Garden. *After fifty years, or letters of a grandfather*, Edinburgh, Thomas Nelson, 1893.

Blaikie, William Garden. *Thomas Chalmers* (Famous Scots series), Edinburgh, Oliphant, Anderson & Ferrier, 1896.

Blomfield, Alfred. *A memoir of Charles James Blomfield, Bishop of London, with selections from his correspondence*, London, John Murray, 1863.

Bogue, David. 'To the Evangelical Dissenters who practise infant baptism', *Evangelical Magazine*, September 1794, 378-80.

Bonar, Andrew A. *Memoir and remains of Robert Murray M'Cheyne*, Edinburgh, Oliphant, Anderson & Ferrier, 1892.

Bonar, Andrew A., and Robert Murray M'Cheyne. *Narrative of a mission of enquiry to the Jews from the Church of Scotland in 1839*, Edinburgh, William Whyte, 1844.

Boston, Thomas. *Human nature in its fourfold state*, Paisley, Alexander Weir, 1769.

(Braidwood, William.) *Faith and works contrasted and reconciled in six letters to a Christian friend; containing remarks on a late address by Dr Chalmers*, Glasgow, Andrew and James Duncan, 1816.

Brewster, David. *More worlds than one: the creed of the philosopher and the hope of the Christian*, London, John Murray, 1854.

Brown, William. *History of the propagation of Christianity among the heathen since the Reformation*, 3rd ed., 3 vols, Edinburgh, William Blackwood, 1854.

Brown, William Laurence. *A comparative view of Christianity and of the other forms of religion which have existed, and still exist in the world, particularly with regard to their moral tendency*, Edinburgh, W. Tait, 1826.

Bryce, James. *The preaching of the gospel, the efficient means of diffusing among mankind a knowledge of the true God. A sermon preached at the opening of the Church of St Andrew, in Calcutta, March 1818*, London, T. & G. Underwood, 1818.

Bryce, James. *A sketch of native education in India, under the superintendence of the Church of Scotland, with remarks on the character and condition of the Hindus, as these bear upon the question of conversion to Christianity*, London, W. Blackwood & Sons, 1839.

Bryce, James. *A sketch of the state of British India with a view of pointing out the best means of civilizing its inhabitants, and diffusing the knowledge of Christianity throughout the Eastern World, being the substance of an essay upon these subjects to which the University of Aberdeen adjudged Dr Buchanan's prize*, Edinburgh, G. Ramsay, 1810.

Bryce, James. *Ten years of the Church of Scotland, from 1833 to 1843, with historical retrospect from 1560*, London, W. Blackwood & Sons, 1850.

Buchanan, Claudius. *Christian researches in Asia*, London, Chidley & Baynes, 1840.

Buchanan, Robert. *The ten years' conflict, being the history of the Disruption of the Church of Scotland*, Glasgow, Blaikie and Son, 1870.

Burns, Robert. *An essay on the office and duties of the eldership in the Church of Scotland*, Paisley, J. Neilson, 1818.

Burns, Robert. *Hints on ecclesiastical reform addressed to the lay eldership of the Church of Scotland*, Edinburgh W. Whyte, 1831.

Burns, Robert. *Historical dissertation on the law and practice of Great Britain and particularly of Scotland with regard to the poor*, Glasgow, Young, Gallie & Co., 1819.

Burns, Robert. *A letter to the Rev Dr Chalmers of Glasgow, on the distinctive characters of the Protestant and Roman Catholic religions: occasioned by the publication of his sermon for the benefit of the Hibernian Society*, Paisley, Stephen Young, 1818.

Campbell, George. *Lectures on systematic theology and pulpit eloquence*, London, William Baynes, 1824.

Campbell, John McLeod. *The nature of the atonement and its relation to remission of sins and eternal life*, London, Macmillan, 1878.

Canton, William. *A history of the British and Foreign Bible Society*, London, John Murray, 1904.

Carus, William. *Memoirs of the life of the Rev Charles Simeon*, London, Hatchard, 1847.

Charteris, Archibald Hamilton. 'The church of the nineteenth century to 1843', in *The Scottish Church from the earliest times to 1881*, St Giles' lectures, first series, Edinburgh, W. & R. Chambers, 1881, 289-320.

Charteris, Archibald Hamilton. *A faithful churchman. Memoir of James Robertson*, Edinburgh, R. & R. Clark, 1897.

Cleland, James. *Enumeration of the inhabitants of the City of Glasgow and County of Lanark for the government census of 1831*, Glasgow, J. Smith, 1832.

Cleland, James. *The rise and progress of the City of Glasgow*, Glasgow, J. Brash, 1820.

Cleland, James. *Statistical tables relative to the City of Glasgow*, Glasgow, James Lumsden, 1823.

Cockburn, Henry. *Journal of Henry Cockburn, being a continuation of Memorials of his time, 1831-1854*, Edinburgh, Edmonston & Douglas, 1874.

Cockburn, Henry. 'Review of T. Chalmers, *Statement in regard to the pauperism of Glasgow from the experience of the last eight years'*, *Edinburgh Review*, 81, October 1824, 228-58.

Collins, William. *The Church of Scotland the poor man's church*, Glasgow, Glasgow Association for Promoting the Interests of the Church of Scotland, 1835.

Connell, John. *A treatise on the law of Scotland respecting the erection, union and disjunction of parishes; the manses and glebes of the parochial clergy, and the patronage of churches*, Edinburgh, Peter Hill, 1818.

Connell, John. *A treatise on the law of Scotland respecting tithes and the stipends of the parochial clergy*, Edinburgh, Peter Hill and Archibald Constable, 1815.

Conolly, M. F. *Biographical dictionary of eminent men of Fife*, Cupar-Fife, J. C. Orr, 1866.

Cook, George. *The life of the late George Hill, Principal of St Mary's College, St Andrews*, Edinburgh, Constable, 1820.

Cox, Samuel Hanson. *Interviews: memorable and useful; from diary and memory reproduced*, New York, Harper and Brothers, 1853.

Cunningham, John. *The church history of Scotland from the commencement of the Christian era to the present time*, Edinburgh, James Thin, 1882.

Day, Lal Behari. *Recollections of Alexander Duff, and of the mission college which he founded in Calcutta*, London, Thomas Nelson, 1879.

Defence of the Rev Dr Chalmers: addressed to the thinking and unprejudiced part of the inhabitants of Glasgow, Glasgow, Andrew Young, 1823.

Dewar, Daniel. *Letter to Sir James M Riddell, being a brief memorial on the state of the Highlands and on the objects to which the parliamentary grant of one hundred thousand pounds for building churches in Scotland should be applied*, Edinburgh, Ogle, Allardice & Thomas, 1819.

Douglas, James. *Hints on missions*, Edinburgh, William Blackwood, 1822.

'Dr Chalmers', *Methodist Quarterly Review*, 1(2), April 1847, 306-8

Duff, Alexander. *Evangelistic theology. An inaugural address delivered in the New College Edinburgh, on Thursday 7th November 1867*, Edinburgh, Andrew Elliot, 1868.

Duff, Alexander. *India and India missions: including sketches of the gigantic system of Hinduism*, Edinburgh, John Johnstone, 1839.

Duff, Alexander. *Missions the chief end of the Christian church*, Edinburgh, John Johnstone, 1839.

Duff, Alexander. *New era of the English language and English literature in India; or, an exposition of the late Governor-General of India's last act*, Edinburgh, John Johnstone, 1837.

Duff, Alexander. 'Statement of the plan and objects of the General Assembly's mission in India', *Calcutta Christian Observer*, December 1835, 651-6.

Duncan, John M. *The parochial ecclesiastical law of Scotland revised by Christopher N. Johnston*, Edinburgh, Bell & Bradfute, 1903.

Duns, John. *Science and Christian thought*, London, Religious Tract Society, 1866.

The Earl of Aberdeen's correspondence with the Rev Dr Chalmers and the secretaries of the Non-intrusion Committee: from 14th January to 27th May 1840, Edinburgh, William Blackwood, 1840.

Edwards, Jonathan. *The works of Jonathan Edwards*, with a memoir by Sereno E. Dwight, revised and corrected by Edward Hickman, 1834, Edinburgh, Banner of Truth, 1974.

Erskine, Thomas. *An essay on faith*, Edinburgh, Waugh & Innes, 1823.

Erskine, T. *Remarks on the internal evidence for the truth of the Christian religion*, Edinburgh, Waugh & Innes, 1820.

Examination of the eight resolutions adopted by a meeting of gentlemen in the Tontine room, Glasgow, 3d November, 1813, after discussing the merits of a bill to be brought into parliament anent building and endowing additional churches in the city of Glasgow. Addressed to Robert Muirhead, Esq., preses of that meeting, Glasgow, J. Hedderwick, 1813.

Fraser, William. *Memoir of the life of David Stow, founder of the training system of education*, London, James Nisbet, 1868.

A free critique on Dr Chalmers's discourses on astronomy; or, an English attempt to 'grapple it' with Scotch sublimity, London, printed for the author, 1817.

Fuller, Andrew. *The principal works and remains of the Rev Andrew Fuller; with a new memoir of his life, by his son, the Rev A. G. Fuller*, London, H. G. Bohn, 1852.

Gilfillan, George. *Life of the Rev William Anderson, Glasgow*, London, Hodder & Stoughton, 1873.

Gordon, George Hamilton (Fourth Earl of Aberdeen). *Selections from the correspondence of the 4th Earl of Aberdeen, 1838-1845, concerning the affairs of the Church of Scotland* (privately published, n.d. Copy in King's College Library, University of Aberdeen).

Gordon, Margaret M. *The home life of Sir David Brewster*, Edinburgh, Edmonston & Douglas, 1870.

Goudie, Gilbert. *The diary of the Reverend John Mill, minister of the parishes of Dunrossness, Sandwick and Cunningsburgh in Shetland, 1740-1803*, Edinburgh, Scottish History Society, 1889.

Graham, J. A. *The missionary expansion of the reformed churches*, Edinburgh, R. & R. Clark, 1898.

Grant, Alexander. *The story of the University of Edinburgh*, London, Longmans Green, 1884.

Grant, James. *Memoirs of Sir George Sinclair, Bart., of Ulbster*, London, Tinsley brothers, 1870.

Gurney, Joseph John. *Chalmeriana: or colloquies with Dr Chalmers*, London, Richard Bentley, 1853.

Guthrie, David K., and Charles J. *Autobiography of Thomas Guthrie and memoir*, London, Isbister, 1874.

Guthrie, Thomas. *A plea for ragged schools; or, prevention better than cure*, Edinburgh, J. Elder, 1849.

Haldane, Alexander. *The lives of Robert Haldane of Airthrey, and of his brother, James Alexander Haldane*, Edinburgh, W. P. Kennedy, 1855.

(Haldane, James Alexander). *Two letters to the Rev Dr Chalmers on his proposal for increasing the number of churches in Glasgow*, Glasgow, Adam Black, 1818.

Hanna, William. *Letters of Thomas Erskine of Linlathen*, Edinburgh, David Douglas, 1878.

Hanna, William. *Memoirs of the life and writings of Thomas Chalmers*, Edinburgh, Thomas Constable, 1849-1852.

Hay, James, and Henry Belfrage. *Memoir of the Rev Alexander Waugh*, Edinburgh, William Oliphant, 1839.

Henderson, Henry F. *The religious controversies of Scotland*, Edinburgh, T. & T. Clark, 1905.

(Heron, Robert). *Account of the proceedings and debate in the General Assembly of the Church of Scotland, 27th May 1796; on the overtures from the provincial synods of Fife and Moray respecting the propagation of the gospel among the heathen*, Edinburgh, Alex. Lawrie, 1796.

Hetherington, W. M. *Memoir and correspondence of Mrs Coutts, widow of the late Rev Robert Coutts, Brechin*, Edinburgh, Johnstone & Hunter, 1854.

Hill, George. *Lectures in divinity*, Edinburgh, William Blackwood, 1854.

Hill, George. *Theological institutes*, Edinburgh, Bell and Bradfute and Peter Hill, 1803.

Horne, C. Silvester. *The story of the L M S 1795-1895*, London, London Missionary Society, 1895.

How best to reduce the poor rates; or, Dr Chalmers and the Eberfeld system of poor relief, Glasgow, Arthur Wilson, 1909.

Hunter, Robert. *History of the missions of the Free Church of Scotland in India and Africa*, London, Thomas Nelson, 1873.

Hutchison, Matthew. *The Reformed Presbyterian Church in Scotland. Its origin and history 1680-1876*, Paisley, J. & R. Parline, 1893.

Inauguration of the New College of the Free Church, Edinburgh; November 1850, with introductory lectures on theology, philosophy and natural science, Edinburgh, Johnstone & Hunter, 1851.

Inglis, John. *To the people of Scotland. The letter of a committee of General Assembly of the Church, relative to the propagation of the gospel in foreign parts, and, more immediately, in the British provinces of India*, Edinburgh, John Waugh, 1826.

Irvine, A. *Substance of a speech, delivered before the Commission of the General Assembly of the Church of Scotland, which met in April last, on the state of religion, and the necessity of erecting new parishes, in the Highlands and Islands of Scotland*, Edinburgh, Anderson & Macdowall, 1819.

Johnstone, Christopher, N. *Handbook of Scottish church defence*, Edinburgh, James Hitt, 1892.

Kinniburgh, Robert. *Fathers of Independency in Scotland; or, biographical sketches of early Scottish Congregational ministers, A. D. 1798-1851*, Edinburgh, A. Fullarton, 1851.

Lapslie, James. *Letters addressed to the Magistrates and Council of Glasgow, and the heritors of landward parishes within the bounds of the Presbytery of Glasgow, anent accommodation in parish churches*, Glasgow, W. Lang, 1811.

Lee, John. *Lectures on the history of the Church of Scotland*, Edinburgh, William Blackwood, 1860.

Letter of instructions from the directors of the Scottish Missionary Society to their missionaries among the heathen, Edinburgh, A. Balfour, n.d.

Lockhart, John Gibson. *Peter's letters to his kinsfolk*, Edinburgh, William Blackwood, 1819.

Love, John. *Letters of the late John Love, minister of Anderson, Glasgow*, Glasgow, William Collins, 1838.

Love, John. *Sermons, preached on various occasions; with fifteen addresses to the people of Otaheite; and a serious call respecting a mission to the river Indus*, Edinburgh, Robert Ogle and Oliver & Boyd, 1846.

Lovett, Richard. *The history of the London Missionary Society 1795-1895*, London, Henry Frowde, 1899.

M'Cosh, James. *The Scottish philosophy, biographical, expository, critical, from Hutcheson to Hamilton*, London, Macmillan, 1875.

M'Cosh, James. *A tribute to the memory of Dr Chalmers. By a former pupil*, Edinburgh, John Johnstone, 1847.

M'Crie, G. G. *The confessions of the Church of Scotland: Their evolution in history.* The seventh series of Chalmers lectures, Edinburgh, Macniven & Wallace, 1907.

MacFarlan, D. *Declaration by the committee of the Constitutional Party in the Church of Scotland in reference to the present state of ecclesiastical controversy in the Church and its relations to the government and constitution of the country*, Edinburgh, J. Goldie, 1843.

MacFarlane, James. *The late secession from the Church of Scotland*, Edinburgh, William Blackwood, 1846.

Macgill, Stevenson. *Discourses and essays on subjects of public interest*, Edinburgh, Waugh & Innes, 1819.

MacKay, W. S. 'The late Dr Ewart', *Oriental Christian Spectator*, November 1860, 436-7.

MacKelvie, William. *Annals and statistics of the United Presbyterian Church*, Edinburgh, Oliphant, 1873.

M'Kerrow, John. *History of the foreign missions of the Secession and United Presbyterian Church*, Edinburgh, Andrew Elliot, 1867.

M'Kerrow, John. *History of the Secession Church*, Glasgow, A. Fullarton, 1841.

(MacLean, Archibald.) *Thoughts on the calls and invitations of the gospel*, Edinburgh, Schaw and Pillans, 1797.

MacLeod, Donald. *Memoir of Norman MacLeod*, London, Daldy, Isbister & Co., 1876.

MacLeod, Norman. 'Dr Chalmers at Eberfeld', *Good Words*, January 1860, 5-8.

Macpherson, John. *The doctrine of the Church in Scottish theology.* The sixth series of Chalmers lectures, Edinburgh, Macniven & Wallace, 1903.

Massie, J. W. *The Evangelical Alliance; its origin and development*, London, John Snow, 1847.

Masson, David. *Memories of two cities, Edinburgh and Aberdeen*, Edinburgh, Oliphant, Anderson & Ferrier, 1911.

Masterman, N. ed. *Chalmers on charity. A selection of passages and scenes to illustrate the social teaching and practical work of Thomas Chalmers*, Westminster, Archibald Constable, 1900.

Matheson, J. J. *A memoir of Greville Ewing, minister of the gospel, Glasgow*, London, John Snow, 1843.

Mathieson, William Law. *Church and reform in Scotland: a history from 1797 to 1843*, Glagow, J. Maclehose and Sons, 1916.

Maxwell, Alexander. *Plurality of worlds: or letters, notes and memoranda, philosophical and critical; occasioned by 'A series of discourses on the Christian revelation viewed in connection with the modern astronomy' by Thomas Chalmers*, London, 1820.

Mearns, Duncan. *Principles of Christian evidence illustrated by an examination of arguments subversive of natural theology and the internal evidence of Christianity advanced by Thomas Chalmers in his 'Evidence and authority of the Christian revelation'*, Aberdeen, A. Brown, 1818.

Memoir of John Adam, late missionary at Calcutta, London, J. Cross, 1833.

Millar, J. H. 'The revival of churchmanship in Scotland', *The divine life in the Church*, Scottish Church Society Conferences, second series, vol. 2, Edinburgh, J. Gardner Hitt, 1895, 67-76.

Miller, Hugh. *The two parties in the Church of Scotland, exhibited as missionary and anti-missionary; their contendings in these opposite characters in the past and their statistics now*, Edinburgh, John Johnstone, 1841.

Mitchell, J. Murray. *Memoir of the Rev Robert Nesbit, missionary of the Free Church of Scotland*, London, James Nisbet, 1858.

More, Hannah. *Practical piety; or, the influence of the religion of the heart on the conduct of the life*, London, Cadell and Davies, 1817.

Morley, John. *The life of William Ewart Gladstone*, London, Macmillan, 1905.

The new statistical account of Scotland by the ministers of the respective parishes, under the superintendence of a committee of the Society for the benefit of the Sons and Daughters of the Clergy, Edinburgh, William Blackwood, 1845.

Noble, Samuel. *The astronomical doctrine of a plurality of worlds irreconcilable with the popular system of theology, but in perfect harmony with the true Christian religion: being a lecture delivered April 13, 1828, at the New Jerusalem Church, Cross Street, Hatton Garden. With an appendix including additional strictures on Dr Chalmers*, London, J.S. Hodson, 1828.

Orme, William. *Memoirs including letters and select remains of John Urquhart, late of the University of St Andrews*, London, James Nisbet, 1869.

Paterson, James. *Address by Mr James Paterson of the University of St Andrews and afterwards of Highbury College London, at his public designation as a missionary to India; which took place in the Congregational Chapel, St Andrew's, 21 December, 1831. With the substance of the charge delivered by Mr Lothian*, Cupar-Fife, G. S. Tullis, 1832.

Patrick, David, and Francis Hindes Groome, eds, *Chambers' biographical dictionary*, Edinburgh, W. & R. Chambers, 1897.

Pearson, Hugh. *Memoirs of the life and writings of the Rev Claudius Buchanan*, Oxford, University Press, 1817.

Rainy, Robert and James Mackenzie. *Life of William Cunningham*, London, T. Nelson, 1871.

Ranken, Alexander. *Institutes of theology; or, a concise system of divinity*, Glasgow, James Brash, 1822.

Ranken, Andrew. *A letter addressed to the Rev Dr Chalmers, occasioned by his frequent allusions to the 'impregnable minds of certain conveners and councilmen,' on the subject of pauperism in the city of Glasgow; accompanied with official documents*, Glasgow, James Hedderwick, 1830.

Renwick, Robert, ed. *Extracts from the records of the Burgh of Glasgow with charters and other documents*, 10, 1809-1822, Glasgow, The Corporation of Glasgow, 1905.

Renwick, Robert, ed. *Extracts from the records of the Burgh of Glasgow with charters and other documents*, 11, 1823-1833, Glasgow, The Corporation of Glasgow, 1906.

Report of the Bible Society of Fife and Kinross Shires for the year ending 24th August, 1813; with a list of subscriptions & benefactions to that date, Cupar, R. Tullis, 1814.

Robertson, Harry. *The Scotch minister's assistant, or a collection of forms for celebrating the ordinances of marriage, baptism and the Lord's supper, according to the usage of the Church of Scotland, with suitable devotions for church and family worship*, Inverness, Young and Imray, 1802.

Rosebery, Lord. *Dr Chalmers. An address delivered on April 14, 1915, in commemoration of the centenary of his first connection with Glasgow*, Edinburgh, David Douglas, 1915.

Ross, James. *William Lindsay Alexander, his life and work*, London, James Nisbet, 1887.

Ryland, J. E. *The life and correspondence of John Foster*, London, Jackson and Walford, 1846.

Sage, Donald. *Memorabilia domestica; or, parish life in the North of Scotland*, Wick, W. Rae, 1889.

Sanial, S. C. 'Early history of St Andrew's Kirk, Calcutta', *Bengal Past and Present*, 10, 1915, 195-210.

Scott, Hew. *Fasti Ecclesiae Scoticanae. The succession of ministers in the Church of Scotland from the Reformation*, Edinburgh, Oliver & Boyd, 1915-1928.

Sherwood, J. M. ed. *Memoirs of Rev David Brainerd: missionary to the Indians of North America*, New York, Funk & Wagnalls, 1885.

Sinclair, John. *The statistical account of Scotland. Drawn up from the communications of the ministers of the different parishes*, Edinburgh, William Creech, 1791-1799.

Sloane, William Milligan, ed. *The life of James McCosh*, Edinburgh, T. & T. Clark, 1896.

Small, Robert. *History of the congregations of the United Presbyterian Church from 1733 to 1900*, Edinburgh, David M. Small, 1904.

Smith, George. *The life of Alexander Duff*, London, Hodder & Stoughton, 1879.

Sprott, George W. *The doctrine of schism in the Church of Scotland*, Edinburgh, William Blackwood & Sons, 1902.

Statement from the Session of St John's Parish, Glasgow, to the directors of the Town's Hospital, in regard to the management of their poor, Glasgow, William Collins, 1836.

Statement relative to church accommodation by the Scottish Central Board for vindicating the rights of Dissenters, Edinburgh, J. Wardlaw, 1835.

Stephen, James. *Essays in ecclesiastical biography*, London, Longmans, Green, Reader and Dyer, 1867.

Stephen, Leslie, and Sidney Lee. *Dictionary of national biography*, London, Smith, Elder & Co., 1885-1900.

Story, Robert Herbert, ed. *The Church of Scotland, past and present: its history, its relation to the law and the state, its doctrine, ritual, discipline and patrimony*, London, William Mackenzie, 1890.

Struthers, Gavin. *The history of the rise, progress and principles of the Relief Church*, Glasgow, A. Fullarton, 1843.

The subordinate standards and other authoritative documents of the Free Church of Scotland, published by authority of the General Assembly, London, T. Nelson, 1850.

Tasker, W. *Dr Chalmers' territorial church, West-port, Edinburgh*, (reprinted from the *Home and Foreign Record of the Free Church of Scotland*, December 1850).

Tayler, W. Elfe. *Passages from the diary and letters of Henry Craik of Bristol*, London, J. F. Shaw, 1866.

Tulloch, John. *Movements of religious thought in Britain during the nineteenth century,* Fifth series of St Giles' lectures, London, Longmans Green, 1885.

Turner, Alexander. *The Scottish secession of 1843: being an examination of the principles and narrative of the contest which lead to that remarkable event*, Edinburgh, Paton and Ritchie, 1859.

van Voght, Baron Caspar. *Account of the management of the poor in Hamburgh since the year 1788. In a letter to some friends of the poor in Great Britain*, Edinburgh, 1795.

Walker, James. *The theology and theologians of Scotland*, Cunningham lectures 1870-71, Edinburgh, T. & T. Clark, 1872.

Walker, John. *The faith and hope of the gospel vindicated. A letter to a friend in Glasgow containing brief remarks on Dr Chalmers' late address to the inhabitants of Kilmany*, Glasgow, James Hedderwick, 1816.

Warneck, Gustav. *Outline of a history of Protestant missions from the Reformation to the present time*, Edinburgh, Oliphant, Anderson & Ferrier, 1906.

Watson, Jean L. *Life of Andrew Thomson, minister of St George's Parish, Edinburgh*, Edinburgh, James Gemmell, 1882.

Watson, Richard. *Works*, 7, London, John Mason, 1835.

Weir, Robert W. *A history of the foreign missions of the Church of Scotland*, Edinburgh, R. & R. Clark, 1900.

Wilberforce, Robert Isaac, and Samuel. *The life of William Wilberforce*, London, John Murray, 1838.

Wilberforce, William. *A practical view of the prevailing religious system of professed Christians in the higher and middle classes in this country contrasted with real Christianity, with an introductory essay by Daniel Wilson*, Glasgow, William Collins, 1833.

Wilson, John. *Index to the Acts and Proceedings of the General Assembly of the Church of Scotland*, Edinburgh, William Blackwood, 1871.

Wylie, James A. *Disruption worthies. A memorial of 1843*, Edinburgh, T. C. Jack, 1881.

BIBLIOGRAPHY 7

Printed sources post-1920

Altick, Richard D. *The English common reader. A social history of the mass reading public 1800-1900*, University of Chicago Press, 1957.

Beaver, R. Pierce. 'The concert of prayer for missions. An early venture in ecumenical action', *Ecumenical Review*, 10, 1957, 420-27.

Bell, Alan, ed. *Lord Cockburn. A bicentenary commemoration 1779-1979*, Edinburgh, Scottish Academic Press, 1979.

Benz, E. 'Pietist and Puritan sources of early Protestant world missions', *Church History*, 20, 1951, 29-55.

Berg, Johannes van den. *Constrained by Jesus' love: an enquiry into the motives of the missionary awakening in Great Britain in the period between 1698 and 1815*, Kampen, J. H. Kok, 1956.

Berkhof, Louis. *The history of Christian doctrines*, London, Banner of Truth Trust, 1969.

Best, Geoffrey. *Temporal pillars. Queen Anne's Bounty, the Ecclesiastical Commissioners and the Church of England*, Cambridge University Press, 1964.

Best, Geoffrey. 'The Scottish Victorian city', *Victorian Studies*, 11, March 1968, 329-58.

Birtwhistle, N. Allen. 'Founded in 1786. The origins of the Methodist Missionary Society', *Proceedings of the Wesley Historical Society*, 30, June 1955, 25-9.

(Blaikie, A.W.) *Letters and journals of Anne Chalmers*, Chelsea Publishing Co., 1922.

Boer, Harry R. *Pentecost and Missions*, London, Lutterworth, 1961.

Breward, Ian. *The work of William Perkins*, Abingdon, Sutton Courtenay Press, 1970.

British Museum general catalogue of printed books, London, Trustees of the British Museum, 1960-1966.

Brooke, John and Mary Sorensen, eds. *The Prime Minister's papers: W E Gladstone, I: Autobiographica*, London, Royal Commission on Historical Manuscripts, HMSO, 1971.

Brown, Callum G. 'The Sunday-school movement in Scotland, 1780-1914', *Records of the Scottish Church History Society*, 21(1), 1981, 3-26.

Brown, Ford K. *Fathers of the Victorians. The age of Wilberforce*, Cambridge University Press, 1961.

Brown, Stewart J. 'The Disruption and urban poverty: Thomas Chalmers and the West Port operation in Edinburgh, 1844-47', *Records of the Scottish Church History Society*, 20(1), 1978, 65-89.

Brown, Stewart J. *Thomas Chalmers and the Godly Commonwealth in Scotland*, Oxford University Press, 1982.

Burleigh, J. H. S. *A church history of Scotland*, London, Oxford University Press, 1960.

Cage, R. A. 'The making of the old Scottish poor law', *Past and Present*, 69, November 1975, 113-18.

Cage, R. A. and E. O. A. Checkland. 'Thomas Chalmers and urban poverty: the St John's parish experiment in Glasgow, 1819-1837', *Philosophical Journal*, 13(1), 1976, 37-56.

Cairns, David. 'Thomas Chalmers' Astronomical discourses: a study in natural theology?' *Scottish Journal of Theology*, 9, 1956, 410-21.

Calder, James Morrison. *Scotland's march past. The share of Scottish Churches in the London Missionary Society*, London, Livingstone Press, 1945.

Cameron, James K. *The First Book of Discipline*, Edinburgh, St Andrew Press, 1972.

Cameron, Nigel M. de S. ed. *Dictionary of Scottish Church History and Theology*, Edinburgh, T. & T. Clark, 1993.

Campbell, Andrew J. *Two centuries of the Church of Scotland 1707-1929*, Paisley, Alexander Gardner, 1930.

Cant, Ronald Gordon. *The University of St Andrews. A short history*, Edinburgh, Scottish Academic Press, 1970.

Carey, William. *An enquiry into the obligations of Christians to use means for the conversion of the heathens*, London, Carey Kingsgate Press, 1961.

Chadwick, Owen. *The Victorian Church*, London, Adam & Charles Black, 1970.

Chambers, D. 'The Church of Scotland's foreign mission scheme: Evangelical revival or Moderate revival?' *Journal of Religious History*, 9(2), 1976, 115-38.

Chambers, D. 'The Church of Scotland's Highlands and Islands' education scheme, 1824-1843', *Journal of Educational Administration and History*, 7(1), 1975, 8-17.

Chambers, D. 'The Church of Scotland parochial extension scheme and the Scottish Disruption', *Journal of Church and State*, 16, 1974, 263-86.

Chambers, Don. 'Doctrinal attitudes in the Church of Scotland in the pre-Disruption era: the age of John McLeod Campbell and Edward Irving', *Journal of Religious History*, 8(2), 1974, 159-82.

Chambers, Don. 'The Kirk and the colonies in the early 19th century', *Historical Studies,* 16(64), 1975, 381-401.

Chambers, Don. 'Prelude to the last things: the Church of Scotland's mission to the Jews', *Records of the Scottish Church History Society*, 19(1), 1975, 43-58.

Checkland, S. G. *The Gladstones. A family biography 1764-1851*, Cambridge University Press, 1971.

Checkland, S. G. and E. O. A. *The poor law report of 1834*, Harmondsworth, Penguin, 1974.

Cheyne, A. C. '1815: Chalmers in Glasgow's time of turmoil', *Life and Work*, July 1978, 23f., 28.

Cheyne, A. C. '1824: The Kirk votes for a world-wide gospel', *Life and Work*, August 1978, 22-4.

Cheyne, A. C. *The transforming of the Kirk*, Edinburgh, Saint Andrew Press, 1983.

Cheyne, A. C., ed. *The practical and the pious. Essays on Thomas Chalmers (1780-1847)*, Edinburgh, St Andrew Press, 1985.

Clark, G. Kitson. *Churchmen and the condition of England 1832-1885*, London, Methuen, 1973.

Clark, Ian D. L. 'The Leslie controversy, 1805', *Records of the Scottish Church History Society*, 14(3), 1962, 179-97.

Clarke, W. K. Lowther. *A history of the SPCK*, London, SPCK, 1959.

Couper, W. J. 'The Moravian Brethren in Scotland', *Records of the Scottish Church History Society*, 5, 1935, 50-72

Cowan, R. M. W. *The newspaper in Scotland. A study of its first expansion 1815-1960*, Glasgow, George Outram, 1946.

Cox, James T. and D. F. M. Macdonald, eds. *Practice and procedure in the Church of Scotland*, Edinburgh, Church of Scotland, 1976.

Cunningham, William. *Historical theology*, London, Banner of Truth Trust, 1960.

Cunnison, J. and J. B. S. Gilfillan, eds. *The third statistical account of Scotland, Glasgow*, Glasgow, Collins, 1958.

Davie, George Elder. *The democratic intellect. Scotland and her universities in the nineteenth century*, Edinburgh University Press, 1964.

Davies, G. C. B. *The first Evangelical bishop. Some aspects of the life of Henry Ryder*, London, Tyndale Press, 1958.

Davies, Gareth and Lionel A. Ritchie. 'Dr Chalmers and the University of Glasgow', *Records of the Scottish Church History Society*, 20(3), 1980, 211-22.

Davies, Ronald E. 'Robert Millar – an eighteenth-century Scottish Latourette', *Evangelical Quarterly*, 62(2), 1990, 143-56.

Dell, Robert S. 'Social and economic theories and pastoral concerns of a Victorian archbishop', *Journal of Ecclesiastical History*, 16(2), 1965, 196-208.

Drummond, Andrew L. *The Kirk and the Continent*, Edinburgh, Saint Andrew Press, 1956.

Drummond, Andrew L. and James Bulloch. *The Church in late Victorian Scotland 1874-1900*, Edinburgh, St Andrew Press, 1978.

Drummond, Andrew L. and James Bulloch. *The Church in Victorian Scotland 1843-1874*, Edinburgh, St Andrew Press, 1975.

Drummond, Andrew L. and James Bulloch. *The Scottish Church 1688-1843*, Edinburgh, St Andrew Press, 1973.

Escott, Harry. *A history of Scottish Congregationalism*, Glasgow, Congregational Union of Scotland, 1960.

Fawcett, Arthur. *The Cambuslang Revival*, London, Banner of Truth Trust, 1971.

Ferguson, William. *Scotland 1689 to the present*, Edinburgh, Oliver & Boyd, 1968.

Ferguson, W. 'Social problems of the nineteenth century', *Scottish Historical Review*, 41, 132, 1962, 55-8.

Finlayson, D. 'Aspects of the life and influence of Thomas Erskine of Linlathen', *Records of the Scottish Church History Society*, 20(1), 1980, 31-45.

Fleming, J. R. *A history of the Church in Scotland 1843-1874*, Edinburgh, T. & T. Clark, 1927.

Fletcher, Irene M. 'The fundamental principle of the London Missionary Society', *Transactions of the Congregational Historical Society*, 19, 1960-1963, 138-46, 192-8, 222-9.

Foot, M. R. D., ed. *The Gladstone diaries, volume I, 1825-1832,* Oxford, Clarendon Press, 1968.

Foot, M. R. D., ed. *The Gladstone diaries, volume II, 1833-1839*, Oxford, Clarendon Press, 1968.

Foot, M. R. D. and H. C. G. Matthew, eds. *The Gladstone diaries, volume III, 1840-1847*, Oxford, Clarendon Press, 1974.

Foot, M. R. D. and H. C. G. Matthew, eds. *The Gladstone diaries, volume IV, 1848-1854*, Oxford, Clarendon Press, 1974.

Foster, John. 'A Scottish contributor to the missionary awakening: Robert Millar of Paisley', *International Review of Missions*, 37, 1948, 138-45.

Foster, John. 'The bicentenary of Jonathan Edwards' "Humble attempt"', *International Review of Missions*, 37, 1948, 375-81.

Gibson, A. J. H. *Stipend in the Church of Scotland*, Edinburgh, William Blackwood, 1961.

Gillispie, Charles Coulston. *Genesis and geology. A study in the relations of scientific thought, natural theology, and social opinion in Great Britain, 1790-1850*, New York, Harper and Row, 1959.

Godwin, William. *Enquiry concerning political justice and its influence on modern morals and happiness*, Harmondsworth, Penguin, 1976.

Gray, W. Forbes, ed. *Lord Cockburn, Memorials of his time*, Edinburgh, Robert Grant, 1946.

Gunson, Niel. *Messengers of grace: evangelical missionaries in the South Seas, 1797-1860*, Melbourne, Oxford University Press, 1978.

Havard-Williams, P. *Marsden and the New Zealand mission*, Dunedin, University of Otago Press, 1961.

Hayes A. J. and D. A. Gowland, eds. *Scottish Methodism in the early Victorian period. the Scottish correspondence of the Rev Jabez Bunting 1800-57*, Edinburgh University Press, 1981.

Henderson, G. D. *The claims of the Church of Scotland*, London, Hodder and Stoughton, 1951.

Henderson, G. D. *The nature of the Church*, Aberdeen, The University Press, 1948.

Henderson, G. D. *Scots confession, 1560 (Confessio Scoticana) and Negative confession, 1581 (Confessio Negativa)*, Edinburgh, Church of Scotland Committee on Publications, 1937.

Henderson, G. D. 'Thomas Chalmers as a preacher', *Theology Today*, 4(3), 1947, 346-56.

Henderson, Ian. 'Thomas Chalmers', in R. S. Wright ed., *Fathers of the Kirk*, London, Oxford University Press, 1960, 129-42.

Hewat, Elizabeth G. K. *Vision and achievement 1796-1956. A history of the foreign missions of the Churches united in the Church of Scotland*, London, Thomas Nelson, 1960.

Hilton, Boyd. *The Age of Atonement: the influence of Evangelicalism on social and economic thought 1795-1865*, Oxford, Clarendon Press, 1988.

Hogg, James. *The private memoirs and confessions of a justified sinner* (edited with an introduction by John Carey), Oxford University Press, 1970.

Hopkins, H. E. *Charles Simeon of Cambridge*, London, Hodder and Stoughton, 1977.

Houghton, W. E. *The Wellesley index to Victorian periodicals 1824-1900*, University of Toronto Press, 1966.

Howse, Ernest Marshall. *Saints in politics. The 'Clapham Sect' and the growth of freedom*, London, George Allen and Unwin, 1971.

Hutton, J. E. *A history of Moravian missions*, London, Moravian Publication Office, 1922.

Inglis, K. S. *Churches and the working classes in Victorian England*, London, R. & K. Paul, 1963.

Johnson, Christine. *Developments in the Roman Catholic Church in Scotland 1789-1829*, Edinburgh, John Donald, 1983.

Jones, M. G. *The charity school movement. A study of eighteenth century Puritanism in action*, Cambridge University Press, 1938.

Jones, M. V. 'The sad and curious story of Karass 1802-1835', *Oxford Slavonic Papers*, NS 8, 1975, 53-81

Jong, J. A. De. *As the waters cover the sea: Millennial expectations in the rise of Anglo-American missions 1640-1810*, Kampen, J. H. Kok, 1970.

Keir, David. *The House of Collins*, London, Collins, 1952.

Kilpatrick, John. 'The records of the Scottish Missionary Society, 1796-1848', *Records of the Scottish Church History Society*, 10, 1950, 196-210.

Kinross, John. *Discovering battlefields of Scotland*, Aylesbury, Shire publications, 1976.

Laird, M. A. 'The legacy of Alexander Duff', *Occasional Bulletin of Missionary Research*, 3(4), 1979, 146-9.

Laird, M. A. *Missionaries and education in Bengal 1793-1837*, Oxford, Clarendon Press, 1972.

Lamb, John A. 'Aids to public worship in Scotland 1800-1850', *Records of the Scottish Church History Society*, 13, 1958, 172-85.

Lang, Peter Redford Scott. *Duncan Dewar. A student of St Andrews 100 years ago. His accounts. With a commentary.* Glasgow, Jackson, Wylie & Co, 1926.

Laws, Gilbert. *Andrew Fuller. Pastor, theologian, ropeholder*, London, Carey Press, 1942.

Leat, Diana. 'Social theory and the historical construction of social work activity: the role of Samuel Barnett', in Peter Leonard, ed., *The sociology of community action*, Sociological review monograph 21, University of Keele, November 1975.

Leishman, James Fleming. *Matthew Leishman of Govan and the Middle Party of 1843*, Paisley, Alexander Gardner, 1924.

Levitt, Ian and Christopher Smout, *The state of the Scottish working-class in 1843*, Edinburgh, Scottish Academic Press, 1979.

Lochhead, Marion. *Episcopal Scotland in the nineteenth century*, London, John Murray, 1966.

Louden, R. Stuart. *The true face of the Kirk. An examination of the ethos and traditions of the Church of Scotland*, Oxford University Press, 1963.

McCaffrey, John F. 'Thomas Chalmers and social change', *Scottish Historical Review*, 60, 1981, 32-60

Machin, G. I. T. 'The Disruption and British politics, 1834-43', *Scottish Historical Review*, 51, 1972, 20-51.

Machin, G. I. T. *Politics and the churches in Great Britain 1832 to 1868*, Oxford, Clarendon Press, 1977.

MacInnes, John. *The Evangelical movement in the Highlands of Scotland, 1688 to 1800*, Aberdeen University Press, 1951.

Maciver, Iain F. 'The Evangelical party and the eldership in General Assemblies, 1820-1843', *Records of the Scottish Church History Society*, 20(1), 1978, 1-13.

Maciver, Iain F. '"I did not seek...but was sought after": The election of Thomas Chalmers to the Chair of Divinity at Edinburgh

University, October 1827', *Records of the Scottish Church History Society*, 20(3), 1980, 223-30.

Mackichan, D. *The missionary ideal in the Scottish churches.* The Chalmers lectures delivered in 1926, London, Hodder and Stoughton, 1927.

Mackie, J. D. *A history of Scotland*, Harmondsworth, Penguin, 1969.

MacLaren, A. Allan. *Religion and social class. The Disruption years in Aberdeen*, London, Routledge & Kegan Paul, 1974.

MacLaren, A. Allan, ed. *Social class in Scotland: past and present*, Edinburgh, John Donald, n.d.

MacLean, Donald. 'Scottish Calvinism and foreign missions', *Records of the Scottish Church History Society*, 6(1), 1938, 4-12.

Macleod, John. *Scottish theology in relation to church history since the Reformation*, Edinburgh, Banner of Truth Trust, 1974.

Malthus, Thomas Robert. *An essay on the principle of population* and *A summary view of the principle of population*, edited with an introduction by Anthony Flew, Harmondsworth, Penguin, 1970.

Martin, Roger. *Evangelicals united*, Metuchen, NJ, Scarecrow, 1983.

Maxwell, William D. *A history of worship in the Church of Scotland*, Oxford University Press, 1955.

Mechie, Stewart. *The church and Scottish social development, 1780-1870*, London, Oxford University Press, 1960.

Mechie, Stewart. 'Church extension in Scotland in the last two centuries', *Expository Times*, 66, 1955, 136-7.

Meek, D. E. 'Scottish Highlanders, North American Indians and the SSPCK: some cultural perspectives', *Records of the Scottish Church History Society*, 23(3), 1989, 378-96.

Mitchison, Rosalind. 'The making of the old Scottish poor law', *Past and Present*, 63, 1974, 58-93.

Mitchison, Rosalind. 'The making of the old Scottish poor law', *Past and Present*; 69, 1975, 119-21.

Morrell, J. B. 'The Leslie affair: careers, kirk and politics in Edinburgh in 1805', *Scottish Historical Review*, 54, 157, 1975, 63-82.

Mowat, Charles Loch. *The Charity Organisation Society 1869-1913. Its ideas and work*, London, Methuen, 1961.

Murray, Iain H. *The Puritan hope*, London, Banner of Truth Trust, 1971.

Myklebust, Olav Guttorm. *The study of missions in theological education*, Oslo, Egede Institute, 1955.

Newell, J. Philip. 'Scottish intimations of modern Pentecostalism: A J Scott and the 1830 Clydeside Charismatics', *Pneuma*, 4(2) 1982, 1-18.

Newell, J. Philip. '"Unworthy of the dignity of the Assembly": the deposition of Alexander John Scott in 1831', *Records of the Scottish Church History Society*, 21(3), 1983, 249-62.

Noll, Mark A. 'Revival, enlightenment, civic humanism and the development of dogma: Scotland and America, 1735-1843', *Tyndale Bulletin*, 40, 1989, 49-76.

Nuttall, Geoffrey F. 'Northamptonshire and the modern question: a turning point in eighteenth-century Dissent', *Journal of Theological Studies*, NS16, 1965, 101-23.

Owen, W. T. *Edward Williams, 1750-1813. His life, thought and influence*, Cardiff, University of Wales Press, 1963.

Parkinson, C. Northcote. *The law and the profits*, London, John Murray, 1963.

Paton, William. *Alexander Duff, pioneer of missionary education*, London, SCM, 1923.

Payne, E. A. 'The evangelical revival and the beginnings of the modern missionary movement', *Congregational Quarterly*, 21, 1943, 223-36.

Philip, Adam. *Thomas Chalmers, apostle of union*, London, James Clarke, 1929.

Piggin, Stuart. *Making Evangelical missionaries 1789-1858: The social background, motives and training of British Protestant missionaries to India*, Abingdon, Sutton Courtenay Press, 1984.

Piggin, Stuart. 'Sectarianism versus ecumenism: the impact on British churches of the missionary movement to India c.1800-1860', *Journal of Ecclesiastical History*, 27(4), 1976, 387-402.

Piggin, Stuart, and John Roxborogh. *The St Andrews Seven*, Edinburgh, Banner of Truth Trust, 1985.

Pollock, John. *Wilberforce*, London, Constable, 1977.

Port, M. H. *Six hundred new churches. A study of the Church Building Commission, 1818-1856, and its church building activities*, London, SPCK, 1961.

Potts, E. Daniel. *British Baptist missionaries in India 1793-1837. The history of Serampore and its missions*, Cambridge University Press, 1967.

Prebble, John. *The Darien disaster*, London, Secker & Warburg, 1968.

Rack, H. D. 'Domestic visitation: a chapter in early nineteenth century evangelism', *Journal of Ecclesiastical History*, 24(4), 1973, 357-76.

Ramsay, Jack. 'Scottish Presbyterian foreign missions - a century before Carey', *Journal of the Presbyterian Historical Society*, 39(4), 1961, 201-18.

Rice, Daniel F. 'An attempt at systematic reconstruction in the theology of Thomas Chalmers', *Church History*, 48(2), 1979, 174-88.

Rice, Daniel F. 'Natural theology and the Scottish philosophy in the thought of Thomas Chalmers', *Scottish Journal of Theology*, 21, 1971, 23-46.

Riesen, Richard A. '"Higher criticism" in the Free Church Fathers', *Records of the Scottish Church History Society*, 20(2), 1979, 119-42.

Robb, George. 'Popular religion and the Christianization of the Scottish Highlands in the eighteenth and nineteen centuries', *Journal of Religious History*, 16(1), 1990, 18-34.

Rosman, Doreen. *Evangelicals and culture*, London, Croom Helm, 1984.

Ross, J. M. *Four centuries of Scottish worship*, Edinburgh, St Andrew Press, 1972.

Rouse, Ruth and Stephen Charles Neill. *A history of the Ecumenical Movement 1517-1948*, London, SPCK, 1954.

Rowell, Geoffrey. *Hell and the Victorians*, Oxford, Clarendon Press, 1974.

Roxborogh, W. J. 'Letters to an evangelical publisher in nineteenth century Scotland: the Johnstone papers', *Bulletin of the Scottish Institute of Missionary Studies*, 18, 1976, 3-18.

Sandeen, Ernest R. *The roots of Fundamentalism. British and American millenarianism 1800-1930*, University of Chicago Press, 1970.

Saunders, L. J. *Scottish democracy 1815-1840. The social and economic background*, Edinburgh, Oliver & Boyd, 1950.

Scherer, James A. *Justinian Welz. Essays by an early prophet of mission*, Grand Rapids, Eerdmans, 1969.

Scotland, James. *The history of Scottish education*, University of London Press, 1969.

Semmel, Bernard. *The Methodist revolution*, London, Heinemann, 1974.

Sefton, H. R. 'St Mary's College, St Andrews in the eighteenth century', *Records of the Scottish Church History Society*, 24(2), 1991, 161-80.

Sefton, H. R. 'The Scotch Society in the American Colonies in the eighteenth century', *Records of the Scottish Church History Society*, 17, 1971, 169-84.

Shaw, Duncan. 'The moderatorship controversy in 1836 and 1837', *Records of the Scottish Church History Society*, 17, 1970, 115-30.

Sher, Richard and Alexander Murdoch, 'Patronage and party in the Church of Scotland, 1750-1800', in Norman Macdougall ed., *Church, politics and society: Scotland 1408-1929*, Edinburgh, John Donald, 1983, 197-220.

Sibree, James. *London Missionary Society. A register of missionaries, deputations etc, from 1796 to 1923*, London, London Missionary Society, 1923.

Sjölinder, Rolf. *Presbyterian reunion in Scotland 1907-1921. Its background and development*, Edinburgh, T. & T. Clark, 1962.

Smith, Alexander. *The third statistical account of Scotland. The County of Fife*, Edinburgh, Oliver and Boyd, 1952.

Smith, Crosbie. 'From design to dissolution: Thomas Chalmers' debt to John Robison', *British Journal for the History of Science*, 12, 1979, 59-70.

Smith, Donald C. *Passive obedience and prophetic protest: social criticism in the Scottish Church, 1830-1945*, New York, Peter Lang, 1987.

Smout, T. C. *A century of the Scottish people, 1830-1950*, London, Collins, 1986.

Smout, T. C. *A history of the Scottish people, 1560-1830*, Glasgow, Collins, 1969.

Strachan, C. Gordon. *The Pentecostal theology of Edward Irving*, London, Darton, Longman & Todd, 1973.

Sutherland, J. A. *Victorian novelists and publishers*, University of London, Athlone Press, 1976.

Swift, Wesley F. *Methodism in Scotland. The first hundred years*, London, Epworth, 1947.

Thirkell, Alison. *Auld Anster*, Anstruther, Buckie House Gallery, n.d. (c.1976).

Thompson, David M. *Nonconformity in the nineteenth century*, London, Routledge & Kegan Paul, 1972.

Turner, Harold W. *Profile through preaching, IMC research pamphlet no 13*, London, Edinburgh House Press, 1965.

Vidler, A. T. *The Church in an age of revolution, 1789 to the present day*, Harmondsworth, Penguin, 1974.

Voges, F. 'Moderate and Evangelical thinking in the later eighteenth century: differences and shared attitudes', *Records of the Scottish Church History Society*, 22(2), 1985, 141-57.

Walls, A. F. 'The nineteenth century missionary as scholar', in Nils E. Bloch-Hoell, ed., *Misjonskall og forskerglede. Festskrift til Professor Olav Guttorm Myklebust*, Oslo, Universitetsforlaget, 1975, 209-28.

Walsh, John. 'Origins of the evangelical revival', in G. V. Bennett and J. D. Walsh, eds, *Essays in modern English church history in memory of Norman Sykes*, London, Adam & Charles Black, 1966, 132-62.

Ward, J. T. 'The factory reform movement in Scotland', *Scottish Historical Review*, 41, 132, 1962, 100-123.

Watt, Hugh. '"Moderator, Rax me that bible"', *Records of the Scottish Church History Society*, 10(1), 1948, 54f.

Watt, Hugh. *New College Edinburgh. A centenary history*, Edinburgh, Oliver and Boyd, 1946.

Watt, Hugh. 'The praying societies of the early eighteenth century', *The Original Secession Magazine*, February 1934, 49-53.

Watt, Hugh. *The published writings of Dr Thomas Chalmers, 1780-1847*, Edinburgh, privately printed, 1943.

Watt, Hugh. *Thomas Chalmers and the Disruption*, Edinburgh, Thomas Nelson, 1943.

Welch, P. J. 'Bishop Blomfield and church extension in London', *Journal of Ecclesiastical History*, 4(2), 1953, 203-15.

White, Gavin. '"Highly preposterous": origins of Scottish missions', *Records of the Scottish Church History Society*, 19(2), 1976, 111-24.

Willey, Basil. *The eighteenth-century background. Studies on the idea of nature in the thought of the period*, Harmondsworth, Penguin, 1972.

Withrington, Donald J. 'The 1851 census of religious worship and education: with a note on church accommodation in mid-19th-century Scotland', *Records of the Scottish Church History Society*, 18(2), 1973, 133-48.

Withrington, Donald J. 'The Disruption: a century and a half of historical interpretation', *Records of the Scottish Church History Society*, 25(1), 1993, 118-33.

Withrington, Donald J. 'Non-church-going, c.1750 - c.1850: a preliminary study', *Records of the Scottish Church History Society*, 17(2), 1970, 99-113.

Withrington, Donald J. 'The SPCK and Highland schools in the mid-eighteenth century', *Scottish Historical Review*, 41, 132, 1962, 89-99.

Wolfe, J. N. and M. Pickford. *The Church of Scotland. An economic survey*, London, Geoffrey Chapman, 1980.

Yuille, George, ed. *History of the Baptists in Scotland from pre-Reformation times*, Glasgow, Baptist Union Publications Committee, 1926.

BIBLIOGRAPHY 8

Theses

Bain, Colin M. *The social impact of Kirkcaldy's industrial revolution, 1810-1876*, PhD, University of Guelp, 1973 (Kirkcaldy public library).

Blakey, Ronald Stanton. *The Scottish minister of the nineteenth century - his life, work, and relations with his people*, MTh, University of Glasgow, 1972.

Brackenridge, R. Douglas. *Sunday observance in Scotland 1689-1900*, PhD, University of Glasgow, 1962.

Cage, Robert A. *The Scottish poor law, 1745-1845*, PhD, University of Glasgow, 1974.

Chambers, Don. *Mission and party in the Church of Scotland, 1810-1843*, PhD, University of Cambridge, 1971.

Cox, Richard B. Jr. *The nineteenth century British Apocrypha Controversy*, PhD, Baylor University, 1981 (Cambridge University Library).

Davidson, Allan Kenneth. *The development and influence of the British Missionary movement's attitudes towards India, 1786-1830*, PhD, University of Aberdeen, 1973.

Enright, William Gerald. *Preaching and theology in Scotland in the nineteenth century: a study of the context and content of the evangelical sermon*, PhD, University of Edinburgh, 1968.

Gilbert, Alan D. *The growth and decline of non-conformity in England and Wales with special reference to the period before 1850: A historical interpretation of statistics of religious practice*, DPhil, Oxford, 1973.

Gunson, W. Niel. *Evangelical missionaries in the South Seas, 1797-1860*, PhD, Australian National University, 1959.

Horsburgh, William. *The renaissance of churchmanship in the Church of Scotland, 1850-1920*, PhD, University of St Andrews, 1947.

Huie, Wade Prichard Jr. *The theology of Thomas Chalmers*, PhD, University of Edinburgh, 1949.

Kirkland, William Matthews. *The impact of the French revolution on Scottish religious life and thought with special reference to Thomas Chalmers, Robert Haldane and Neil Douglas*, PhD, University of Edinburgh, 1951.

Maciver, Iain Finlay. *The General Assembly of the Church, the state, and society in Scotland: some aspects of their relationships, 1815-1843*, MLitt, University of Edinburgh, 1976.

Montgomery, Alfred Baxter. *The Voluntary Controversy in the Church of Scotland, 1829-1843, with particular reference to its practical and theological roots*, PhD, University of Edinburgh, 1953.

Murray, Nancy Uhlar. *The influence of the French Revolution on the Church of England and its rivals 1789-1802*, DPhil, University of Oxford, 1975.

Orr, J. M. *The contribution of Scottish missions to the rise of responsible churches in India*, PhD, University of Edinburgh, 1967.

Phillips, H. P. *The development of demonstrative theism in the Scottish thought of the nineteenth century*, PhD, University of Edinburgh, 1951.

Piggin, Frederic Stuart. *The social background, motivation, and training of British Protestant missionaries to India, 1789-1858*, PhD, University of London, 1974.

Reeve, D. P. *Interaction of Scottish and English evangelicals, 1790-1810*, MLitt, University of Glasgow, 1973.

Rice, Daniel Frederick. *The theology of Thomas Chalmers*, PhD, Drew University, 1970.

Robertson, George Booth. *Spiritual awakening in the north-east of Scotland and the Disruption of the Church in 1843*, PhD, University of Aberdeen, 1970.

Smith, Donald C. *The failure and recovery of social criticism in the Scottish church, 1830-1950*, PhD, University of Edinburgh, 1964.

Williams, Henry Howard. *The religious thought of Thomas Erskine of Linlathen: its origin, nature and influence*, PhD, University of Leeds, 1951.

Willmer, Haddon. *Evangelicalism 1785 to 1835*, Hulsean Prize Essay, University of Cambridge, 1962.

BIBLIOGRAPHY 9
Scottish Missionary sermons, 1795-1820

This list includes a few titles from outside the period, but unless they are of special interest it does not contain sermons preached for the SSPCK or for the LMS in London. With these exceptions, what follows is as complete a list as possible of the missionary sermons published in Scotland during this period. Where possible the denomination[1] and location of the preacher are given in brackets. Most of these sermons can be found in New College Library Edinburgh, or the National Library of Scotland. In one or two instances the reference has been taken from a review.

Baird, George Husband (CS, University of Edinburgh). *The universal propagation and influence of the Christian religion*, 1795.
Balfour, Robert (CS, Lecropt). *The salvation of the heathen necesary and certain*, Glasgow Missionary Society, 14 April 1796.
Black, Alexander (CS, Marischal College Aberdeen). *On the progressive diffusion of divine knowledge*, Aberdeen, 1824.
Black, David (CS, Lady Yester's, Edinburgh). *The duty of seeking the things which are Jesus Christ's*, Edinburgh Missionary Society, 1803.
Blinshall, James (CS, Dundee). *The evidence of the future publication of the gospel to all nations*, Edinburgh, 1780, SSPCK.
Brodie, John (Relief, Aberdeen). *Preaching the gospel the great means appointed by God for the salvation of men*, Aberdeen, 1798.
Brown, John (AS, Biggar). *The danger of opposing Christianity and the certainty of its final triumph.* Edinburgh Missionary Society, 2 April 1816, Edinburgh, 1816.
Burns, William (CS, Dundee). *The propriety of immediate exertions for propagating Christianity urged: A sermon preached in St Andrew's church before the Dundee Missionary Society formed for propagating the gospel among heathen and unenlightened nations on Monday April 25, 1808*, Dundee, 1808.
Burns, William Hamilton (CS, Dundee). *Moravian missions illustrated and defended*, Aberdeen, 11 April 1814.

---

[1] Abbreviations:
      AS   Associate Synod of Burghers
      CS   Church of Scotland
      GAS   General Associate Synod of Anti-Burghers
      C   Congregational (Independent)

Campbell, Robert (AS, Stirling). *The glory of Christ displayed in the conversion of the nations: a sermon preached before some members of the Society in Stirling for promoting the spread of the gospel among the heathen, on Sabbath evening, 5 January 1800, to which is added some general strictures on a pamphlet entitled 'The New-light examined' by William Porteous DD*, Edinburgh, 1800.

Chalmers, Thomas (CS, Kilmany). *The two great instruments appointed for the propagation of the gospel and the duty of the public to keep them both in vigorous operation; A sermon preached before the Dundee Missionary Society on Monday the 26 October 1812*, Dundee, 1813.

Chalmers, Thomas (CS, Kilmany). *The utility of missions ascertained by experience: A sermon preached before the Society in Scotland for Propagating Christian Knowledge at their anniversary meeting in the High Church of Edinburgh, on Thursday, June 2, 1814*, Edinburgh, 1815.

Colquhoun, Malcolm (CS, Gaelic Dundee). *Predictions concerning the person and kingdom of Messiah illustrated*, Second general meeting of the Dundee Society for Propagating the Gospel among the Heathen, June 1797.

Davidson, Thomas (CS, Tolbooth, Edinburgh). *The glory of God displayed in the building up of Zion: a sermon preached in Lady Glenorchy's chapel before the Edinburgh Missionary Society, March 30 1802*, Edinburgh, 1802.

Dickson, David (CS, St Cuthberts, Edinburgh). *The influence of learning on religion: A sermon preached before the Society in Scotland for Propagating Christian Knowledge, June 3, 1818*, Edinburgh, 1814.

Dickson, David, Snr. (CS, Trinity, Edinburgh). *The purpose of Christ respecting his people among the gentiles. A sermon preached before the Edinburgh Missionary Society, Edinburgh 30 July 1799*, Edinburgh, 1799.

Douglas, Neil (Relief, Dundee). *Messiah's glorious rest in the latter days: a sermon delivered in the Associate Church before the Missionary Society, Dundee, May 1, 1797, and in the Relief Church, Dove-hill, Glasgow, May 2*, Dundee, 1797.

Duncanson, Andrew (AS, Airdrie). *Divine agency necessary to the propagation of Christianity. Sermon at Campbell Street Meeting House, Glasgow, May 17, 1796.*

Ewing, Greville (CS, Lady Yester's Edinburgh). *A defence of missions from Christian societies to the Heathen world. A sermon preached before the Edinburgh Missionary Society, Thursday, February 2, 1797*, Edinburgh, 1797.

Ewing, Greville (C, Glasgow). *The ignorance of the heathen and the conduct of God towards them*, London Missionary Society, 1803.

Findlay, John (CS, Paisley High). *The universal diffusion of knowledge with its happy effects*, London Missionary Society, 1799.

Fleming, Thomas (CS, Lady Yester's, Edinburgh). *The nature, imporatance and right exercise of Christian zeal: a sermon preached before the Edinburgh Missionary Society, 4 April 1809.*

Fraser, Alexander (CS, Kirkhill). *The superior liberality of the scheme of redemption: a sermon, preached before the Northern Missionary Society, at their first meeting in the Church of Tain, August 27, 1800*, Edinburgh, 1800.

French, James (CS, East Kilbride). *The effectual and universal influence of the cross of Christ*, Glasgow Missionary Society, 8 November, 1796.

Glass, Laurence (AS, Aberdeen). *All things gathered together in one in Christ, a sermon preached before the Aberdeen Society for Foreign Missions, June 11, 1805*, Aberdeen, 1805.

Glenn, William (EMS Missionary). *The establishment of the mountain of the Lord*, Edinburgh Missionary Society, 3 April 1817.

Gray, James (GAS, Brechin). *The last charge of an ascending redeemer: or the duty of Christians in promoting the spreading of the gospel explained and enforced. A sermon on Mark 16:15*, Edinburgh, 1819.

Grey, Henry (CS, St Cuthbert's Chapel of ease, Edinburgh). *The diffusion of Christianity dependent on the exertions of Christians. A sermon preached in Lady Glenorchy's Chapel before the Edinburgh Missionary Society. 2 April 1818*, Edinburgh, 1818.

Hall, Robert (AS, Kelso). *The state of the heathen world disclosed...a sermon preached before the Kelso Bible Association*, Edinburgh, 1815.

Hunter, Andrew (CS, University of Edinburgh). *Christ drawing all men unto him. A sermon preached before the Edinburgh Missionary Society in Lady Glenorchy's Chapel on Thursday July 20, 1797.*

Inglis, John (CS, Old Greyfriars, Edinburgh). *A sermon preached in the Old Greyfriars Church, Edinburgh, December 10, 1826 when a collection was intimated under the authority of the General Assembly in aid of the propagation of the gospel*, Edinburgh, 1826.

Inglis, John (CS, Old Greyfriars, Edinburgh). *The grounds of Christian hope in the universal prevalence of the Gospel*, June 5, 1818, SSPCK, 1818.

Irving, Edward (CS, London). *For missionaries after the apostolical school a series of orations*, London, London Missionary Society, 1825.

Jamieson, John (AS, Scone). *The certainty of the gospel being sent to the heathen, and the danger of refusing to promote its progress. A sermon preached before the Dundee Missionary Society, August 1, 1799*, Dundee, 1799.

Johnston, Bryce (CS, Holywood, Dumfries). *The divine authority and encouragement of missions from Christians to the heathen: a sermon preached before the Dumfries Missionary Society in the Church of Holywood, on Thursday the 16 of November 1797*, Dumfries, 1797.

Johnstone, James (AS, Rathillet). *The pastoral care of Jesus over the heathen a sermon preached before the Dundee Society for Propagating the Gospel among the Heathen, 18 October 1796*, Dundee, 1796.

Kennedy, Thomas (CS, St Madoes). *Encouragement to missions: A sermon preached before the Perth Society for Propagating the Gospel among Heathen and Unenlightened Nations, 26 June 1797*, Perth, 1797.

Kennedy, Thomas (CS, St Madoes). *The success of evangelical missions in the universal spread of the gospel the peculiar work of God. A sermon preached in St Andrew's Church Dundee, for the benefit of the mission in Russian Tartary, 20 October 1806*, Dundee, 1806.

Kennedy, Thomas (CS, St Madoes). *The divine authority of missionary societies: A sermon, preached in St Andrew's Church, Dundee, before the Missionary Society for the benefit of missions to the heathen, 28 October, 1811*, Dundee, 1811.

Lawson, George (AS, Selkirk). *A sermon preached before the Edinburgh Missionary Society, at their anniversary meeting, April 19, 1808, (Romans 11:31)*, Edinburgh, 1808.

Love, John (CS, Anderston, Glasgow), *A serious call respecting a mission from Glasgow to the river Indus, addressed to Christians in Glasgow and in Western and Northern parts of Scotland*, Glasgow, Maurice Ogle, 1820.

Macrie, Thomas (GAS, Edinburgh). *The duty of Christian societies towards each other in relation to the measures for propagating the gospel, which at present engage the attention of the religious world*, Edinburgh, 1797.

McDiarmid, John (Relief, Aberdeen). *The propagation of the gospel important and necessary*, Aberdeen, 1799.

M'Lagan, James (CS, Auchtergaven). *The obligation of Christians to evangelize the heathen. A sermon preached before the Perthshire Missionary Society*, Perth, R. Morrison, 1816.

Noel, Gerard (Church of England, Rainham, Kent). *The duty of imparting Christianity to the heathen: a sermon preached in St George's Episcopal Chapel, York Place; on Sunday November 30, 1817 for the benefit of the Church of England Missionary Society*, Edinburgh, 1818.

Paul, William (CS, St Cuthbert's, Edinburgh). *The influence of the Christian character upon the propagation of Christianity*, Edinburgh, SSPCK, 1797.

Peddie, James (AS, Edinburgh). *The perpetuity, advantages and universality of the Christian religion: a sermon preached before the Edinburgh Missionary Society, Bristo Street Meeting-House, Thursday November 18, 1796.*

Peebles, William (CS, Newton-upon-Ayr). *The universality of pure Christian worship, and the means of promoting it considered. A sermon, preached for the benefit of missions in the Church of Newton-upon-Ayr on September 18, 1796.*

Peters, Alexander (CS, Logie-Pert). *The necessity and obligation of sending the gospel to heathen and unenlightened nations. A sermon preached in St Andrew's Church before the Dundee Missionary Society on Monday evening 27 April, 1807*, Dundee, 1807.

Pirie, Alexander (AS, Glasgow). *The duties and qualifications of a gospel missionary. A sermon preached before the Glasgow Missionary Society, November 7, 1797*, Glasgow, 1797.

Robertson, William (CS, Gladsmuir). *The situation of the world at the time of Christ's appearance, and its connection with the success of his religion considered*, SSPCK, 1755

Russell, John (CS, Kilmarnock). *The nature of the gospel delineated and its universal spread founded upon the declaration of Jesus Christ. A sermon preached in the parish church, Kilmarnock, Thursday August 18, 1796.*

Snodgrass, John (CS, Paisley). *Prospects of providence respecting the conversion of the world to Christ. A sermon preached before the Paisley London Missionary Society, in the High Church of Paisley on Friday, June 10th, 1796*, Paisley, 1796.

Tait, Walter (CS, Tealing), *The conversion of God's ancient people a proper object of Christian solicitude and ground of Christian joy. A sermon preached before the Dundee Auxiliary Society for promoting Christianity among the Jews*, Dundee, 1811.

Thomson, Andrew (CS, St George's, Edinburgh). *The genuine character of the gospel stated and illustrated: a sermon preached before the Edinburgh Missionary Society, 18th April 1815*, Edinburgh, 1815.

Thomson, Andrew (CS, St George's, Edinburgh). *The ultimate and universal prevalence of the Christian religion, June 5, 1817*, Edinburgh, SSPCK, 1817.

Thomson, James (CS, Dundee). *The nature and properties of Christ's kingdom considered as a motive to undertake and as an encouragement to persevere in missionary exertions, Steeple Church, 28 July 1807*, Dundee Missionary Society, Dundee, 1807.

Wardlaw, Ralph (C, Glasgow). *The truth, nature and universality of the gospel. A sermon preached at Stirling on Tuesday 29, 1819, at the anniversary meeting of the Society for Stirlingshire and its vicinity in aid of Missions and other religious objects.*

INDEX

Rutherford Studies in Historical Theology

Church and Creed in Scotland:
The Free Church Case 1900–1904 and its Origins

Kenneth Ross

When the Free Church of Scotland and the United Presbyterian Church united in 1900 to form the United Free Church, a small minority of the Free Church declined to enter the union. Four years later the House of Lords upheld their claim that the name and property of the Free church belonged to them. This important book is an examination of the controversy surrounding the decision, and its origins in the history of the Free Church.

1988 / 412pp / ISBN 0-946068-30-5

The Erosion of Calvinist Orthodoxy:
Seceders and Subscription in Scottish Presbyterianism

Ian Hamilton

This work traces some aspects of the erosion of Westminster Calvinism among Scottish seceders during the years 1773 to 1879. Its main conclusion is that the erosion of Westminster Calvinism within the Scottish Secession was a slow and disputed process. It is argued that although this process did not reach its peak until 1879, a significant departure from Westminster Calvinism occurred during the Atonement Controversy in the 1840s.

1990 / 212pp / ISBN 0-946068-34-8

Thomas Erskine of Linlathen:
His Life and Theology 1788–1837

Nicholas Needham

One of the most significant figures in Scottish theological thought in the early nineteenth century was a layman, Thomas Erskine, who combined his role as Laird of Linlathen with that of a theological writer and correspondent of very considerable influence, in Scotland and further afield. Erskine began as a moderate Calvinist, but in 1828 he published his *Unconditional Freeness of the Gospel* which provoked a storm of criticism for its advocacy of universal pardon. Erskine's final position was that of a Liberal Universalist.

1990 / 543pp / ISBN 0-946068-29-1

The Doctrine of Holy Scripture in the Free Church Fathers
Nicholas Needham

Dr Needham examines the views of Scripture held by five founding fathers of the Free Church of Scotland – Thomas Chalmers, William Cunningham, James Bannerman, Robert Candlish and 'Rabbi' John Duncan. He investigates their views of textual and higher criticism, inspiration and inerrancy, apologetics and the relation between science and Scripture. Whilst noting differences of emphasis and terminology, Dr Needham argues for a substantial harmony between them in all crucial areas.

1991 / 157pp / ISBN 0-946068-39-9

An Ecclesiastical Republic:
Church Government in the Writings of George Gillespie
W.D.J. McKay

This work is the first full-length study of George Gillespie, a key figure in the Westminster Assembly. It considers the nature of the kingship of Christ, the place of the Old Testament in ecclesiology and the structures and leadership of the Church, all issues of contemporary concern.

1997 / 340pp / ISBN 0-946068-60-7

Religious Radicalism in England 1535–1565
C.J. Clement

The author here provides a kaleidoscopic analysis of the radical reforming spirits of the key generation of the English Reformation. Those hitherto lumped together as Anabaptists are here carefully characterized in their own individuality. This comprehensive study ends with an account of the theology of the English Radicals in their relationship to Lollardy, Anabaptism and Anglicanism.

1997 / 448pp / ISBN 0-946068-44-5

The Federal Theology of Thomas Boston
A.T.B. McGowan

In this volume, the author seeks to demonstrate that Thomas Boston was a consistent federal Calvinist, true to the *Westminster Confession of Faith*. The volume interacts with the discussions of the day, in relation to the nature and development of federal theology, but also with current debates in the Calvin/Calvinism argument.

1997 / 248pp / ISBN 0-946068-59-3

Tertullian's Theology of Divine Power
Roy Kearsley

This book traces Tertullian's handling of key doctrines and draws implications for some of today's crucial issues: Trinitarian faith, the status of the creation, gender, authority and power abuse. It takes the agenda of early Christian thought seriously and finds it profoundly relevant for today.

1999 / 190pp / ISBN 0-946068-61-5

Thomas Boston as Preacher of the Fourfold State
Philip Graham Ryken

Thomas Boston, the Presbyterian pastor-theologian, was the most widely published Scottish author of the eighteenth century. *Thomas Boston as Preacher of the Fourfold State* is a historical, practical, and theological study of his preaching ministry, understood against the background of patristic, medieval, Reformation and Puritan theology.

1999 / 372pp / ISBN 0-946068-72-0

Thomas Chalmers: Enthusiast for Mission:
The Christian Good of Scotland and the Rise of the Missionary Movement
John Roxborogh

Enthusiast for Mission tells afresh the inspiring story of Scottish church leader Thomas Chalmers, his conversion, parish experiments, support for overseas mission and struggle for spiritual autonomy up to and beyond the Disruption of the Church of Scotland in 1843.

1999 / 338pp / ISBN 0-946068-49-6

'Rigide Calvinisme in a Softer Dresse':
The Moderate Presbyterianism of John Howe (1630–1705)
David Field

This attractive presentation of the thought of John Howe depicts him as treading a middle path between the rationalizing moralism of Anglicanism and the unflinching high Calvinism of the Westminster divines. Howe restated Calvinism in the face of searching criticisms. This study compares Howe with the Cambridge Platonists, with John Wilkins and with Richard Baxter, and throws light on the theological decline of English Presbyterianism before and after 1700. An important contribution to understanding of early nonconformity.

Forthcoming / ISBN 0-946068-75-5

Rutherford Studies in Contemporary Theology

Actuality and Provisionality:
Eternity and Election in the Theology of Karl Barth

John Colwell

John Colwell's scholarship provides him with the basis for some sharp observations about the more sweeping criticisms of Barth, and shows that this supposedly 'extreme' theologian produces a far more nuanced and subtle account of such topics as the relations of incarnation and atonement, creation and redemption, grace and freedom, than do those who have read and moved rapidly on to provide their own one-sided 'improvements'. The aim of this study is neither to dismiss Barth nor simply to repeat him but to attempt to understand him, and to develop the work of theology in the light of his massive contribution.

1989 / 323pp / ISBN 0-946068-41-0

A Study in the Concept of Transcendence in Contemporary German Theology

Loránt Hegedüs

This important study by the Hungarian theologian, Loránt Hegedüs, was completed during his tenure of a research fellowship at Princeton. Dr Hegedüs relates modern German theological developments to the biblical agenda of the transcendent God and his creation. His thesis is that Christ provides our central focus for considering the transcendence of God.

1991 / 112pp / ISBN 0-946068-40-2

Transcendence and Immanence in the Philosophy of Michael Polanyi and Christian Theism

R.T. Allen

The aim of this study is to explore the themes of God's simultaneous transcendence over and immanence within the universe as formulated on the basis of the philosophy of Michael Polanyi and in Christian Theism; to ascertain how far the former is compatible with the latter; and to show how the former may be used to articulate and illuminate the latter.

1992 / 196pp / ISBN 0-7734-1635-8

The Problem of Polarization:
An Approach Based on the Writings of G.C. Berkouwer

Charles Cameron

The sheer bulk of Berkouwer's Studies in Dogmatics makes the serious reading of his works a most formidable task. The present study seeks to draw together certain key aspects of Berkouwer's thought and relate them particularly to the problem of theological polarization in a way that emphasizes the significance of his theology.

1992 / 597pp / ISBN 0-7734-1633-1

The God Who Fights:
The War Tradition in Holy Scripture

Charles Sherlock

In this volume Dr Sherlock examines the scriptural passages where military language is used of God and the people of God. We would not speak spontaneously of God as a Warrior, or as 'the Lord of hosts', so why did the writers of the Old Testament do this? And why did the New Testament writers take up some of their imagery and bring military terminology into the way they understood the cross of Jesus? Dr Sherlock's study, written in full awareness of what the scholars have said yet simply enough for ordinary people to understand, will help us to answer these questions.

1993 / 445pp / ISBN 0-7734-1653-6

God Does Heal Today:
Pastoral Principles and Practice of Faith Healing

Robert Dickinson

A comprehensive examination of the ministry of healing, this study is thorough, biblical and practical – compulsory reading for every pastor and elder who seeks to minister to those who are ill. Dr Dickinson critically assesses current practices in the church in light of Scripture and leaves no aspect unquestioned. He brings some clear thinking to an area of church life and pastoral practice which has been chaotic and confused, and his analysis is arresting and insightful.

1995 / 343pp / ISBN 0-946068-56-9

Revelation of the Triune God
In the Theologies of John Calvin and Karl Barth

Sang-Hwan Lee

This study grapples in depth with the structure of two of the most influential works in Western theology – Calvin's *Institutes* and Karl Barth's *Church Dogmatics*. It concentrates on the Trinitarian revelation of God as the critical source of Calvin's *summa*, while also clarifying his hold on the oneness of God. In both Calvin and Barth Dr Lee highlights the indispensability of faith for theology. He insists on Barth's freedom from philosophical structural principles such as Hegel's idealism. A comparison of Calvin and Barth argues that differences are a matter of emphasis, particularly in their distinctive nuancing of the threeness and oneness of God. This is a powerful exposition of Reformed revelational theologies.

Forthcoming / ISBN 0-946068-74-7

The Sacrament of the Word Made Flesh:
The Eucharistic Theology of Thomas F. Torrance
Robert Stamps

Professor Tom Torrance is arguably the greatest living British theologian. Dr Stamps' focus on the Eucharist in his prolific and wide-ranging corpus demonstrates the unity of academy and church, of scholarship and worship, in his theology. This work takes us to the very heart of Torrance's theology. Since Christ is the primal sacrament of all God's reality and truth to the church, the Eucharist for Torrance is essentially 'the sacrament of the Word made flesh'. Because Eucharist interacts with other dominant concerns in his thought, this study is a fine introduction to the structural articulation of Torrance's powerful theology.

Forthcoming / ISBN 0-946068-76-3

Rutherford House
17 Claremont Park
Edinburgh EH6 7PJ
Scotland UK

Phone: 0131 554 1206
E-mail: info@rutherfordhouse.org.uk
Web: www.rutherfordhouse.org.uk